A SOCIAL CRITIQUE OF CORPORATE REPORTING

A Social Critique of Corporate Reporting

A semiotic analysis of corporate financial and environmental reporting

DAVID CROWTHER
University of North London

Ashgate

Published by
Ashgate Publishing Limited
Gower House
Croft Road
Aldershot
Hampshire GU11 3HR
England

Ashgate Publishing Company
131 Main Street
Burlington, VT 05401-5600 USA

Ashgate website: http://www.ashgate.com

British Library Cataloguing in Publication Data
Crowther, David
    A social critique of corporate reporting : a semiotic
    analysis of corporate financial and environmental reporting
    1. Corporation reports 2. Social responsibility of business
    3. Industries - Environmental aspects
    I. Title
    657.9'5

Library of Congress Control Number: 2001098451

ISBN 0 7546 1938 9

Printed and bound in Great Britain by Antony Rowe Ltd, Chippenham, Wiltshire

Contents

List of Figures

List of Tables

Chapter 1

The Function of Corporate Reporting

Introduction

This book is concerned with the role of corporate reporting in UK public limited companies.[1] A conventional view of such reporting is that it provides a means for the organisation, or its representatives, to communicate the past actions of the company, the results of those past actions, and the intended future actions of the company. This is undertaken partly to satisfy legal requirements but also in order that any interested party may undertake an evaluation of the effectiveness of the past actions of the company and the expected outcomes of its future activity.[2] Depending upon the perspective one takes, this communication may be to the owners of the business (ie the shareholders), the investors in the business, prospective future investors in the business, or to any permutation or combination of stakeholders who are associated with the business in any way. Indeed this communication may even be to society at large on the basis that all members of society are either present or potential stakeholders in the business (Crowther 1996b).

It is a common assumption that the most significant part of any corporate report is the accounting information which is contained therein. This book however takes a very different view of corporate reporting. The central argument to is that the purpose of corporate reporting has changed from one primarily of stewardship and accountability to shareholders to a more outward looking and forward looking perspective. It will be argued that one of the driving forces for this change in orientation has been the discourse of environmental accounting but that other forces are also involved.

Throughout, reference is made to the managers of a business. In the context of this work the term manager is used as a shorthand term to

1

identify the non-owning salary-taking elite who form the dominant decision taking coalition at the centre of the organisation.[3] Their respective positions may be as directors or as senior managers, and they may have a token ownership in the company.[4] Additionally they may not comprise all the people in the most senior echelons of an organisation; their identification as a part of this group is dependant upon their centrality to the decision making process in the organisation and to the control of the use of resources within the organisation. As such it is evident that the precise grouping of such managers may not be known to external parties but will be clearly identified within any organisation, particularly by managers whether within the group or excluded, and this group of managers will vary in composition from one company to another.

The argument throughout this book is essentially explorative and is concerned with looking at different aspects of the changes in corporate reporting and taking different perspectives in the development of the argument. As such it seeks to provide evidence to negate some of the commonly held conceptions concerning corporate reporting. The argument has been developed without the need to adopt any particular position but rather to focus upon the evidence and arguments within the discourse. Thus the standpoint taken in the development of the argument is that simplification through the identification of underlying structures (Levi-Strauss 1961) with its consequent simplification and omission of data and analysis at variance with the central structure is insufficient to fully develop an understanding. Instead the argument of Deleuze and Guattari (1994) that it is the exceptions and variances which are significant to an understanding is used. Hence the argument is advanced from a post-structuralist perspective on the basis that the world is complex rather than simple and is subject to different interpretations from different perspectives.[5] Indeed it is argued that although post-structuralism and postmodernism are presented as different from structuralism and modernism, they are in fact actually situated within the modernism / structuralism discourse. They are therefore different manifestations of the same discourse, focussing upon the complexity pole of one of the principal binarisms of modernity rather than the simplicity pole. Thus the viewpoint adopted in this book might seem conflicting according to many worldviews but the integrated viewpoint adopted is considered to be coherent and makes for a richer understanding of the subject matter considered. Indeed even the dialectics inherent within structuralism (Levi-Strauss 1972) are accepted and used in the arguments of this book. The development of the argument and the reasons for using the different perspectives selected, and exclusion of other perspectives, are explained and developed within the appropriate chapters within the book.

A starting point for the development of the argument concerning the changing nature and purpose of corporate reporting must however be commenced with a consideration of the historic development of such reporting, as an archaeology.[6]

The Archaeology of Corporate Reporting

It has been argued (Crowther & Carter 1998) that the world changed at the time of the Enlightenment into one in which the individual assumed dominance. It is into this world that modern accounting was born on the basis that there was a need to record the actions of the individual and its effects as a basis for the planning of future action. This need was brought about by the need for a separation of the public and private actions of an individual and the need to record, and account for, the public actions because of the involvement of others in these public actions. Thus the Medieval methods of bookkeeping, with the indistinguishability of public from private actions, was inappropriate to this Modern world in which Capitalist enterprise was beginning to arise. Capitalism required the ability to precisely measure activities and this was the founding basis of management accounting. Indeed it has been argued (Sombart 1915) that capitalism would not have been possible without the techniques of double entry bookkeeping and its subsequent metamorphosis into management accounting. This accounting provided the mechanism to make visible the activities of all involved in the capitalist enterprise and to both record the effects of past actions and the expected results of future actions.

The modern world therefore saw the genesis of the modern firm as a mechanism which enabled individuals to combine in enterprise, and to combine capital and expertise from different individuals. It also saw the concomitant genesis of modern accounting in providing a representation of the actions of the firm, as distinct from the individuals comprising that firm. Thus the archaeology of corporate reporting can be seen to stem from the development of the firm as an individual entity as a means of reporting the activities of the firm to the owners of that firm. Thus the Joint Stock Companies Act 1844 imposed upon firms the requirement to maintain accounts and to produce a balance sheet for shareholders. It was expected that such accounts would be published but this requirement to publish accounts was however repealed by the Joint Stock Companies Act 1856, with such accounts being required only for the internal purposes of the owners of the company. Nevertheless the development of the limited company as a form of enterprise necessitated the development of corporate reporting as a means of communication between the managers of the company and its owners. This need became increasingly apparent with the increasing size of such enterprises and the concomitant divorcing of ownership from management of such enterprises. This in turn was one of the drivers which led to the development of accounting practice and the development of corporate reporting. Thus by 1890 such enterprises were being accounted for on the basis of their being 'going concerns' as one of the main accounting principles (Newman 1979), with accounting practice being based upon a separation of capital from income and profits from trading, both on the basis of a recognition of the divorcing of shareholding from management of the enterprise.

Thus by the start of the twentieth century it had been accepted that firms had a corporate identity which was distinct from that of their owners and that such firms embodied a presumption of immortality (Hein 1978). Alongside this was the acceptance that control of the actions of the firm implied some liability for the effects of those actions and that the divorce of management from ownership necessitated some protection for the owners. This was achieved through the function of the audit of the activities of the firm and the Companies Act 1900 made compulsory the remuneration of such auditors. Although auditors are legally employed by the company it has never been made clear whether they are effectively employed by the shareholders, whose interests they are expected to protect, or by the directors, who have the managing role in the company. It is perhaps for this reason that the question of the impartiality of auditors has remained a constant source of debate into the present.

At the turn of the century it was generally accepted that accounting served the purpose of facilitating the relationship between managers and owners of a business, through its reporting function, but that the general public had no right to such information (Murphy 1979). Thus the Companies Act 1906 stated that there was no requirement for companies to produce financial statements, although the Companies (Consolidations) Act 1908 amended this to require the production of a profit and loss account and balance sheet. This was further amended by the Companies Act 1929 which required the production of these, together with a directors report and an auditors report for the AGM. Subsequent legislation has extended the reporting requirements of companies to the format seen today.[7]

Such corporate reporting has however been extended in addition to the satisfying of legislative requirements. Thus the period up to the Second World War saw an increasing use of accounting information for analysis purposes but with an emphasis upon the income statement. This period also saw the extension of the directors' report to contain information about the company which was not to be found in the financial statements. This information was however primarily concerning the past actions of the company as the emphasis in this period remained firmly upon the reporting of past actions as part of the relationship between the ownership and management of the firm. It is only in the post-war period that this emphasis changed from backward looking to forward looking and from inward looking to outward looking. Gilmore and Willmott (1992) have argued that this was a reflection of the changing nature of such reporting to a focus upon investment decision-making and the need to attract investment into the company in this period of expansion. The emphasis remained firmly upon the needs of the company however and only the emphasis had changed from informing existing investors to attracting new investors. Thus Jordan (1970: 139) was able to claim that:

> The purpose of accounting is to communicate economic messages on the results of business decisions and events, insofar as they can be expressed in terms of quantifiable financial data, in such a way as to achieve maximum understanding by the user and correspondence of the message with economic reality.

The users of such corporate reports, although no longer only the shareholders of the company and its managers, were however still considered to be a restricted set of the population, having specialist knowledge of and interest in such reporting. The identification of such specialists had however been extended to include both the accounting profession and investment professionals. Thus Cyert and Ijiri (1974: 29) were able to claim that:

> Financial statements are not just statements reporting on the financial activities and status of a corporation. They are a product of mutual interactions of three parties: corporations, users of financial statements, and the accounting profession.

while Leach (1975: 13) stated that:

> In recent years there have been enormous changes in public interest in and understanding of financial statements. The informed user of accounts today is no longer solely the individual shareholder but equally the trained professional acting for institutional investors and the financial news media.

Thus there was at this time a general acceptance that corporate reporting should be provided for the knowledgeable professional rather than the individual (Mauntz & Sharif 1961) and in order to satisfy the needs of these professionals corporate reports became more extensive in content, with greater disclosure of financial and other information. This pressure for greater disclosure was not however new and Mitchell (1906) argued that the accounts produced did not give an adequate basis for shareholder judgement.[8] All that has changed is the perception of who the reporting should be aimed at with a widening of the perceived intended audience from managers and shareholders to include other professionals. There was however throughout this time little questioning of the assumed knowledge that the financial information is the most important part of the corporate report. The importance of the financial information contained in the reports has changed however and Lee and Tweedie (1977) claimed that the most important financial information contained in the report was details concerning profits, earnings and dividends. They equally claimed that the economic prospects of the firm are the most important information contained in the report (Lee & Tweedie 1975) but were dismissive of the private shareholder in recording (Lee & Tweedie 1977) that the majority read the chairman's report but nothing else.[9]

Accounting and Corporate Reporting

The archaeology of corporate reporting until the 1970s is simply the archaeology of the financial accounting aspects of reporting, as little else was considered to be of significance and Hein (1978) identifies the steps in such developments as being (in chronological order):

- The balance sheet;
- The profit and loss account;
- Cash reporting and accounting;
- Increasing disclosure of other financial information;
- The development of the notes to accompany the balance sheet and profit and loss account.

The implication of this chronology is that the development took place in a linearly temporal manner; it is of course accepted that this is a simplification but nevertheless it can be accepted as a model of the temporal topography of corporate reporting.[10] No attention was paid to the development of the report itself, although it was recognised that the orientation of the report had changed from past to future and that increasing attention was being paid to the non-financial parts of the report such as the chairman's statement. Instead attention was given to the form of accounting and the application of accounting principles and standards. This was reflected by the establishment of the Accounting Standards Steering Committee in 1969.[11] The primary focus for the accounting of organisations was financial accounting and this accounting was temporally divided, for reporting purposes, into annual periods to provide the subject matter of the annual report. This itself is of course a social construct of the modern era and Clegg, Higgins and Spybey (1990: 61) claim that:

> Another arbitrary – if formally rational – aspect of accounting practice is the choice and weighting of time-frames. Profit is struck on an annual basis, and the time-frame and weighting of anticipated returns can vary greatly. The financial institutions' separation from, and domination of, manufacturers gives yearly accounts a much greater salience than in countries where financial institutions are made much more receptive to manufacturers' requirements, and this in turn highlights the artificial distinction between operating costs and capital outlays.

This focus upon financial accounting as dominant for corporate reporting purposes ignores, of course, the development of management accounting for internal control purposes. More significantly the focus upon the activities of the firm as far as they affected only the firm itself led to a failure to anticipate the wider use of corporate reports by other stakeholders to the firm and the development of environmental accounting.

Equally the focus upon the development of the financial reporting aspects of corporate reporting ignores the development of the semiotic[12] of such reporting and the changing nature of this semiotic. This lack of recognition is despite the acceptance that such reporting had changed over time to become more forward looking, to include more non-financial information including the chairman's report, and to become used by a wider range of people. It is argued in this book that this semiotic of corporate reporting is the most important use of such reporting and the prime vehicle for developing an understanding of such reporting and the changed nature of the reporting itself. Indeed the function of the semiotic is to aid social construction of corporate activity in a way which is mediated through the semiotic (Vygotsky and Luria 1994), in such a way that the interpretation of the reader is controlled from without by the creators of the semiotic.[13] It is further argued that the lack of recognition of the semiotic of corporate reporting has also led to a lack of exploration of the dialectics inherent in such reporting. This work aims to identify these dialectics and explore them in the development of the semiotic of corporate reporting.

This recognition of the use made of the corporate report has of course affected the way in which the report is produced as well as the contents and format of the report itself. Thus the earliest reports consisted merely of the financial reporting information of balance sheet, profit and loss account and increasing amounts of analysis of such information and notes to provide greater detail. The incorporation of the chairman's report provided an acknowledgement that financial information alone was insufficient to explain the actions of the company in the past and its prospects for the future. This was then extended, in recognition of the increasing size and complexity of organisations and the increasing divorce of investment from involvement in management of the organisation, to provide details about the activities and plans of the organisation. At the same time, over the last 25 years the report itself has changed from a plain statement to an increasingly glossy product containing maps, charts and pictures in a multicoloured production designed to have mass appeal. It is this modern form of corporate reporting, in the way produced and used by large publicly quoted companies, which is the subject of analysis as far as this work is concerned. These changes have not affected private companies in the same way, arguably because the ownership and management of such companies are much more closely intertwined.[14]

The Dialectics of Corporate Reporting[15]

From the archaeology of corporate reporting outlined above it is evident that several stages in the format and function of corporate reporting can be identified which show an evolution of such reporting with the passage of time. In each stage the dialectic is concerned with the relationship between the organisation and its environment and is mediated through the production of the annual corporate report. These stages can be classified as follows:

Stage 1: pre – 1940

This stage encompasses the period up until the Second World War and is defined by a dialectic which recognises the distinction between the firm and its environment but chooses to ignore the external environment. In this period corporate reporting was simply an internal transaction to the organisation as a way of communicating between the managers and owners of the business. Indeed the external environment was deliberately excluded from this communication. Moreover the communication which took place was almost entirely retrospective, being simply a reporting of past actions and results. It can be argued therefore that at this time the managers of the organisation recognised their agency relationship with shareholders and were fulfilling their duty to shareholders by reporting upon their actions and the results of those actions. In Stage 1 the results from actions taken were what mattered and the report was merely deemed to be an effective means of communicating those results to the people who needed to know.

Stage 2: 1940 – 1975

In this stage the firm, and the managers of the firm, chose to recognise the existence and importance of the external environment and the need to attract inward investment. Thus the orientation of the report moved towards not just current investors in the firm but also towards potential investors. Part of the purpose of reporting in this stage therefore was to solicit additional members of the firm, in the form of investors. This change necessitated an increasing focus upon future prospects for the firm rather than merely a reporting of past performance. The focus still remained predominantly upon the firm however and the sole purpose of communicating with the external environment was not to achieve a communication with that environment but simply to increase membership of the firm. It can be argued however that the agency relationship between managers and shareholders had started to weaken in this stage and that the relationship was changing so that managers now viewed their relationship as being with any investors in the business (whether shareholder or not) rather than with the current owners of that business. In this way the managers of the business can be described as commencing to subvert their subordinate role, as agents to the owners, in the activities of the firm. In this stage it was both the results of past actions and prospects (for the firm) of future actions which mattered and the report remained merely an effective means of communication.

Stage 3: post 1975

This third stage in the development of reporting is epitomised by the most dramatic change in corporate reporting.[16] No longer was the firm seeking to communicate internally – to members or potential members – but rather the focus was upon the external environment. Indeed no longer did results alone matter, although still contained in the report. Instead the emphasis changed to the future prospects of the business becoming more important than the past performance. Thus the report now became predominantly forward looking and, perhaps more significantly, the forward orientation is not solely upon the economic prospects of the firm but also upon the prospects for the shareholder community in terms of rewards – both dividends and share price increases. Additionally the report now acknowledged the rest of the stakeholder community and sought to demonstrate corporate citizenship by commenting upon relationships with, and benefits accruing to, employees, society, customers and the local community. Indeed the report has tended to become not merely a communication medium but rather a mechanism for self-promotion. Thus the actual results of the firm's past performance were no longer of prime importance but rather the image of the firm is what mattered and the production of the report became the event itself, rather then merely a communication mechanism.

Thus a dialectic seems to exist in corporate performance measurement and reporting.[17] It will be argued that this dialectic is more apparent than real.[18] Nevertheless the dialectic has changed over time as the discourse of environmental accounting has assumed prominence.[19] The use of this dialectic in such reporting will be considered further throughout but in order to explore the dialectic, which has been created within the discourse of corporate reporting, then a vehicle for its exploration is necessary. This vehicle is semiology, as considered in chapter 4.

The dialectic of corporate reporting can therefore be considered in terms of two dimensions of reporting – the internal v external dimension and the backward looking v forward looking dimension. In terms of these two dimensions the primacy of the orientation has changed over time – from internal to external and from backward looking to forward looking – but the dialectic still remains that of the relationship of the firm with its external environment.[20] These issues will be considered in greater detail throughout and it will be argued that part of the resolution of the dialectic has taken place in terms of a metamorphosis of the dialectic into managerial motivations versus stakeholder interests.

The Fourth Stage of Evolution

It is argued that the advent of wide use of the Internet as a means of communication has changed the third stage of the archaeology developed in this chapter into a fourth stage. This stage extends the third stage by the use of this Internet technology. The increasing availability of access to the Internet has had the effect of instigating a discourse which considers the present and likely future impact of this means of communication upon the construction of society and upon the lives of individual members of that society (Rushkoff 1997). This has been considered in detail by Crowther

(2000) who argued that this means of communication has a large potential impact upon corporate reporting. This is because access to use of the Internet can redefine the corporate landscape and change the power relationship between large corporations and individuals. The changes in these power relationships can be profound and even revolutionary. The technology can give individuals the ability to confront large corporations and to have their voice heard with equal volume within the discourse facilitated by cyberspace.

This era can be argued to be the era of electronic communication and reporting. No longer is the company bound by the requirements of paper production of its annual report, although this does still exist and continues to change in accordance with the outline of stage 3. Of greater significance however is the electronic communication of the performance of the company, which incorporates its annual report into a wider range of information concerning the company. As in stage 3, it is the image of the company which matters, and part of that image is created merely by its electronic presence. The nature of that presence is of greater importance however and companies vie with each other to have more elaborate, spectacular and entertaining websites.[21]

Thus all large organisations, and most small ones, have a presence on the world wide web. More significantly all UK plcs make use of this technology to communicate their corporate performance. This communication includes a repetition of their formal corporate reporting but in the context of other information. The way in which this evolving technology can change the argument of this work will be considered in detail in the final chapter.

Corporate Reporting as Simulacra

The change in focus of corporate reporting over time means that the current form of reporting is one in which the report itself is now all that matters and there is no longer any need to consider the actual results of the firm in any detail.[22] Thus it will be argued, with evidence, that these results are now incidental to the purpose of such reporting. Indeed the forward looking nature of such reporting now means that all that is necessary for the production of the report is that the semiotic created makes the present look better than the past, and the future look even more attractive then the present. Indeed this semiotic has now become the principal function of corporate reporting: such reports, or rather the semiotic inherent in such reports, must stand favourable comparison with other reports – either past reports of the organisation or current reports of other organisations.

In this way corporate reports can now be viewed as little more than image creation mechanisms. The image created through the semiotic and the consumption of that image is all that remains of corporate reporting. Thus such reports can be considered to be nothing more than simulacra (Baudrillard 1994) which need have no bearing on anything other than themselves and no reference point other than previous corporate reports. As long as they are consumed as real by their recipients then this consumption suffices to legitimate their existence and disguise the absence of any relationship with corporate activity. This maintenance of the corporate report as simulacrum, through its consumption as real, is an essential part of the maintenance of the dialectic in its present form, and the maintenance of the primacy of managers in organisation hierarchies. This maintenance will be explored in detail throughout this work.

The structure of the rest of the argument falls into three parts:

- A setting of the context of the research problem and the development of a methodology for exploration;
- The consideration of the effects of the discourse of environmental accounting upon corporate reporting;
- The consideration of other factors upon corporate reporting.

These three parts develop the argument from the generally accepted reasons for corporate reporting in terms of the accounting for and communication of performance to the central argument of this work. This concerns the changed nature of corporate reporting and the reasons for such changes with a consideration of the implications for the future. In summary the three parts comprise the following components.

Company reporting was devised initially to make use of accounting information for the dual purposes of providing the legal owners of the business (i.e. the shareholders) with information concerning the activities which had been undertaken by the company, and the results of that activity, and for the satisfaction of legal requirements regarding reporting. In this respect it was assumed that managers acted as agents of the owners of the business and that the reporting function of the annual accounts and report was to inform the shareholders of the actions taken by the managers of the company on their behalf. On this basis therefore the annual report of the company need be little more than a copy of the annual accounts together with supporting notes to aid understanding, and indeed such reports in the early part of this century were little more than this. In recent times however the format and content of the annual report has changed with more information being included in the report and greater information being given concerning the activities of the company and the actions of the managers of the company. Thus the size of company reports has increased and the statement from the chairman has assumed a prominent position in the report. It might be considered that this merely reflects a distancing between ownership of the company, as vested in the shareholders, and the management of the company, undertaken by managers who need not necessarily have any ownership of the company, with this distancing being manifest in the need to provide greater information to the owners who no longer have any part in the management of the company and in the taking of decisions which will affect the future performance of that company.

An examination of the changed nature of corporate reporting, and the changed informational content of such reports, has been undertaken in order to arrive at an understanding of the purpose of such reports in the context of organisational performance. At the same time the role of accounting information in such reports, and the changes in the nature of the use of such accounting information, must necessarily be undertaken, as corporate reports without accounting information are incomplete documents. This consideration of the role of accounting leads to an increased understanding of the relationship between the managers of a company and the performance of that company, as reflected in the annual reporting of that company.

In arriving at such an understanding, the role of accounting in the organisation forms an important precursor. In chapter 2 therefore the role of accounting in an organisation is considered and the way in which it affects organisational performance is analysed. Thus in this chapter the role of accounting within the organisation is considered in the contexts of facilitating the control of organisational activities by the managers of that organisation, the facilitating of accountability of the managers of the organisation to its owners, and the role of accounting in the strategic decision making process of the organisation. These functions of accounting are critiqued and this leads to a consideration of the role of accounting in the reporting of the performance of both the organisation and its management. One focus of this chapter therefore is upon the use of accounting by the managers of the organisation and therefore concentrates upon management accounting and upon the internal perspective of organisational performance.

The conventional use of accounting techniques and information by organisations is founded in the classical liberal paradigm in that it is only the effects of actions taken insofar as they affect the organisation itself which need be taken into consideration. Accordingly accounting only measures these effects of the actions of the organisation and ignores other effects. In terms of the evolution of corporate reporting this was sufficient until managers perceived the need to look outside the company membership into a wider arena. Any organisation however exists in such a wider environment than its own membership and any actions taken by an organisation affect other parts of that environment in addition to itself. It is a recognition of this that led to a different discourse arising within accounting which sought to measure all the effects of the activities of an organisation both within its own domain and without. This discourse has been labelled under various names but in this book is referred to as social and environmental accounting. Chapter 2 therefore also considers the discourse of such accounting and critiques its implications for both accounting and for organisational reporting. One effect of this discourse is that organisations, or more specifically the managers of those organisations, have increasingly sought to report upon their social and environmental performance but have largely failed to incorporate such reporting into the accounting of the organisation. Instead it tends to have been treated as a separate aspect of organisational performance. Implicit within this treatment of the internal and external aspects of organisational performance, it is argued, is an assumption that good financial performance and good environmental performance are mutually exclusive and represent different dimensions of organisational performance. Thus it becomes necessary to manage these two aspects of performance separately and to sacrifice performance along one dimension for the sake of performance along the other. This leads to the establishment of a dialectical aspect of performance which is explored throughout the remainder of the book.

The method chosen to explore the argument in this book is that of semiology and in doing so a semiology of corporate reporting has been developed. This development of a semiology of corporate reporting is achieved in chapters 4 – 8 while the dialectic is explored through both a semiotic analysis and a quantitative analysis of performance. In doing so a methodology needs to be developed and justified and this methodology is developed in chapter 3, which, inter alia, describes, and critiques, the role of semiology in analysing corporate reporting. In developing this semiology the notion of binary opposition is explained and a set of binary opposites developed from corporate reporting. These binary oppositions form the basis for the semiotic analysis in this and subsequent chapters. The analysis of corporate reporting needs to be based upon a sample of companies, for which analysis is undertaken, and in this chapter that sample is chosen and justified, as is the time period of the longitudinal analysis under consideration.

One reason which is often given for the development of environmental reporting is the increased power and significance of stakeholders to the organisation other than shareholders and managers. Chapter 3 therefore also provides an argument for a model of the multidimensionality of stakeholder foci and perspectives based upon the model developed by Crowther (1996b). It has been further argued that these other stakeholders exert pressures upon the organisation which cause the managers to respond through their actions, and one manifestation of this response is an increased level of environmental reporting. In Chapter 3 therefore the role of these stakeholders is also examined in the context of their ability to act as pressure groups. The analysis of environmental pressure groups, through the development of a typology, indicates that pressures from this source do not arise in a way which can be expected to affect environmental reporting.[23] Chapter 4 introduces quantitative evidence which is supported by the qualitative evidence from chapter 5 concerning the role of environmental accounting in organisational performance. Thus the metrics of performance measurement are considered along with the role of accounting in measuring performance, while the implications are considered in chapter 6.

In the next two chapters the emphasis shifts from that of environmental accounting to a consideration of the outward and forward looking nature of corporate reporting. In these chapters therefore the arguments of postmodernism are examined in the context of their implications for organisations and their environments. This involves further exploration of the semiology of corporate reporting through a consideration of the internal versus external binary opposition. Furthermore the role of accounting in legitimating organisational decisions and in supporting the managers of the organisation in their decision making is considered. This consideration is set within the context of the rituals of organisational behaviour as legitimating vehicles and the role of accounting in such ritual behaviour. Such legitimation of organisational behaviour through ritual is based upon the past as setting a precedent for the future and the semiology of corporate reporting is extended in this chapter to an exploration of the past versus future binary opposites within the semiotic. These arguments lead to a conclusion that the two dimensions are not incompatible in terms of performance maximisation.

The concluding chapter sets the analysis into context and considers the generalisability of the arguments which have been developed. This consideration is set in the context of the regulatory, cultural and linguistic variations between different countries and the way in which this may impact upon the analysis. Furthermore this chapter looks at the possible implications of the advent of Internet technology in affecting the relationship between organisations, their managers and other stakeholders.

Notes

[1] These UK limited companies which form the focus of this research are the larger companies which would be expected to be included in the FTSE500 list of companies and it is this area that the analysis is directed. There are difference when smaller plc's are concerned and when private companies are concerned and these difference will be highlighted throughout the book as a means of explaining the central argument of the work.

[2] The undertaking of such evaluations naturally forms one of the principal functions of accounting (see Crowther 1996a).

[3] Thus the terms 'managers' and 'dominant coalition' are used synonymously throughout the remainder of the book, although it is recognised that the equation of these two terms is simplistic.

[4] Principally from the operation of reward structures.

[5] Although it is claimed that the method is primarily post-structuralist, it also includes some significant structuralist elements. Thus it would be perfectly possible to claim that the method is primarily structuralist with some post-structuralist elements included within. This recognition of such ambivalence in terminology is in perfect accord with post-structuralist philosophy.

[6] The term archaeology is used in this book in the manner used by Foucault (1970), as depicting a reconstruction and interpretation of past developments.

[7] This is of course a simplified depiction of the legal framework of corporate reporting and is used to illustrate the main points of the argument rather than to be comprehensive.

[8] It is accepted that until the Companies (Consolidations) Act 1908 there was no legal requirement to produce a profit & loss account and balance sheet and so information might have been inadequate. The point is to show that the desire for further information has been a continuing theme of the discourse.

[9] This claim is in direct contradiction to the claim of Epstein & Pava (1993) that the majority of investors study the income statement and the balance sheet in some detail. This difference may reflect a change over time, a different investigative method, or a cultural difference (Epstein & Pava conducted their study in the USA). Epstein & Pava also studied the non-financial parts of the corporate report and found that some use was made of these also by shareholders.

[10] It is recognised that GAAP, accounting standards, accounting theory and reporting expectations have developed during this period. The effect of these is fully recognised but does not form the major focus of this work. Any consideration of the effect of these developments is therefore not denied but rather considered as incidental to the arguments of this work.

[11] This subsequently metamorphosed into the Accounting Standards Board.

[12] The meaning and use of the term semiotic is considered in detail in chapter 4. The idea of the semiotic forms a central platform of the methodology used in this book.

[13] The creation, interpretation and control of this semiotic forms a main focus of study of this book.

14 It is of course recognised that the reporting requirements of private companies are some what different to those of plcs.

15 The modern dialectic was created by Hegel (1956), whose motivation was to achieve understanding through the dialectic method (Findlay 1958). The Hegelian dialectic flows through history according to Hegel, who believed that we each individually arise out of our past. Accordingly the thesis and antithesis of the dialectic also arise from the past and flow through history towards a resolution, but need not always be evident. Indeed it is argued that this axis of the dialectic can only become evident with hindsight but also that this recognition is necessary before any resolution can take place. Inherent in the exploration of the dialectic of corporate reporting in this book therefore is the development of an understanding of the thesis and antithesis, as a precursor to any consideration of the resolution of the dialectic. This dialectic method was subsequently adapted by Marx (see Cornforth 1971) into dialectical materialism but the Kantian (1934) notion of a dialectic rather focuses upon the inherent contradictions in all scientific principles. It is this Kantian version of dialectics which is used in this book.

16 See the 1975 publication by the Accounting Standards Steering Committee entitled 'The Corporate Report' for an indication of this changing emphasis, affecting both form and content.

17 Although the Hegelian method is not used in this book, this dialectic can be seen to exist in Hegelian terms by considering it in terms of thesis and antithesis.

18 This will be demonstrated in terms of the Kantian inconsistencies existing within the dialectic.

19 See chapters 3 onwards for evidence to support this assertion.

20 This change over time however means that the Hegelian method may appear to provide an appropriate mechanism for the exploration of the dialectics of corporate reporting. Instead however it will be demonstrated that this Hegelian method is not appropriate as this dialectic is a false dialectic. Instead there are other dialectics that appear, as Kantian inconsistencies, within corporate reporting and it is the exploration of these which provide a mechanism for exploring the purpose of corporate reporting.

21 The changes and the effects of these changes upon both the corporate reporting landscape and the dominant coalition within the organisation will be considered in detail in chapter 10.

22 This is not to negate the kinds of analysis undertaken by accountants and the City analysts; instead the point of this work is to focus upon the semiotic.

23 This analysis is supported in this chapter by an argument which resolves the focus of pressures from stakeholders into two types – the organisational pressures of shareholders, investors and analysts and the societal pressures of environmentalists, citizens and society. This therefore provides a justification and motivation for the polarisation of corporate reporting into the financial versus environmental performance dialectic developed previously.

Chapter 2

Measuring and Reporting Performance

The Traditional Discourse of Accounting

Corporate reporting has an internal aspect to it in that communication is not just to the external environment but also is internal to the organisation – that is between the managers and shareholders. There is however a further internal dimension to corporate reporting, predicated in one of the principal uses of accounting information – the planning and control of performance along with the concomitant measurement of that performance.[1] All firms measure their performance and report upon those measurements, and one of the principal vehicles for such measurement is through the use of accounting information. The reporting based upon this measurement is used both externally by the firm in reporting its performance to its owners and other interested parties but also internally in the control of the business and the making of decisions which will affect the future performance of the business. It is therefore possible to identify three distinct areas of business management for which the measurement and reporting of performance is important. These three categories are:

- accounting, which is concerned with control in the business environment; this is an activity which is essentially primarily concerned with the present, and immediate future, as far as the business is concerned.
- accountability, which is concerned with the reporting of the activities and results of the business; this activity is primarily concerned with the past.[2]

- strategic management, which is concerned with the planning of the business's activities and the evaluation of its subsequent performance; this activity is primarily concerned with the future.

It is therefore possible to identify the measurement and reporting of performance for a business as an activity which is temporally contextual, being concerned with the present time as far as the business is concerned but also with the past, for reporting purposes, and the future, for planning purposes. Thus although these three categories of business activity are not mutually independent, and there is inevitably a high degree of interaction between them, it is nevertheless possible to discern these distinct strands in the literature and so to examine them separately. Furthermore all three categories are concerned with the activities of the firm itself and adopt a measurement stance from that viewpoint; moreover it is an agent of the firm which undertakes that measurement. Thus the measurement of performance for an individual firm is based entirely upon the measurement of the effect of its activities upon itself, rather than any recognition that the firm's activities have an effect upon its external environment. This stance as far as performance measurement is concerned is embedded within the implicit assumptions of traditional accounting, stemming as it does from classical liberalism. This conventional view of performance provides a starting point for examining the role of accounting in the measurement and reporting of performance.

In any consideration of corporate reporting these aspects of performance cannot be ignored and so a consideration of the role of accounting is necessary. In this chapter therefore these three function of accounting measures are examined in detail. It will be apparent from this discourse that the principal concern of the discourse is with how accounting can better act as a servant of managers in fulfilling these functions. It is argued in this work however that these functions, although important to organisational behaviour, actually serve the needs of managers through the ability to use accounting information as a means of constructing organisational performance. In the case of accounting this is achieved through technical expertise in the mastery of the use of accounting information.[3]

Accounting as Management Control

Not only is accounting in this context concerned with the present as far as the control of the activities of the firm are concerned, but it is also concerned primarily with the internal activities of the firm. As far as this control of the internal activities of a business is concerned therefore the branch of accounting which has the greatest relevance to this activity is that of management accounting. Scapens (1984) has provided a survey of the major topics in this area, identifying planning, cost classification, control (which he considers to be responsibility accounting), costing and accounting for divisionalised organisations as principal areas of concern.[4] Otley (1984) identifies management accounting as based largely upon micro-economic theory and is concerned about the wider role of accounting in society. He argues that while management accounting is largely a control process there is nevertheless a complementary relationship between accounting systems and organisational design. He too is concerned with the behavioural aspects of accounting and argues that, while budgetary control is used as a major form of performance evaluation, and so budgets have an impact upon people, it is also true that people have an impact upon budgets, including the likelihood of individual biasing of budgets for personal benefit.

There is general agreement that it is impossible to treat management accounting in isolation from the organisational environment in which it operates, and that micro-economic theory of the firm is too superficial in attempting to do so. This point is argued forcibly by Aoki (1984) who states that the traditional economic view of the firm as a black box, with the internal design being irrelevant, run for the benefit of the shareholders is inadequate. He further argues that there are three groups concerned in the firm – the shareholders, the workers and the management – and that rather than the firm being run in the sole interests of one group, the interactions between the groups are crucial in determining the firm's behaviour. In this respect he argues that a bargaining process, depending upon their respective power, acts as a mechanism for resolution; he names this process 'the collective game theory of the firm'. Whilst recognising the importance of different stakeholders in the business and their conflicting aims, this analysis of stakeholders is inadequate in ignoring the respective power of these stakeholders.[5] The importance of power in the behaviour of the stakeholders has however been recognised and analysed further by other writers[6] and this is subject to further discussion later.

Not only is economic theory considered by some to be inadequate to describe the behaviour of a firm but conventional accounting is also considered to be inadequate by some people. Thus Tinker (1985) argues that conventional accounting fails to account satisfactorily for the expropriation and reallocation of wealth between various groups of the stakeholder community and also fails to satisfactorily account for value added and value sacrificed.[7] He proposes several alternatives such as emancipatory accounting or social constituency accounting, without satisfactorily explaining the actual mechanics of their operation. Consequently the main value of this work is in identifying problems with current theory rather than in suggesting alternatives.

The inadequacy of management accounting is emphasised also by Johnson and Kaplan (1987: 254) who argue that the role of management accounting has changed so that it is no longer relevant to managerial needs, stating of management accounting systems:

> Their original purpose of providing information to facilitate cost control and performance measurement in hierarchical organisations has been transformed to one of compiling costs for periodic financial statements.

They further argue (1987: 256) that:

> More important than attempting to measure monthly or quarterly profits is measuring and reporting a variety of non-financial indicators. The indicators should be based on the company's strategy and include key measures of manufacturing, marketing, and R&D success.

It is argued in this book that although one aspect of managerial need is that of internal control of organisational activity and resource allocation, this is not in fact the prime need for accounting information and that the composition of these periodic financial statements (i.e. corporate reports) is necessarily the prime need of managers. Thus it is argued that this transformation of management accounting is actually part of the process of meeting the needs of corporate reporting, with an inevitable, and therefore acceptable, subordination of other roles for management accounting.

Problems with accounting generally have been highlighted by Smith (1992) who is concerned more with financial reporting, arguing that new accounting techniques of doubtful ethical value have been created with the intention of boosting reported profits. Examples he quotes included changes in depreciation calculations and the introduction of brand accounting. He highlights the differing intentions of internal and external reporting and raises the issue of accountability, without considering who the managers of a firm should be accountable to.[8]

While considerable effort was expended during the 1980s in describing the limitations of accounting theory, this activity is relatively easy to do and it is much harder to suggest satisfactory alternatives. Later work has been more constructive in attempting to do so. Thus Hogarth (1993) considers the concept of behavioural decision theory in accounting, recognising such concepts as bounded rationality, the use of heuristic rules, confirmation, and thought as construction, from other areas of management and behavioural science. Thus accounting thought is moving away from the mechanistic view limited to its own domain of earlier times and seeking to make use of knowledge from other arenas. Hogarth however recognises problems with his theory and its application, while Hopper, Storey and Willmott (1987) consider accounting from a dialectical point of view.[9] While broadening the arena of operation of management accounting to consider societal and cultural aspects of accounting, their analysis fails to add to theory insofar as practical application is concerned.

Rappaport (1986), on the other hand, recognises problems with accounting such as the exclusion of risk and of investment requirements from the analysis, and the problems of ignoring the time value of money and not considering dividend policies. He goes on to consider the concept of shareholder value and how this can be created and sustained.[10] His suggestions are related to the determination of business strategies which create value, and with the relationship between business performance and executive compensation. He distinguishes usefully between absolute and relative performance and suggests that it is the incremental value of performance which is of significance. He also reminds that the criteria for the evaluation of performance are those of validity, verifiability, controllability and communicability. His analysis therefore recognises some of the limitations of accounting theory but is practical rather than esoteric in suggesting courses of action to take to improve the situation. The main problem with his analysis however is that it is a return to economic theory in the suggestion that shareholder value is the only concern of a firm, whereas there seems to be a general acceptance of the importance of the wider stakeholder community.

While considering the wider context in which accounting operates however it is important to consider Chern's (1978) reminder of the forgotten assumptions of accounting, namely that the bottom line is a measure of benefit to the organisation and that a benefit to the organisation is also a benefit to society. It is thus important not to neglect the positive aspects of accounting as far as organisational control is concerned and not to forget about the needs and expectations of the owners of a business in any consideration of other stakeholders. Indeed Hofstedt (1976) also issues a reminder that the past may not predict the future and so current paradigms, based on the past, should not be accepted without question. Robson (1992) also provides a reminder of some of the qualities of accounting, stating that rather than accounting being explained as metaphor, it should be explained as inscription to enable action at a distance.[11]

These practical uses of accounting, as a means of running a business, contrast with the search by some writers for a philosophical base for accounting and a place for it in a wider societal context. For example, Morgan (1988) considers a variety of metaphors used for accounting such as ideology, history or language, and argues that accounting is an interpretative art. He argues that while accountants view themselves as objective appraisers of reality, in actual fact they construct reality in a limited and one-sided way and there is therefore a tension between the accountant's view of the world and the world itself in a wider sense.

Exploration of the use of accounting therefore seems inevitably to need to include both its practical techniques and their application, and its use in an organisational setting. Thus there is a need to consider accounting information not as facts but as having a meaning, and limitations, within the context within which it is employed. Swanson (1978) suggests that all organisational information needs to be examined in terms of its importance to the relationship between the organisation and its environment. He argues that much information is two-faced, being both internally and externally based and directed and can influence therefore both organisational self-learning and organisational self-delusion.

The search for a wider framework in which to study accounting has been undertaken by several writers, including Laughlin (1987) who concluded that accounting systems in their organisational contexts are technical phenomena. He therefore recommended that Critical Theory be used as a methodology. Tinker (1988) on the other hand adopted a panglossian approach to accounting theory, quoting Barnes (1982) who argued for a constructionist approach. Tinker identifies the traits of ideology which pervade accounting theory and lead to an underestimation of the consequences of factual indeterminacy, as well as an inherent conservatism which favours the status quo, and a failure to deal with beneficial interests. He considers that the key accounting theories in use are based upon agency theory and transaction cost theory, evaluating the weakness in relying upon these theories but failing to suggest alternatives.

The changing role of management accounting is affected by the needs for accounting information for corporate reporting purposes and the consideration of the role, and techniques, or management accounting is inevitable affected by this. Thus the discourse concerning the needs for control purposes of management accounting is subordinate to this need, and therefore considered no further in this book.

Accounting Techniques in Practice

Other writers have been more concerned with the practical evaluation of accounting in operation and Mak (1989) conducted a study which demonstrated that the consistency between different levels of control systems is related to financial performance and also that appropriate control systems depend to some extent upon perceived environmental uncertainty. Other writers are more concerned with the budgetary process as an essential part of the control mechanism.[12] The involvement of organisational politics in the budgetary process is recognised by Covalenski and Dirsmith (1986) who argue that, rather than budgeting being an enabler of rational decision making, the budgeting process helps to construct reality and is used as a mechanism of legitimation for intended action. The budgeting process therefore is inextricably bound up with the behavioural aspects of an organisation and is partly concerned with determining what action the organisation should decide to take and partly determined by the course of action the organisation has already decided to take. The traditional view of a linear relationship between strategy, budgeting and implementation therefore appears to be overly simplistic and actual behaviour is more complex than theory would suggest.

In considering budgeting systems as part of the control process of an organisation it is necessary to consider the framework in which control operates and this is identified by Otley and Berry (1980) as having four constituents: objectives, predictive models, measures and choices of action. Machin (1983) considers the budget to be a mechanism of the management control system while Vickers (1967) considers that control is concerned with distinguishing between what is and what ought to be, and taking steps towards the latter. Otley (1980) follows his work with Berry by considering not only the constituents of a control framework but also the need for an ability and a motivation to act. He considers the applicability of contingency theory for the analysis of management accounting systems, particularly with regard to the effects of technology, organisational structure and the environment. Ouchi (1979) considers that the mechanisms of control are: market mechanisms, ie prices (both external and internal to the firm); bureaucratic mechanisms, ie rules; and clan mechanisms, ie traditions.

The key features of budgetary control are considered by Buckley and McKenna (1972) to be: a yardstick for comparison; the quantitative transfer of information; and formalisation. They do however consider the motivational aspects of budgets in terms of motivational theories. This is considered further by Briers and Hirst (1990) who argue that information can be used in a variety of ways, and by Macintosh (1985) who considers the negative consequences of budgeting in terms of leadership style, group dynamics and participation in the process of budgeting. Otley and Berry (1979) argue that budgets tend to have skewed assessment of risk and that the best estimate is not always the average. Birnbeg, Turopolec and Young (1983) recognise the existence of uncertainty in the budgeting process and argue that accountants seek to reduce uncertainty by structuring tasks and measuring outputs. They also consider that accountants use a variety of methods which distort the information systems, such as filtering, smoothing and biasing information and focusing upon particular aspects. Thus the budgeting system as part of the control process of an organisation is not a simple system and needs to be considered in behavioural terms as well as technical and quantitative terms.

Some writers have been concerned with the rate of return as a measure of control.[13] In considering the role of accounting in the control process, and the role of the control process in the management of an organisation, it is important to recognise the purpose of management accounting. This has been described by Emmanuel, Otley and Merchant (1985) as having three aspects, namely: a scorecard of performance; attention directing towards significant factors; and an aid to decision making. Kaplan (1984) suggests that cost accounting techniques used in management accounting may no longer be relevant because of the changed nature of firms and the much lower labour content of products. He also argues that it is apparent that profit is being used as a means of motivating managers and evaluating short-term performance, and therefore there is a need for new measures of performance. This point is reiterated by Govindarajan and Gupta (1985) who maintain that long run criteria contribute to organisational effectiveness rather than short-term criteria. On the other hand the use of capital budgeting techniques as a long-term performance measure does not necessarily facilitate long term performance.[14]

The discourse surrounding the application of accounting techniques in practice is extensive and continuous; the preceding examples are only a part of that discourse and are included for illustrative purposes. It is argued here that while this discourse continues it serves to create a level of distraction which obscures the way in which management accounting itself has been subverted to serve the needs of corporate reporting. There is an inevitable encouragement in the prolonging of this discourse concerning the practical application of accounting techniques from organisations. This encouragement comes both from the accounting profession itself, in the mistaken belief (Crowther & Carter 1998) that technical expertise enhances the status of the profession, and from managers, in the belief that this transfers attention from the subversion of organisational accounting.

Accounting in an Organisational Context

It seems apparent therefore that there is a need to consider the role of accounting and accounting systems in the management of organisations both mechanistically and contextually. This point is made by Hopwood (1983), who considers the difficulties of accounting in terms of the context in which it operates. He identifies factors such as competing interpretations of the accounting for events, and tensions between the different facets of an organisation, as well as arguing that accounting attempts to fulfil both reflective and constitutive roles, and that difficulty is created by the external origins of internal accounting. Spicer and Ballew (1983) argue that organisational structure is a significant determinant of the effectiveness of management accounting and control systems because structure can affect the following: information transfer needs within the firm; the need for internal governance structures, such as transfer pricing rules; the level of formal and informal participation within the firm; and the ability of firm members to seek personal goals contrary to organisational goals. Marcus and Pfeffer (1983) consider power to be important to the effectiveness of accounting and control systems, which they state can be implemented more easily if they are consistent with other sources of power, the dominant organisational culture and paradigm, and shared judgements about technical certainty and goal congruence.

In an empirical study of management accounting systems following take-overs or mergers Jones (1985) identified these factors as being integral to the successful absorption of the companies taken over or merged, but having dysfunctional aspects concerning personal stress levels and resistance. Hedberg and Jonsson (1978) argue that organisations have fixed repertoires of behavioural programs and that the accounting information system filters away conflicts and ambiguities, and therefore kills initiative, while Dermer (1988) argues that the control exercised by managers is limited because of the organisations rules and underlying beliefs and behaviours. Gordon and Miller (1976) argue that accounting information systems need to consider the wider environment and take into consideration not just accounting information but also environmental information, organisational attributes and managerial decision making styles. Argyris (1990) argues that people are involved in the control process and that they use the human theory of control rather than technical theories and this can inhibit the operation of the control process. Simons (1964) however states that the control system can not only help implement strategy but can also aid in the strategy formulation process.

The role of accounting in organisational performance cannot therefore be explored without a consideration of the people involved in the control process and the effects of accounting systems on their behaviour, and vice versa. The main people involved with the control of an organisation are its managers. In large organisations the management of the business is normally divorced from its ownership and Williamson (1970) argues that this hinders its control and decision making processes and leads to internal inefficiencies. It also raises the question of executive remuneration and its link to performance.[15] Other features of large organisations of concern to Williamson are resource allocation and the social costs of conglomeration. These questions of ownership, control and resource allocation must however be considered in the context of where power resides within the organisational decision making process.

One factor of importance to all organisations however, which comes from its control system, is the factor of performance evaluation. To evaluate performance it is necessary to measure performance and Churchman (1967) states that measurement needs the following components: language to express results; specification of objects to which the results will apply; standardisation for transferability between organisations or over time; and accuracy and control to permit evaluation. Accounting information inevitably has a role to play in the evaluation of performance but Govindarajan (1984) suggests that a strong fit between environmental uncertainty and performance evaluation style is associated with higher business unit performance and the higher the level of environmental uncertainty the more subjective will be the approach to evaluation. As long ago as 1956 Ridgway considered the dysfunctional aspects of performance measurement and suggested that the use of purely quantitative measures of performance led to undesirable consequences for organisational performance.[16]

Considerations of the role of accounting in the control of business operations therefore can be seen to be concerned with both the appropriateness of the use of accounting for such control and on the appropriateness of particular techniques in the control process. The discourse however recognises that accounting in isolation is insufficient for the control of business operations and that the context in which accounting is used is also important to the effectiveness of its use. Indeed the context determines just how accounting information is used, either within the organisation or externally to that organisation. There is a general recognition in the discourse that accounting and people are inseparable in any consideration of organisational decision making and performance, with each affecting the other. There is however an implicit assumption of agency theory insofar as it is assumed that all managers in a firm are seeking to maximise benefit for the owners of the business and the discourse need only be concerned with how best to achieve this. This discourse is broadened by a consideration of the firm in terms of its wider stakeholder community in terms of issues of accountability.

Accountability

In addition to accounting for the activities of an organisation, with its attendant problems previously discussed, it is necessary that an organisation reports on its activities. This is necessary not just to satisfy statutory requirements but also to inform the owners of the business, and other investors, who are increasingly divorced from the management of the business in larger organisations, what has happened in the business and how it has performed. There is also increasingly a perceived need to report upon the activities and plans of the organisation to a much wider community of stakeholders and to thereby place the organisation within a community and societal setting. Such reporting naturally is based upon the past actions of the organisation, as it is only activity which has taken place which can be reported upon, although such reporting also is concerned with the present and with plans for the future.[17] Nevertheless this aspect of performance is predominantly backwards looking, and is based upon financial accounting rather than management accounting. Furthermore this aspect of performance is concerned primarily with the representation of the organisation to its external environment and so has an outward focus, rather than the internal focus of control.

Reporting therefore, as far as an organisation is concerned, is partly concerned with its accountability and partly with satisfying its informative and public relations needs; in any event reporting is concerned with the performance of the organisation both in the immediate past and planned for the immediate future. Beaver (1989) has identified some changing trends in reporting and highlights a rapid growth in reporting requirements and changes in existing requirements, with less emphasis on earnings and more on soft data and a greater emphasis on disclosure.[18] Eccles (1991) concurs and states that there has been a shift from treating financial figures as the foundation of performance measurement to treating them as part of a broader range of measures. He warns however that this change in reporting requirements needs a new information architecture and also that there is danger in publishing too much information as this can give assistance to an organisation's competitors.

Lee and Parker (1979) trace the development of financial reporting and view the changes which have taken place as being due to the influences of pressure groups rather than the legislative framework, which they consider to be reactive rather than prescriptive. Aryana (1979: 267) concurs with this interpretation of the influence of pressure groups on the changing reporting of organisational activity and states:

> The development of data (provided by accountants) is affected by the conflicting interests of its suppliers (management), its consumers (mainly shareholders and creditors), regulatory agencies and accounting bodies.

McDonald and Puxty (1979) on the other hand maintain that companies are no longer the instruments of shareholders alone but exist within society and so therefore have responsibilities to that society, and that there is therefore a shift towards the greater accountability of companies to all participants. Recognition of the rights of all stakeholders and the duty of a business to be accountable in this wider context therefore has been a relatively recent phenomenon and the economic view of accountability only to owners has only recently been subject to debate to any considerable extent.

Purdy (1983) identifies that not only is there pressure for a general review of corporate reporting but that there have been new types of accounting responding to this pressure. Among others he mentions the treatment of cash flow accounting, the distribution to different groups, and the reporting of organisational activity in terms of value added. He discerns two worrying trends however in the subordination of shareholders' rights to the needs of the company and its survival, and in the tendency for this to lead to short term satisficing and risk reduction rather than to profit maximisation. This implicit assumption that profit maximisation is, or should be, the aim of a firm is a return to neo-classical economic theory and it is worth remembering that Clark (1957: 218) pointed out that profit maximisation is a difficult concept to define, leaving room for the incorporation of good citizenship, when he stated:

> Corporate business must still consider profits, and it has an obligation to do as well by its equity investors as it reasonably can. But when economic theorists describe business as 'maximising profits' they are indulging in an impossible and unrealistic degree of precision. The further a firm's policies extend into the future, the less certain can it be just what policy will precisely 'maximise profits'. The company is more likely to be consciously concerned with reasonably assured survival as a paramount aim, and beyond this, to formulate its governing policies in terms of some such concept as 'sound business', usually contributing to healthy growth...
>
> Where there is this margin of uncertainty as to precisely what policy would 'maximise profits', there is room for management to give the benefit of the doubt to policies that represent good economic citizenship. And it seems that an increasing number of managements are giving increasing weight to this kind of consideration.

The debate about profit maximisation was considerable among economists during this period with Baumol (1959), Cyert and March (1963) and Williamson (1967) being among writers considering the problems of profit maximisation. Others (eg Robinson 1964) argued that firms were not necessarily profit maximisers in all circumstances.

As far as reporting is concerned however Bell (1984) found by using an experimental methodology that the form of presentation does affect the confidence that decision makers have in their judgement of company performance. He found that quantification adds weight to their confidence, thereby demonstrating that while soft issues might be increasing in importance there is still a need for hard accounting data. Bhaskar and McNamee (1983) suggest that organisations have multiple objectives in performance evaluation and reporting and that these are fundamentally irreconcilable and so proxy goals and measures are used as surrogates.[19] Changing information needs and the use of surrogate measures and goals were found to be a feature of non-profit organisations by Greenberg and Nunamaker (1987: 332) who state:

> Without a doubt, the use of multiple performance measures in evaluating and controlling non profit activities is commonplace. These multiple measures can be viewed as short-run objectives in themselves, or as surrogates for more ill-defined non-measurable goals.

They also make the point that performance evaluation starts with the determination of what constitutes a good performance. Laughlin and Puxty (1983) adopt a worldview stance and consider the different viewpoints of the users of information and the providers of information, suggesting that problems are caused by the different viewpoints of these two distinct classes of users.

This need to recognise that people are involved in the reporting process and in the accounting process as well as in the running of organisations is explored at length by Hopwood (1974) who is concerned with the behavioural implications of accounting for control and for performance evaluation. He states that accounting systems are just one way of processing information, maintaining that the accounting function is influenced by the needs and attitudes of the individuals involved as well as by group processes and pressures from the wider social and economic environment. He argues that while accounting data is used for the evaluation of performance, different approaches can have different effects and lead to different conclusions being drawn. He also argues that budgetary targets can lead to a satisficing tendency[20] and that controls can lead to defensive behaviour, whereas participation can lead to greater satisfaction and increased performance, and social factors can influence behaviour as much as organisational rules. His thesis therefore is that human beings are inextricably involved in the control and reporting processes and that these processes cannot be studied other than within this context. Thus in this way the arguments from economics made by Baumol (1959), Cyert and March (1963) *et al.* have been transferred from the domain of economics to the domain of accounting.

The Accountability of Complex Organisations

The point concerning the involvement of people in the reporting processes of organisations is made also by Mitroff (1983), who examines the firm from a stakeholder perspective. He states that the assumption that the behaviour of organisations can be understood in terms of a relatively small number of internal and external stakeholders is too simplistic, as is the assumption that stakeholder behaviour can be understood in terms of economic properties.[21] His Jungian exploration of the behaviour of individuals in the measurement and reporting of organisational performance is significant in providing a motivation for managerial behaviour. Whether this Jungian explanation of behaviour is accepted or not however, it is important to remember that, just as organisations are complex due to their composition of individual people, so too are individuals who are not uni-dimensional but rather are complex and unpredictable in their behaviour and motivation and that this has implications for organisational control and reporting.

In contrast Williamson (1975) considers organisations to be complex due to their size, which leads to uncertainty, bounded rationality and information impactedness.[22] He argues that the extent of these factors determines the likelihood of organisational failure and that there are organisational limits to the size of a firm brought about by such factors as diseconomies of scale, communication distortion and bureaucratic insularity. He states that multidivisionalism is a method of overcoming this but that there are still limits to size because of difficulties of communication, resource allocation and lack of entrepreneurial opportunities. He argues therefore that organic growth beyond a certain size leads to failure, thereby limiting the effective size of a firm. In fact it is argued here that this organisational failure framework provides one further mechanism by which the effect of the needs of corporate reporting upon accounting can be explained.

While businesses are complex organisations, because of the human element of their composition, it is nevertheless still a fact that organisations, as businesses, continue to exist and function and that there remains a need to account for their behaviour, evaluate their performance and report upon it. In order to evaluate performance it is necessary to determine the constituents of good performance and the use of performance indicators as a means of determining this is increasing in importance. Oakland (1989) reminds that to be useful a performance indicator must be measurable, relevant and important to the organisation's performance. Such indicators must also be meaningful to anyone seeking to evaluate performance and the cost of obtaining the information must not outweigh its value. Brewster (1994) makes the point that it is not a simple process to identify good performance indicators and that a comparative measure against the performance of other organisations can give misleading signals and cause resources to be focused on the wrong things.

In measuring performance, while it is evident that the interests of the wider stakeholder community are of increasing concern, it is nevertheless important that the interests of the owners of a business, ie the shareholders, are not neglected because these owners expect some return on their investment commensurate with the level of risk to which they are exposed. Rappaport (1992: 89) challenges the assumption that stock market prices, as a measure of shareholder return, are dependent upon short term results, stating that:

> ...managers continue to believe that stock prices are driven by short term accounting numbers despite research evidence to the contrary.

He considers that stock market value in the long term is dependent upon achieving competitive advantage and states (1992: 90):

> Maximum returns for current shareholders will materialise only when managers maximise long term shareholder value and deliver interim results that attest credibility to the sustainability of competitive advantage.

He identifies the perceived conflict between achieving competitive advantage and creating shareholder value when he states (1992:85):

> Increasingly, companies are becoming polarised into two camps: those who consider shareholder value the key to managing the company and those who put their faith in gaining competitive advantage.

but challenges this assumption, stating (1992: 86):

> Long term productivity lies at the root of both sustainable competitive advantage and consistent results for the shareholder.

Nevertheless for him the performance of a company is evaluated solely in terms of shareholder value.[23]

A different perspective upon performance evaluation has been proposed by Kaplan and Norton (1992) with the development of their balanced scorecard approach. They argue that traditional measurement systems in organisation are based upon the finance function and so have a control bias but that the balanced scorecard puts strategy and vision at the centre. They identify four components of the balanced scorecard, each of equal importance, and each having associated goals and measures.[24] They argue (1993: 135-6) that measurement is an integral part of strategy, stating:

> Today's managers recognise the impact that measures have on performance. But they rarely think of measurement as an essential part of their strategy. For example, executives may introduce new strategies and innovative operating processes intended to achieve breakthrough performance, then continue to use the same short-term financial indicators they have used for decades, measures like return on investment, sales growth, and operating income.

and

> Effective measurement, however, must be an integral part of the management process.

They maintain that the balanced scorecard is a way of evaluating performance which recognises all the factors affecting performance and it is certainly true that an external perspective, in the shape of customers, is included in this framework which is lacking from Rappaport's shareholder value analysis.

This discourse is predicated in the assumption that accountability is only to the owners of the business and fails to consider accountability in a wider context. Moreover the discourse makes the assumption that accountability can be achieved through the reporting of performance in accounting terms without recognising one of the main points surrounding the central argument of this book, that such accounting has ceased to have a major significance in the reporting of organisation performance.

Accountability in a Wider Context

The evaluation of performance is however partly concerned with the measurement of performance and partly with the reporting of that performance, and with the greater importance being given to social accountability the changing reporting needs of an organisation are also being recognised. Thus Birnbeg (1980) states that accounting is attempting to supply various diverse groups, with different needs for information, and that there is a need for several distinct types of accounting to perform such a function. Similarly Gray (1992) considers the limitations of the traditional economic base for accounting and questions some of its premises such as: the desirability of growth; the existence of rational economic man; the exclusion of altruism; and the ignoring of the way in which wealth is distributed. He argues that there is a need for a new paradigm with the environment being considered as part of the firm rather than as an externality and with sustainability and the use of primary resources being given increased weighting. Rubenstein (1992) goes further and argues that there is a need for a new social contract between a business and the stakeholders to which it is accountable, and for a business mission which recognises that some things go beyond accounting.

Monks and Minow (1991) consider that power is an essential component of accountability and that corporations are externalising machines suited to self-preservation. They therefore argue that when faced with conflicting pressures a company will act in the interests of self-preservation with lower risk but less benefit being chosen. They also argue that the power of businesses is increasingly being consolidated into the hands of the executives rather than owners and that social accountability is not a feature of such organisations.[25]

Different perspectives therefore exist concerning the extent of disclosure of performance data, the need for reporting and the framework in which such reporting takes place. These differing perspectives however all evaluate practice from a particular viewpoint rather than from the multiple perspective stance of addressing the needs of multiple groups of stakeholders. There is recognition that these different groups require different information and that this poses a problem for accounting and for reporting, but little consideration has been given to an analysis of this problem and ways of its resolution. The various suggestions noted regarding different methods of accounting all seek to satisfy one viewpoint and perceived need at the expense of others. Organisations attempting this task of meeting differing requirements need to consider first their own position in the community and the values upon which they are founded. This was recognised by Selznick (1957: 136) who stated:

> Truly accepted values must infuse the organisation at many levels, affecting the perspective and attitudes of personnel, the relative importance of staff activities, the distribution of authority, relations with outside groups, and many other matters. Thus if a large corporation asserts the wish to change its

role in the community from a narrow emphasis on profit-making to a large social responsibility (even though the ultimate goal remains some combination of survival and profit-making ability), it must explore the implications of such a change for decision making in a wide variety of organisational activities.

The ethical implications of a firm's behaviour were considered by McCoy (1985: 87) who considers ethics to be at the core of business behaviour, stating:

> Dealing with values requires continual monitoring of the surrounding environment, weighing alternative courses of action, balancing and (when possible) integrating conflicting responsibilities, setting priorities among competing goals, and establishing criteria for defining and evaluating performance. Along with these goes learning ways to bring this ethical reflection directly and fully into the processes by which policy is made, implemented, and evaluated. Increasingly, skills in dealing with values as integral components of performance and policy-making are being recognised as central for effective management in a society and a world undergoing rapid change.

The way in which a business performs in terms of its ethical behaviour, and identified place in society as a whole, is determined by its relationship with its stakeholder community. It is also to some extent determined by, as well as to some extent determining, the culture of the organisation. Kotter and Heskett (1992) consider corporate culture and show how this can lead to good business performance but also to bad business performance and a lack of ability to change to match changing environmental conditions. They consider that effective leadership is crucial to success. Success, like good performance, is always of course a subjective construct depending upon the perspective of the evaluator.

Nevertheless business performance is dependent not only upon such factors as the accounting systems and behavioural aspects of organisational behaviour but more crucially upon the planning aspects of organisational behaviour, and this is the role of strategic management.

Strategic Management

Strategy is concerned with planning and Ackoff (1974) identified the principles of planning as being participative, holistic and continuous. Planning is by its nature a future oriented activity but planning for that future depends upon, *inter alia*, an understanding of the present. Accounting information, based upon the measurement and reporting of performance in the present and recent past, gives a basis to that understanding that is both quantified and determinate. Planning is however also concerned with the control of an organisation, and it is assumed that managers are in control of the organisation, which functions as a cybernetic system. Dermer (1986) however argues that this managerial control is an illusion and that the cybernetic model needs revising. He argues that the existence of multi-interest groups necessitates a multi-rational approach and that political relationships within the organisation are important. Mason and Swanson (1979) argue for a systems approach to understanding organisational behaviour with information being influential as well as informative. They argue that this systems approach leads to three levels of planning and measurement for the organisation: at the organisational level, the individual level and the societal level. Dermer (1988) defines organisational order as a sustained pattern of behaviours and beliefs, and argues in favour of a pluralistic model of the organisation.[26]

Organisations are therefore generally considered to be complex and individualistic, being a composite of the various interests interacting, and made up of people. Attempts have however been made to categorise organisations according to their manifest patterns of behaviour and Miles and Snow (1978) believe that organisations can be grouped into four distinct types depending upon the adaptive behaviour used to maintain an effective alignment with their environment. The basic ideas which lead to this categorisation are that organisations act to create their environment, management's strategic choices shape the structure and processes of the organisation, and structure and process constrain strategy, so that organisational behaviour is based upon the strategic choices made by managers. They describe the process of organisational adaptation as being concerned with the solving of three problems: the entrepreneurial problem which is concerned with the acceptance of the product and market domains of the organisation; the engineering problem which is concerned with the creation of systems of control for the organisation; and the administrative problem which is concerned with reducing uncertainty. Based upon these premises they identify four types of organisation: defenders, prospectors, analysers and reactors.[27]

This analysis shows the importance to the organisation of awareness of the external environment and of the need to handle the uncertainty of this environment in a definite way. It suggests that there are a variety of ways of doing so, but that the organisation's structure must fit its strategy, which must in turn be aligned to the environment.[28]

These analyses tend to suggest that strategic management needs to be flexible and responsive but that planning is at the core of successful strategic management. Mintzberg (1994) however suggests that although planning is perceived to be necessary in order to control and co-ordinate activities and to ensure that the future is taken into account, in actual fact strategic planning, as an activity, is of no benefit to an organisation in developing its strategy for dealing with the future but rather has a limited role in explaining the present.[29] His position is very much against the formal planning process as a means of determining the strategy of an organisation. This position was previously adopted by Peters and Waterman (1982) who claimed that, as man is not rational, a rational model of the organisation is not appropriate.[30] Goold and Quinn (1990) examine the strategic control process and suggest that a formal control process has both advantages and disadvantages. Advantages which they suggest include: it forces greater realism into the planning process; it encourages higher standards of performance; it defines responsibilities; and it provides motivation for business unit managers. Disadvantages include: inflexibility in responding to the environment; the possibility of misdirection of motivation and resources towards wrong goals; and added cost and bureaucracy to the control process.

Planning, Control and Strategic Determination

There is considerable doubt therefore concerning the value of planning as a formal process for strategic management. The question of evaluating strategic performance is equally subject to debate and Chakravarthy (1986) suggests that traditional measures of performance based upon profitability are inadequate for evaluating strategic performance.[31] Kimberley, Norling and Weiss (1983: 251) also make this point and argue that traditional measures do not necessarily even measure some aspects of performance and can certainly lead to inadequate and misleading evaluations of performance, stating:

> Traditional perspectives on performance tend to ignore the fact that organisations also perform in other, less observable arenas. Their performance in these arenas may in some cases be more powerful shapers of future possibilities than how they measure up on traditional criteria. And, paradoxically competence in the less observable arenas may be interpreted

as incompetence by those whose judgements are based solely on traditional criteria. Particularly in the case of organisations serving the interests of more than one group where power is not highly skewed and orientations diverge, the ability to develop and maintain a variety of relationships in the context of diverse and perhaps contradictory pressure is critical yet not necessarily visible to the external observer.

It appears therefore that it is difficult to identify the determinants of the level of performance of an organisation[32] and this point is made by Child (1974, 1975) who examines both the universality theory and the contingency theory of organisational behaviour and finds support for both theories.

Kay (1993) considers organisational performance in terms of added value and suggests measures such as comparison of historic and current costs, measurement of shareholder value and cash flow, and capital costs and the equivalence of financial measures of performance. He argues that strategy involves identifying a firm's distinctive capabilities and applying them to appropriate markets.[33] Stacey (1991) on the other hand argues that business organisations are feedback mechanisms and that parameters in the performance feedback mechanism need to take account of instability as well as stability, irregularity and random shocks, adapting to as well as shaping customer requirements, and an awareness that small changes escalate over time.[34]

Any theory of organisational behaviour however must take into account the fact that organisations consist of people, who plan, control and manage a business and also interact with each other. Likert (1967) recognises this in advocating a recognition of the human element of management while Ouchi (1981) advocates a change in management style to include communication, involvement of people, and trust in relationships, suggesting that while these were present in the best run American companies they were missing from others.[35]

In studying managerial work Mintzberg (1973) describes it as 'characterised by brevity, variety and fragmentation'. He describes the basic purpose of management as: to ensure efficient production, to design and maintain stability and to act as an informational link between the organisation and its environment, thereby ensuring that the organisation serves the ends of its owners.[36]

Kotter and Heskett (1992) identified four factors which shape managerial behaviour: the competitive and regulatory environment; leadership and its efforts to articulate and implement a business vision and strategy; the formal structure, systems, plans and policies of the organisation; and the corporate culture. They describe culture as consisting of shared values and behavioural practices and argue that the fit between culture and business context determines the performance of an organisation. They cite research which demonstrates a fourfold increase in performance as far as revenue growth is concerned and a twelve fold increase in performance as far as stock price growth is concerned for firms which have performance enhancing cultures as compared with those which do not. The importance of culture is also stressed by Hampden-Turner (1990), who considers also that an organisation's culture can either enhance performance or destroy performance depending upon how it operates in the organisation.

Culture, Strategy and Control

While culture is considered by these writers as being crucial to the performance of a business, it is only one aspect of performance determination, and to some extent culture determines management style while to some extent management style also determines culture. Thus the fact that management is able to alter both culture and management style is therefore important in determining business performance. Goold and Campbell (1987) identify three different types of business each with their own management style and label these three types as strategic planning, financial control and strategic control companies.[37]

Campbell, Devine and Young (1990) are concerned with the mission of an organisation and have developed the Ashridge Mission Model which suggests that a company needs to define its mission in terms of its purpose, strategy, standards, behaviours and values. They argue that defining the mission of an organisation enhances performance by developing better strategic thinking, greater commitment to shared corporate goals, ethical behaviour and a greater awareness of the importance of the various stakeholders.

These various writers tend to imply a unidimensional approach to understanding organisational behaviour and that understanding and manipulating the key variable, whether it be mission, culture or the planning function, is sufficient to achieve good organisational performance. The reality however is that organisations are more complex than this and Child (1984) identifies several problems in defining what constitutes good performance. Thus he considers that there are multiple dimensions to performance and good performance in one dimension may result in poor performance in another. He also argues that the time span to be considered in evaluation is important and that good performance in the short term may not equate to good performance in the longer term, and vice versa. This suggestion poses problems for many of the measurement systems of corporate performance which tend to utilise immediate measures to indicate performance levels, thereby leading to short term behaviour.[38] Child considers organisational behaviour and performance in terms of control, distinguishing control over means and methods from the exercise of power in terms of control over processes. He argues that there are dimensions of control needed to satisfy a range of criteria, and that control can be formal or informal, centralised or decentralised, bureaucratic or person centred and this control can be control over output or over culture, and that all these aspects contribute towards organisational performance. The aspects of control are considered further by Flamholtz, Das and Tsui (1985) who consider control in terms of the structure and culture of an organisation and its external environment. They argue that a control system needs to include planning and definitions of outcomes and measurement, with feedback, evaluation and rewards elements. They argue therefore that a control system needs to be cybernetic but that the context in which control operates requires an open system, but more importantly recognise that control systems are not totally internal to the organisation but must take into account the external environment and the interaction of the organisation with its environment.

Neimark and Tinker (1986) argue for a dialectical approach to management control systems stating that management accounting is based upon neo-classical economics and therefore has the following problems: the absence of a historical perspective and a feedback mechanism; a separation of the control system from the environment, which is incompletely specified; and a view of performance as being non-problematic. They argue that control systems are agents of social change and that problems are solved by the interplay of the various forces concerned. Neu (1992) argues that managers in selecting strategies focus upon a small number of variables and that managers are embedded in social relations (individual, institutional and societal) and that therefore manager's choices are social constructions rather than the conclusions of rational analysis as is normally assumed. Brunsson (1993) considers the question of rationality further, suggesting that there are things which can be said but not done and things which can be done but not said, and that there is a difference between truth as an absolute and truth in practice. He also states that those in control are influenced by their constituency and that the need for consistency and routinisation often outweigh the need for control and that control therefore is often justification of behaviour and reasoning for actions is often just hypocrisy.[39]

Accounting and Business Performance

It seems clear therefore that while a business is an entity insofar as it is perceived to act as a whole towards the fulfilment of the particular objectives which it has, it is in reality a composite entity which consists of an association of individuals each working, at least in theory, towards a commonalty of shared purpose. The actuality is different to this in that common purpose is often not clearly identified and articulated and that the individuals are not necessarily working totally towards that common purpose, particularly when this purpose conflicts with or diverges from their individual motivations and objectives. This is particularly apparent when these individuals are considered within the context of the stakeholder community because the different stakeholder groupings have different desires and different motivations which are often in conflict with those of other stakeholders. These conflicts need to be resolved in some fashion in order for the business to function and it is obvious that, as businesses do actually function, that they end up being resolved by some means.

It is inevitable however that these conflicting needs and desires lead to tensions within the organisation, and that the organisation can therefore be considered to be a dynamic entity which exists around the conflicting tensions of these needs and desires. Various attempts have been made by writers to explain the operation of these tensions and the resulting organisational behaviour. These attempts have been made using the various theories of micro-economics, psychology, deconstruction and critical theory but none seems to have satisfactorily explained all the resulting behavioural variables.

Although organisations can be seen to be composite organisations with accounting running through the organisation as a basis for the planning and control of organisational activity as well as the measurement of performance, considerable debate surrounds the use of accounting by an organisation. Nevertheless the various uses of accounting as a basis for the measurement of past performance, the control of present performance, and the planning of future performance bind the whole organisation throughout time into a unified whole and thereby relegate the debate concerning the use of accounting by that organisation into one concerning the applicability of, and implementation of, the various techniques of accounting. This binding of the organisation into a unified whole is however only possible at the expense of simultaneously separating the organisation from its external environment. Thus accounting, when used traditionally, considers solely the organisation itself and the effects of that organisation's actions only upon itself, rather than recognising any interaction between the organisation and its environment.

Just as the functioning of an organisation however can be seen to be a composite of its various constituents, so too does this reflect upon the performance of the business and the multiple facets of that performance. It is clear that the determination of good performance is dependent upon the perspective from which that performance is being considered and that what one stakeholder grouping might consider to be good performance may very well be considered by another grouping to be poor performance.[40] The evaluation of performance therefore for a business depends not just upon the identification of adequate means of measuring that performance but also upon the determination of what good performance actually consists of. Just as the determination of standards of performance depends upon the perspective from which it is being evaluated, so too does the measurement of that performance, which needs suitably relevant measures to evaluate performance, not absolutely as this has no meaning, but within the context in which it is being evaluated. From an external perspective therefore a very different evaluation of performance might arise, but moreover a very different measurement of performance, implying a very different use of accounting in that measurement process, might arise.

Conclusions

Much research has been undertaken into the various methods of measuring performance and there is a general recognition that traditional accounting measures do not necessarily provide adequate tools for such measurement. Various additional methods, both based upon accounting and quantitative analysis and upon more qualitative analysis, have been proposed within the literature. It seems however that it is generally accepted that this problem has not been resolved, and so the research continues. Accounting however still has a place at the centre of the organisation as part of the control system and as part of the evaluation system. The planning function of strategic management still remains as the key to the successful operation of a business, even if the constituent parts of planning are subject to debate.

The question of accountability and the reporting of performance is one which has opened up recently in terms of who the business is accountable to, and what should be reported upon, to whom, and in what form. This debate concerns one of the central aspects of performance evaluation. The three key areas of this accounting research therefore, namely planning, control and reporting, can be seen to be crucial to the investigation of organisational performance evaluation, to be considered separately and collectively.

The evaluation in this chapter shows the diverse strands of accounting research, all of which are predicated on the assumption that better use of accounting techniques will lead to better organisational performance. It has been argued however that this discourse of accounting is in fact not the sole determinant of organisational performance, and in fact has the effect of obfuscating the usurpation of both accounting and organisational decision making by managers for the purpose of corporate reporting.

Notes

[1] This dimension of accounting is generally referred to as management accounting. See Crowther (1996a) for a fuller consideration of this role of management accounting.

[2] This category will incorporate the main purposes of financial accounting and reporting.

[3] This technical expertise does not necessarily reside in the managers themselves, who are in the majority not qualified accountants. Their expertise is principally in the mobilisation of the resources of reported accounting information and the ability to call upon the expertise of the accountants within the organisation to undertake the necessary tasks of accounting in the required manner.

[4] The key concepts which he identifies are concerned with uncertainty, information costs, behavioural aspects of accounting, and contingency theory. He argues that cost allocations are arbitrary and lead to sub-optimality of performance, with a concentration upon short-term decision making.

[5] When considering power in the context of a disciplinary practice of surveillance (Foucault 1977) through the use of the reporting mechanisms of accounting, it is clear that the majority of power resides in the managers of the organisations who control and distribute this reporting to other stakeholders in the manner they choose. It is recognised however that legislatory and regulatory requirements provide a limit to their ability to control this information and pose demands upon the reporting framework.

[6] See particularly Russell (1992) and Clegg (1989) for a consideration of and an analysis of the distribution of power within society at large. This analysis applies equally to organisations as micro-societies.

[7] He argues that these failures lead to social alienation amongst stakeholders and that there is a need to change accounting to meet the actual needs of society.

[8] It is not the intention of this book to suggest the resolution of this problem of accountability; rather it is the attention to consider the ways in which this is reflecting in corporate reporting.

[9] They identify shortcomings in the traditional framework of accounting in dealing with the treatment of distributional conflicts, tensions in management control systems and with the cultural and ideological specificity of accounting. At the same time they introduce into the discourse the concept of accounting as social construction.

[10] The differences in accounting, and in consequent reported results of organisational performance between traditional accounting and accounting for shareholder value, are considered in some detail in Crowther, Davies & Cooper (1998).

[11] He explains that such inscription enables the translation of elements within their context and that viewed this way accounting has the following qualities: mobility by enabling the actor and his setting to be divorced; stability by the use of conventions which eliminate contextual dependencies thereby making information recognisable to all users; and combinability by enabling the accumulating and aggregating of data.

[12] Wildavsky (1975) describes budgeting as a means of translating financial resources into human purposes, thereby focusing upon the need to have a mechanism for determining and monitoring actual performance within an organisation. He describes the budgetary process as a plan but states that it tends to be based largely upon the past and is mostly incremental. Because of these problems and the involvement of the budgetary process in the politics of the organisation he subsequently (1984) identifies a tendency amongst budget holders to ask for resources over and above those actually required, as part of the negotiating process of reaching budget agreement.

[13] Thus Dearden (1969) evaluates return on investment as a measure of performance and highlights both technical drawbacks (including the differing methods of transfer pricing, the use of book values and a tendency to over-simplification) and implementation constraints (including the difficulty of setting equitable profit objectives and the difficulty of assigning responsibility). He therefore demonstrates the limitations to the use of ROI as a means of evaluating divisional performance, suggesting that the use of either residual income or two-step pricing would provide a means of overcoming these deficiencies. Emmanuel and Otley (1976) on the other hand criticise the value of residual income as a means of evaluating performance, arguing that not only is it possible to be evaluated only after the event but also that there is a danger in evaluating

individual divisional performances while neglecting the total performance of the organisation, forgetting that this is the key criterion. Similarly Emmanuel and Gee (1982) argue that transfer pricing can be a fair and neutral process while Watson and Baumler (1975) argue that transfer pricing can either enhance differentiation or facilitate integration in the whole organisation depending upon its use. On the other hand Grabski (1985) considers the different transfer pricing models existing, such as the economic, mathematical programming and behavioural models, considering their respective applicability and concluding that they can each have different effects depending upon their mode of application. Jarrett (1983) is concerned with the limitations of internal rate of return as a method of evaluating performance and determining the allocation of resources. He states that the uses of net present value (NPV) and net future value lead to different results and that the greater uncertainty in future cash flows and the longer lives of assets lead to greater uncertainty, and therefore to less reliability being attached to the financial information contained in financial reporting. Scapens (1979) on the other hand suggests that maximising economic profit leads to NPV maximising decisions and stresses the difference between operating and investment decisions. Spicer (1988) however distinguishes between central and diversified decisions and states the need to take into consideration incentives, risk, and conflicts of interest. Technical limitations as well as behavioural variables therefore seem to limit the value of accounting as a means of controlling a business and measuring its performance. Swieringa and Weick (1987) recognise this and argue that ROI and variance analysis are treated as aids to decision making but they can also directly affect motivation and commitment, can induce short-termism and groupthink, and can also eliminate options as well as articulating them.

[14] This point is made by Lister (1984) and repeated by Haka, Gordon and Pinches (1985) who state that sophisticated capital budgeting techniques do not necessarily lead to superior performance.

[15] Executive remuneration schemes are outside the scope of this work.

[16] Various investigations have been undertaken into the actual practice of organisations concerning performance measurement and evaluation. Thus Fitzgerald, Johnston, Brignall, Silvestro and Voss (1991) considered service businesses and suggested that business unit performance needs to be measured in relation to the objectives identified in the planning process. A variety of measures were used and were linked to the competitive environment, the service type, business strategy and the motivation and reward structure. Davis, Coates, Emmanuel, Longden and Stacey (1992) considered multinational companies and found that a variety of financial and non-financial measures were in use, linked to organisational culture, but suggested that these measures could result in risk minimising behaviour and short term decision making rather than optimal behaviour. Jackson (1986) considered the public sector and identified difficulties in setting measures appropriate to consumer needs but sufficiently standardised

to be implemented. It therefore appears that a variety of performance measures are used and that there is widespread recognition of the need to link these to the strategy of the organisation and to the needs of the stakeholder community. It is also recognised that this is a difficult process which has not necessarily been adequately addressed.

[17] See Crowther (1996b) for a detailed consideration of accounting's use in this respect.

[18] He claims that there has been a shift from an economic view of income to an informational perspective with a recognition of social implications of an organisation's activities, a distinctly different perspective from that of Lee & Tweedie (1975).

[19] They suggest that these multiple objectives are reflected in the new information needs of users of information thereby leading to changes in the types of data collected and analytical tools used.

[20] See Wildavsky (1984) and Birnbeg et al (1983), inter alia, referred to previously.

[21] He argues that Jungian analysis shows that each individual is not a single stakeholder but rather a complex of multiple stakeholders in terms of archetypes and ego-types, each responding differently. He therefore argues that managerial behaviour is determined by these internal-to-the-psyche stakeholders and their interplay, which exerts influence upon the behaviour of individuals, both as individuals and as members of groups, organisations, businesses and society.

[22] This concept is developed within his Organisational Failure Framework.

[23] He had made this point previously in 1981 when he considered the limitations of accounting techniques such as ROI and earnings per share as a way of evaluating company strategy. He argued that a shareholder value approach, based upon discounted cash flow analysis, was the correct way of evaluating alternative company strategies, stating that the ultimate test of a corporate plan was whether it creates value for the shareholders and that this was the sole method for evaluating performance.

[24] The four components are: financial perspective – how does the firm look to shareholders; customer perspective – how do customers perceive the firm; internal business perspective – what must the firm excel at; and innovation and learning perspective – can the firm continue to improve and create value.

[25] Taylor (1989) on the other hand considers local authorities and the framework in which they operate, arguing that rather than the conventional trustee or user needs models in existence a world view conceptual model is appropriate. He argues that this model gives a social perspective and understands the individual as a member of society rather than seeking to understand the societal processes as a result of individual processes. Ogden and Bougen (1985) consider the disclosure of accounting information to trade unions and state that different conceptualisations of the relationship between management and employees can generate different conclusions regarding the disclosure of accounting information during industrial relations bargaining. They argue that increased disclosure can

lead to reduced opposition from employees, greater commitment and loyalty and increased legitimacy for intended action.

[26] He identifies the key elements of this model as leadership (ie management), citizenship (ie the various stakeholders), institutions (the formal and informal patterns of relating) and ideologies (the patterns of belief). He argues that the system of control for such an organisation consists of four components: managerially imposed regulations; self-regulatory activities; co-operation sufficient to permit commonalty rather than goal attainment; and a fit which implies accommodation among the various interest groups.

[27] According to Miles & Snow (1978) defenders perceive the environment as stable, are finance and production dominated and aim to grow incrementally through market penetration. For them planning is concerned with problem solving and performance evaluation is achieved by comparing present performance with that of previous time periods. Prospectors are concerned with finding and exploiting new product and market opportunities and they are creators of change. They are people centred with a low degree of structural formalisation, and marketing and research and development are the dominant functions. Planning is concerned with problem finding and performance evaluation is achieved by comparison with similar organisations. Analysers are followers of change rather than initiators and undertake extensive market surveillance to achieve this. They tend to operate a matrix structure with marketing and production being the dominant functions. Planning for these organisations is all important and therefore intensive and comprehensive, and performance evaluation tends to be by means of comparison of actual performance against plans and budgets. Reactors, the final grouping, tend not to have a clearly articulated strategy and the strategy - structure relationship does not change to meet changing environmental conditions. They are therefore viewed as unsuccessful organisations, with failure being their ultimate destination.

[28] This point is made also by Clegg and Fitter (1981) who identify, via a case study methodology, that problems within an organisation stem from the structure of that organisation being unable to cope with the environmental uncertainty and from inappropriate managerial responses and choices.

[29] He identifies various problems for the planning function regarding the information available and suggests that hard information is limited in scope, much information is too aggregated to be of value and that generally information is too unreliable and arrives too late to be of use for planning. He also identifies various pitfalls for the planning process, including: planning tends to be incremental; it ignores or cannot cope with discontinuities; it is inflexible and constrains freedom of action; it can lead to a lack of commitment from managers excluded from the planning process; and it substitutes calculation for commitment. Mintzberg suggests that although strategy may be a plan it is more than this, including a pattern (therefore including emergent strategies) and a

perspective and thus not able to be formally composed from a rigorous planning system.

[30] This is because: the analytical approach is abstract and heartless and has an in-built conservative bias; it is negative in outlook, abhors mistakes and denigrates the importance of values; it leaves no place for internal competition and does not value experimentation. They argue that success is achieved by managing ambiguity and paradox, tolerating failure, allowing organisational fluidity and evolution, and accepting the importance of culture. They argue their case by means of examples of successful companies, but with the benefit of hindsight it can be seen that this success was ephemeral rather than sustainable and a more rigorous approach to understanding sustainable strategic success is needed.

[31] He argues that, rather than using conventional financially based measures, use should be made of alternative measures, and he suggests composite measures. He also suggests that rather than the conventional perspective of market based evaluation of performance, alternative perspectives are needed which recognise the need to satisfy multiple stakeholders.

[32] This difficulty arises for a variety of reasons but primarily because of the need to satisfy the differing needs of a diverse group of stakeholders.

[33] He also argues that strategy concerns the relationship between the firm and its competitors, customers and suppliers and that strategic management therefore needs an external focus rather than the internal focus of a planning model.

[34] He argues that rather than the traditional mechanistic, organic or power models of an organisation what is needed is the scientific chaos model. This model he claims recognises the following factors: complex patterns of behaviour; extreme sensitivity to change; hidden patterns; chaos is essential to innovation; and innovation emerges at critical points in the life cycle of the organisation. The implications of this model for strategic planning are that: long term financial models are of little value; probabilistic models only help in the short term; long term forecasts and simulations are impossible; long term plans make no contribution to the business; and short interval control is vital. This model would seem to imply a total refutation of the value of planning and while it is true that plans become less reliable the further into the future they are projected this does not necessarily equate with their being valueless. Nevertheless a recognition of the existence of unpredictable events and behaviours is important and this seems to be the real value of chaos theory to organisational management and planning.

[35] He labelled this theory as Theory Z to distinguish it from, and imply its superseding of, Theories X and Y of McGregor (1960) concerning human behaviour, and implying that there was a logical progression in understanding human behaviour in the work place from theory X to Y to Z.

[36] He identified three types of role for the manager – the interpersonal, informational and decisional roles – and subdivided these into eleven job types, arguing that the manager needed to fulfil each of these roles at various points in his work. He also suggested ways to manage more efficiently, including the

sharing of information, ensuring the role taken fits the situation, and dealing with coalitions, thereby recognising that the manager must deal with multiple perspectives in the performance of his job in the same way as an organisation must deal with the multiple perspectives of the wide stakeholder community.

[37] They suggest that financial control companies are dominated by the centre with tight control, and actual performance compared with budget and a short term emphasis upon profitability and share price growth. Strategic control companies are also dominated by the centre but the emphasis is upon business planning rather than financial performance, with separate business units having autonomy in achieving plans. Financial control companies tend to grow through acquisition whereas strategic control companies grow organically but at a slower rate. For strategic control companies relative changes in performance are more important than absolute measures of profitability or share price. Strategic planning companies take a longer term view and are interested in building competitive advantage. The centre provides support rather than control and these companies are interested in sales growth through market development rather than in share price growth, assuming that this will follow in the long term from developing the competitive advantage of core businesses. Whilst this analysis of different business behaviour provides a perspective on the different types of management it does seem to be very much a restatement of the work of Miles and Snow (1978) previously cited.

[38] This supports the findings of Coates, Davis, Longden, Stacey and Emmanuel (1993) previously cited.

[39] This argument might be considered to be somewhat cynical but it does focus upon the rationality of behaviour, both assumed and actual, and that declared and actual reasoning might not be the same. It also calls attention to the behavioural considerations not just of organisational control but of the whole operating of organisations. This sets the various aspects of organisational behaviour within the context of interpersonal behaviour and indicates that the various aspects of organisational performance cannot be studied mechanistically but must take the human element into account. The whole discourse surrounding strategic development and implementation however is based upon the assumption that the process is complex. By implication therefore the people who undertake such tasks are fulfilling a difficult role on behalf of the organisation and its shareholders and stakeholders.

[40] As identified by Child (1984), previously cited.

Chapter 3

Accounting for Social and Environmental Performance

Introduction

The traditional view of accounting, as far as an organisation is concerned, is that the only activities with which the organisation should be concerned are those which take place within the organisation,[1] or between the organisation and its suppliers or customers. Consequently it is considered that these are the only activities for which a role for accounting exists. Here therefore is located the essential dialectic of accounting – that some results of actions taken are significant and need to be recorded while others are irrelevant and need to be ignored. This view of accounting places the organisation at the centre of its world and the only interfaces with the external world take place at the beginning and end of its value chain. These interfaces comprise of, at the commencement of the organisational processing cycle, resources acquisition (raw materials, labour capital etc) and, at the end of the cycle, selling its wares (goods or services) and distributing a share of the value created through its transformational process to its owners (i.e. shareholders). This view of accounting is particularly pertinent for management accounting, which is essentially concerned with the transformational process within the organisation, and the management of that transformational process.

It is apparent however that any actions which an organisation undertakes will have an effect not just upon itself but also upon the external environment within which that organisation resides. In considering the effect of the organisation upon its external environment it must be recognised that this environment includes both the business environment in which the firm is operating, the local societal environment in which the

51

organisation is located and the wider global environment. This effect of the organisation can take many forms, such as:

- the utilisation of natural resources as a part of its production processes;
- the effects of competition between itself and other organisations in the same market;
- the enrichment of a local community through the creation of employment opportunities;
- transformation of the landscape due to raw material extraction or waste product storage;
- the distribution of wealth created within the firm to the owners of that firm (via dividends) and the workers of that firm (through wages) and the effect of this upon the welfare of individuals.

It can be seen from these examples that an organisation can have a very significant effect upon its external environment and can actually change that environment through its activities. It can also be seen that these different effects can in some circumstances be viewed as beneficial and in other circumstances be viewed as detrimental to the environment. Indeed the same actions can be viewed as beneficial by some people and detrimental by others.[2] This is why planning enquiries or tribunals, which are considering the possible effects of the proposed actions by a firm, will find people who are in favour and people who are opposed. This is of course because the evaluation of the effects of the actions of an organisation upon its environment are viewed and evaluated differently by different people.

Accounting however traditionally remains focused upon the actions of the organisation and ignores the effects of the organisation upon its external environment.[3] A growing number of writers however have recognised that the activities of an organisation impact upon the external environment and have suggested that one of the roles of accounting should be to report upon the impact of an organisation in this respect. Such a suggestion first arose in the 1970s and a concern with a wider view of company performance is taken by some writers who evince concern with the social performance of a business, as a member of society at large. This concern was stated by Ackerman (1975) who argued that big business was recognising the need to adapt to a new social climate of community accountability but that the orientation of business to financial results was inhibiting social responsiveness. McDonald and Puxty (1979) on the other hand maintain that companies are no longer the instruments of shareholders alone but exist within society and so therefore have responsibilities to that society, and that there is therefore a shift towards the greater accountability of companies to all participants.

Recognition of the rights of all stakeholders and the duty of a business to be accountable in this wider context therefore has been largely a relatively recent phenomenon.[4] The economic view of accountability only to owners has only recently been subject to debate to any considerable extent. It is recognised however that some owners of businesses have always recognised a responsibility to other stakeholders and this is evident from the early days of the Industrial Revolution. Thus, for example, Robert Owen (1816, 1991) demonstrated dissatisfaction with the assumption that only the internal effects of actions need be recorded through accounting. Furthermore he put his beliefs into practice through the inclusion within his sphere of industrial operations the provision of housing for his workers at New Lanark. Others went further still and Jedediah Strutt and his sons of Belper, for example, provided farms to ensure that their workers received an adequate supply of milk, as well as building accommodation for their workforce which was of such high standard that these dwellings remain highly desirable in the present.[5] Similarly the Gregs of Quarry Bank provided education as well as housing for their workforce. Indeed Salt went further and attempted to provide a complete ecosphere for his workers. Thus there is evidence from throughout the history of modernity that the self-centred approach of accounting for organisational activity was not universally acceptable and was unable to satisfactorily provide a basis for human activity. It is however upon this inadequate foundation that the basis of traditional accounting rests.

The Development of Social Accounting

Implicit in this concern with the effects of the actions of an organisation on its external environment is the recognition that it is not just the owners of the organisation who have a concern with the activities of that organisation. Additionally there are a wide variety of other stakeholders who justifiably have a concern with those activities, and are affected by those activities. Those other stakeholders have not just an interest in the activities of the firm but also a degree of influence over the shaping of those activities. This influence is so significant that it can be argued that the power and influence of these stakeholders is such that it amounts to quasi-ownership of the organisation. Indeed Gray, Owen and Maunders

(1987) challenge the traditional role of accounting in reporting results and consider that, rather than an ownership approach to accountability, a stakeholder approach, recognising the wide stakeholder community, is needed.[6]

The desirability of considering the social performance of a business has not always however been accepted and has been the subject of extensive debate. Thus Hetherington (1973: 37) states:

> There is no reason to think that shareholders are willing to tolerate an amount of corporate non-profit activity which appreciably reduces either dividends or the market performance of the stock.

while Dahl (1972: 18) states:

> ....every large corporation should be thought of as a social enterprise; that is an entity whose existence and decisions can be justified insofar as they serve public or social purposes.

Nevertheless the performance of businesses in a wider arena than the stock market and its value to shareholders has become of increasing concern. Fetyko (1975) considers social accounting as an approach to reporting a firm's activities and stresses the need for identification of socially relevant behaviour, the determination of those to whom the company is accountable for its social performance and the development of appropriate measures and reporting techniques. Klein (1977) also considers social accounting and recognises that different aspects of performance are of interest to different stakeholder groupings, distinguishing for example between investors, community relations and philanthropy as areas of concern for accounting. He also considers various areas for measurement, including consumer surplus, rent, environmental impact and non-monetary values. While these writers consider, by implication, that measuring social performance is important without giving reasons for believing so, Solomons (1974) considers the reasons for measuring objectively the social performance of a business. He suggests that while one reason is to aid rational decision making, another reason is of a defensive nature.

Unlike other writers, Solomons not only argues for the need to account for the activities of an organisation in term of its social performance but also suggests a model for doing this, in terms of a statement of social income. His model for the analysis of social performance is as follows:

Analysis of Social Performance

	£
Statement of Social Income:	
Value generated by the productive process	XXX
+ unappropriable benefits	XXX
- external costs imposed on the community	XXX
Net social profit / loss	XXX

Fig 3.1 Analysis of Social Performance

While Solomons proposes this model, which seems to provide a reasonable method of reporting upon the effects of the activities of an organisation on its external environment, he fails to provide any suggestions as to the actual measurement of external costs and benefits. Such measurement is much more problematic and this is one of the main problems of any form of social accounting – the fact that the measurement of effects external to the organisation is extremely difficult. Indeed it can be argued that this difficulty in measurement is one reason why organisations have concentrated upon the measurement through accounting of their internal activities, which are much more susceptible to measurement.

In this respect, Gray, Owen and Maunders (1987) consider social reporting in terms of responsibility and accountability and distinguish between the internal needs of a business, catered for by management accounting, and the external needs, which are addressed for shareholders by financial reporting but largely ignored for other stakeholder interests. Social accounting is an attempt to redress this balance through a recognition that a firm affects, through its actions, its external environment (both positively and negatively) and should therefore account for these affects as part of its overall accounting for its actions.

The evaluation of the performance of an organisation is partly concerned with the measurement of performance and partly with the reporting of that performance, and with the greater importance being given to social accountability the changing reporting needs of an organisation are also being recognised. Thus Birnbeg (1980) states that accounting is attempting to supply various diverse groups, with different needs for information, and that there is a need for several distinct types of accounting to perform such a function. Similarly Gray (1992) considers the limitations of the traditional economic base for accounting and questions some of its premises.[7] Rubenstein (1992) goes further and argues that there is a need for a new social contract between a business and the stakeholders to which it is accountable, and a business mission which recognises that some things go beyond accounting. Ogden and Bougen (1985) on the other hand consider the disclosure of accounting information to trade unions and state that different conceptualisations of the relationship between management and employees can generate different conclusions regarding the disclosure of accounting information during industrial relations bargaining.[8]

The Gaia Hypothesis

While the discourse of accounting was developing the notion of greater accountability to stakeholders during the 1970s, other developments were also taking place in parallel. Thus in 1979 Lovelock produced his Gaia Hypothesis in which he posited a different model of the planet Earth; in his model the whole of the ecosphere, and all living matter therein, was co-dependant upon its various facets and formed a complete system. According to this hypothesis, this complete system, and all components of the system, was interdependent and equally necessary for maintaining the Earth as a planet capable of sustaining life. This Gaia hypothesis was a radical departure from classical liberal theory which maintained that each entity was independent and could therefore concentrate upon seeking satisfaction for its own wants, without regard to other entities. This classical liberal view of the world forms the basis of economic organisation, provides a justification for the existence of firms as organs of economic activity and provides the rationale behind the model of accounting adopted by society. The Gaia hypothesis however implied that interdependence, and a consequent recognition of the effect of ones actions upon others, was a facet of life. This consequently necessitates a different interpretation of accountability in terms of individual and organisational behaviour and reporting.

Given the constitution of economic activity into profit seeking firms, each acting in isolation and concerned solely with profit maximisation, justified according to classical liberalism, it is inevitable that accounting developed as organisation-centric, seeking merely to measure and report upon the activities of the firm insofar as they affected the firm. Any actions of the firm which had consequences external to the firm were held not to be the concern of the firm. Indeed enshrined within classical liberalism, alongside the sanctity of the individual to pursue his own course of action, was the notion that the operation of the free market mechanism would mediate between these individuals to allow for an equilibrium based upon the interaction of these freely acting individuals and that this equilibrium was an inevitable consequence of this interaction.[9] As a consequence any concern by the firm with the effect of its actions upon externalities was irrelevant and not therefore a proper concern for its accounting.

The Gaia hypothesis stated that organisms were interdependent[10] and that it was necessary to recognise that the actions of one organism affected other organisms and hence inevitably affected itself in ways which were not necessarily directly related. Thus the actions of an organism upon its environment and upon externalities was a matter of consequence for every organism. This is true for humans as much as for any other living matter upon the planet. It is possible to extend this analogy to a consideration of the organisation of economic activity taking place in modern society and to consider the implications both for the organisation of that activity and the accounting for that activity. As far as profit seeking organisation are concerned therefore the logical conclusion from this is that the effect of the organisation's activities upon externalities is a matter of concern to the organisation, and hence a proper subject for accounting in terms of organisational activity.

While it is not realistic to claim that the development of the Gaia Theory had a significant impact upon organisational behaviour, it seems perhaps overly coincidental to suggest that a social concern among business managers developed at the same time that this theory was propounded. It is perhaps that both are symptomatic of other factors which caused a re-examination of the structures and organisation of society. Nevertheless organisational theory has, from the 1970s, become more concerned with all the stakeholders of an organisation, whether or not such stakeholders have any legal status with respect to that organisation. At the same time within the discourse and practice of accounting there has been a growth in concern with accounting for externalities and for the effects of the actions of the firm upon those externalities. One externality of particular concern is that of the environment; in this context the environment has been defined to include the complete ecosphere, rather than merely the human part of that ecosphere. These concepts form part of the foundations of a concern with environmental accounting.

Environmental Accounting

The approach to measuring organisational activity through an accounting for the actions of a firm in relation to the external environment, and the impact of those activities of the firm upon external stakeholders, is generally known as environmental accounting. Such accounting recognises that the actions taken by a firm impact upon its external environment and consequently can be, and should be, accounted for. This is in contrast with the traditional view of accounting that what happens to the firm is of relevance to the firm, and should therefore be accounted for, while what happens outside the firm, whether affected by the firm or not, is irrelevant to the firm and not therefore a proper subject for accounting as far as the firm is concerned. Forms of accounting which reflect the actions of the firm upon its external environment are generally labelled social accounting, which has been defined as:

> ...the process of communicating the social and environmental effects of organisations' economic actions to particular interest groups within society and to society at large, beyond the traditional role of providing a financial account to the owners of capital, in particular, shareholders. Such an extension is predicated upon the assumption that companies do have wider responsibilities than simply to make money for their shareholders.
> (Gray, Owen & Maunders 1987: ix)

and as:

> Voluntary disclosures of information, both qualitative and quantitative made by organisations to inform or influence a range of audiences. The quantitative disclosures may be in financial or non-financial terms.
> (Mathews 1993: 64)

The essential features of such social accounting therefore can be stated to be firstly that it is an attempt to report upon the effects of the actions of the firm upon the societal environment which is external to the firm itself, secondly that it is aimed at an audience external to the firm and thirdly that it is voluntary in nature. In this respect it differs from traditional accounting in terms of its audience and its voluntary nature. One consequence of this is that not all firms feel the need for reporting this aspect of their operations and such reporting as does take place is by no means uniform in its approach.

One subset of social accounting is that form of accounting which is concerned with reporting the actions of the firm insofar as they relate to the environment in a physical rather than social sense. This is collectively known as environmental accounting and has been defined in the following terms:

> ...it can be taken as covering all areas of accounting that may be affected by the response to environmental issues, including new areas of eco-accounting. (Gray, Bebbington & Walters 1993: 6)

while Schaltegger, Muller and Hinrichsen (1996: 5) make the following statement

> Environmental accounting can be defined as a sub-area of accounting that deals with activities, methods and systems for recording, analysing and reporting environmentally induced financial impacts and ecological impacts of a defined economic system.

Just as the definitions of such forms of accounting vary from one person to another, so too does the way in which such accounting is operationalised within different firms. Indeed this variation can be found not just through inter-firm comparison but also through longitudinal study. Environmental accounting is a relatively recent phenomenon and Mathews (1997) suggests that its roots go back only to the 1970s. Since that time interest in such accounting has grown considerably and the applications, perceived relevance and techniques of environmental accounting have developed considerably. Indeed the purposes of environmental accounting have also changed and Schaltegger et al (1996) state that such forms of accounting were used in the past to placate external environmental activists but are now regarded as an important source of information for the internal management of the firm. No proof however is offered for this statement and it will be suggested later that neither environmental activists nor the internal management processes of the firm have any significant influence upon the development of environmental accounting. Rather it will be argued that the prime use of environmental accounting data is for the production of reports for external consumption instead of for internal decision making purposes.

It can be seen however that difficulties surround the nature and purposes of environmental accounting. This is equally true with regard to the nature and purpose of traditional accounting, and the appropriateness of any measures suggested for either. Nevertheless it is clear that social and environmental accounting is significantly different from traditional accounting because of its attempt to include an accounting for the effects of the actions of the organisation upon the external environment. Thus the organisation, although recognised to be a discrete entity, is only one part of a system which transcends the organisational boundary and negates the internal / external binarism of traditional accounting. This different focus both distinguishes such accounting from its traditional relative and leads to the need for different measures of performance.

Growth in the techniques offered for measuring environmental impact, and reporting thereon, has continued throughout the last twenty-five years, during which the concept of environmental accounting has existed. However the ability to discuss the fact that firms, through their actions, affect their external environment and that this should be accounted for has often exceeded within the discourse any practical suggestions for measuring such impact.[11] At the same time as the technical implementation of environmental accounting and reporting has been developing the philosophical basis for such accounting has also been developed. Thus Benston (1982, 1984) and Schreuder and Ramanthan (1984a, 1984b) consider the extent to which accountants should be involved in environmental accounting while Donaldson (1982) argues that such accounting can be justified by means of the social contract as benefiting society at large. Others (eg Batley & Tozer 1993, Geno 1995) have argued that sustainability is the cornerstone of environmental accounting while Gray and Collison (1991) have stated that environmental auditing should be given prominence.

More critical authors (eg Cooper & Scherer 1984, Laughlin & Puxty 1986) have viewed traditional accounting, from a labour process perspective, as a mechanism to support the dominance of capital over labour interests. Such authors have tended to view social and environmental accounting as a mechanism for benefiting non-traditional users of accounting information.[12] Similarly Power (1991) argues that there is a need to prevent the institutionalisation of such accounting by its adoption and absorption by the accounting profession into normal accounting.[13] Such critical views however conflict with the declared aims of environmental accounting of measuring and reporting upon the effect within the external environment of the activities of the firm. In order to do so effectively, environmental accounting needs to be absorbed within mainstream accounting and utilised by practising accountants as a part of their normal activities. Environmental accounting cannot therefore be both a radical vehicle for change (Maunders & Burritt 1991, Puxty 1991) as well as a mechanism for incorporating externalities into the reporting of the firm through its accounting.[14]

Environmental accounting can be seen to be a topical issue from a variety of perspectives but to be useful in measuring and reporting upon the impact of the actions of the firm it must necessarily be absorbed into the repertoire of accounting practitioners and into the systems of organisational control and reporting, rather than remaining as a critical external discourse.

A Framework of Environmental Accounting

Although it has been stated earlier that the disclosure of the actions of the firm in terms of their impact upon the external environment is essentially voluntary in nature this does not necessarily mean that the actions themselves are always voluntary. Nor does it mean that all such disclosure is necessarily voluntary. The regulatory regime which operates in the UK means that certain actions must be taken by firms which affect their influence upon the external environment. Equally certain actions are prevented from being taken. These actions and prohibitions are controlled by means of regulation imposed by the government of this country – both the national government and local government. For example all proposed building of new industrial premises is controlled by planning regulations and when this proposed planning involves designated green belt land then this can also involve public enquiries. Such enquiries also arise when the proposal is for new mining, either open cast or deep mining. Acceptance of any such proposals is generally dependant upon the plans, including proposed actions to protect local communities and the environment, and, in the case of mining, steps required to be taken to repair the environment once the activities have ceased. Equally regulations govern the type of discharges which can be made by organisations, particularly when these are considered to cause pollution. Such regulations govern the way in which waste must be disposed of and the level of pollutants allowed for discharges into rivers, as well as restricting the amount of water which can be extracted from rivers.

The regulatory regime which operates in this country is continuing to change and become more restrictive as far as the actions of an organisation and its relationship with the external environment are concerned.[15] It seems reasonable to expect these changes to continue into the future and concern for the environmental impact of the activities of organisations to increase. These regulations tend to require reporting of the activities of organisations and such reporting also involves an accounting connotation. This accounting need is both to satisfy regulatory requirements but also to meet the internal needs of the organisation as the managers of that organisation, in both controlling current operations and in planning future business activities, must have accounting data to help manage the organisational activities in this respect. The growth of environmental data, as part of the management information systems of organisations, therefore can be seen to be, at least in part, driven by the needs of society at large, as reflected in the regulations imposed upon the activities of organisations. As the extent of regulation of such activities can be expected to increase in the future therefore the more forward looking and proactive organisations might be expected to have a tendency to extend their environmental impact reporting in anticipation of future regulation, rather than merely reacting to existing regulation.

It cannot reasonably be argued however that the increase in stature and prominence accorded to environmental accounting and reporting among organisations is driven entirely by present and anticipated regulations. To a large extent the external reporting of such environmental impact is not determined by regulations – these merely require reporting to the appropriate regulatory body. Nor can it be argued that the increasing multinational aspect of organisational activity, and the consequent need to satisfy regulatory regimes from different countries, has alone driven the increased importance of environmental accounting. Organisations which choose to report externally upon the impact of their activities on the external environment do so voluntarily, and in doing so they must expect to derive some benefit from this kind of disclosure. The kind of benefits which organisations can expect to accrue through this kind of disclosure will be considered later in this chapter. At this point however we should remember the influence of stakeholders upon the organisation and it can be suggested that increased disclosure of the activities of the organisation is a reflection of the growing power and influence of stakeholders, without any form of legal ownership, and the recognition of this influence by the organisation and its managers.

The Objectives of Environmental Accounting

The objective of environmental accounting therefore is to measure the effects of the actions of the organisation upon the environment and to report upon those effects. In other words the objective is to incorporate the effect of the activities of the firm upon externalities and to view the firm as a network which extends beyond just the internal environment to include the whole environment. In this view of the organisation the accounting for the firm does not stop at the organisational boundary but extends beyond to include not just the business environment in which it operates but also the whole social environment. Environmental accounting therefore adds a new dimension to the role of accounting for an organisation because of its emphasis upon accounting for external effects of the organisation's activities. In doing so this provides a recognition that the organisation is an integral part of society, rather than a self contained entity which has only an indirect relationship with society at large. This self-containment has been the traditional view taken by an organisation as far as their relationship with society at large is concerned, with interaction being only by means of resource acquisition and sales of finished products or services. Recognition of this closely intertwined relationship of mutual interdependency between the organisation and society at large, when reflected in the accounting of the organisation, can help bring about a closer, and possibly more harmonious, relationship between the organisation and society. Given that the managers and workers of an organisation are also stakeholders in that society in other capacities, such as consumers, citizens and inhabitants, this reinforces the mutual interdependency.

Environmental accounting also provides an explicit recognition that stakeholders other than the legal owners of the organisation have power and influence over that organisation and also have a right to extend their influence into affecting the organisation's activities.[16] This includes the managers and workers of the organisation who are also stakeholders in other capacities. Environmental accounting therefore provides a mechanism for transferring some of the power from the organisation to these stakeholders and this voluntary surrender of such power by the organisation can actually provide benefits to the organisation. Benefits from increased disclosure and the adoption of environmental accounting can provide further benefits to the organisation in its operational performance, beyond this enhanced relationship with society at large. These benefits, it is argued, can include:

- an improved image for the organisation which can translate into additional sales;

- the development of environmentally friendly or sustainable methods of operation which can lead to the development of new markets;
- reduced future operational costs through the anticipation of future regulation and hence a cost advantage over competitors;
- decreased future liabilities brought about through temporal externalisation;
- better relationships with suppliers and customers which can lead to reduced operational costs as well as increased sales;
- easier recruitment of labour and lowered costs of staff turnover.

It needs to be recognised however that there are increased costs of instituting a regime of environmental accounting and that these additional costs need to be offset against the possible benefits to be accrued. These increased costs are concerned with the development of appropriate measures of environmental performance and the necessary alterations to the management information and accounting information systems to incorporate these measures into the reporting system. This is particularly problematical for the organisation in terms of justification because the increased costs are readily quantifiable but the benefits are much more difficult to quantify.

This leads to one of the main problems with the accounting for externalities through social and environmental accounting. This problem is concerned with the quantification of the effects of the activities of the organisation upon its external environment. This problem revolves around four main areas:

- determining the effects upon the external environment of the activities of the organisation;
- developing appropriate measures for those effects;
- quantifying those effects in order to provide a comparative yardstick for the evaluation of alternative courses of action, particularly in terms of an accounting based quantification;
- determining the form and extent of disclosure of those quantification so as to maximise the benefits of that disclosure while minimising the costs of the disclosure and minimising the possibility of knowledge of the firms operational activities being given to competitors.

These are problems which have been addressed by proponents of this form of accounting but it is fair to say that these problems have primarily been recognised to exist rather than being satisfactorily solved.

Those that argue in favour of an increased extent of disclosure in this area tend to consider the advantages of the disclosure from the point of view of external stakeholders rather than from the point of view of the organisation itself. Indeed one of the features of the environmental accounting discourse is the polarisation of views between those concerned with the firm, and its owners and managers, and those concerned with the environmental, and thereby certain external stakeholders. The management of stakeholders, and the business on behalf of all stakeholders, is one mechanism for reinforcing the organisational boundary, which becomes less important under a social accounting perspective. Indeed it will be argued that this polarisation of perspectives is an important component of organisational performance reporting. Accordingly it is increasingly apparent that these environmental issues are recognised by organisations as being of importance and the extent of environmental reporting by organisation is increasing and seems likely to increase further in the future.[17]

Before the development of any appropriate measures can be considered it is first necessary for the organisation to develop an understanding of the effects of its activities upon the external environment. The starting point for the development of such an understanding therefore is the undertaking of an environmental audit. An environmental audit is merely an investigation and recording of the activities of the organisation in order to develop this understanding (Kinnersley 1994). Indeed BS7750 is concerned with such audits in the context of the development of environmental management systems. Such an audit will address, inter alia, the following issues:

- the extent of compliance with regulations and possible future regulations;
- the extent and effectiveness of pollution control procedures;
- the extent of energy usage and possibilities increasing for energy efficiency;
- the extent of waste produced in the production processes and the possibilities for reducing such waste or finding uses for the waste necessarily produced;
- the extent of usage of sustainable resources and possibilities for the development of renewable resources;
- the extent of usage of recycled materials and possibilities for increasing recycling;
- life cycle analysis of products and processes;
- the possibilities of increasing capital investment to affect these issues;

- the existence of or potential for environmental management procedures to be implemented.

Once this audit has been completed then it is possible to consider the development of appropriate measures and reporting mechanisms to provide the necessary information for both internal and external consumption. These measures need to be based upon the principles of environmental accounting, as outlined below. It is important to recognise however that such an environmental audit, while the essential starting point for the development of such accounting and reporting, should not be viewed as a discrete isolated event in the developmental process. Environmental auditing needs to be carried out on a recurrent basis, much as is financial or systems auditing, in order to both review progress through a comparative analysis and to establish where further improvement can be made in the light of progress to date and changing operational procedures.

The Principles of Environmental Accounting

In order to understand the rationale for environmental accounting, and the basis on which it is suggested that such accounting operates, it is necessary therefore to consider the principles upon which environmental accounting operates. There are three basic principles (Schaltegger et al 1996) to environmental accounting:

- sustainability;
- accountability;
- transparency.

and each will be considered in turn.

Sustainability

Sustainability is concerned with the effect which action taken in the present has upon the options available in the future. If resources are utilised in the present then they are no longer available for use in the future, and this is of particular concern if the resources are finite in quantity. Thus raw materials of an extractive nature, such as coal, iron or oil, are finite in quantity and once used are not available for future use. At some point in the future therefore alternatives will be needed to fulfil the functions currently provided by these resources. This may be at some point in the relatively distant future but of more immediate concern is the fact that as resources become depleted then the cost of acquiring the remaining resources tends to increase, and hence the operational costs of organisations tend to increase.[18]

Sustainability therefore implies that society must use no more of a resource than can be regenerated. This can be defined in terms of the carrying capacity of the ecosystem (Hawken 1993) and described with input – output models of resource consumption. Thus the paper industry for example has a policy of replanting trees to replace those harvested and this has the effect of retaining costs in the present rather than temporally externalising them. Similarly motor vehicle manufacturers such as Volkswagen have a policy of making their cars almost totally recyclable. Viewing an organisation as part of a wider social and economic system implies that these effects must be taken into account, not just for the measurement of costs and value created in the present but also for the future of the business itself.

Measures of sustainability would consider the rate at which resources are consumed by the organisation in relation to the rate at which resources can be regenerated. Unsustainable operations can be accommodated for either by developing sustainable operations or by planning for a future lacking in resources currently required. In practice organisations mostly tend to aim towards less unsustainability by increasing efficiency in the way in which resources are utilised. An example would be an energy efficiency programme.

Accountability

Accountability is concerned with an organisation recognising that its actions affect the external environment, and therefore assuming responsibility for the effects of its actions. This concept therefore implies a quantification of the effects of actions taken, both internal to the organisation and externally. More specifically the concept implies a reporting of those quantifications to all parties affected by those actions. This implies a reporting to external stakeholders of the effects of actions taken by the organisation and how they are affecting those stakeholders. This concept therefore implies a recognition that the organisation is part of a wider societal network and has responsibilities to all of that network rather than just to the owners of the organisation. Alongside this acceptance of responsibility therefore must be a recognition that those external stakeholders have the power to affect the way in which those actions of the organisation are taken and a role in deciding whether or not such actions can be justified, and if so at what cost to the organisation and to other stakeholders.

Accountability therefore necessitates the development of appropriate measures of environmental performance and the reporting of the actions of the firm. This necessitates costs on the part of the organisation in developing, recording and reporting such performance and to be of value the benefits must exceed the costs. Benefits must be determined by the usefulness of the measures selected to the decision-making process and by the way in which they facilitate resource allocation, both within the organisation and between it and other stakeholders. Such reporting needs to be based upon the following characteristics:

- understandability to all parties concerned;
- relevance to the users of the information provided;
- reliability in terms of accuracy of measurement, representation of impact and freedom from bias;
- comparability, which implies consistency, both over time and between different organisations.

Inevitably however such reporting will involve qualitative facts and judgements as well as quantifications. This qualitativeness will inhibit comparability over time and will tend to mean that such impacts are assessed differently by different users of the information, reflecting their individual values and priorities. A lack of precise understanding of effects, coupled with the necessarily judgmental nature of relative impacts, means that few standard measures exist. This in itself restricts the inter-organisation comparison of such information. Although this limitation is problematic for the development of environmental accounting it is in fact useful to the managers of organisations as this limitation of comparability alleviates the need to demonstrate good performance as anything other than a semiotic.

Transparency

Transparency, as a principle, means that the external impact of the actions of the organisation can be ascertained from that organisation's reporting and pertinent facts are not disguised within that reporting. Thus all the effects of the actions of the organisation, including external impacts, should be apparent to all from using the information provided by the organisation's reporting mechanisms. Transparency is of particular importance to external users of such information as these users lack the background details and knowledge available to internal users of such information. Transparency therefore can be seen to follow from the other two principles and equally can be seen to be a part of the process of recognition of responsibility on the part of the organisation for the external effects of its actions and equally part of the process of transferring power to external stakeholders.

Reporting Environmental Effects

Although topical at the present time, environmental accounting has been shown to be a relatively recent phenomenon. As such it has by no means met with universal acceptance as an aspect of the activities of a firm which is of importance and worthy of involvement in by members of the firm, as far as accounting in this manner is concerned. The perceived benefits of such accounting to organisations has not been demonstrated to such an extent that all organisations consider such measurement and reporting would benefit them, although this view is being modified over time. Increasingly organisations are seeking to measure environmental impact and to report upon it both internally and externally. Indeed there is an increasing acceptance that environmental issues have a direct relationship with the economic success of an organisation. This view of the perceived irrelevance of environmental information however is particularly prevalent amongst accountants. Thus Frost and Wilmhurst (1996) report the findings of a survey among practising accountants in which they found that not only were the majority of accountants not involved in environmental management issues but a only minority believed that such environmental information was important to users of annual reports. Equally Quellette (1996) reported that traditional accounting used by firms provided inadequate information on environmental impact and costs and this resulted in ill-informed management decisions.

Exactly how such environmental information can be quantified and incorporated into traditional company accounting is a matter of some debate. Current accounting practice, as enshrined within the Statements of Standard Accounting Practice (SSAPs) is essentially focused upon the firm as the subject for accounting. Thus SSAPs specifically exclude accounting for costs which will not be incurred by the firm. If accounting in such a manner were to be allowed in practice then the problems of how to quantify environmental impact would become of significance. In this respect Hooks (1996) argues that the accounting profession has a responsibility to address this issue and to develop a means of accounting which establishes a balance between accounting for profit and accounting for environmental impact. She argues that this accounting would be wider than the current practises regarding disclosure, which appear to be linked to a desire to create an appropriately environmentally conscious image rather than any true concern with environmental impact.[19] Similarly Howard (1996) argues that ethical behaviour, corporate governance and environmental accounting are inextricably intertwined in determining the performance of a firm. Indeed these arguments are slowly becoming embedded into professional practice and the ICAEW (1993) have produced guidelines which recommend that organisations publish their environmental objectives in ways which are open to the measurement of performance and give details of expenditure on specific objectives.

There have been many claims that the quantification of environmental costs and the inclusion of such costs into business strategies can significantly reduce operating costs by firms; indeed this was one of the main themes of the 1996 Global Environmental Management Initiative Conference. Little evidence exists that this is the case but Pava and Krausz (1996) demonstrate empirically that companies which they define as 'socially responsible' perform in financial terms at least as well as companies which are not socially responsible.[20] Similarly in other countries efforts are being made to provide a framework for certification of accountants who wish to be considered as environmental practitioners and auditors.[21] Azzone, Manzini and Noci (1996) however suggest that despite the lack of any regulatory framework in this area a degree of standardisation, at least as far as reporting is concerned, is beginning to emerge at an international level. If this is the case then it can be expected to become reflected in the regulatory frameworks at national levels in due course. It can equally be argued that firms which regard themselves as successful can afford to devote more effort towards being socially responsible as they progress upwards through a form of Maslow's hierarchy.

Bailey and Soyka (1996) claim that environmental accounting provides a firm with a set of tools which can help the firm with both improving the quality of the environment and with improving business performance and hence profitability. They significantly however fail to address the problems of quantification which beset attempts to account for environmental impact suggesting, by implication, that environmental engineers and the techniques of TQM have already solved these problems.[22] Milne (1996) suggests that management accounting is deficient in that it ignores the impact of the firm upon the biophysical environment.[23] Birkin (1996) on the other hand argues in favour of the adoption of environmental management accounting, which he defines as a set of techniques concerned with the provision and interpretation of information to aid managerial decision making and which takes into account effects upon the external environment. While both writers argue for their individual preferred techniques both again significantly fail to explain such techniques in a way which can be applied in practise by firms concerned with the effects of their actions upon the external environment. Jones (1996) suggests that any method of accounting for biodiversity should be based upon the concept of stewardship rather than ownership.

Similarly Ranganathan and Ditz (1996) state that when environmental issues are quantified they are more likely to be included in the business decision-making process and can therefore help to improve the performance of firms, when measured by traditional accounting means. They recognise however that existing management accounting systems are deficient in this respect but argue that incorporating environmental accounting information into existing accounting information systems need not necessitate a major overhaul of such systems. Again such statements are made without any evidence and without the kind of detail needed to allow such changes to be made to the systems of other firms.

As well as a concern with environmental accounting from the point of view of the internal use of such information for decision making purposes, of equal concern is the use of environmental accounting information for external reporting purposes. In this respect it can be argued that the incorporation of environmental information into the annual reports of firms reflects the concern of the evaluators of such information for investment purposes with the wider scope of organisational activity. Such concern can be seen to be reflected in the discourse concerning environmental issues which is taking place in society at large and is reflected in the media. Equally however it can be argued that the inclusion of such information into the corporate reporting system, as manifest in the annual reports, is a reflection of the desire of firms, and their managers, to address a wider audience through their reports than merely the traditional investors in the firm, either actual or potential. This wider audience can be considered to be those members of society at large who are concerned with the environment and with environmental issues. This will include environmental pressure groups and their individual members as well as other individual members of society. At one level it can be argued that this reflects a recognition by the firm and its managers that the wider external stakeholder community has an interest in the firm and the effect of its actions upon the environment.

At another level however it can be argued that these individual members of society, whether members of environmental pressure groups or not, also may be stakeholders in the firm in other roles; for example they may well be customers, or potential customers, or suppliers or employees. As stakeholders may well have multiple roles in their interaction with an organisation it becomes impossible to separate out the reasons for an organisation desiring to increase the extent of its environmental reporting, except in terms of the creation of a semiotic for the maintenance of managerial hegemony. It is also impossible to ascertain whether or not the firm is seeking to address a different audience, or merely seeking to address differing concerns of the same traditional audience, its owners or potential investors. Nevertheless, as Jones (1996) reports, the extent of environmental reporting, in terms of the number of firms engaged in such reporting, has grown rapidly since 1990 and continues to grow. Similarly KPMG (Management Accounting 1996) confirm this growth in environmental reporting but state that it differs considerably in terms of just what is reported. They argue that a lack of standards, coupled with an uncertainty as to whom such reporting is directed, has led to this wide variation in environmental reporting.[24] Gamble, Hsu, Jackson and Tollerson (1996) on the other hand argue, based upon empirical research, that environmental reporting is not increasing in coverage but that there are national differences. Beaver (1989) however has identified some changing trends in reporting and highlights a rapid growth in reporting requirements and changes in existing requirements, while Eccles (1991) concurs.[25]

Disclosure in Corporate Reporting

An examination of the external reporting of organisations does however demonstrate an increasing recognition of the need to include environmental information and an increasing number of annual reports of companies include some information in this respect. This trend is gathering momentum as more organisations perceive the importance of providing such information to external stakeholders. It has been suggested however (Till & Symes 1999) that the inclusion of such information does not demonstrate an increasing concern with the environment but rather some benefits to the company itself.[26] One trend which is also apparent however is the tendency of companies to produce separate environmental reports. In this context such reports are generally termed environmental reports although in reality they include both reporting upon environmental impact and upon social impact. Thus the terms social accounting and environmental accounting tend to have been conflated within the practice of corporate reporting and the two terms used interchangeably for the form of performance measurement and reporting which recognises and reports upon the effects of the organisation's actions upon its external environment.

    While these reports tend to contain much more detailed environmental information than is contained in the annual report the implication of this trend is that such information is required by a separate constituency of stakeholders than the information contained in the annual report. This suggests an impression therefore that environmental information is not necessary for the owners and investors in a business but is needed by other stakeholders. This therefore leads to a further suggestion that organisations view environmental issues as separate from the economic performance of the business rather than as integral to it. This conflicts with some of the arguments and findings considered above which suggest the need for the integration of environmental and economic performance within the accounting needs of a business for the sake of continuing future performance. It does however highlight the problematic nature of environmental accounting and some of the problems associated with environmental impact measurement which will be considered later in this book. It will be argued in later chapters that this separation is an essential part of the maintenance of the dialectic of corporate reporting.

    There appears to have been a resurgence of public interest and concern about the environment in recent years and this is being reflected in corporate reporting. Adams (1992: 106-7) explains this resurgence of interest as follows:

> In Britain during the last four decades, within a market economy driven by consumer preference and purchasing capacity, greater economic leisure has provided the opportunity to both analyse and reflect on the underlying nature and direction of a demand led economic system. There is an increasing requirement for information on the social and environmental impact of corporate policy and appraisal effects. The movements for healthy eating, ethical investment and, above all environmental concern have played a big part in awakening the consumer's social awareness.... The very process by which the majority in the West have become affluent is increasingly being questioned by some of its beneficiaries. Can we go on like this? Is it sustainable? Is the whole system flawed and ultimately self destructive? These questions are being asked not just by pressure groups but also by individuals, by business, by governments and global institutions.

These concerns have led to the general opinion that there is something different about environmental information which deserves reporting in its own right rather than being subsumed within the general corporate reporting and lost in the organisation-centric norm of corporate reporting. This opinion is based upon a recognition that:

> The environment (which is a free resource to individual businesses) is increasingly being turned into a factor that does carry costs. Primarily as a result of requirements imposed by current or probable future government regulation on pollution control, but also to some extent because of the wider concern of the public, who can affect a business's profitability by their behaviour as consumers, employees, and investors, there is a financial impact that needs to be accounted for.   (Butler, Frost & Macve, 1992: 60)

These kinds of argument support the practice of corporate reporting in suggesting a general agreement that environmental accounting is distinct from traditional accounting.

The Dialectic of Corporate Performance Reporting

The discourse of corporate performance measurement therefore, together with the practice in terms of organisational reporting, suggest that social performance measurement and reporting (including environmental reporting) is very different from traditional performance reporting, and that the use of accounting in such measurement and reporting is therefore very different. Indeed it will be demonstrated that the two concerns resolve into a polarisation into a concern with financial performance on the part of investors and environmental performance on the part of pressure groups. Furthermore it seems to be generally accepted that the concerns of the two forms of reporting are very different. Thus traditional corporate reporting is assumed to be for shareholders and be concerned only with the internal effects of the organisation's activities. Environmental reporting on the other hand is assumed to be for other stakeholders and to be concerned primarily, if not exclusively, with the effects of the organisation's activities on its external environment.

Moreover, by implication, the concerns of one must be at the expense of the concerns of the other as the two are assumed to be mutually exclusive. Thus the managers of an organisation must manage two conflicting dimensions of corporate performance in order to satisfy the needs of different stakeholders – or at least this dialectic must appear so.[27] This has enabled these managers to adopt the environmental perspective in the maintenance of the dialectic between internal and external aspects of performance, and thereby demonstrate their competence in management of the organisation.

Notes

[1] Essentially the only purpose of traditional accounting is to record the effects of actions upon the organisation itself.

[2] See Child (1984) and Crowther (1996b) regarding the different dimensions of performance.

[3] Indeed this is consistent with financial accounting theory, and its concern with the boundary of the organisation, and with GAAP.

[4] Mathews (1997) traces its origins to the 1970s although arguments show that such concerns can be traced back to the Industrial Revolution.

[5] Indeed the earlier workers' accommodation provided by Richard Arkwright, arguably the instigator of the Industrial Revolution, at Cromford, Derbyshire, remain equally desirable.

[6] The benefits of incorporating stakeholders into a model of performance measurement and accountability have however been extensively criticised. See for example Freedman & Reed (1983), Sternberg (1997, 1998) and Hutton (1997) for details of this ongoing discourse.

[7] Gray in particular argues that there is a need for a new paradigm with the environment being considered as part of the firm rather than as an externality and

with sustainability and the use of primary resources being given increased weighting.

[8] They argue that increased disclosure can lead to reduced opposition from employees, greater commitment and loyalty and increased legitimacy for intended action. This evidence therefore seems to suggest that greater disclosure of information can actually bring about benefits to the organisation as well as to the stakeholders involved. This is in line with the concepts of social and environmental accounting which are concerned with greater disclosure of the activities of an organisation but with an emphasis upon disclosure of actions and the way in which they impact upon the external environment.

[9] This assumption of course ignores the imbalances in power between the various parties seeking to enact transaction through the market.

[10] In actual fact Lovelock claimed in his hypothesis that the earth and all its constituent parts were interdependent. It is merely an extension of this hypothesis to claim the interrelationship of human activity whether enacted through organisations or not.

[11] For example Ramanathan (1976) suggested using the concept of social overhead to be offset against reported results from traditional measures of income, without suggesting how this might be calculated, while Dierkes & Preston (1977) suggest a model for such accounting based entirely upon non-financial quantification. Equally Mathews (1984) proposed a conceptual model for the categorisation of various forms of socially oriented disclosure which included the separation of socially responsible accounting from total impact accounting, while Bebbington (1993) has attempted to consider models for sustainability accounting.

[12] In other words stakeholders other than the professionals for whom external reporting has been considered to be effected.

[13] His view is that radical critique can only be effected from outside the dominant discourse. This is in contrast to the argument of Derrida (1978) as well as failing to appreciate the purpose of such accounting – to hold the organisation accountable through its reporting to all of its stakeholders.

[14] The academic discourse of environmental accounting debates this dilemma to a great extent but this dilemma is not translated into the discourse of corporate reporting. My reading of the academic discourse is that there is general agreement concerning what is desirable in such accounting and the debate is concerned with the means of achieving that outcome – whether incremental change or revolutionary change is the preferred means of securing the desired outcome.

[15] In other words the extent of regulation in this area has increased in recent years and is continuing to increase.

[16] See Rubenstein (1992), cited earlier, for fuller details of this argument.

[17] But see Deegan & Rankin (1999) for a consideration of the deficiencies of current environmental reporting.

[18] Similarly once an animal or plant species becomes extinct then the benefits of that species to the environment can no longer be accrued. In view of the fact that many pharmaceuticals are currently being developed from plant species still being discovered this may be significant for the future.

[19] This is of course part of the maintenance of the semiotic of environmental responsibility referred to earlier.

[20] It is accepted however that different definitions of socially responsible organisations exist and that different definitions lead to different evaluations of performance between those deemed responsible and others.

[21] For example the Canadian Institute of Chartered Accountants is heavily involved in the creation of such a national framework.

[22] This is perhaps a reflection of the engineering background of the authors and the implicit certainty embedded within the discourse of TQM, rather than a genuine suggestion that the problems besetting the accounting community in this respect have been solved elsewhere.

[23] He argues that the making of decisions affecting the environment requires a multidisciplinary approach which needs the inclusion of non-accounting information as well as the development of new accounting techniques. He suggests as examples social cost – benefit analysis and non-market valuation techniques.

[24] This issue of the target audience of such reporting will be the subject of further consideration later.

[25] These changes are principally concerned with the use of a broader range of measures of performance together with an increasing recognition of the social implications of organisational activity.

[26] Till & Symes consider Australian companies where there are tax effects of environmental actions and disclosure benefit companies with increased disclosure. The cultural and legal environments differ from country to country and in the UK such benefits do not accrue. Nevertheless the lack of altruism, or concern for stakeholders, needs to be borne in mind when considering such increased environmental reporting.

[27] It is not suggested that the increasing prominence of social and environmental aspects of corporate performance since the 1970s has been promulgated by managers, any more than the Gaia Hypothesis has been so promulgated. Rather it is argued that the timing of these societal concerns, which are also reflected in corporate reporting, has been convenient for managers.

Chapter 4

Semiology and Statistics: A Methodology for Analysis

Introduction

The previous two chapters have shown, by means of literature review, that there is a perceived dichotomy between financial performance and environmental performance, which represent two incompatible dimensions of performance. As such it is implicit that good performance along one dimension must be at the expense of good performance along the other dimension. If this is the case then it must be expected that this is apparent from an investigation of corporate reports and will be reflected not just in the accounting part of the report but also in the other part of the report. This is therefore testable and it is the purpose of this work to test this assumption. Furthermore it is intended to test the assumption that corporate reports are intended to be outward looking and forward looking documents designed to meet the needs of a wide range of stakeholders of the organisation.

In order to test these assumptions it is first necessary to develop a set of hypotheses, which are testable, and then to develop a method for testing these hypotheses. Thus the following two propositions have been developed which need to be developed into testable hypotheses:

- There is a dichotomy between financial performance and environmental performance which represent two incompatible dimensions of performance.
- Corporate reports are intended to be outward looking and forward looking documents designed to meet the needs of a wide range of stakeholders of the organisation.

The second proposition must be viewed as a corollary of the first, stemming from the fact that environmental accounting is designed to meet the needs of this wide range of stakeholders. It is therefore necessary to develop a hypothesis to test the first statement before developing one to test the second.

Development of Hypotheses

The performance of an organisation is reflected in its annual reporting in both financial terms, through its balance sheet and profit and loss account and associated notes,[1] and in the reports from the chairman and directors and the overview of the company performance and prospects.[2,3] Additional information is also given in the Environmental Report of the organisation when this is produced.[4] The dichotomy between the two dimensions of performance is such that it would suggest that good performance in both dimensions of performance cannot be achieved. This performance can be tested by a consideration of the following hypotheses:

Hypothesis 1

There is a significant difference between the financial performance of different organisations.

Hypothesis 2

There is a significant difference between the environmental performance of different organisations.

Hypothesis 3

There is a negative correlation between the financial performance and the environmental performance of the same organisations.

These hypotheses are designed to identify that there are differences in both financial and environmental performance between companies (hypotheses 1 and 2) and the expectation of the incompatibility of good performance in both dimensions would lead to the negative correlation suggested in hypothesis 3. These hypotheses are subject to quantitative testing.

Hypothesis 4

The annual reports of companies will consider both dimensions of performance in terms of the written reports.

Hypothesis 5

The written parts of the annual report will favour the dimension of performance for which performance has been better.

Corporate reports contain written aspects as well as accounting aspects and these written aspects are subject to much less regulation. Accordingly it would be expected that these parts of the reports would focus upon those aspects of performance which reflect best upon the organisation and its performance. These hypotheses are intended to test this assumption and, as such, are subject to qualitative testing.

As far as the second statement, regarding the outward and forward looking focus of the annual report, is concerned this can be subject to qualitative testing though a consideration of the following hypotheses:

Hypothesis 6

The written reports have greater prominence that the financial reports in the corporate report.

Hypothesis 7

The written reports consider future prospects to a greater extent than past performance.

Hypothesis 8

The reporting documents as a whole show evidence of being designed to meet the needs of a wide range of external stakeholders.

The written parts of the reports are less concerned with the stewardship role of reporting and are more concerned with the image of the organisation. This will tend to be future oriented and concerned with the image of the organisation as far as a wide range of stakeholders is concerned.

Confirmation of these hypotheses will provide evidence in support of the propositions stated above and hence evidence in support of the position of this book regarding the changed nature of corporate reporting.

As far as testing these hypotheses is concerned the methods used in this research are a quantitative analysis of reported performance for hypotheses 1 – 3 and a qualitative analysis for hypotheses 4 – 8. The precise methods are explained below, after an explanation as to how the multiple perspectives of all stakeholders can be resolved into the two dimensions of financial and environmental performance.

Dimensions of Performance

While the various stakeholder needs for performance evaluation may seem disparate and incompatible, it is only by recognising that performance exists in multiple dimensions and for multiple purposes that the needs of an organisation for its measurement and reporting of performance can be addressed.[5] There is a need therefore to recognise these aspects of performance and to synthesise them into a system of performance evaluation in order for appropriate measures to be devised. In order to do so it is suggested that the different aspects of performance can be considered as dimensions, each of which provides one axis for the multi-dimensional matrix of performance evaluation into which this framework is compiled. The three dimensions identified (Crowther 1996b) are:

- the perspective dimension;
- the purpose dimension;
- the focus dimension.

For each dimension a number of perspectives exist which can be summarised in the following tables:

The Perspective Dimension	
Stewardship	asset conservation
Ownership	shareholder value
Stakeholder	power and accountability
Employee	rewards and motivation
Environmental	sustainability
Social	disclosure and community effect
Managerial	strategy formulation and implementation
Resource Allocation	planning
Worldview	holism

Table 4.1 The Perspective Dimension

The Purpose Dimension

Strategy formulation
Strategy implementation
Control
Accountability
Valuation
Legal
Informative : public relations
Informative : prospective customers
Defensive

Table 4.2 The Purpose Dimension

The Focus Dimension

Internal v External
Short term v Long term
Past v Future

Table 4.3 The Focus Dimension

Each of these three dimensions is of importance to all stakeholders in the evaluation process, although each component within each dimension is only relevant to some parties. These three dimensions are not however independent of each other and each interacts with the other two dimensions. These interactions between the three can be viewed in the form of a matrix reflecting their interaction and interdependence. This system is of necessity multidimensional but the following matrix is an attempt to synthesise these needs into a workable model for understanding the differing needs in the evaluation of performance.

Analysis of the various factors which are significant for the evaluation of performance shows that these can be categorised into three dimensions: perspective, purpose and focus, each of which interacts with the other two dimensions

Perspective	Focus			
	Past	Future	Internal	External
stewardship	x		x	
ownership	x	x		x
stakeholder	x	x	x	x
employee	x		x	
environmental		x		x
social		x		x
managerial		x	x	x
resource allocation	x	x	x	
worldview	x	x	x	x

Table 4.4 The Perspective Dimension and Focus

Purpose	Focus			
	Internal	External	Short term	Long term
strategy formulation	x	x		x
strategy implementation	x		x	
control	x		x	
accountability		x	x	
valuation	x	x	x	
legal	x	x	x	
informative : PR		x	x	x
informative: prospective customers		x	x	
defensive		x	x	x

Table 4.5 The Purpose Dimension and Focus

Purpose	Focus				
	Steward ship	Owner ship	Stake holder	Employee	Environmental
strategy formulation		x			
strategy implementation					
control	x			x	
accountability	x	x	x		x
valuation		x		x	
legal	x		x		
informative : PR			x		x
informative : prospective customers					
defensive		x			

Purpose	Focus			
	Social	Managerial	Resource allocation	Worldview
strategy formulation		x	X	X
strategy implementation	X	X	X	
control		X	X	
accountability				X
valuation				
legal	x			
informative : PR	X			x
informative : prospective customers	X			X
defensive	X			

Table 4.6 The Focus Dimension and Perspective

Modelling the Performance Evaluation Determinants

This provides a framework for analysis which indicates that the evaluation of performance operates in multiple dimensions and that the way in which the performance of an organisation is evaluated depends upon the person undertaking that analysis. Thus there is no such thing as 'the one' evaluation which demonstrates the performance of an organisation to be good or bad; any evaluation must necessarily be performed within a context. This framework also indicates that there are a variety of pressures upon an organisation, which will influence the activities of that organisation and hence the mechanisms it uses to measure and evaluate its performance. These pressures will inevitably feed into the performance reporting systems and the dominant coalition within the organisation seeks to balance up its needs with those of the other stakeholders to the organisational performance. Given that the dominant coalition is constantly mutating, as the respective stakeholders to the organisation gain and lose power in their struggle for a voice in the performance of the organisation, it is argued that it can be expected that the organisational performance reporting system also mutates to reflect these changes in the constituency, and therefore requirements, of that dominant coalition.

Once it is recognised therefore that there are multiple dimensions of performance, and that there are a variety of pressures acting upon the organisation, there is a need to consider how these different, and often conflicting, pressures are resolved and eventually manifest themselves in the actual reporting systems of an organisation. The framework developed (Crowther 1996b) explains the existence of tensions in the organisation's performance measurement and reporting systems but fails to explain how these tensions are resolved and eventually manifest themselves in the reporting systems of the organisation. In order to explain this resolution of these tensions it is therefore necessary to develop a model of how the organisation reacts to these pressures in the development of its performance reporting system. It is equally necessary to recognise how the managers of the organisation, as the operators of the performance reporting system, react to the various pressures and operationalise these pressures in the development of a reporting system. The development of such a model will help explain the operational behaviour of an organisation and the way in which these tensions are resolved, as well as explaining the determining factors in the changing reporting mechanisms, and critical factors to report upon, for an organisation.

Any such model, in order to be of value in explaining organisational behaviour and the behaviour of the operators of the reporting system, must aim to be generic in form. Equally, in order to have practical application, this model must provide a representation of the diverse and conflicting pressures identified in the framework for analysis of these pressures. It is necessary therefore to examine these different constituents of the pressures for performance measurement and evaluation and also the different dimensions along which these pressures are manifest and to seek for commonalties in their manifestation. This can be achieved through a consideration of how these pressures are manifest and then through the clustering of the factors under main headings.

It is argued that the three dimensions of performance interact with each other and cannot be considered in isolation and so a starting point is to consider these dimensions of performance in the form of a Venn diagram and then to consider the interactions. Thus a Venn diagram as follows can be constructed:

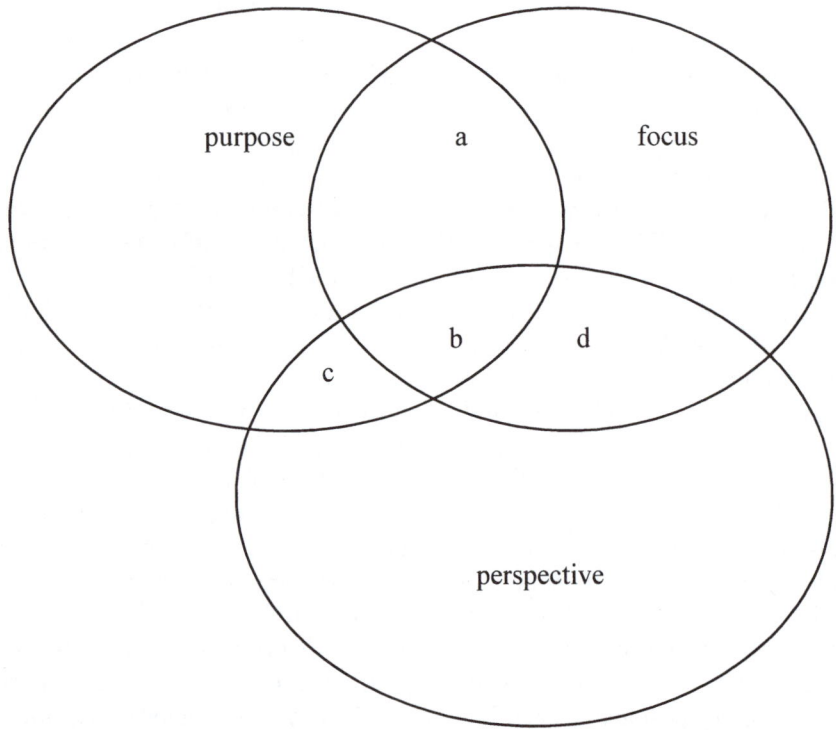

Fig 4.1 Interactions Between the Dimensions of Performance

In such a diagram the interactions between the dimensions can be identified as follows:

- area a - interactions between the purpose and focus dimensions
- area b - interactions between the purpose and perspective dimensions
- area c - interactions between the perspective and focus dimensions

- area d - interactions between the 3 dimensions of purpose, perspective and focus

This diagram provides a model which indicates the interaction of the three dimensions, and obviously the areas of overlap will be the most significant in the determination of the factors affecting organisation performance measurement and reporting. Equally area d where all three dimensions interact with each other will be the most significant area of influence. This model does not however provide anything other then a representation of these interactions and significantly does not provide any indication of the respective sizes of these areas of interaction. Additionally it does not provide any indication of which factors fall into which areas of interaction, and therefore of which factors are the most significant determinants of performance measurement and reporting. In order to achieve this aim it is necessary to examine each factor in each dimension in details and to consider the effect of these factors on the interaction between dimensions. Reference to the framework shows that it is postulated that all factors in the perspective and focus dimensions interact with the focus dimension but with different factors of the focus dimension. The focus dimension therefore can be considered to be not a dimension as such but rather as a set of polarities, thus:

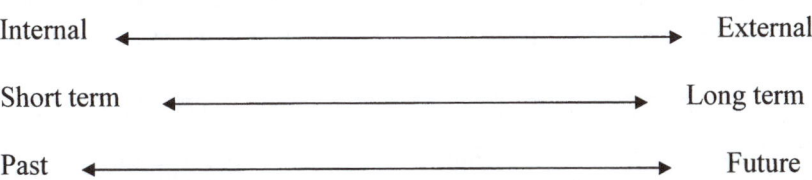

Internal ←——————————————————→ External

Short term ←——————————————————→ Long term

Past ←——————————————————→ Future

Equally it can be seen that the short term – long term and the past – future polarities are both temporal in nature, with the short term – long term polarity being subsumed within the extended temporality of the past – future polarity. It is therefore possible to eliminate the short term – long term polarity and concentrate upon the two remaining polarities. These represent the temporal focus of the organisation (i.e. past – future) and the reporting polarity (i.e. internal – external) and it is possible to consider the interaction of the factors from the perspective dimension and the purpose dimension with each of these two polarity functions from the focus dimension.

This focus dimension, when considered in this manner can be used to construct a model of the focus of an organisation's performance measurement and reporting structure, as follows:

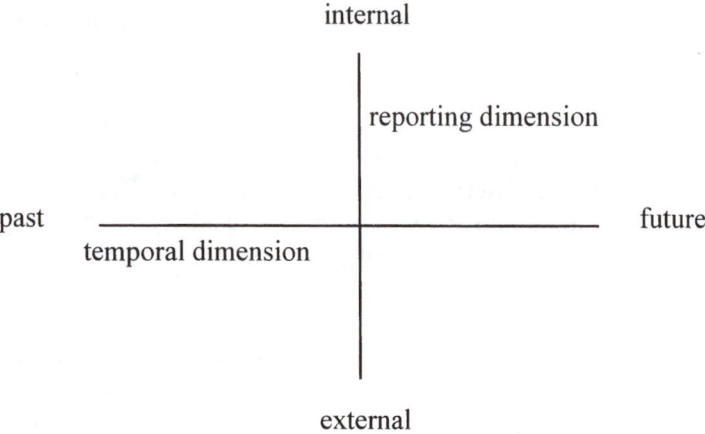

Fig 4.2 Dimensions of Organisational Reporting

Taking the factors from the two dimensions of perspective and purpose, it is possible to consider their interactions along these two polarised dimensions from the focus dimension in order to consider the main interactions of these factors.

Thus in considering the temporal polarity first the interactions of the factors can be seen to be as follows:

polar focus		
past	future	past and future
stewardship control accountability valuation legal	employee environmental social strategy formulation strategy implementation informative defensive	ownership stakeholder resource allocation worldview

Table 4.7 Temporal Polar Focus

In this figure the factors identified as both past and future can be considered not to be polarised but to operate along the continuum. Such factors therefore are excluded from the analysis following, as not leading to any particular interaction, but rather as being common to all interactions.

Similarly by considering the factors in relationship to the reporting polarity the interactions can be identified as follows:

polar focus		
internal	external	internal and external
stewardship employee resource allocation strategy formulation strategy implementation control legal	ownership environmental social worldview accountability valuation informative	stakeholder defensive

Table 4.8 Reporting Polar Focus

In this figure the factors identified as both internal and external can be considered not to be polarised but to operate along the continuum. Such factors therefore are excluded from the analysis following, as not leading to any particular interaction, but rather as being common to all interactions.

This analysis therefore establishes the polarity of the various factors from the perspective and purpose dimensions in terms of the temporal and the reporting axes resolved from the focus dimensions. It is however necessary to translate this analysis into a two dimensional matrix of interactions as part of the process of developing a model of the factors influencing organisational performance measurement and reporting. Further analysis is therefore necessary to explore these interactions and to identify which factors can be considered to reside in each quadrant of the dimensional model depicted in Fig 4.2. In doing so the factors which are polarised to either end of each axis become the significant factors rather than those which have been identified as continuous along the axis. This is because such factors will inevitably sit in several quadrants of the model and hence obscure the analysis and attempt to determine the locus of operation for each of the four quadrants.

This further two dimensional analysis therefore suggests the following:

internal past	internal future	external past	external future
stewardship control legal	employee strategic resource allocation	valuation	environmental social informative defensive

Table 4.9 Two Dimension Analysis of Focus

The dimensional model developed as figure 4.2 can now be transformed into a 2 x 2 matrix and the relevant factors inserted into each part of the matrix. This matrix can be considered to be a performance evaluation matrix of an organisation. This matrix reveals the following:

internal past stewardship control legal	internal future employee strategic resource allocation
external past valuation	external future environmental social informative defensive

Fig 4.3 Factors in the Performance Evaluation Matrix

A consideration of this matrix as two halves, concerned with respectively the internal and the external focus of the organisation suggests an analysis as follows:

Internal focus:

This focus is concerned with managerial behaviour within the organisation and with how the organisation controls and manages its resources, plans for the future and operationalises that planning.

External focus:

This focus is concerned with how the organisation, and the managers of that organisation as the operators of the organisation's behaviour, reacts with the external environment and the pressures generated from that environment.

In this respect, therefore, it is argued that the external focus can be deemed to represent the pressures exerted upon the organisation from the environment in which it is operating while the internal focus can be deemed to represent the mechanisms for the managers of the firm to respond to those pressures and to organise the factors of production accordingly in response to those pressures. It is possible therefore to suggest that the external focus is active upon the organisation while the internal focus is essentially reactive to the pressures from the external environment.

Further analysis of the matrix by consideration of each quadrant separately, in terms of organisational performance evaluation, suggests that the focus of attention for each quadrant can be explained as follows:

Internal past:

This quadrant is concerned with the accounting and financial reporting aspects of organisational performance. It is concerned with control of the business and with the reporting of what has happened. The factors in this quadrant therefore are essentially passive and reactive to the factors in the other quadrants which will influence managerial behaviour in the shaping of organisational behaviour and hence in the determination of the performance which is reported on through the factors in this quadrant. This quadrant can therefore be symbolised as the financial reporting quadrant.

Internal future:

The focus of managerial attention will be in this quadrant, which is concerned with the planning functions of managerial behaviour. This planning will determine organisation performance, which will in turn affect the reporting functions of the internal past quadrant. The planning decisions made by managers in addressing the strategic issues affecting the organisation will to a large extent be determined by an analysis of the factors from the external focus and the pressures which are imposed, or perceived to be imposed, from these quadrants. This quadrant can therefore be symbolised as the planning quadrant.

External past:

The focus of attention upon this quadrant will be that of investors in the business, both as owners and as lenders of debt. Concern will be with ensuring security for the debt and with ensuring that the activities of the firm are such that growth occurs, in whatever terms are deemed appropriate (eg sales, turnover, return on capital employed, earnings per share). This is so that investment in the organisation can be demonstrated to be a worthwhile endeavour. Equally concern will be with projecting the patterns of past performance into the future in order to ensure that any investment in the business will continue to generate rewards sufficiently to merit such investment. This quadrant therefore can be symbolised as the investment quadrant.

External future:

The concerns of this quadrant are with the environment in which the organisation is operating. Environment in this context can be taken to include the competitive environment in which the organisation is operating, the societal environment in which the organisation exists and the ecological environment upon which the organisation impacts through its activities. The external stakeholders to the organisation will therefore be primarily concerned with this quadrant and pressure from such stakeholders will be manifest here, demanding a response from the organisation and its managers depending upon how these pressures are perceived and evaluated by the organisation managers. This quadrant can therefore be symbolised as the environment quadrant.

Using the symbolism developed from this analysis therefore it is possible to reconstruct the performance evaluation matrix used for this analysis in order to show the focus of attention as far as organisational performance is concerned of each of the quadrants of the matrix. This can be depicted as follows:

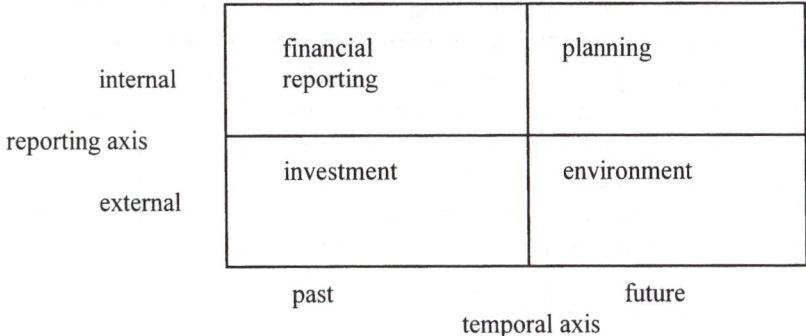

Fig 4.4 Symbolic Factors in the Performance Evaluation Matrix

From this matrix depicting the prime motivators for each quadrant it is then possible to consider the principal actors for each of the quadrants. These can be identified as follows:

Financial reporting quadrant:

This quadrant is the preserve of accounting and so the principal actors in this quadrant will be accountants, controlling the operations of the organisation and reporting upon the activities of the organisation. It is recognised however that operational management will be involved in the control of operations and that not all reporting will be financial in nature. The nature and extent of such reporting will however be determined by the activities of the organisation and the pressures exerted from elsewhere in the performance evaluation matrix.

Planning quadrant:

Managerial activity in the organisation will be concentrated in this quadrant and so the principal actors are managers. Managerial activity will be concerned with evaluating the pressures from the external quadrants, reconciling these conflicting pressures and transforming this evaluation into a plan of action. This plan will in turn determine the activities of the financial reporting quadrant.

Investment quadrant:

Present and future investors in the business will be the principal actors in this quadrant. In a large business all investment activity will tend to be channelled through the banking and City institutions and will be determined to some extent by the activities of those institutions and the analysis undertaken by the members of those institutions. The City, at least as far as the UK is concerned, can thus be considered to be the mediating mechanism for this quadrant and hence can be taken to represent the principal actor in this quadrant. For an international perspective however the actor for this quadrant needs to be more generically termed and hence the term investment analyst is used to represent this quadrant.

Environment quadrant:

As far as the competitive environment is concerned the actions of competing organisations will exert pressures on the organisation which the managers of that organisation will attempt to anticipate and to react to. Other pressures of a societal nature and of an environmental nature will be exerted by pressure groupings of various types. A typology of environmental pressures has been developed below and so at this point it is sufficient to identify the principal actors in this quadrant as competitors and pressures groups.

Stakeholders in the Environmental Pressure Game

In considering the effect of environmental pressures upon an organisation, and the consequent effects upon the performance measurement and reporting systems of the organisation, it is important to recognise that these pressures, while arising from some of the stakeholders, in the widest context, to that organisation, actually arise from a variety of different sources.[6] It is equally important to recognise that such environmental influences affect different organisations in different ways and to different extents. Thus for example the environmental pressures upon an organisation engaged in oil recovery or open cast mining will be quite different to those upon an organisation engaged in retailing or in food processing. Not only will the pressures be different for different industrial sectors but they will also differ according to geographical location of the industry and according to temporal factors influencing the local communities concerned and the society at large. Thus it can be expected that due to the differing natures of the environmental pressures being exerted, and the respective strengths of those pressures, organisations will respond differently. It could be expected however that organisations operating in similar industrial sectors and in similar physical and temporal localities would be subject to very similar environmental pressures. Similar pressures upon similar organisations could be expected to be manifest in similar reactions to those pressures, both in terms of changes in operating procedures and in terms of changes in performance measurement and reporting systems. If these similarities in responses to environmental pressures are not evident then it is necessary to investigate the organisations in greater detail in order to elucidate the reasons for these differences in response patterns. First however it is necessary to consider the types of environmental pressures to which an organisation is subject. This is achieved through the construction of a typology of environmental pressures.

One pressure to which all organisations are subject is that of the legal environment within which the organisation operates. While it might be expected that this environment is identical for all organisations, in actual fact this is not the case. As far as the UK is concerned this environment consists of three distinct components – UK legislation, EC legislation, and regulatory frameworks. Regulatory frameworks tend to be specific to individual industrial sectors and also to distinct parts of the country geographically. Thus the building industry has a specific regulatory framework in the form of building regulations but this varies from one part of the country to another. This depends to some extent upon the involvement of the local authority but is also because some parts of the country are classed as National Parks and have building restrictions to discourage such activity while other parts of the country are classed as development areas where such activity is positively encouraged. Sanctions applied for non-conformity with the regulations can either be in the form of punishment for breach of the regulations or rewards for compliance. Thus farming, for example, has a regulatory framework which involves sanctions for particular activities (e.g. fines for polluting rivers), complete freedom in other areas (e.g. no planning restrictions for agricultural buildings), and rewards in the form of grants or subsidies for compliance with certain regulation (such as 'set aside' or conforming to milk quotas). This regulatory framework is specific to this industry and does not apply to others. Some industries operate self-regulatory frameworks while others have frameworks imposed. Thus these regulatory frameworks affect different industries differently.

The framework of legislation on the other hand can be expected to apply to all industries and all firms within an industry to a similar extent. In general terms this is true but it needs to be acknowledged that the impact of such legislation is to some extent dependent upon the perceived geographical location of any particular firm. Thus one firm might be a wholly UK based organisation and hence pay particular regard to UK legislation. Another firm in the same industry might regard itself primarily as based in another country within the EC and hence pay regard not just to UK legislation but also to EC legislation, and also to the legislation of the other EC country in which it is based. Yet another firm might regard itself as truly global and be prepared to move its operations around the world to exploit legislative differences. One further facet of the legislative framework in which a firm operates which might be important to the way in which that firm operates and reports on performance is the difference between extant legislation and anticipated legislation. The framework is subject to a process of continual change and modification, the impact of which is to gradually increase the statutory requirements for conformity.[7] While extant legislation needs to be complied with this is not true of anticipated legislation, which may never achieve actuality. Nevertheless some firms seek to anticipate such legislation, either because of the costs and time scales involved in achieving compliance or because they believe that positioning themselves in the forefront of environmental developments will give them some competitive advantage. Thus the reaction of all firms, even in the same industrial sector, will by no means be universally similar.

Another part of the operating environment of an organisation involves its relationships with the media, and this is of crucial importance as far as pressure groupings are concerned. While in theory the media provides a source of information on current events, in actual fact the role of the media in the context of environmental pressure is far from that of a neutral reporting mechanism.[8] Environmental issues are regarded as newsworthy by the media, and hence used by this industry to provide a vehicle for selling its own products and services, while at the same time purporting to provide impartial news coverage. This is implicitly recognised by all the stakeholders involved in these environmental issues and so all seek to exploit the possibility of media coverage for their own purposes.[9] Thus firms will seek to broadcast their environmental impact when seen to be positive while seeking to hide less positive aspects. Conversely pressure groups will seek to provide newsworthy coverage of issues which are important to their own agendas, rather than seeking to rank such issues according to environmental impact priority. Thus media involvement becomes a weapon for all stakeholders to use to meet their own agendas rather than an impartial method of evaluating issues, and some stakeholders have recognised this and exploited it to a greater extent than have others.

A Typology of Environmental Pressures

There are a variety of pressures acting upon organisations in terms of performance, and these can be viewed as representing different dimensions of performance. In order to consider the way in which the various stakeholders affect organisational behaviour and reporting systems it is possible to construct a typology of environmental pressures. The typology can be constructed in 2 dimensions by a consideration of the focus of the pressure grouping along two axes, with one axis being concerned with focus and ranging from narrow focus on specific issues to a broad focus upon a wide range of environmental issues. The other axis represents the extent of the influence of the pressure group on organisational performance measurement and reporting systems, and this can be considered to be the dependant variable in a causal relationship. In general terms it is postulated that the broader the focus of the pressure group the greater influence it will have upon the organisational reporting systems. It is not possible at present to postulate the kind of relationship but merely that there will be a relationship. This relationship can be represented thus:

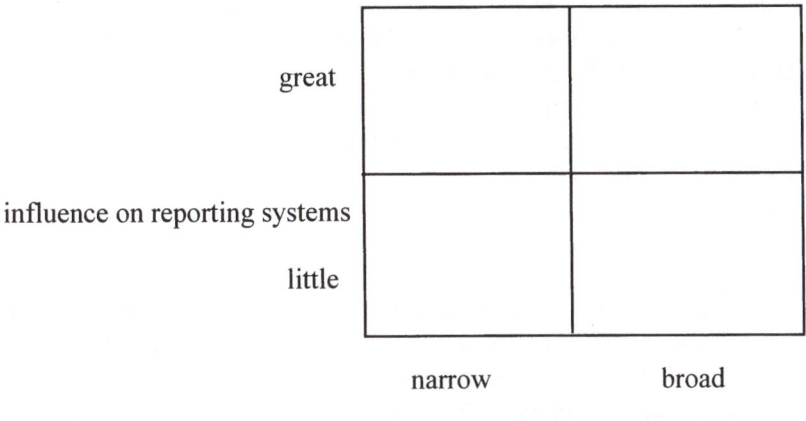

Fig 4.5 Pressure Group Profiles

Using this representation a typology can be constructed which is based upon the aims of the particular types of pressure groupings. However 6 different categories of pressure group can be identified.

a) International environmental organisations

This grouping naturally contains the largest organisations and also those organisations which tend to have the greatest public profile. This profile is achieved partly because they have the resources to generate such a profile through campaigning and partly because they have the skills to exploit the media to ensure maximal coverage. The declared aim of such groups is the protection of the global environment in its broadest context and probably the most familiar of such organisations would be Greenpeace and Friends of the Earth. Such organisations operate at all levels from the global, when considering issues such as nuclear testing by the French or whaling by anyone, to a national level when dealing with such issues as the disposal of North Sea oil platforms, and also to a local level when dealing with community issues such as the provision of cycle paths for a local community. The modus operandi of these organisations is to target specific organisations through specific campaigns and to use their resources, even illegitimately if this increases their impact, for specific ends. These campaigns have the effect of polarising opinion about the specific issues they are concerned with and using the emotional power of 'the environment' to achieve success. This is sometimes regardless of whether or not the scientific arguments can withstand scrutiny, as in the case of the disposal of the Brent Spar oil platform. Nevertheless such organisations have had a significant impact upon the operating procedures of certain businesses, and hence their performance reporting systems, while leaving other businesses untouched.

b) Specific purpose organisations

These organisations tend to be organised on either an international basis or a national basis, depending upon their objectives, but the distinguishing feature is the limitation of their purpose to the achieving of a particular objective. Thus an international organisation, such as the World Wildlife Fund, is concerned with the protection of wildlife globally while a national group, such as the Royal Society for the Protection of Birds, is concerned solely with bird life in the UK, extending its operation overseas only to the extent that what happens to migratory birds overseas can impact upon their welfare in the UK. Other organisations are UK based but concerned with issues overseas, such as Programme for Belize, which is concerned with the preservation, through acquisition, of the rain forest in Belize. Still other organisations purport to be international while being totally UK based. An example of such an organisation is Compassion in World Farming which, despite its name, is concerned primarily with farm animal welfare in the UK and to a lesser extent the EC. These organisations all tend to operate through the mobilising of mass opinion and only seek to exert influence on business organisations when these organisations have a direct impact upon the issue with which they are concerned.[10] Such issues tend to be discrete issues of limited temporal extent, such as the construction of a new reservoir or mine. Their impact upon organisational performance and reporting systems therefore is likely to be limited in extent.

c) *Illegitimate instruments of terrorism*

The use of terrorism[11] as a means of securing political ends has an extensive history and some record of effectiveness.[12] Success has a tendency to change the discourse surrounding such activity from one of illegitimacy to one of legitimacy. The use of terrorist organisation and methods has been extended in recent years to the arena of environmental issues. This has been manifest in the violent and destructive tactics of organisations such as the Animal Liberation Front, the obstructive tactics of such people as Ecoprotestors in their opposition to road building programs,[13] and the disruptive tactics of such people as Reclaim the Streets in gaining maximum media coverage from their non-violent program of closing major streets in London for periods of time or in affecting the 1998 G8 summit in Birmingham. The discourse surrounding environmental terrorism is one of illegitimacy, depending upon whether one considers that the ends justify the means or not. Their impact upon legitimate organisations tends to be one of increasing transaction costs for the firms targeted, or for society at large, rather than any long term change in performance measurement and reporting. Chaliand (1987) has argued that a successful terrorist organisation needs a base in society which extends beyond its membership and needs popular support in order to exist and achieve results. One way to negate the power base of such an organisation is to subsume the aims of the organisation within popular discourse and thereby negate its impact. The environmental impact reporting of an organisation is one way of achieving this subsumption and perhaps is one reason why such protest groups have had little impact upon organisational behaviour.

d) *Local groups*

Large numbers of local groupings exist for the purpose of exerting pressure on organisations because of concern about a particular environmental issue.

Such groups tend to have a purely local interest in a particular environmental issue and to be concerned with a particular locality. Examples would include groups concerned with the protection of a particular site from use in the building or extractive industries. Other examples include both groups concerned with pressure for reducing traffic congestion through the construction of a bypass and conversely groups concerned with preventing the construction of a bypass because of its environmental impact.[14] The essential feature of such groups is their temporary nature due to their concern with a specific aim; once their objective is past and their pressure group has met with either success or failure then the reason for their existence ceases. At this time the grouping tends to disintegrate, although individuals active within such a group may well feel motivated to become involved in further environmental issues through joining or starting another pressure group. Due to the ephemeral nature of these local issues groups and the fact that they tend be concerned with purely local issues, the impact which they have upon organisational performance reporting systems tends to be minimal, unless the issues can be brought to general public attention and gain the involvement of some larger group.

e) Individual action

Large numbers of people, as individuals, are concerned about environmental issues, either in general or about specific issues, but do not associate with others in a pressure group. This does not necessarily mean that such people do not take any action but rather that the action taken is not in concert with others. Thus individuals acting alone often take action in the form of lobbying by writing to influential people, writing to the organisation concerned and writing to members of parliament asking for action to be taken, or not taken, depending upon the issues in hand and the institution which they are contacting. Equally individuals acting alone often ignore the dominant economic rationality[15] and act in a non-price discriminatory manner in selecting the goods and services which they choose to consume because of their concern about the environmental impact of certain organisations as opposed to others. Thus the debate concerning genetically modified foods available in supermarkets has been affected by individuals choosing not to purchase such foods.[16] This has had the effect of some supermarkets (e.g. Sainsbury's) making alternatives available and other supermarkets (e.g. Somerfield's) excluding such foods from their stores.

f) Individuals as customers

Individuals acting alone are customers of some organisations and their actions can affect the behaviour of those organisations. Indeed this is one course of action selected by some of the larger pressure groups through attempting a boycott of the services of particular organisations. Thus, for example, Europe-wide boycotts of Shell petrol stations by individuals had some affect upon the company changing its mind about its proposed disposal of the Brent Spar oil platform. Equally, campaigns exist from time to time to boycott the purchase of the goods of certain food producers because of concern regarding fishing policy for some of the food products used by that producer – e.g. catching tuna by line rather than net because of the adverse impact upon dolphins caused by the use of nets. Such campaigns can influence the organisations concerned and change their operating procedures, and hence their performance reporting, but in doing so it needs to be recognised that the power relationship is significant. Individual customers acting alone have little power to influence large organisations and it requires significant numbers of individuals acting in the same way to exert sufficient influence to bring about a change in policy. It is for this reason that success through acting in this way tends to be limited and to be focused upon one issue at a time.

Not all customers of organisations however are individuals and many organisations have other organisations – often large and hence powerful organisations – as their customers. Pressure from such customers can provide a very powerful motive for changing operating procedures and reporting systems. Thus for example retailing companies can take decisions not to stock certain goods – such as British beef, tuna caught by nets rather than lines, or goods which are excessively packaged – and affect the policies of the producers of these products very directly. These retailers may be responding to pressure brought upon them by individuals acting as customers or may be taking a proactive stance because of the expectation of longer term competitive advantage. Whatever the reason such organisations are in a position to affect the performance of their supplying organisations. Customer power can therefore vary from low to high depending upon the power of the individual customer.

Using this typology of environmental pressure it is possible therefore to use the matrix postulated in Fig 4.5 to construct a depiction of environmental pressure relationships which indicates which type of pressure group is likely to have the greatest impact upon organisational performance and reporting systems. This can be represented thus:

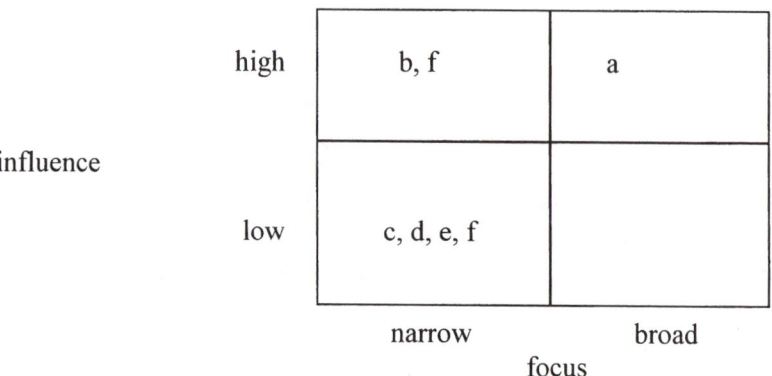

Fig 4.6 Suggested Pressure Group Influence

key:
a - international environmental organisations
b - specific purpose organisations
c - illegitimate instruments of terrorism
d - local groups
e - individual action
f - customers

        In terms of the methods used by these groupings to achieve their objectives it is possible to categorise such activities as follows:

* lobbying, of organisations and influential others;
* attention directing through the seeking of media attention and support;
* direct action, both legitimate and illegitimate.

Conflicting Objectives

It can be seen from this typology that not all environmental pressure groups have the same objectives, other than the generic one of concern for the environment in some form or other. Indeed these groups may well come into conflict with each other as their proposed courses of action for protecting the environment are in direct opposition to each other. This in itself suggests that the desired courses of action which need to be taken for ultimate environmental benefit, both by society at large and by individual organisations within that society, have not been firmly established either scientifically or economically. Thus Button (1990), Folmer (1990),

Elkington (1990) and Markandya (1990) are each separately able to arrive at a different definition of sustainability in terms of environmental economic activity and each consider effectiveness in environmental protection differently, without any of them feeling the need to disagree with any of the others.

Given this difficulty in arriving at any agreement of the significant environmental issues, and the necessary course of action needed to minimise the environmental impact of any action which might be taken, the effectiveness of environmental pressure groups needs to be questioned. Often these groups are separately pressuring organisations to take diverse courses of action, which may well be in conflict with each other. Such a confused state of affairs can make it difficult for an organisation, whatever the general inclination of its dominant coalition, to take decisive action to protect the environment through its activities. Often therefore such an organisation is forced to take action in response to pressure, regardless of whether or not it is believed to be beneficial to the environment.[17] Equally this uncertainty provides a legitimate reason for an organisation not to respond to any pressure from environmental groups and to respond instead to pressure from other sources, such as the City through the financial markets.[18]

It is clear however that environmental factors are of increasing importance to the economic activities of business organisations and need to be responded to in some form. Indeed some organisations, and an increasing number, are taking a proactive stance through the development of an environmental policy[19] as part of their platform of corporate strategy. It can be argued that in doing so they believe that they are securing a long term sustainable competitive advantage over other organisations not taking such a stance. It is argued here however that this is a part of the maintenance of the dialectic between financial and environmental performance, which is a necessary part of the supporting of managerial primacy. Thus an explanation of the way in which all external pressures from stakeholders is developed shows that they can all be resolved into two types – financial pressures and environmental pressures.

The determinants of what makes one organisation respond to such environmental pressure and another in the same industrial sector not respond, or respond differently, is often argued to be dependant upon the goals of the organisation itself. In this respect it is argued that such a response is shaped by the effect upon the organisation of its customers, as representing society at large, who ultimately affect the organisation's performance rather than by the effect of environmental pressure groups. In order to illustrate this effect it is therefore necessary to consider the semiotic of environmental reporting.

The Performance Evaluation Matrix

The performance evaluation matrix can therefore be reconstructed to represent the principal actors in the domain of organisational performance. This can be modelled therefore as follows:

	accountants	managers
internal		
external	investment analysts	competitors pressure groups

reporting axis

past   future

temporal axis

Fig 4.7 Principal Actors in the Performance Evaluation Matrix

It has previously been postulated that the internal focus part of the performance evaluation matrix is essentially reactive while the external focus is essentially active upon the organisation. This active focus is the one which therefore provides factors which will determine the organisation's response to these pressures and hence the performance measurement and reporting systems of the organisation. Based upon this view of the operating of the performance evaluation matrix it can further be postulated that competitors to the organisation do not directly exert any pressures for performance upon the organisation in an intentional manner. Such pressure as is exerted by competitors may be direct but is essentially unintended and can be regarded as a coincidental by product of their own activities in seeking to resolve their own performance evaluation matrix. In considering this matrix therefore as the operators affecting performance of the organisation it is reasonable to argue that the exclusion of competitors from this analysis of operators leads to a more accurate representation of intentional actors as far as any particular organisation is concerned. Consequently this matrix can be again reconstructed to indicate the principal operators affecting the performance of an organisation. The performance evaluation matrix, in terms of operators, will therefore become:

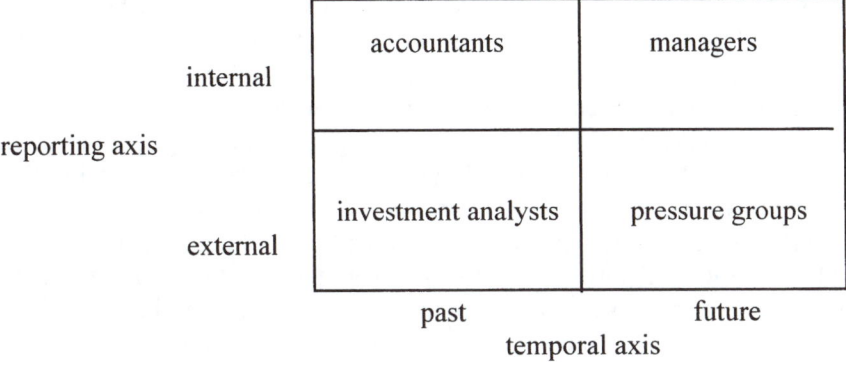

Fig 4.8 Operators in the Performance Evaluation Matrix

This matrix therefore can be used to represent the main factors in the determination of the performance evaluation and reporting systems of an organisation. This matrix does not however describe how the various factors interact with each other and determine how an organisation responds to the tensions between the various factors. In order to achieve this end it is necessary to decompose this matrix. It has previously been suggested that the factors in the internal part of the matrix respond to the factors in the external part of the matrix. It is therefore possible to classify these factors as follows:

drivers of the performance reporting system:
• investment analysts;
• pressure groups.

reactors of the performance reporting system:
• accountants;
• managers.

From this classification it is possible to construct an explanation of how the various factors affect the performance measurement and reporting system of an organisation. It is suggested that external pressure is exerted upon an organisation from both investment analysts and from environmental pressure groups. It is further suggested that the pressure from these two groups is often in conflict as the investment analysts pressurise for growth, in whatever terms are deemed appropriate, while environmental pressure groups press for the recognition of societal and environmental needs. These needs often manifest themselves in the form of additional costs to the business in a drive for sustainability and accountability. The conflicting demands of these two groups therefore create a tension in the organisation as it seeks to resolve this conflict and order its business to reconcile these conflicting needs.

The way in which these conflicting demands are resolved and reconciled will depend upon how they are evaluated within the organisation, and this is one of the roles of the management of the organisation. This will depend to some extent upon the nature of the firm itself and how it is constituted. In this respect the structure of the firm, its culture, information systems and technological focus will all be significant determinants of this evaluation by the management of the firm. There will thus be an interaction between the nature of the individual organisation and its managers which will together lead towards the determination of a performance reporting system for the organisation. The behaviour of managers in this respect will be determined in part therefore by the context in which they are operating (i.e. the nature of the firm) and in part by their own individual personalities. Both factors will be a part of the mechanisms for resolving the tensions inherent a model of performance reporting.

The managers of a firm therefore are not simply reactors in this process, acting merely as functionaries in the reconciling of the tensions caused by the conflicting needs of the external environment. In actual fact the managers themselves have a positive role to play in shaping the performance reporting system in a way which this model does not indicate. It would be more realistic therefore to depict the performance measurement and reporting system as a reactor to the pressures exerted from the external environment and the managers of the organisation as a moderating influence upon the reporting system.

This therefore provides an explanation of how the forces acting upon an organisation from its external environment affect the performance measurement and reporting system of that organisation. It is also suggested that it provides an explanation of why similar firms in the same industrial sector respond differently to what might be expected to be the same kinds of pressures and so report upon performance differently. This difference is caused by the internal operating of the organisation and the way in which the pressures are recognised, evaluated and responded to. This can be expected to result in different reporting styles and even to the adoption of different reporting measures depending upon the responses taken by the firm and its managers to these pressures.

This explanation not only gives a basis for explaining differences in reporting, and why they might arise, but also gives a means of testing the validity of the explanation through the examination of its operation in different organisations operating in the same industrial sector. It also provides a means of comparison of the effects of these pressures upon reporting styles between sectors. Such testing is of course essential to determine the validity of this model of performance measurement and reporting. It therefore becomes necessary to identify industrial sectors in which to examine the operations of this model and to develop an instrument to measure the effects of the different pressures and how they become manifest in the performance reporting system.

In considering performance reporting it is essential to recognise that this includes both measures of financial reporting and of non-financial reporting and that the pressures exerted from investment analysts and from pressure groups will affect both types of reporting. It must be remembered however that the term investment analyst is being used as representative of all the investment interest stakeholders acting upon the organisation and their evaluation will be concerned primarily with financial measures of performance. Non-financial measures will be of interest to these parties only insofar as they can be used as a guide to an extrapolation of future financial performance. The use of non-financial measures to report upon performance therefore can be taken to indicate a response by the organisation to the pressure exerted by the pressure group stakeholders. In terms of performance reporting therefore this can be depicted as follows:

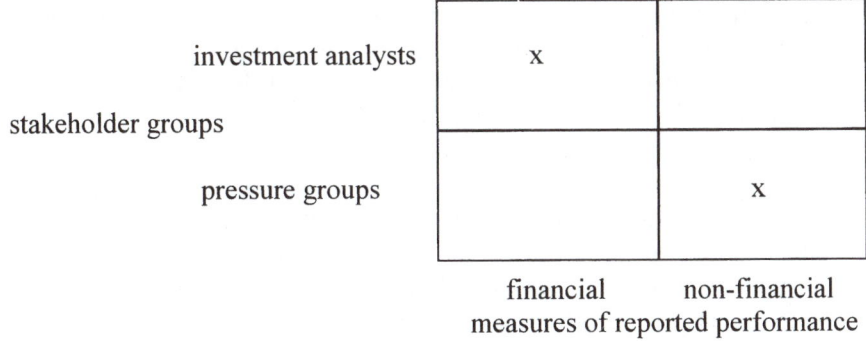

Fig 4.9 Significance of Performance Measures Reported

The identification of measures of reported performance in this manner, while not absolute in its categorisation, will give some basis for the construction of an instrument for the measurement of the effect of the pressures exerted from the different stakeholder groupings.[20]

Selecting the Sample for Analysis

In order to test the hypotheses developed above it is necessary to make use of a selection of corporate reports from which, through analysis, to test these hypotheses. Selection is necessary because the numbers of organisations producing reports is so large that a study of the whole population is neither practical nor necessary. The analysis undertaken is deliberately based upon UK companies in order to eliminate any problems from the use of different natural languages, such as would be found with continental European reporting, and problems with cultural differences and differing legislative requirements, which may be found in all non-UK corporate reports.[21]

Even from among UK based companies it is necessary to restrict the analysis to a sample of companies, due to the number of companies producing annual reports. Selection of companies has therefore been based upon the following argument. In selecting such a sample of companies there are two main criteria to be considered:

- The companies selected must be of sufficient size that published reports are readily available and the companies must have been in existence for a sufficient period of time to enable a longitudinal study to be undertaken. This latter criterion therefore necessitates the exclusion of recently formed companies. Furthermore it excludes those companies which are not public limited companies because the relationship between managers and owners is likely to be close, such that managerial motivations are different.

- The companies selected must have social or environmental considerations which raise issues affecting their operational performance and which affect stakeholders in addition to the shareholders of the company. In this respect it must be stated that all companies have such social and environmental considerations which they need to address, although these are more overt for some companies than they might be for others. The companies selected are not restricted therefore through the satisfaction of this criterion.

With these criteria in mind it was decided to select a sample from several different industrial segments within the UK. To ensure that published reports, and ancillary secondary data, are readily available it has been decided to select companies which are domiciled in the UK, and hence subject to UK reporting requirements. By ensuring that all the companies selected in the sample are subject to UK reporting requirements it is possible to undertake a comparative analysis without the need to consider external variables such as different regulatory requirements. It also ensures that cultural variables brought about by differing national conventions are excluded from the analysis. It was also decided to select companies which are all within the FTSE-500 listing of companies. Again this is to ensure that the companies selected are of comparable size and to exclude possible variations brought about by the fact that companies of different sizes are seeking to address, through their reporting, different constituencies in terms of owners, investors and potential investors. Given that all companies to be selected in the sample for analysis are part of the FTSE-500 group of companies, it is reasonable to assume that their owners and investors are largely the same group of people, comprising largely institutional investors, and that investment is mediated by means of the same City located investment markets. Moreover the managers are likely to be in the main a distinct group of non-owning salaried individuals.[22] This controlling of extraneous variables to the analysis enables a concentration upon the variables of concern in this analysis.

As previously stated social and environmental considerations affect all companies to a greater or lesser extent but in some industries such issues have a much greater prominence and an equally greater profile as far as society at large is concerned. Thus extractive industries probably have environmental considerations which have a greater impact as far as society at large is concerned than any other type of business. Indeed from among the extractive industries then it is probably true that oil companies have the highest profile as far as environmental considerations are concerned. This is brought about by several factors, including:

- The importance of oil to the economies of all industrial countries and the need to transport that oil from place of extraction to place of use, with the requirement for processing along the way. This imperative to transport and process the oil makes this industry more vulnerable to accidents.
- The use of oil as a political weapon by the oil producing states (e.g. OPEC) who have manipulated oil prices for political purposes from the 1970s onwards. The arguments regarding the justified or non-justified use of this natural resource in this way are irrelevant for the purpose of raising the profile of this industry. Other political uses of oil have had

more direct and serious environmental impacts such as when Saddam Hussein, as part of his defence of the Iraqi invasion of Kuwait, discharged large quantities of oil into the Persian Gulf and subsequently released large quantities (some of which was set on fire) onto the Kuwaiti land.

- The track record of oil producing companies to have oil spillage, either as a result of accidents, indifference or poor maintenance of extractive, refining and transportation infrastructures. Examples of accidents largely involve ships and range from the Torrey Canyon in 1969 to the Amoco Cadiz in 1993. Indifference and poor maintenance has been evident in both Alaska and in Siberia.

- The emphasis placed upon the oil industry by environmental pressure groups such as Greenpeace. This evidence is manifest in many forms, not least the public pressure brought to bear upon Shell regarding the disposal of the Brent Spar storage facility.

Other high profile industries, from an environmental perspective, include the nuclear industry. From a UK perspective this industry has not been in the private ownership domain for any great length of time and has been discounted for that reason. This fact, together with the relatively few companies involved in this industry, make it too small and unusual a sample for purposes of comparative analysis.

Other major industries with significant social or environmental concerns include the chemical and pharmaceutical industries. Not only have these industries been targeted by a whole range of environmental pressure groups but they have also been subject to much research in the recent past.[23]

For the purposes of this analysis it was decided to exclude such high profile industries from consideration and to concentrate upon other industries. It will be argued that this selection of a sample from other industries which have significant social or environmental issues facing them but which do not have the high public profile of the above industries will enable an analysis to be undertaken which will be more readily generalisable. It is argued that this is because the industries selected are much closer to the norm as far as British industry, and the stakeholder considerations facing them, are concerned. For the purposes of comparison two diverse industries were selected for analytical comparison. In the event three industries have been selected, two of which share a common problem regarding social and environmental issues. The industries selected are:

- The water industry which has environmental issues as far as pollution, public access and land use are concerned, together with a variety of social issues surrounding supply.
- The food producing and retailing industries, which taken together have a common problem with the use of packaging material and its subsequent disposal. In this respect for the purposes of this analysis these two industries have been considered as one due to this sharing of the common problem regarding packaging.

These two industries therefore comprise the industrial segments to be used for the analysis, and it is necessary from within these industries to select an appropriate sample of companies who will form the subject of this analysis. This selection has been undertaken as follows:

The Water Industry Sector

Generally speaking the companies in the water industry can be classified into two distinct types:

- water supply companies;
- water and sewerage companies.

All these companies, of either type, provide services to a distinct geographical area. As such these companies can be considered to be monopoly companies based upon the concept of a natural monopoly as identified by Mill (1848). Any competition therefore between companies is restricted to competition addressed to their investment community, and possibly also to their wider societal stakeholder community rather than being competition to attract customers, although steps are currently underway to facilitate competition geographically between these companies. In this respect these companies make an ideal sample to evaluate their responses to their stakeholders through reporting to these two stakeholder groupings as well as society at large.

Water supply companies are generally small in size and are mostly excluded from the FTSE-500 listing for this reason. Water and sewerage companies, on the other hand, are all large in size and are all included within the FTSE-500. Furthermore to a large extent they are comparable in size and thus form an ideal set of companies for comparative analysis. All of these companies were formed in 1989 as a result of the government privatisation programme, although the organisations themselves had been in existence since 1974 when there had been a reorganisation of the local provision of public services. This reorganisation combined some of the function of local authorities with those of water boards and various other public sector organisations to form regional water authorities. At that time nine regional water authorities were formed to cover the whole of England, together with one for Wales as a whole and one for Scotland, with various small water authorities remaining as anomalies for a variety of reasons. The 1989 privatisation programme transferred, at the same time, all the English and the one Welsh water authorities into private ownership through public sale of shares in the public limited companies created for this purpose. All were large enough to enter the FTSE-500 listing of companies and, given their shared history, can be considered to comprise a relatively homogenous group, at least until the time of their privatisation. Since that time there is evidence that they have sought to differentiate themselves from each other, possibly to attract investment funds and possibly in preparation for the enforced competitive environment in service provision announced at that time but without any associated timescale.

These water and sewerage companies therefore comprise one set of companies for the analysis to be undertaken. One advantage of using this set of companies is that the 10 companies in this classification comprise the whole population and it is therefore unnecessary to select a sample from within the population. The sample for analysis therefore comprises the whole population of English and Welsh water and sewerage companies. These are as follows:

Company	Turnover (£million)
Anglia Water plc	660
Hyder plc[24]	652
Northumbrian Water Group plc	344
Severn Trent plc	1157
Southern Water plc	425
South West Water plc	314
Thames Water plc	1194
North West Water Group plc[25]	1839
Wessex Water plc	241
Yorkshire Water plc	580

Table 4.10 Sample of Water Companies

Two of these companies were however taken over during 1996 by other companies. Thus Northumbrian Water Group plc was acquired by

Lyonnaise Europe plc and merged with two smaller water supply companies, North East Water plc and Essex and Suffolk Water plc, to form a new Northumbrian Water Group. This new company is 100% owned by Lyonnaise Europe plc and so is no longer a quoted company and has no share price information nor individual reporting requirement. Similarly Southern Water plc has been acquired by Scottish Power plc, after a competitive bid from Southern Electric plc, and also, as a wholly owned subsidiary, is no longer a quoted company and has no share price information nor individual reporting requirement. These two acquisitions effectively reduce the sample size for water and sewerage companies to the following 8 companies:

- Anglia Water plc;
- Hyder plc;
- Severn Trent plc;
- South West Water plc;
- Thames Water plc;
- United Utilities plc;
- Wessex Water plc;
- Yorkshire Water plc.

As these companies were all floated at the same time in 1989 then the question of a longitudinal study and the determination of an appropriate time period for such a study has been determined by circumstances. Each has a record of operation and publication of annual reports dating back to the end of their first financial year in 1990. It was decided to ignore the first year of operation for these companies, as possibly being unrepresentative, due to the aftermath of their transfer from the public to the private sector and to undertake a longitudinal study starting at the beginning of the financial year commencing in 1990 and finishing with the financial year ending in 1996. Thus a 6 year period of study has been selected for this analysis. Selecting a 6 year period of study effectively reduces the sample size from 10 companies to 8 companies. For most purposes this difference has little practical effect but in order to enhance the analysis to be undertaken and to provide additional perspectives then this analysis has been extended to include the full sample of 10 companies, but necessarily restricted to a 5 year period of analysis (1990 – 1995). This extended analysis is not used for the statistical analysis undertaken in Chapter 5 but is used for the subsequent analysis undertaken throughout the rest of the book.

The circumstantial determination of this 6 year period for longitudinal study therefore also determines the period of study for other firms in the other sectors included in this analysis, although again in some instances further analysis using the 5 year period identified above has been used. Although all the water and sewerage companies have the same year end date of 31st March the year end date for the other companies selected varies considerably between March and December. It has therefore been decided to select the 6 years ending at some point in the period mid 1996 to mid 1997, with the annual reports becoming available at some point up to the end of 1997. Although it is recognised that differing year end dates may affect any statistical analysis to be undertaken, because of changing economic and political circumstances, it is felt that the selection of a 6 year data set will largely eliminate these problems.

The Food Supply and Retailing Industry Sector[26]

Although, as mentioned previously, it was decided to treat these two sectors as one from the point of view of analysis, because of the common problem shared in terms of packaging and its disposal, for the purpose of selecting a sample of companies for analysis these companies have been treated as two distinct sectors. Accordingly a sample has been chosen from each sector. The two sectors from which samples were chosen therefore are the food retailing and food manufacturing sectors.

One determining factor in selecting a sample from each of these two industrial sectors is the length of time the company has been in existence, which must be sufficient for a longitudinal study over the same time period as that of the water and sewerage companies. Another factor is that each company within a sector must be of comparable size. In this respect it must be recognised that the degree of homogeneity in size which exists in the Water sector is not possible in any other sector, apart from the privatised electricity distribution sector. The diversity in size of the companies selected in these two sectors is therefore, of necessity, much greater. In addition sectoral specific criteria were applied to the selection of appropriate companies to comprise the sample as follows:

Food retailers

The companies selected were required to be generally recognised household names and operate through a sufficient number of retail outlets that they could be regarded as having national coverage. All of the companies selected must be primarily food retailing companies but it is recognised that all of them sell products other than food. The criterion for selection was inclusion in the FTSE sector classified as food retailers, with the consequent interpretation that this form of retailing is their prime activity and their main source of revenue. The adoption of all these criteria meant that only a sample of 8 companies was available, comprising the whole population of companies meeting these criteria. The companies selected for analysis therefore are as follows:

Company	Turnover £million
Argyll Group plc	6500
Asda Group plc	6042
Iceland Group plc	1375
Kwik Save Group plc	3512
Wm Morrison Supermarkets plc	2111
Nurdin & Peacock plc	1660
J Sainsbury plc	12050
Tesco plc	12094

Table 4.11 Sample of Food Retailing Companies

Food manufacturers

From this sector the companies were required to be manufacturers in the sense of processing food which was then branded and sold through retail outlets. Such companies, for selection purposes, were also required to produce a diverse range of such branded goods in order to qualify for selection, but the number of different brands under which the goods produced were marketed was deemed to be irrelevant. Essentially this differentiates such companies from those manufacturing single ranges of goods, such as Thorntons plc which manufactures entirely chocolate products of a luxury nature or A G Barr plc which manufactures primarily soft drinks. Equally this differentiated such companies from those engaged in raising or importing food (either with or without any associated processing) of either an animal nature (e.g. Bernard Matthews plc) or of a vegetable nature (e.g. Geest plc). These companies are therefore essentially manufacturers of food products, rather than merely engaged in the food production industry. The classification of companies deemed acceptable in this sector is determined by their classification in the Stock Market listings. From within the group of companies which matched all the selection criteria a sample of 10 companies was selected. The size of the sample was selected to match the size of the water industry population. The sample selected therefore comprised the following companies:

Company	Turnover £million
The Albert Fisher Group plc	1698
Associated British Foods plc	5707
Cadbury Schweppes plc	5115
Dalgety plc[27]	4335
Hazlewood Foods plc	766
Northern Foods plc	1947
Tate & Lyle plc	4510
Unigate plc	2134
Unilever plc	33522
United Biscuits (Holdings) plc	3436

Table 4.12 Sample of Food Manufacturing Companies

The total sample selected for analysis from these three industrial sectors therefore comprises 26 companies, but increases to 28 companies for the purpose of certain further analysis.

Measuring Financial Performance

In order to evaluate the performance of the firms selected for analysis from the point of view of investors and potential investors, it is first necessary to select the appropriate measures to be used in the analysis. At this point therefore it is necessary to consider the reported measures which are available because they are reported in the annual reports of companies, can be calculated from the information so reported, or are otherwise available in the public domain. From this information it is then necessary to decide which measure(s) should be selected for the purposes of this analysis.

Traditionally performance measurement systems have been based upon accounting numbers such as EPS (earnings per share) or ROCE (return on capital employed). The shortcomings of these measures are well documented and Ezzamel and Hart (1989) and Rappaport (1986), amongst others, have criticised such measures for promoting a short term focus for managerial actions. Indeed Rappaport also argues that accounting profit fails to measure changes in the economic value of the firm for a variety of reasons, including the exclusion of risk, a failure to consider dividend policy and the ignoring of the time value of money.

Despite these limitations to traditional measures however there is widespread belief in the UK that share prices are driven by the capitalisation of a company's earnings per share at an appropriate price earnings ratio multiple (e.g. Stewart 1991). Indeed a number of writers have described an apparent fixation with EPS and Rappaport (1986) in the USA states that '...in both corporate reports and the financial press, there is an obsessive fixation on earnings per share (EPS) as the scorecard of corporate performance.' Similarly in the UK Marsh (1990) reports upon a survey which found that '...81% (of UK finance directors) believed that EPS was the main basis for the valuation of share prices'.

The Accounting Standards Board have sought to reduce the emphasis placed upon EPS, primarily through FRS3 (Financial Reporting Standard No 3), which requires a number of changes to be made to the presentation of the profit and loss account as well as the calculation of EPS and the definition of extraordinary items. FRS3 paragraph 52 states:

> It is not possible to distil the performance of a complex organisation into a single measure. Undue significance, therefore, should not be placed on any one such measure which may purport to achieve this aim.

Soon after FRS3 was published however the Institute for Investment Management and Research (IIMR) published guidance under which maintainable EPS could be calculated. The IIMR argued that this maintainable EPS statistic was the key indicator of corporate performance, thereby providing further evidence that EPS is considered to be the dominant measure of corporate performance. More recently still the Sunday Times (August 11 1996) reported the results of a survey of the top 200 UK companies, conducted jointly with Braxton Associates, which found that most companies are still using EPS as the key target for guiding their business.

The nature of the discourse regarding the measurement and evaluation of corporate performance has however broadened in recent years with the adoption of different perspectives and this has been reflected in the changing nature of corporate reporting.[28] The discourse therefore seems to have moved away from the concerns of shareholders in the firm and away from the economic rationale for accounting and towards a consideration of the wider stakeholder environment. At the same time however these concerns cannot be ignored and part of the discourse has seen a return to economic values in assessing the performance of the firm. Thus Rappaport (1986) recognises some of the problems with accounting but goes on to consider the concept of shareholder value and how this can be created and sustained. He develops a methodology of shareholder value based upon his previous work where he argues (1992) that a shareholder value approach[29] is the correct way of evaluating alternative company strategies, stating that the ultimate test of a corporate plan is whether it creates value for the shareholders, and that this is the sole method of evaluating performance.

The return to a consideration of the importance of economic value and to the theory of the firm is based upon the assumption that maximising the value of a firm to its shareholders also maximises the value of that firm to society at large. Within the discourse therefore the concept of shareholder value is frequently mentioned and there is acceptance of the need to account for shareholder value within the practitioner community. Indeed the annual reports of companies regularly expound the virtue of creating value for shareholders and it is frequently cited as a corporate objective. This objective can simply be defined as being achieved when the rate of return obtained within a business exceeds the cost of obtaining funds.

The concept of shareholder value as an objective appears to be widely accepted within the accounting community but its use as a quantified evaluation is less often found in practice. This, it can be argued, is because the managers of a firm are preoccupied with other objectives such as growth in size, turnover, market share or accounting returns, which are more easily measured. The achievement of objectives such as these is also often correlated with managerial rewards but less so with increasing shareholder value (Williamson 1963). Indeed Jensen and Meckling (1976) use agency theory to demonstrate how following managerial interests can lead to higher rewards for those managers at the expense of a reduction in the value of the company.

Problems arise from the use of accounting measures as a means of evaluating company performance. Stewart (1991) and Brealy and Myers (1991) separately consider how the use of earnings per share can be of doubtful value in achieving this end, both because of the different calculations used for the same accounting measure and because of the adoption of different accounting measures. Equally Fisher and McGowan (1983) show that ROI, ROA and ROE suffer from the same problem.

A recent development in the quest for a tool to measure shareholder value has been the concept of economic value added,[30] which has been advocated (Stewart 1991) as a better measure to assess corporate performance and the creation of shareholder value than conventional accounting measures. Indeed Stewart (1994: 73) states that:

> Economic value added is an estimate, however simple or precise, of a business's true economic profit.

Economic value added is claimed to have a number of important advantages over traditional accounting measures, the chief one being that economic performance is only determined after the making of a risk adjusted charge for the capital employed in the business. Critics however argue that while this may be theoretically sound, the need to make arbitrary adjustments to standard accounting numbers in order to put the technique into practice makes the technique of doubtful validity. The application of the technique and the adjustments needed were evaluated by Coates, Davies, Davis, Zafar and Zwirlein (1995) who suggest that simplified calculations produce satisfactorily reliable results.

Mechanisms for calculating economic value added are described by Stewart (1991), who elaborates the standard adjustments[31] needed to transform accounting information into an economic value added calculation. A definition of economic value added can be given simply as operating profits after tax less a charge for capital used to generate these profits. The residual from this calculation is the measure of economic value added and if positive demonstrates that the company has earned a greater return on its capital employed than the opportunity cost of the capital employed, and has hence added value to the company from the viewpoint of shareholders. Opportunity cost is defined in this context simply as the market cost of capital, appropriately weighted between equity and debt capital. If negative the opposite is the case and value has been lost.

Associated with economic value added is the measure market value added[32] which is defined by Stewart (1991) as the market value of the company (i.e. stock price x shares outstanding) minus the economic book value of the capital employed. Stewart argues that this measure is superior to just using market value as a means of assessing the value creating performance of a company because market value can be increased simply by investing as much capital as possible, without consideration of the returns to be achieved from this investment. In theory market value added should reflect the present value of expected future value added and thereby provides a measure of the expectation of shareholder value created. In practice this relationship is not as simple as this because of the factors affecting the operation of the market. It is therefore argued by proponents of these kind of shareholder value analysis techniques that both measures need to be considered together in order to evaluate the value of the techniques of shareholder value analysis in assessing company performance. The two measures together are therefore taken as a representation of shareholder value.

Govindarajan and Gupta (1985) argue that long run criteria contribute to organisational effectiveness rather than short term criteria, whereas Rappaport (1986, 1992) suggests that shareholder value analysis addresses both and maximises both. There is, nevertheless, a considerable body of evidence which suggests otherwise and that a concern with shareholder value added and returns to shareholders leads to a short term focus and lack of regard for the longer term (e.g. Coates et al 1995). Indeed some managerial actions taken to boost short term valuations (e.g. delayering and outsourcing) can be argued to actually reduce long term value, particularly when the product and market development capability is externalised.

The market value added concept recognises that the market value of equity, and changes therein as a result of changed expectations by existing and potential investors, is an important part of the measurement of performance for investment purposes. It equally recognises however that the market value of equity does not by itself constitute a reliable measure of shareholder wealth creation. It does however seek to measure how much a firm has added to or subtracted from its shareholder investment and as such seeks to measure one factor which is of significance to this group of shareholders. It does of course fail to take into account the level of dividend return to shareholders, and in this respect can be considered as completely contrasting with more traditional measures such as EPS, which is concerned entirely with dividend payments. Dividend returns are of course a potentially significant source of wealth creation for shareholders, and for certain companies which adopt high dividend pay out policies the ignoring of such dividends would significantly distort their actual wealth creation potential.

For the purposes of the analysis to be undertaken here, what is of concern from the point of view of the evaluation of performance, based upon reported financial figures, is what might be of interest to the group of stakeholders which is under consideration. From this point of view therefore it is sufficient to dismiss measures such as ROCE and economic value added as being concerned with the internal measurement of performance; the investor group of stakeholders can be expected to be interested in performance as reflected in the external environment. It is equally appropriate to dismiss market value added as this is a corollary of economic value added, and Stewart (1991) claims that the two measures need to be considered together. Changes in performance from the perspective of the external environment can be considered to be manifest through changes in the value of shares (i.e. in capital growth or diminution), and in returns via dividend payment. An appropriate measure therefore to use in this analysis is one which reflects both of these two aspects of performance when viewed from an external perspective on investment. One such measure exists which aggregates performance in terms of these two factors and that is the measure of total shareholder returns (TSR). This is the measure which has been selected therefore to use for the evaluation of performance from the perspective of investors.

There are many ways to calculate total shareholder returns but for the purposes of this analysis it is defined as the increase in market capitalisation over a predefined period plus the total dividend paid in the period, expressed as a percentage of the market capitalisation at the start of that period. Thus the calculation reflects not just changes in share price during the period but also is adjusted for any share issues or buy backs during the period in order to reflect more truly the returns to any holder of an individual share.

Measuring environmental performance

Financial performance comprises one aspect of performance as far as the dichotomy to be tested is concerned. The other aspect of performance which is of interest is that of social and environmental performance. Accordingly it is necessary to consider the measures of social and environmental performance which are reported by the companies subject to analysis. From this it is possible to decide upon a measure which is appropriate to use for comparative analysis. In the case of this dimension of performance however the situation is rather different to that of financial performance. In this case rather than having a variety of measures available, all acceptable for such analysis, and deciding upon the most appropriate measure, there is in fact no measure which exists and is universally recognised as an appropriate measure. It is therefore necessary firstly to consider what measures are available and to consider their appropriateness for the purpose of this analysis.

In this context therefore it is important to recognise that, with the absence of any particular measure of environmental performance, there are a variety of measures which, it is argued, have a relationship with such performance but which do not necessarily fully reflect the extent of such performance. Such measures must therefore be considered to be merely surrogate measures for this dimension of performance, which provide some method of deriving a commonality in the evaluation of such performance. From the possible measures which are available, four measures have been considered and the relative merits of each measure as an indicator of social and environmental performance have been evaluated. The four measures are:

- lines of text;
- charitable donations;
- size and frequency of environmental reports;
- number of measures reported.

Each of these, and the meaning of each, is considered in detail in chapter 5. From these measures it is argued that it is appropriate to construct a composite measure which reflects for each company the environmental performance of that company.

The Language of Accounting

Accounting has often been described as the language of business (Davidson, Schindler & Weil 1974) and, as such, provides the technology by which an organisation may be represented by and to its stakeholders. The technology of this accounting language also provides a means by which the owners and managers of a business can communicate with each other, plan for the future, control the implementation of that planning and report upon the subsequent performance. This consideration of accounting as the language of business has been extended by Belkaoui (1978) who argues that accounting is not just the language of business but is actually a language in its own right, satisfying the grammatical and lexical characteristics of a language. On the basis of this argument that accounting is a language rests some of the problems of interpretation of accounting information. This is because accounting is not the native language[33] of any person and so all users of the accounting language suffer from the interpretation problems of all users of a second language.

The acceptance of accounting as a language explains some of the interpretative difficulties with accounting data, but these difficulties can also be explained by the way in which accounting is used. Thus accounting as a language is capable of being studied linguistically in order to understand its use in practice. Language is a means of communication between people sharing a common culture, or at least sufficient commonality to enable communication to take place. This cultural commonality can be in terms of a societal culture or, as in the case of corporate reporting, in terms of a business culture. Thus accounting as the universal language of business enables this communication to take place regardless of the original native language of the parties[34] to the communication process. In this communication such language provides not merely a representation of objects and events which the communicator of information has in mind but also a representation of the desires, intentions and goals of the communicator. These are either consciously embedded into the communication according to the communicator's intentions or unconsciously embedded despite the communicator's intentions. As such these intentions are subject to analysis and interpretation.

In order for communication to take place it is necessary for the language used to have some formal structure to ensure common understanding, and this is the function of syntax and grammar, as well as of the meaning ascribed to individual words. In this respect accounting as a language has a clearly defined syntax and grammar with very specific rules concerning usage. Indeed it can be argued that this is one of the strengths of accounting language which enables precise communication between individuals, spatially or temporally separated from each other, to such an extent that the communicators of information using the language of accounting can be certain that the recipients will understand the content of the message.

In speech, as opposed to written language, this formal structure of language is simpler and the rules are often broken, with meaning being partly given by contextual information as well as speech content. Thus it is possible for a conversation to be understood by all parties to it which would be meaningless if written down and shown to a third party because the vital contextual and implied content of the communication is missing. Accounting as a language however differs from all other languages, other than dead languages such as Egyptian hieroglyphs, in that it has no spoken form but consists entirely of a written form. In this respect therefore accounting language equates to Bernstein's (1961) elaborated code and has no comparable restricted code, other than perhaps in terms of the shorthand used by accounting practitioners. Such shorthand can however be considered to be nothing more than a special case of the elaborated code used by technical experts in the language. Halliday (1978) argues that the format of this code both determines social structure and is determined by such social structure and that the use of language socialises the child into the adult. This analogy can be extended to the use of accounting language where it can be argued that the familiarity with the use of accounting language socialises the organisational child into the organisational adult able to take his or her place in the management of an organisation.[35]

Linguistic studies have shown that language is used to identify social class (e.g. Labov 1966, Klein 1965, Hewitt 1982) but that language also defines identity much more narrowly in terms of the social group to which one belongs. This view has been identified by Le Page (1968: 194) who stated:

> Each individual creates the systems for his verbal behaviour so that they shall resemble those of the group or groups with which from time to time he may wish to be identified.

Thus this view suggests that language acts like a membership card and assumes that language usage and behaviour is adopted to gain membership. A contrary argument from feminist discourse however suggests that language is used as a source of power and dominance, and is used in this manner by the dominant group in order to exclude others. Thus Lakoff (1975: 136) considers language in the context of power and dominance, stating:

> The language of the favoured group, the group that holds the power, along with its non-linguistic behaviour, is generally adopted by the other group, not vice versa.

Thus the power of accounting in organisations can be based upon the argument that accounting is a language and therefore that knowledge of the language,[36] and acceptance of the precepts upon which it is based, can be used to give or withhold power within the organisation. Decisions are made in an organisation by those with the information necessary to make the decisions (or at least by those who perceive themselves to be in possession of that information) and the power necessary to enforce that decision. Thus Finkelstein (1992) argues that strategic choice in an organisation is dependant upon the power of the top management team. Accounting information provides a mechanism for giving power to that team, or enabling the team to take power, as it provides a source of expert and referent power.

The precision of accounting as a language, together with its existence only in terms of the elaborate code of its written form, suggest that there should be little problem in the interpretation of information conveyed through the use of accounting language. It must be recognised however that accounting language is rarely used for communication solely through that language, except between one accountant and another. When the communication is intended to be between non-accountants then the use of accounting language is normally accompanied with the use of another language, being the native language of at least one party to the communication. Thus accounting information for organisations is normally communicated partly in the language of accounting and partly in another language.

Corporate Reporting and Accounting

Corporations produce annual reports which are designed to provide a representation of the existence of that corporation at a point in time, the year end position.[37] In some respects these corporate reports are produced to satisfy the statutory reporting requirements for that organisation.[38] They are also designed to provide the legal owners of the organisation[39] with a statement of how the organisation has been managed on their behalf. Corporate reports are produced on an annual basis (with possible interim reports also) and hence provide a statement of the corporation's existence over time, which enables comparison from one time period to another. Each annual report is however a statement in its own right, designed to inform the owners at that point in time, regardless of whether or not they were owners at the time of the last report. Such reporting however has been extended in use to providing a statement of the activities of the organisation over the past period, and plans for the future, to any person or body who is interested. Thus such reporting is made freely available to anyone who requests such reports and can be considered to address not just shareholders but any stakeholder, or potential stakeholder of the organisation.

Corporate reporting can therefore be said to provide a representation of the organisation to the outside world and such reporting is the subject matter of this book. When communication between an organisation and its external environment is undertaken in the form of published corporate reports then such reporting is undertaken partly in the language of accounting and partly in the appropriate natural language of the organisation's perceived principal territorial location. This location may either be defined in terms of its location of operation, in terms of its location of ownership, or in other terms; the exact choice of location is determined by the authors of the corporate report – in other words the managers of the organisation who can be expected to make the selection according to their own needs and interests. These two languages used are also accompanied by visual representations of the organisation and its activities designed to increase the meaning of the representation so provided. This composite communication set can be considered in total and, as such, provides the basis for a semiotic analysis and interpretation of corporate reporting.

The Origins of Semiotics

Semiology, or semiotics,[40] has been defined simply as 'the study of signs' (Guiraud 1975). This description however must be viewed as being overly simplistic. In actual fact semiology can be considered to be the study of the creation of the symbolic and its subsequent signification. Thus semiology has been further defined as 'a science which studies the life of signs within society' (Saussure 1966). Semiotics can therefore be considered to be a study of communication and more particularly the study of communication acts or events – a study of the message itself and its relationship with the recipient of that message. According to semiotic theory therefore communication is determined by the interrelationship between the message itself and the recipient of that message. In this respect therefore, as Derrida (1978) argues, the writer of the message ceases to have any significance once the message has been written, as interpretation is entirely determined by this interplay between the message and its recipient. In other words meaning is in the interpretation of the message by the recipient and the intentions of the writer are therefore irrelevant. This inevitably places a heavy burden upon the recipient of the message in extracting meaning from that message but it also places a heavy burden upon the writer of the message. Thus rather than being irrelevant to the message, the writer of the message is in fact central to the message itself as (s)he must endeavour to ensure that the meaning wished to be imparted is actually the one which is extracted by the recipient rather than any alternative meaning.

In spoken communication this is a relatively simple exercise as the speaker knows something about the hearer, has a general understanding of the context in which the communication is being made, and receives feedback which enables the message to be modified during its transmission. When the message is transmitted in written form, either as text or as pictures, however, the situation is very different as there is no framing context for the message, or rather a different framing context for each reader, and no relationship between the writer and the reader other than the message itself. The message itself therefore becomes the sole form of mediation between the writer and the reader and thereby assumes the dominant role in the communication. This message therefore becomes the totality of the communication act, and the communication event becomes the relationship between the message and the reader of that message. Semiotics therefore is the study of both the communication act and the communication event.

Semiotics has its origins in linguistic theory and a perennial debate since its acceptance within the discourse of communication has been one of whether semiotics is merely a subset of linguistic theory or whether, since its scope is much greater than linguistics and encompasses linguistics within its scope, it is a meta-level of analysis, of which linguistics comprises one subset.[41] In this study the communication act is encapsulated within the corporate reports produced by the organisations being studied, ie the annual reports and associated environmental reports produced. Within this communication act there are three transmission devices, two of which are linguistic and one of which is non-linguistic. These devices are:

- The natural language used in communication – in the case of the reports considered this is the language of English.
- The language of accounting, considered by Belkaoui (1978) to be a language in its own right.
- The non-linguistic devices used within the act, comprising pictures, graphs, colours etc. which are an integral part of the communication event.

These three devices combine within the reports to make the communication act, and thereby the text. As such the text, which is to be semiotically analysed, comprises all three communication devices when used together.

Postmodern analysis of society and its organs therefore provides a mechanism for the semiotic analysis of external reporting. In this context Baudrillard (1988) claims that there is a need to break with all forms of enlightened conceptual critiques and that truth in the postmodern era is obsolete, while Fish (1985) claims that truth and belief are synonymous for all practical purposes. In terms of any external reporting of organisational performance therefore this would suggest that the meaning of any such reported performance becomes whatever it is interpreted to mean. This interpretation will depend upon the perspective of the person performing that interpretation, and the purpose for which that interpretation is undertaken. Thus a postmodern perspective is in perfect accord with the semiotic arguments considered above. This need for interpretation naturally places a heavy emphasis upon the interpretative ability of the receiver of the reported information as well as presupposing that this receiver understands the language of the reporting system sufficiently well to be able to extract meaning from this information. It also provides an opportunity for those undertaking the reporting to structure the information reported in such a manner as to facilitate their desired manner of interpretation. It is clear therefore that in seeking to analyse the reporting of organisational performance from the multiple perspectives of those seeking to undertake such analysis there is a need to consider an organisation's performance reporting structure from a postmodernist standpoint separately from that of the prevailing dominant hegemony. In order to do so this requires a reconsideration of the purpose of such reporting within the context of the text produced and its consumption by the various stakeholders involved in the communication event.

Approaches to Semiotic Analysis

The roots of semiotics stem from two distinct strands of literature – the linguistic work of Saussure and the philosophical work of Peirce. Each source leads to a slightly different mode of analysis

Saussure (1966) identified a sign as dyadic, having two sides – the signifier and the signified: the signifier being the material object and the signified being its associated mental concept. The inseparability of these two aspects of the sign led to his diagrammatic representation:

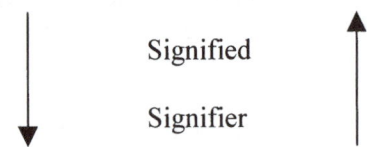

Signified

Signifier

Fig 4.10 The Saussurian Dyadic

Thus Saussure's understanding of the process of communication is based upon an assumption of the transfer of mental concepts through the signs produced.

Peirce (1958), on the other hand, developed a triadic theory of the signs based upon the triple relationship of the representamen, the object and the interpretant. In his theory the representamen is the sign itself, the object is that which the representamen stands for and the interpretant is the significate effect of the sign.

Saussurian semiology must necessarily be undertaken in the context of a wider system of meaning external to the sign itself. In this mode of analysis the sign itself is part of a flow of meaning and is interpreted contextually and individually by each individual participating in the communication event. Peircian semiotics on the other hand functions on the basis that each sign is self-contained and able to generate further signs, with associated meanings, from within itself. Thus the Peircian approach has its own internal dynamic associated with both the sign and its interpretation which is often referred to as an unlimited semiosis. Peirce's system of semiotics has been extensively critiqued by Habermas (1971) because of his assumption that every individual is able to produce his own semiotic from the communication event. Thus the semiotic is infinitely variable, as any event would not produce the same semiotic for each individual. He states (1971: 138-9):

> Not every communication, however, is merely the subsumption of the individual under an abstract universal, or what is in principle mute subjection to a public monologue that everyone can produce for himself. On the contrary, every dialogue develops on an entirely different basis, namely that of the reciprocal recognition of subjects who identify one another under the category of selfhood and at the same time maintain themselves in their non-identity. The concept of the individual ego includes a dialectical relationship between the universal and the particular, which cannot be conceived in the behavioural system of instrumental action.

For static signs, such as advertisements, this Peircian method of semiotic analysis provides the most suitable method of interpretation and understanding of meaning. For corporate reporting, the subject matter of this book, however the sign is not static but is contextual to the organisation, its external environment and its audience. Moreover each individual corporate report produces not just one sign but rather a multiplicity of signs each of which are contextually dependant upon the other signs produced. It is for this reason that Saussurian methodology is considered to be the most appropriate method of analysis and is used in this book to develop a semiotic understanding of corporate reporting.

The semiology of Saussure has been developed extensively by later writers, but one significant analysis has been undertaken by Lacan (1977) who argued that human beings are entirely enmeshed within the sign and its subjectivity, thereby making the separation of the signifier and the signified impossible.[42]

Actors and Audience on the Semiotic Stage

Although accounting information is of necessity central to the script of corporate reporting in order to satisfy the statutory obligation of such organisations to report upon their activities, in reality its place within the script has been somewhat marginalised by the other purposes of corporate reporting.[43] The satisfying of statutory obligations requires little more than the production of a simplified set of accounts with accompanying notes. If performance reporting for statutory purposes was therefore central to the script of corporate reporting then such reports would be simple documents. This is evidenced by the fact that many of the annual corporate reports for private companies, or for family owned businesses,[44] are simple in content and style and aim merely to satisfy statutory obligations. For large quoted public limited companies however this is not the case and all such companies produce annual reports which contain material far in excess of the minimum requirements. Also in style and presentation they can be seen to appeal to an audience quite different to the Registrar of Companies, who requires a statutory return. Thus, just as Johnson and Kaplan (1987) argue that the use of accounting information for internal control purposes has been subordinated to the need for the compilation of accounts for external reporting purposes, it is argued here that such compilation and reporting has been subordinated to the need to produce corporate reports for other purposes.[45] The purpose of this semiotic analysis therefore is to identify such purposes and to explore the interactions between the various actors and audiences for the communication event involving such corporate reporting.

This semiotic analysis is based upon the premise that such interactions take place upon a stage, labelled the semiotic stage, and that the corporate report can be considered to be the script which determines the interactions between the participants. Every script needs an author and in the context of the corporate reports considered it is clear that the authors of such scripts are primarily internal to the organisation.[46] Although many people may be involved in the production of such corporate reports, not least of which may be accountants within the organisation who are concerned with the compilation of accounting data into an appropriate form for inclusion within the script, it is clear that the ultimate editors of the script consist of the dominant coalition of management who will ensure that the finished text meets with their approval. Thus this dominant coalition, although acting in an editorial role, can be considered to be the authors of this script.[47]

In a conventional view of corporate reporting time is considered in a linear manner so that the authors produce the script which is then presented to the audience. The audience, ie the readers of the script, in this linear depiction therefore have no involvement in the script but are merely passive recipients. This can be depicted thus:

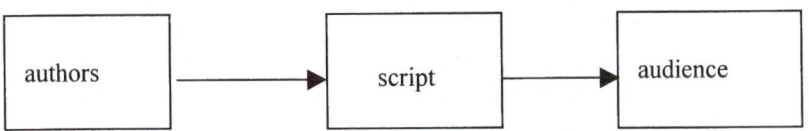

Fig 4.11 A Conventional View of Corporate Reporting

According to this view there is merely a linear movement of the text from the authors to the audience. In this conventional view of corporate reporting there is therefore no communication event but merely a script passed from one person to another. At the same time as the script is passed the burden of interpretation of the meaning of the script is also passed and this burden falls entirely upon the recipient to make of the script what (s)he will.

A semiotic view of corporate reporting however takes a very different view and removes the linear constraint assumed within a traditional view of temporality. With this view the communication event is viewed as an interaction between the audience and the script but moreover as an interaction between the authors and the audience using the script as a mediating mechanism. These interactions take place upon what is defined here as the semiotic stage which encompasses the communication event. This stage can be depicted thus:

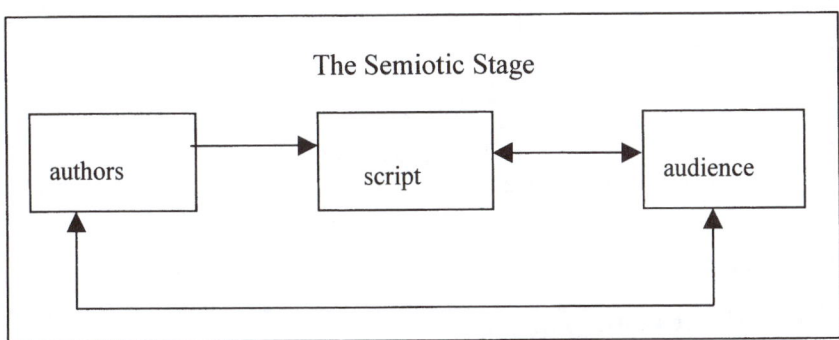

Fig 4.12 A Semiotic View of Corporate Reporting

Furthermore this semiotic stage is extended by the authors of the script utilising another mediating mechanism in their interactions with the audience. This further mediating mechanism is that of the press,[48] which the authors use as an attention directing mechanism to the key salient parts of the scripts and to draw attention to the script itself. This mediating mechanism is however complicated by the fact that the authors of the script have no direct control over it and can only interact by communicating with the press and hoping that the press will, not just communicate with the audience, but rather communicate in the way desired by the authors.

It is perhaps for this reason that such organisations devote considerable effort to fostering what they consider to be suitable and desirable relations with the press in order to be able to exert pressure and control upon this mediating mechanism for communication. Despite the self proclaimed independence of this press it remains unclear to what extent such control is in fact exerted. Nevertheless for the purposes of this analysis it is assumed that no such control exists and that the press in fact acts as a one way mediating mechanism between the authors of the corporate script and the audience. The complete semiotic stage can therefore be depicted thus:

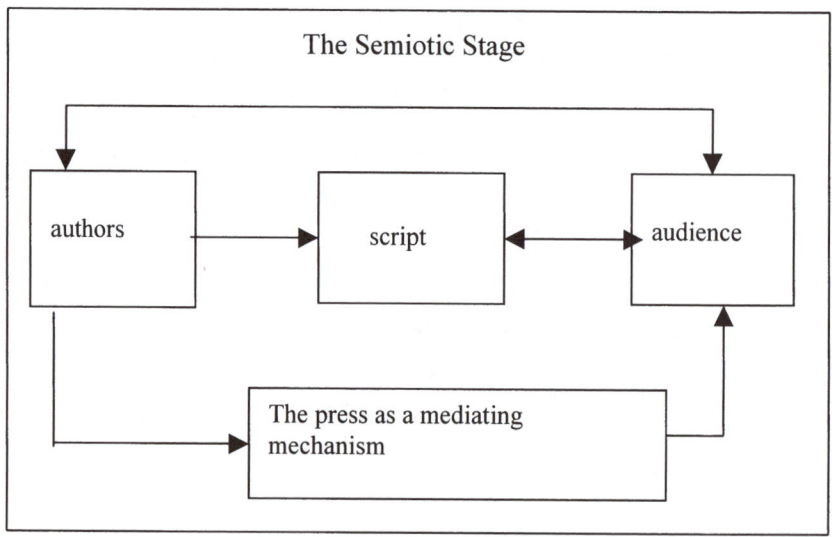

Fig 4.13 The Semiotic Stage

As far as the audience is concerned, just as for any other script, the authors cannot control the make up of that audience. Hence it becomes important for the script to be designed on the basis of universal appeal to all potential audiences. This is one reason why the style of the script has developed to encompass more than the transmission of information regarding organisational activities to the legal owners of the organisation and has been extended to provide information to all stakeholders.[49]

Interpreting the corporate reporting event in the form of a script designed to appeal to an unknown audience increases its likeness to a cinema film script rather than to a play (Crowther, Cooper & Carter 2001). In a film enactment there is no direct communication between the actors and the audience – the film is created in advance of the audience receiving it, whereas in a play the script unfolds afresh at each enactment and the audience reaction can affect this unfolding. One of the essential differences between a film and a play is that in a film the narrative is provided in part as a series of snapshots of events which link together through the audience participation in the interpretation of the otherwise disjointed narrative (Carroll 1980). This narrative provides a framework for the whole film in a symbolic form (Wright 1975). This can be likened to corporate reporting where each individual report provides a series of snapshots of organisational activity and performance over the preceding period and each corporate report, as a whole, provides a snapshot of organisational existence in a temporal sequence.

In the corporate reporting script it is apparent that the authors of the script have a starring part in the action. Others with parts to play include the press, employees, customers and their pressure groups, shareholders, City analysts and the government. In many respects this makes for an unusual script because the primary actors are also the authors of the script while the other cast members also comprise the audience to the film. Metz (1974) identifies that a film script is aimed at the audience rather than the participants and in this case the script unfolds by aiming the script at the audience while also involving them in the script in minor roles.

The Extent of Semiotic Analysis

In developing the semiology of corporate reporting the issues concerned in the analysis are the reporting of activities and performance both to the owners of the business and to all other parts of the audience. The analysis undertaken of these companies selected therefore is concerned with investigation of the way these companies report both in terms of traditional financial performance and in terms of their impact upon society at large, either socially or environmentally. It is also concerned with the way in which these companies address the reporting requirements of various constituencies among the readership of their reports, the audience to the script. The analysis is therefore undertaken both at a societal level and at a sectoral level as well as longitudinally. At the sectoral level the analysis is both inter-sectoral and intra-sectoral.

The documents which form the script for the organisation, in this analysis, include all the performance - related publications of the organisation which are produced periodically for external consumption by all sectors of the audience.[50] Other publications, such as advertising and public relations material, are excluded from being considered as part of the corporate reporting script. Thus all these documents together are considered, both individually and collectively, to be the script for analysis for each company in the sample. This analysis is undertaken in terms of the effect of the script in terms of the semiotic stage considered earlier.

It is recognised however that the restriction of the analysis to this sample of companies might limit the generaliseability of the analysis whereas it is claimed in this work that the same insights can be gained whatever the sample of companies chosen. For this reason therefore, although the analysis is principally based upon this sample of companies, illustrations from a wide range of other companies are used throughout the analysis in order to overcome this limitation.

Traversing the Semiotic Stage

Language consists simply of a system of differences (Saussure 1966) and this led to his identification of the binary opposite of *langue* and *parole*. These were considered by Barthes (1967) as being synonymous with language and speech. This notion of binary opposition has however been extended into a binary opposition of scheme and usage (Hjelmslev 1963). It is this notion of binary opposition which provides a mechanism for meaning construction, through categorisation, in the semiotic exploration of a text. This binary opposition provides a structure to the text and the construction of a text as an integral structure is tantamount to the recognition of its constituent pairs of binary opposites (Greimas 1990). Furthermore what is important is not the binary opposites themselves but rather the meaning already existing within them (Greimas and Rastier 1968). Berger (1982) supports this notion of binary opposition as a mechanism for discovering meaning within a text and claims that the reading of a text semiotically implies an understanding of the binary opposites embedded within them, while Baudrillard (1988) regards the notion of binarism as an essential and sacred part of the text. The examination of binary opposites therefore provides a mechanism for traversing the semiotic stage and examining the communication event surrounding the text and its actors.[51]

The rationale for using this notion of binary opposition as a means of exploring corporate reporting is based upon the argument of Fish (1972) who states that reading is an activity in which meanings are an event in the readers' consciousness. For him the text is discourse which challenges the reader to confront problems and questions which cannot readily be resolved into a reassuring harmony (Belsey 1980). Fish (1972: 1-2) defines this as dialectical, stating:

> A dialectical presentation .... is disturbing, for it requires of its readers a searching and rigorous scrutiny of everything they believe in and live by. It is didactic in a special sense; it does not preach the truth, but ask that its readers discover the truth for themselves, and this discovery is often made at the expense not only of a reader's opinions and values, but of his self-esteem.... For the end of a dialectical experience is (or should be) nothing less than a *conversion*, not only a changing, but an exchanging of minds.

Fish therefore sees the reader as participant in the text but places the author firmly in control of the discourse.[52] He also proposes the exploration of the dialectic through the tensions inherent[53] in its binary oppositions[54] and this is the method which is adopted in this book.[55]

The semiotic analysis undertaken is based upon the identification and exploration of the binarisms inherent in the script. The selection of particular binary pairs will be explained in the relevant parts of this book when this analysis is undertaken. The exploration is based upon the selection of data which is used to show the inconsistencies in the script and this is manifest in both he linguistic and the non-linguistic parts of the script. Thus a databank of text excerpts from the corporate scripts and a databank of images has been compiled which is used to explore the inconsistencies and tensions within the script. These databanks are used as a means for exploring the binarisms and the inherent inconsistencies throughout the semiotic analysis. These databanks provide an access to the code (Bernstein 1961) of corporate reporting while an exploration of the inconsistencies provides an opportunity to break this code (Singh 1999) and arrive at an understanding of meaning. Thus it is possible to arrive at an understanding of the performed (Munro 1999a) order in terms of an interplay of these artefacts and the agendas inherent within the organisation.

Thus an understanding of the account which is being offered in the text can be arrived at though a consideration of the different accounts on offer – the traditional and the different. As Munro (1996: 4) states:

...it is important to appreciate that there is never just a single story-line on offer. Accounts involve an intricate, and continuous, process of embedding accounts in other accounts, one in which a multiplicity of readings is always possible.

The exploration of the binarisms, in terms of inconsistencies in the reported script, allows therefore for the deriving of an understanding of the tension inherent in the text from the viewpoint of the different stakeholders to the reporting script and thereby an exploration of the hypotheses developed earlier. The texts and images selected for analysis from within the corporate reporting script have been chosen to effect this exploration.

Notes

[1] These are required by legislation enshrined within the Companies Acts and as expressed through GAAP.

[2] There is a limited legal requirement to report in this manner. Custom and precedent, as shown in the archaeology of corporate reporting, in Chapter 1 shows the development of this part of the report.

[3] These are collectively termed the written reports in the remainder of this book, unless identified separately.

[4] When produced this report is normally produced as a companion publication to the annual report.

[5] See Crowther 1996b for full details of these differing needs.

[6] See Crowther 1996b for full details of these sources.

[7] This has been illustrated in the public sector by such writers as Pollitt (1990) and Hoggett (1996).

[8] See for example the article 'ICI heads list of worst polluters' (*The Times* 22/3/99) which provides a list of the 10 worst polluting organisations, as determined by the Environment Agency. This list includes 2 water companies who are within the sample selcted for analysis in this work.

[9] See for example the article 'Windfall tax plea against penalising good performers' (*The Times* 26/6/97) which provides an account of the arguments by Wessex Water against the imposition of a windfall tax (see Chapter 4) on good performers. Interestingly Wessex Water is one of the 10 companies named as polluters in the article referred to in footnote 8, thereby indicating the way in which the press is attempted to be used as a mediating mechanism on the semiotic stage.

[10] The limited power of registered charities to engage in political activity is recognised but ignored, as irrelevant, for the purposes of the development of this typology.

[11] The term terrorism is used here to imply illegal and disruptive activity, rather than to imply the use of physical violence.

[12] Consider for example the protest against the Poll Tax.

[13] See Crowther & Cooper (2001) for a consideration of the tactics of ecoprotestors.

[14] See Crowther & Cooper (2001) for a consideration of the role of ecoprotest in local community activity opposing the building of roads.

[15] Thus they focus upon their own utility and select their purchase and consumption patterns accordingly, rather than purely upon price. This is in perfect accord with the arguments of Marshall (1947) and earlier economists.

[16] A particularly good example is the debate concerning genetically modified foods which has led several supermarket chins to announce that they will stop using such foods in their own label products.

[17] As was the case for example with Shell and the Brent Spar oil platform.

[18] See for example the article 'Shell challenged on green audit' (*The Times* 11/4/97).

[19] See for example the B & Q (1997) publication 'Environmental Paint Policy' produced as part of its general environmental policy.

[20] It is recognised that this resolution of the different perspectives upon performance into two is highly structuralist in its method. It does however explain the dialectic between traditional and environmental accounting and reporting in terms of a dialectic between two different sets of stakeholders. Moreover it explains the nature of corporate reporting and its division into the financial performance based annual report and the environmental performance based environmental report. As such it also provides a set of binarisms for the exploration of the semiotic.

[21] This necessarily restricts the semiology to a British semiology but considerations of generaliseability to other environments will be considered in chapter 10.

[22] This group has been termed the dominant coalition, and it is recognised that they may well have an ownership of shares in the company arising from their managerial duties as part of their executive remuneration package.

[23] See for example Azzone et al (1996) who documents much such research.

[24] Hyder plc was formerly known as Welsh Water plc prior to its expressed preference for a Welsh language name.

[25] North West Water Group plc is now known as United Utilities plc after the acquisition of NORWEB plc, a regional electricity company covering a very similar geographical area.

[26] This definition is based upon the classification of companies provided in the FTSE index.

[27] It should be noted that Dalgety plc is substantially concerned with the production of pet foods. Nevertheless the company is also engaged in the production of foods for human consumption and has been included in the sample because, irrespective of the end consumer, pet foods are also purchased by humans and the same manufacturing processes, and consequent environmental issues, apply. Other companies in this sample are engaged, to a greater or lesser extent, in

activities other than food manufacture but have been included because of their Stock Market classification as food manufacturers.

[28] For example, Beaver (1989) states that there has been a shift from an economic view of corporate performance measurement to an informational perspective with a recognition of the social implications of an organisation's activities. Similarly Eccles (1991) states that there has been a shift from treating financial figures as the foundation of corporate performance measurement to treating them as part of a broader range of measures, while McDonald and Puxty (1979) maintain that companies are no longer the instruments of shareholders alone but exist within society and so have responsibilities to that society. Others (e.g. Tinker 1985) argue for a changed basis for accounting to reflect these changes.

[29] See Crowther, Davies & Cooper 1998 for a critique of this technique.

[30] The term Economic Value Added is copyrighted to Stern Stewart & Co.

[31] The Stern Stewart methodology involves up to 192 adjustments.

[32] The term market value added is also copyrighted to Stern Stewart & Co.

[33] In using the term native language it is intended to mean the language which a person speaks in their everyday communication. Accounting as a language has of course not only the problem that it is not spoken as a native language but also that it is a written language rather than a spoken one.

[34] See Robson (1992) for a consideration of the role of accounting in communication across distance.

[35] This analogy of the socialisation process in relation to language is of course a restricted interpretation and ignores the arguments of Bourdieu (1984) regarding the use of language as a cultural good in the socialisation process but is considered to be sufficient as accounting is nothing more than a written form of communication. As such it contains cultural capital only when read.

[36] Knowledge in this context implies the ability to read the language (i.e. to understand accounting reports) rather than to write the language. This function requires the technical proficiency of the accountant of an organisation.

[37] See Clegg, Higgins & Spybey (1990) regarding the artificial dividing up of time to meet this need.

[38] See chapter 1 for a consideration of these legal requirements.

[39] That is the shareholders who are generally not involved in the operational activities of the organisation.

[40] The two terms were created independently. Semiology is the term used by Saussure while semiotics is the term used by Peirce. In this book the term semiology is preferred to describe the method while the singular noun and adjective applied throughout is the term semiotic, which applies to both method terms.

[41] Hervey (1982) argues that this debate is sterile and that while semiotics can be considered to be simply 'looking in other areas of communication for the properties first encountered in natural languages' it is also 'defined by explicit reference to the non-linguistic'. In this particular analysis this debate is ignored

because it is felt not to be relevant to the development of a semiology of external reporting.

[42] Lacan developed these arguments further in the context of his psychoanalysis, but this inextricable enmeshment of the person as an individual within the semiotic of any sign is at variance with the argument of Derrida above. The adoption of a Lacanian perspective would necessitate a consideration of the motivations of the actors involved in the semiotic, and these are absent from this analysis. Consequently the Derridan position is adopted in this book.

[43] This marginalisation might seem to conflict with the statutory purposes of corporate reporting but it will be argued that the usurpation of such reporting for other purposes has relegated this statutory purpose to a relatively less significant position within the corporate reporting script.

[44] See for example the annual reports of companies such as Astech Educational Solutions Ltd (a private company which produces no more than is needed to satisfy legal requirements) or A. G. Barr plc (a family dominated plc) as an illustration of the differences.

[45] This is not to deny that corporate reports are used by such people as investment analysts for financial analysis, but merely to argue that this is no longer the only major purpose of the production of these reports.

[46] It is recognised that the services of external professionals, such as photographers, may be used in order to enhance the visual presentation but only within the control of internal members of the organisation.

[47] It is recognised however that the auditors of the company have a role in this editorial process such that they need to be satisfied that the reporting creates a true and fair view of the company's past performance.

[48] In this context the press is defined not just as those people who produce business and financial reporting for newspapers, television and magazines but also those members of City institutions who produce their own analysis, interpretation and forecasting of the financial affairs and business activities of corporations.

[49] That is to say all significant stakeholders.

[50] Thus the text for each company will include the annual reports produced for all the years of the longitudinal analysis, all interim reports produced during this period and all other reports produced. These other reports chiefly comprise of environmental reports, which have been produced by most of the companies in the sample at least once during the time period under consideration, and often on a periodic basis which is occasionally annual.

[51] It is accepted that when dealing with the semiotic of such reporting from the viewpoint of the multiple stakeholders concerned with such a script that there are multiple interpretations, and therefore multiple voices involved. The essential feature of the consideration of such binarisms – which equate to dialectics – is that a focus upon the extreme position of each binarism facilitates the extraction of meaning.

[52] This view coincides with the arguments concerning semiotics advances earlier in this chapter.

[53] These inherent tensions form the Kantian dialectic which provides a basis for analysis.

[54] Fish does not actually use the term binary opposition but concentrates instead upon the tensions that exist within the text. His use of this equates to the concept of binary opposition which is used in this book.

[55] Although the mode of analysis for this consideration of the semiotics of corporate reporting has been selected as that of exploring the binary opposites in the semiotic, it is recognised that other modes of analysis are used in semiotics to different effect. The Piercian mode of analysis has been considered and rejected previously as inappropriate, but other modes also exist. For example Sebeok (1994) argues for the study of the semiotic in terms of the signs of the text and the meaning to be attached to each sign. He identifies six different types of sign: signal, symptom, icon, index, symbol and name. It would be possible to analyse the texts of the corporate reports by classifying the signs within them into these various categories but it is considered that this would not add to the analysis as it would only result in the same kinds of conclusions being drawn. Consequently this type of analysis is recognised as a possibility but excluded from this particular analysis. Equally Barthes (1972, 1977) and Eco (1994) make use of an unstructured mode of analysis through consideration of the text in totality and the meaning of the text as a whole. This mode of analysis is useful in a consideration of the overall meaning of corporate reporting but fails however to gather the diverse meanings inherent in a complex text such as a corporate report and so is not considered appropriate for the development of the semiology of corporate reporting. A Saussurian analysis based upon exploration of the binary oppositions inherent in the text is considered to be the most appropriate form of analysis and is therefore used in the semiotic analysis undertaken in this work. This provides a means of exploring the Kantian inconsistencies in the script.

Chapter 5

The Environmental Discourse: the Quantitative Evidence

Measuring Financial Performance

For the purposes of the analysis to be undertaken in this chapter, what is of concern from the point of view of the evaluation of performance, based upon reported financial figures, is what might be of interest to the groups of stakeholders under consideration. An appropriate measure therefore to use in this analysis is one which reflects the appropriate aspect of performance when viewed from an external perspective on investment. One such measure exists which aggregates performance in terms of these two factors and that is the measure of total shareholder returns (TSR)[1]. This is the measure which is to be to used for the evaluation of performance from the perspective of investors.

There are many ways to calculate total shareholder returns but for the purposes of this analysis it is defined as the increase in market capitalisation over a predefined period plus the total dividend paid in the period, expressed as a percentage of the market capitalisation at the start of that period. Thus the calculation reflects not just changes in share price during the period but also is adjusted for any share issues or buy backs during the period, in order to reflect more truly the returns to any holder of an individual share.

Taking the six year period under consideration therefore (or a five year period for two of these companies), the TSR for the water companies in the sample can be seen to be as follows, when calculated on an annual basis:

Company			TSR per cent				
	1991	1992	1993	1994	1995	1996	ave
Anglian	3.86	60.65	25.10	-8.66	25.13	4.15	18.37
Hyder	9.05	62.48	38.51	-0.92	11.92	2.84	20.65
Northumbrian	5.89	79.57	30.20	7.04	64.42	-	37.42
Severn Trent	7.03	58.53	39.69	-8.61	37.72	3.79	23.02
Southern	4.11	63.59	49.81	-10.24	24.79	-	26.41
South West	3.60	65.06	37.42	-15.58	9.59	22.80	20.48
Thames	2.31	59.10	24.16	-11.81	23.42	15.25	18.74
Utd Utilities	6.67	51.71	29.97	-2.42	24.16	14.47	20.76
Wessex	41.22	61.35	23.45	-14.93	17.26	13.03	23.56
Yorkshire	14.15	56.99	21.18	-8.92	19.33	25.85	21.43
Mean	9.79	61.90	31.95	-7.05	25.77	12.77	23.08

Table 5.1 TSR for Water Companies

The homogeneity of this group of companies can be seen from the fact that the performance of the group year by year has been roughly similar insofar as the highest annual TSR for all companies was in 1992 while the lowest for all companies, except for Northumbrian, was in 1994. Average annual TSR was between 18 per cent and 27 per cent for all companies except Northumbrian (37.42 per cent). Further evidence of homogeneity within this group of companies is provided by the fact that in 1994 the average TSR was negative (-7.05 per cent) and for all companies, except for Northumbrian, the TSR for that year ranged between –0.92 per cent and –15.58 per cent. Similarly in 1992 the average TSR for the group was 61.90 per cent and the range was between 51.71 per cent and 79.57 per cent.

The homogeneity of this group of companies can be contrasted with the range and variation of returns which were reported for the other two groups of companies in the sample. Figures for the food retailing group of companies are as follows:

Company	TSR per cent						
	1991	1992	1993	1994	1995	1996	ave
Argyll	20.83	46.54	-27.01	2.23	33.07	22.93	16.43
Asda	-63.31	79.98	7.53	26.03	68.49	13.59	22.05
Iceland	51.59	53.36	-13.73	-10.28	2.01	-34.97	8.00
Kwiksave	25.22	38.16	-17.79	-7.52	-4.47	-29.52	0.68
WMorrison	34.96	97.11	-32.62	29.23	1.08	16.60	24.39
Nurdin&P	-3.52	14.28	9.28	-5.79	-1.58	43.22	9.31
Sainsbury	27.73	53.72	-19.25	-4.41	-1.36	2.65	9.85
Tesco	5.65	13.34	-10.47	21.77	23.90	22.99	12.86
Mean	12.39	49.56	-13.01	6.41	15.14	7.19	12.95

Table 5.2 TSR for Food Retailing Companies

For this group of companies the dispersion of reported TSR is much greater. For example in 1991 the highest reported TSR is 51.59 per cent (Iceland) while the lowest is -63.31 per cent (Asda), and for 1992 the highest is 97.11 per cent (W. Morrison) and the lowest is 13.13 per cent (Tesco). Indeed the average TSR for the individual companies ranges from 0.68 per cent to 24.39 per cent. While looking at individual years in isolation it can be seen that, with the exception of 1992, at least 2 companies showed a negative TSR in every year but that different companies showed negative TSRs in different years and that every company showed a negative TSR in at least one year. The homogeneity of this group of companies is therefore apparently much less than the group of water companies.

A comparison of the food manufacturing group of companies selected for analysis shows the following position:

Company	1991	1992	TSR per cent 1993	1994	1995	1996	ave
ALFisher	-35.31	-15.77	31.29	-21.96	10.71	-1.34	-5.40
AssBrFood	15.78	12.53	14.54	3.59	34.89	33.89	19.20
Cadbury	40.78	6.80	20.87	-11.70	32.40	-4.19	14.16
Dalgety	15.96	30.14	8.61	-9.36	11.77	-2.77	9.06
Hazlewood	34.14	-12.65	6.31	-18.01	-6.63	15.79	3.16
NorthFood	79.47	4.73	-8.26	-4.20	-15.08	25.44	13.68
Tate&Lyle	52.66	4.46	3.27	9.83	16.40	4.90	15.25
Unigate	6.09	20.88	29.45	-3.25	29.95	7.10	15.04
Unilever	36.24	24.45	10.70	-0.79	17.46	9.99	16.34
UtdBiscuit	29.85	-4.03	7.02	-4.07	-16.79	-12.14	-0.06
Mean	27.57	7.15	12.38	-5.99	11.49	7.67	10.04

Table 5.3 TSR for Food Manufacturing Companies

For this group of companies also the dispersion of reported TSR is much greater than it is for the water companies. For example in 1991 the highest reported TSR is 79.47 per cent (Northern Foods) while the lowest is −35.31 per cent (A L Fisher) while for 1993 the position is reversed with the highest TSR being 31.29 per cent (A L Fisher) and the lowest is −8.26 per cent (Northern Foods). Indeed the average TSR for the individual companies ranges from −5.40 per cent to 16.34 per cent while looking at individual years in isolation shows that in every single year at least 1 company showed a negative TSR but that different companies showed negative TSRs in different years and that every company showed a negative TSR in at least one year. The homogeneity of this group of companies is therefore apparently much less than the group of water companies.

These differences can be seen by a comparison of the mean TSR for each group, according to sector. These figures are as follows:

Sector	TSR per cent						
	1991	1992	1993	1994	1995	1996	ave
Water	9.79	61.90	31.95	-7.05	25.77	12.77	23.08
Food Retailing	12.39	49.56	-13.01	6.41	15.14	7.19	12.95
Food Manf	27.57	7.15	12.38	-5.99	11.49	7.67	10.04

Table 5.4 Mean TSRs for Groups

From this comparison it is possible to see the wide range of returns to shareholders which have been reported for these companies. This range is wide not just between sectors but also between years within each sector. In each sector the maximum annual return is at least 33 per cent (and up to 70 per cent) higher than the lowest annual return. In each sector the lowest annual return is negative, but not necessarily in the same year for all sectors.

It is inevitable when using a measure such as Total Shareholder Returns, which incorporates into the measure a factor based upon the market valuation of shares, that the returns reported cannot be based entirely upon the performance of the company itself in isolation from the economy as a whole, as reflected in the Stock Market. Indeed the Stock Market valuation of shares is a crucial part of the returns to shareholder as growth in the business, and hence in its future profit earning potential (and hence return distributional potential) is reflected entirely through the price for stock as set by the trading taking place in the Stock Market. However it is essential to recognise that this trading reflects not just the activity of each individual company being traded, in terms of reported performance and anticipated future performance, but also reflects the activity, and anticipated future activity, of the economy as a whole. In other words when the perceived prospects for the economy are gloomy then the value of the Stock Market in total tends to reduce, and the price of individual stocks tends to diminish. When this happens then an individual stock can be expected to show a negative return, when measured in terms of TSR, regardless of what is being reported concerning the performance of that individual company. In times of optimism then the converse is the case and individual companies can in this case be expected to show high TSRs, regardless of their individual reported performances and expectations of future performances.

Oscillations in the value of the Stock Market as a whole therefore interfere with reported TSR for individual companies when looked at on a year by year basis. The question as to whether actual performance of companies reflects the expectations expressed through this operation of the Stock Market, and in optimistic times reported performance is higher than in pessimistic times when recorded through internal measures of performance such as ROCE or EVA, is irrelevant from the point of view of this analysis. While returns to shareholders is of concern for this analysis, and changes in the Stock Market generally inevitably change returns to individual shareholders at particular points in time, one problem with any analysis which includes these changes is that such changes affect individual companies in different ways and at different times. This has the effect of making a comparison of different companies and groups of companies more difficult. For example every company in the sample shows a large variation in TSR from one year to another and all companies except one (Northumbrian Water) show a negative TSR in at least one year of the period under consideration. The fact that the majority show a negative TSR in approximately the same period around 1994 suggests that this result is caused by some extraneous factor which affected the Stock Market as a whole, rather than factors affecting each individual company in isolation.

The year in which this negative TSR is reported however, as well as the size of the negative TSR, is different for different companies. The size of the negative TSR for any particular company can be affected by the perceived performance and expected future performance of that individual company, within the context of the overall expectations of the economy as a whole, and this can explain differences in the size of reported negative TSRs. One further factor which can affect these negative TSRs, in terms of size, and will certainly affect the timing of such TSRs is the year end date of respective companies in the sample. Depending upon when the year end of a particular company is in relationship to sudden shocks to the Stock Market as a whole, which have the effect of changing valuations of all stocks within the market, then this can place the reported change in a different financial year. More importantly however this timing can change the reported effect of the sudden shock. Typically what happens is a sudden shock which adversely affects all share prices followed by a period of realignment in which the prices gradually return to the normal levels from before the shock. Thus the extent of the deviation from the norm is greater the closer the time is to the actual shock. Companies with financial year end close to the shock will report greater reductions in share price and therefore greater negative TSRs than those reporting at a time further away from the shock and in which the return to normality is underway. In other words the size of reported TSR for any individual company in any particular time period is a function of the economy as a whole rather than just a function of the reported performance of that particular company.

For comparative purposes therefore it becomes important to seek an appropriate measure which as far as possible eliminates such external effects from the calculation of shareholder returns. TSR when calculated on a year by year basis plainly does not achieve this aim but over a period of time it can be expected that oscillations in reported TSR for any company will average out. Thus the effect of extraneous events will become subsumed within the average performance of the market as a whole. This average performance for the market as a whole over time shows a gradual increase in valuations and it is therefore possible to perform a comparative evaluation between companies based upon these averages. It is therefore intended to use average TSR over the period of the sample (i.e. 1991 – 1996) as the means of comparison of the companies in the sample.

One way of calculating average TSR is to take a simple mean of the 6 years data. While this might be satisfactory for most purposes, one of the problems with this approach is that previously mentioned whereby annual figures might be either exaggerated or diminished due to the timing of the end of the financial year in relationship to any sudden shock to which the Stock Market in general has been subject. Additionally using this method of averaging means that the calculation of TSR for each year is based upon the market valuation at the end of the previous year, and this too heightens the problem of making more extreme the calculations. An alternative approach therefore is to base the calculation upon the market valuation at the beginning of the 6 year period and to calculate TSR from then for the whole six year period as cumulative shareholder returns and then to average this total over the period by means of an annuity based calculation of annual TSR.

Taking the water companies as an example comparison of the average TSR using each method is as follows:

Company	mean per cent	annuity per cent
Anglian	18.37	16.38
Hyder	20.65	18.71
Severn Trent	23.02	20.73
South West	20.48	17.78
Thames	18.74	16.77
Utd Utilities	20.76	19.53
Wessex	23.56	21.21
Yorkshire	21.43	19.89

Table 5.5 Average TSR for Water Companies

Inevitably the annuity method of calculation produces a lower calculation of annual average TSR than does the mean method, but arguably it also emphasises the relative homogeneity of the group. It also means that the measurement of performance for all companies is commenced from the same base period and finishes at the same time. The effect of any extraneous factors which affect the Stock Market as a whole during this period are thereby excluded from the calculations. It is considered therefore that the annuity based method of calculating TSR, based upon the start of the period under examination (i.e. from the commencement of the 1990-91 financial year) provides a basis for comparison of companies which best removes extraneous fluctuations, caused by economic factors, from the calculation of TSR. It is for this reason therefore that this basis of calculating average annual TSR for each company is to be used. Based upon this method of calculation, the average annual TSR for each company in each sector has been calculated. As it is intended to use a five year period for some of the analysis these figures are also shown for comparative purposes.

The comparative figures for water companies are as follows:

Company	TSR 6 yrs per cent	TSR 5 yrs per cent
Anglian	16.38	19.96
Hyder	18.71	22.85
Northumbrian	-	34.23
Severn Trent	20.73	25.36
Southern	-	23.37
South West	17.78	21.70
Thames	16.77	20.45
Utd Utilities	19.53	23.88
Wessex	21.21	25.96
Yorkshire	19.89	24.33

Table 5.6 Five Year Annuity TSR for Water Companies

The figures for food retailing companies are as follows:

Company	TSR 6 yrs per cent	TSR 5 yrs per cent
Argyll	13.71	16.67
Asda	9.38	11.36
Iceland	2.99	3.60
Kwiksave	-2.00	-2.40
W Morrison	18.22	22.25
Nurdin & Peacock	8.15	9.86
Sainsbury	7.40	8.94
Tesco	12.15	14.75

Table 5.7 Five Year Annuity TSR for Food Retailing Companies

The figures for food manufacturing companies are as follows:

Company	TSR 6 yrs per cent	TSR 5 yrs per cent
A L Fisher	-7.91	-9.42
Associated British Foods	18.66	22.80
Cadbury Schweppes	12.58	15.28
Dalgety	8.31	10.05
Hazlewood	1.67	2.00
Northern Foods	9.88	11.97
Tate & Lyle	14.12	17.17
Unigate	14.35	17.45
Unilever	15.76	19.19
Utd Biscuits	-1.14	-1.37

Table 4.8 Five Year Annuity TSR for Food Manufacturing Companies

These figures therefore provide the basis for a comparative evaluation of financial performance from the point of view of investment in the businesses. It should be noted that the figures based upon a 5 year analysis of performance are almost uniformly higher than those based upon a 6 year analysis of performance, reflecting the annuity basis of calculation. A simple t test to compare the two sets of figures, for those companies for which both sets of data exist, shows that t = 7.58. This is significant at the 0.001 level, showing that the two sets of data come from different populations. It is therefore necessary to treat the sample on either a 6 year period basis or a 5 year period basis. It is not possible to mix the data from the two sets for analytical purposes.

This result conforms to expectations and also conforms to a visual scan of the data. It therefore provides evidence for analysing the smaller sample of water companies for comparative purposes. When the larger sample over a reduced period of time is used for analysis then this data will merely be used for further refinement and explanation rather than to suggest that the results supercede or conflict with the basic analysis.

The sample of water companies to be used for statistical analysis therefore becomes a sample size of 8. This is the same sample size as the sample of food retailing companies. The sample of food manufacturing companies however is of 10 companies. For purposes of comparative analysis it seems reasonable to reduce this sample size also to 8. It has been decided therefore to eliminate two companies from the sample and the two selected are:

- Dalgety – on the basis that this company, although classed as a food producer in the Financial Times classification of companies by sectors, is actually largely concerned with the manufacture of pet foods. Indeed in press commentary the company is normally described as a pet food company.
- Unilever – on the basis that this company, although classed as a food producer in the Financial Times classification of companies by sectors, has substantial interests in other activities such as detergents, deodorants and chemicals.

The sample of companies for which statistical analysis is to be undertaken therefore is:

- Water:
    Anglia
    Hyder
    Severn Trent
    South West
    Thames
    United Utilities
    Wessex
    Yorkshire
- Food retailing:
    Argyll
    Asda
    Iceland
    Kwik Save
    Morrison
    Nurdin & Peacock
    Sainsbury
    Tesco
- Food manufacturing:
    Albert Fisher
    Associated British Foods
    Cadbury Schweppes
    Hazlewood
    Northern Foods
    Tate & Lyle

Unigate
United Biscuits

Comparing Financial Performance

The first part of the analysis to be undertaken is concerned entirely with reported financial performance, based upon total shareholder returns. The purpose of this analysis is to consider any differences with respect to this performance between the different industrial sectors. This kind of analysis for the three sectors together can be made by means of a 1 way ANOVA for unrelated designs.

This shows a factor which is significant at the $p = 0.01$ level but not at the $p = 0.001$ level. This therefore suggests that the three samples are significantly different and that the level of TSR depends upon industrial sector. The evidence from this sample is not however overwhelming and so further analysis is needed, looking at the relationship between the three sectors.

It is less clear however, from merely looking at the data, if this significant difference applies to all three sectors or, if there is a difference only between one sector and the other two. It is therefore necessary to investigate this by considering any differences between sectors in terms of the difference between each pair of two sectors. This gives three separate analyses, as follows:

- Water – Food retailing
- Water – Food manufacturing
- Food retailing – Food manufacturing

It is therefore necessary to investigate the possibility of differences between each of these pairs of sectors in turn, using an appropriate statistical technique. For this kind of analysis this technique is a t test for unrelated design. The analysis is as follows:

Water – Food Retailing

Calculation of t values and significance results in a value of $t = 2.78$ which is significant at the 0.01 level and so it can be assumed that the differences between these two groups of companies is such that they are from different populations. In this case this suggests that for these two sectors the level of TSR is dependant upon sector. This finding supports the conclusion which would be drawn from a simple observation of the data. The meaning of this finding will be considered once the other two comparisons have been made. This analysis produces however a factor which is not significant at any higher levels of probability.

The fact that the difference between these two samples is not significantly different at high levels of probability might be regarded as somewhat surprising given the nature of the numbers. This must be attributed to the fact that the sample size is very small and the standard deviation, at least for the food retailing sample, is relatively large. This is one of the problems when dealing with small samples. One course of action would be to increase the sample size, which could therefore be expected to show a significant difference for a larger data set. This is not possible in this case as the sample size is determined by the number of companies in each industrial grouping which meet the criteria for selection.

One way to provide supporting evidence for the difference between the two groups is to treat the data sets as not parametric and to perform a Mann - Whitney test on the data. This gives a results of $U = 3$ which is significant at the 0.01 level and so it can be assumed, on the basis of this test, that the differences between these two groups of companies is such that they are from different populations. This is of course not a statistical proof but merely supporting evidence for the assertion made. In this case therefore this supports the assertion that for these two sectors the level of TSR is dependant upon sector. This finding also supports the conclusion which would be drawn from a simple observation of the data. While not necessarily statistically valid this further analysis has been undertaken to overcome the problem of small data samples and add weight to the arguments from other analyses. The meaning of this finding also will be considered in the context of an evaluation incorporating the analysis from the other two comparisons.

Water – Food Manufacturing

Calculation of t values and significance for these samples gives a value of $t = 1.01$ which is not significant at any level. The fact that the difference between these two samples is not significantly different might be regarded as somewhat surprising given the nature of the numbers. This must be attributed to the fact that the sample size is very small and the standard deviation, at least for the food manufacturing sample, is relatively large. This is one of the problems when dealing with small samples. One course of action would be to increase the sample size, which could therefore be expected to show a significant difference for a larger data set. This is not possible in this case as the sample size is determined by the number of companies in each industrial grouping which meet the criteria for selection.

Again one way to provide supporting evidence for the difference between the two groups, as considered previously, is to treat the data sets as not parametric and to perform a Mann - Whitney test on the data. This also gives a result of U = 3 which is significant at the 0.01 level and so again it can be assumed, on the basis of this test, that the differences between these two groups of companies is such that they are from different populations. In this case, although again not a valid statistical assertion, this supports the assertion that for these two sectors the level of TSR is dependant upon sector. This finding also supports the conclusion which would be drawn from a simple observation of the data. While not necessarily statistically valid this further analysis has been undertaken to overcome the problem of small data samples and add weight to the arguments from other analyses. The meaning of this finding also will be considered in the context of an evaluation incorporating the analysis from the other two comparisons.

Food Retailing – Food Manufacturing

For these samples calculation of t values and significance gives a result of t = 0.067 which is insignificant at the 0.2 level and so it can be assumed that the differences between these two groups of companies is such that they are not from different populations. In other words the differences within the groups are greater than the differences between the groups and there is therefore no clear distinction between the two groups. This supports the argument advanced earlier that these two sectors are related because of their sharing of common problems and issues related to packaging. It therefore seems reasonable from the point of view of analysis to consider these two sectors as belonging to a single population. The meaning of this finding will be considered in the context of an evaluation incorporating the analysis from the other two comparisons.

Having considered the problems of small data sets previously however and sought to overcome the problem by treating the data sets as not parametric and therefore performing a Mann - Whitney test on the data, it seems appropriate for this comparison to also perform the same test. This gives a result of U = 29 which is not significant at any level and so it can be assumed, on the basis of this test also, that the differences between these two groups of companies is such that they are not from different populations. In other words this test supports the findings of the t test for this comparison. Again the significance of this will be considered in the context of the meaning of all the analysis undertaken.

Although when undertaking an anova test of the three sectors together it was found that there was a significant difference between the sectors, it can be seen that in reality there is only a difference between the water sector and the food retailing and manufacturing sectors. These latter two sectors show no significant difference between them. An examination of the data in isolation, by simple observation, makes it is possible to see the differences found through analysis. It is in fact not surprising that the results of the comparison of the water and the two food sectors, the retailing and manufacturing sectors, shows them to be significantly different. Indeed it would be surprising if it were not the case. Nor is it surprising that there is no significant difference between the food retailing and the food manufacturing sectors. Indeed the similarity of the results in terms of TSR is such that it would be reasonable to treat these two sectors as one group. Given the argument for using these two sectors, ie that they shared a common problem in terms of packaging, it is not surprising that it seems possible to make this statement, at least within the context of total shareholder returns. The question as to whether or not these two sectors comprise one group or two will be returned to at various points during the subsequent analysis and discussion.

The question therefore arises as to what makes the water industry different from the other two industrial sectors to such an extent that the returns to shareholders can be demonstrated to be significantly different. It is of course possible that the nature of the operational efficiency of this industry is such that the firms can make a higher level of profit, and hence returns to shareholders in this industry. It is to be expected that differing industries have differing norms in this respect. The hypothesis of a perfect market for investment however, as mediated through the Stock Exchange, would, if accepted as reality, mitigate against this difference as it would have the effect of normalising the shareholder returns of all companies towards the average for the market. This is particularly relevant when it is realised that the bulk of the returns to shareholders from the measure of TSR is composed of changes in share price. In a perfect market changes in share price reflect investors' expectations of future dividends, discounted to present values, and a perfect market would tend to equalise these expectations of the future in terms of share price. The only circumstances which would cause this normalisation to be varied would be the following:

- A situation could arise which caused the returns from one company (as reflected in share price changes) to differ from the norm. This would however only apply in the short term until the normalising tendency of the market could correct this deviation. Such a situation could not apply over the longer term and would not be possible over the 6 year period of this analysis. Equally this argument would only apply to one company and could not apply to a whole sector, unless that short term effect applied to the whole sector. It therefore seems appropriate to dismiss this possibility as providing any explanation.

- The share price is a reflection of the expectation of investors with regard to future dividends. If in any year the returns to shareholders in the form of dividend paid in that year was considerably different to the expectations, as reflected in share price, then this could cause the calculated TSR for that particular year to be different to the market norm. It is reasonable to accept that this situation could apply to an individual company in a particular year but, as the analysis applies to a 6 year period, then in order for this to account for the difference between the water and the other sectors it would be necessary to suppose that this situation applied in every year (or virtually every year) to every company (or to virtually every company) in the water sector. This circumstance would be necessary to account for the differences based upon cumulative returns for the sector and to account for the sectoral difference as opposed to a single company difference. This seems to be such an unlikely situation that it can be rejected as providing an explanation.

It seems reasonable therefore to conclude that the perfect market hypothesis does not apply and so it is necessary to consider alternative explanations for the sectoral differences which exist. Having argued that the perfect market hypothesis does not exist in this context however it is equally necessary to accept that this lack of a perfect market will allow some variations to exist between companies and between sectors. It is not however reasonable to accept that the lack of a perfect market causes such imperfections in the market as to account for the significant level of differences reported. It must be supposed that the market does actually provide some kind of mediating mechanism to, at least to a certain extent, bring about a limited form of normalisation. This kind of imperfection would provide an explanation for the differences between returns for different companies in the same sector, and for the differences between the food retailing and food manufacturing sectors. It does however not seem to explain the difference between the water sector and the other two sectors. It therefore becomes necessary to seek an alternative explanation.

One factor which can explain the difference between different sectors of the market is that concerning the level of risk which applies, or is perceived to apply, to different sectors. Sectors with a higher level of risk associated with then can expect to give a greater return to shareholders as a reward to bearing that risk. This can help explain the similarity within a sector and the difference between one sector and another. It has already been stated however that water companies are each in a monopoly situation with regard to supply of their products. It is equally true that the product which they supply is a commodity product which is in constant demand. Moreover that demand is steadily increasing over time. It does not seem to be therefore a particularly risky business from a trading perspective and this too fails to account for any difference between this and the other sectors.

Risk can however be manifest in other forms than that relating to trading conditions. For example a company which continually demonstrates abnormal returns to its shareholders can be subject to a take-over bid for this reason. In this respect it is perhaps significant that two of these water companies have been acquired in the recent past while several others have been subject to bids which have been prevented as being against the interest of consumers. Equally a company which is cash rich can be subject to a take-over bid for this reason, and again it is perhaps significant that some of the water companies have so much cash, and so little that they wish to do with that cash, that they have embarked upon share buy back schemes.

Abnormal returns can also be a result of abnormal trading conditions and it is reasonable to argue that the water industry is subject to abnormal trading conditions for the following reasons:

- There has been a major restructuring of these companies following their privatisation. This has been to such an extent that their operating costs have fallen year by year. Indeed this restructuring has been expected and the Office of Water Regulation has expected such restructuring to happen and has built in calculations regarding the expected results in the level of prices set. If the level of operational costs falls for any company at a faster rate than that expected, and allowed for, in the pricing structure then the company will make abnormal returns. Expectations of this continuing to happen in the future will cause share prices to rise, and this seems to have happened.
- These companies are subject to regulation regarding the prices which they are able to charge for their core services. This regulation allows for periodic reviews which can cause a step change in expected profits. This can have the result that while returns are particularly high at the present time there is considerable uncertainty as to the future. This in turn can have the effect that the risk of investment is perceived to be

higher and normalisation towards market averages does not happen because of the unquantifiable uncertainty regarding the future. Again there is evidence that this may well be the case for this industry. This has been of particular significance during 1996 and 1997 with the prospect of a change in government bringing a political dimension into the risk associated with these companies. Indeed the Labour Party, as part of its electioneering, announced the imposition of a one-off windfall tax on the profits of privatised utilities. This tax was subsequently implemented. The political climate under which these companies operate therefore can be seen to be considerable more uncertain than most other industries.

- The companies operating in this industry are monopolies and as such can be expected to exploit their monopoly situation to earn abnormal returns. It would appear that this provides at least part of the explanation for the difference between this sector and the others considered.

Further evidence that the returns to shareholders in the water industry are different to those in other sectors of the economy is provided by the press comment over recent years. This comment purports to reflect public opinion and comments abound regarding the excessive profits made by these companies. For comparison there is not a single comment in the press concerning excessive returns to shareholders with regard to either of the other two sectors being studied in this analysis during the period under consideration. This in itself suggests that there is a difference between the water sectors and the food retailing and manufacturing sectors, or at least there is a general perception amongst both the public and the press of a difference, and this in itself supports the argument for treating the sectors as being different in terms of total shareholder returns for purposes of this analysis, and supporting the finding from the analysis already considered.

The exceptional nature of the returns to shareholders of water companies was also acknowledged by Ian Byatt, Director General of the Office of Water Regulation (Ofwat). In a speech to the Liverpool Economic and Statistical Society in March 1997 he stated:

> Water companies have, like other utilities, substantial returns to their shareholders. The Centre for Regulated Industries has calculated that the real (post inflation) return to shareholders in water companies from 1989 to 1997 was 23 per cent a year on average. Most of this accrued in the early years (particularly between 1989 and 1992) or as a result of take-over. The annual average real return since the 1994 price reviews, excluding companies taken over was 9.75 per cent, less than half of the return since 1989.

Even a cursory glance at the figures for the TSR of the water companies shows that they do not bear out the statement made by Byatt. Admittedly 1992 was a year of exceptional shareholder returns, possibly caused by the low returns during the preceding year. Equally 1994 was a year in which shareholder returns were, with the exception of Northumbrian Water, universally negative. It would be reasonable to suggest that this was due to the effect of the periodic review undertake by Ofwat during this year. Returns for other years post-1992 however remain high and it is difficult to suggest that returns can be separated into pre- and post-1992 with a discernible difference in returns to shareholders in each period, or that returns after the 1994 review are different to those prior to the review. The remarks made by Byatt therefore need be interpreted in the context of his role and can be taken to imply that regulation of the industry is effective. For comparative purposes therefore the returns pre- and post-1992 are considered separately. A calculation of the average returns in each period shows the following:

Company	TSR per cent	
	1991-2	1993-6
Anglian	32.25	11.43
Hyder	35.76	13.09
Northumbrian	42.73	33.88
Severn Trent	32.78	18.15
Southern	33.85	21.45
South West	34.33	13.56
Thames	30.70	12.76
Utd Utilities	29.19	16.55
Wessex	51.28	9.70
Yorkshire	35.57	14.36
Average	35.84	16.49

Table 5.9   Water Company TSRs Analysed

Using a simple average of the years in each of the time periods, it is possible to see that the averages seem to be quite different. It must be recognised however that 1994 was an exceptional year which affected the average for the latter period in a significant manner. Nevertheless if a statistical analysis is undertaken to determine if the two sets of data are significantly different then this reveals a value of t = 3.69. This difference is significant at the 0.01 level but not significant at the 0.001 level. This finding therefore suggests that the two samples are significantly different but the case is not absolutely proved. This test has been conducted using a simple mean of the TSR values for pre-1992 and post-1992 in order to test out the assertion made by the Director General of Ofwat. Using a simple mean is considered to be the most appropriate method in these circumstances, given the limited amount of data to construct an annuity based TSR average. If an annuity basis of calculation was made however then it is considered that these differences would be even less significant. Given these finding then there is no reason to suppose that abnormal returns were not made in the post-1992 period, despite Byatt's assertions, again reinforcing the conclusion drawn earlier that his comments therefore need be interpreted in the context of his role and can be taken to imply that regulation of the industry is effective.

The analysis undertaken shows that financial performance is different for different companies and is also different between the sectors which have been analysed. The implications of this will be considered after the environmental performance of the companies has been analysed.

Measuring Environmental Performance

Financial performance comprises one aspect of performance as far as the dialectic under consideration is concerned. The other aspect of performance which is of interest from the point of view of this analysis, and which comprises the other part of the dialectic, is that of social and environmental performance. Accordingly it is necessary to consider the measures of social and environmental performance which are reported by the companies subject to analysis. From this it is possible to decide upon a measure which is appropriate to use for comparative analysis. In the case of this dimension of performance however the situation is rather different to that of financial performance. In this case rather than having a variety of measures available, all acceptable for such analysis, and deciding upon the most appropriate measure, there is in fact no measure which exists and is universally recognised as an appropriate measure. It is therefore necessary firstly to consider what measures are available and to consider their appropriateness for the purpose of this analysis.

In this context therefore it is important to recognise that, with the absence of any particular measure of environmental performance, there are a variety of measures which, it is argued, have a relationship with such performance but which do not necessarily fully reflect the extent of such performance. Such measures must therefore be considered to be merely surrogate measures for this dimension of performance, which provide some method of deriving a commonality in the evaluation of such performance. From the possible measures which are available, four measures have been considered and the relative merits of each measure as an indicator of social and environmental performance have been evaluated. The four measures are:

- lines of text;
- charitable donations;
- size and frequency of environmental reports;
- number of measures reported.

Each of these, and the meaning of each, is considered in detail below. From these measures it is argued that it is appropriate to construct a composite measure which reflects for each company the environmental performance of that company.

Lines of Text

Each company has within its annual report a variety of statements concerning the importance of social / environmental issues to that company and concerning the performance of the company in terms of such issues. It is reasonable to argue that the more text that is devoted to such issues the greater is their perceived importance to that company. On that basis therefore the number of lines of text devoted to such issues within the annual report have been counted and reported, thereby providing a measure of the relative importance of such issues.

Given that the annual reports of the different companies, and even of the same company from one year to another, differ considerably in terms of layout, size of print face used and number of columns of text on one page it has been necessary to adjust the measure from a simple count of number of lines. The count has therefore been adjusted to equate to the number of lines of text printed in normal type size and filling the whole of the page (i.e. no columns).

The result for water companies for all years is as follows:

Company			No of lines				
	1991	1992	1993	1994	1995	1996	ave
Anglian	26	29	39	27	35	34	32
Hyder	0	0	0	0	0	0	0
Northumbrian	0	0	0	3	13	0	3
Severn Trent	8	7	9	6	4	18	9
Southern	11	25	28	30	16	8	20
South West	22	32	23	32	29	42	30
Thames	8	7	7	6	33	33	16
Utd Utilities	0	4	0	40	71	32	25
Wessex	21	38	55	27	18	24	31
Yorkshire	8	6	5	39	31	24	19
Mean	10	15	17	21	25	22	18

Table 5.10 Water Company Lines of Text

The result for food retailing companies for all years is as follows:

Company			No of lines				
	1991	1992	1993	1994	1995	1996	ave
Argyll	0	0	0	0	0	0	0
Asda	0	0	0	0	0	0	0
Iceland	0	0	13	10	14	17	9
Kwiksave	5	4	8	7	1	7	5
WMorrison	0	0	0	0	0	0	0
Nurdin&P	0	0	0	0	0	0	0
Sainsbury	8	12	19	33	25	24	20
Tesco	27	8	15	21	23	32	19
Mean	5	3	7	9	8	10	7

Table 5.11 Food Retailing Company Lines of Text

The result for food manufacturing companies for all years is as follows:

| Company | No of lines | | | | | | |
	1991	1992	1993	1994	1995	1996	ave
ALFisher	0	0	0	0	5	17	4
AssBrFood	0	0	0	17	17	17	9
Cadbury	17	26	30	26	32	28	27
Dalgety	0	14	9	30	15	10	13
Hazlewood	14	12	12	23	17	10	15
NorthFood	0	0	0	0	0	0	0
Tate&Lyle	0	7	0	0	9	7	4
Unigate	0	0	0	0	0	0	0
Unilever	14	29	40	33	23	28	28
UtdBiscuit	19	19	12	14	31	17	17
Mean	6	11	10	14	15	13	13

Table 5.12 Food Manufacturing Company Lines of Text

A summary of each of the three sectors shows the following:

| Sector | No of lines | | | | | | |
	1991	1992	1993	1994	1995	1996	ave
Water	10	15	17	21	25	22	18
Food Retailing	5	3	7	9	8	10	7
Food Manf	6	11	10	14	15	13	13

Table 5.13 Sector Analysis Lines of Text

It can be seen from this data that there is a considerable difference between sectors and even between companies within one sector. These differences are possibly significant and so it was decided to incorporate this measure into the composite measure constructed as a measure of environmental performance.

Charitable Donations

All, or virtually all, companies make charitable donations in the course of their operations and these donations need to be reported in the annual reports of those companies. It is not however necessary to report as to the purpose of such charitable donations nor as to the recipients of such donations, except when a company wishes to make a virtue of a particular donation by mentioning it specifically in the script of the report. It is not therefore possible to identify whether any donation is for a social or for an environmental purpose. Nevertheless it is reasonable to argue that the extent of charitable giving on the part of companies demonstrates the extent of concern with the external environmental in one form or another. In other words it is argued that the greater the donations as a proportion of income the greater is the concern of the company with its external environment. While this concern is with the external environment in its widest definition it is also reasonable to argue that social and environmental issues are inevitably reflected in this concern and comprise the majority of such donations. Lacking any further information therefore it seems reasonable to argue that the manifestation of such concern is proportionate to concern with other aspects of the external environment. On this basis therefore it seems reasonable to argue that the extent of charitable donations provides a proxy measure for the extent of concern with social and environmental issues and this is the reasoning behind including such a measure in this analysis.

Given that the companies being considered in this analysis differ considerably in size it is necessary to translate the absolute figures reported in the accounts into a relative measure. This has been achieved by measuring the charitable donations of the companies in relation to their income and hence the measure used shows the charitable donations as a percentage of sales income, thereby providing such a relative measure.

The figures for the water companies in the sample for the years under consideration are as follows:

Company	per cent of sales revenue						
	1991	1992	1993	1994	1995	1996	ave
Anglian	0	0.011	0	0	0.003	0.016	0.005
Hyder	0.009	0.010	0.011	0.009	0	0	0.007
Northumbrian	0.188	0.188	0.077	0.032	0.030	0.026	0.090
Severn Trent	0.018	0.018	0.017	0.017	0.022	0.019	0.019
Southern	0	0.009	0	0.008	0.007	0.007	0.005
South West	0.013	0.022	0.017	0.011	0.010	0.010	0.014
Thames	0.010	0.012	0.011	0.010	0.009	0.010	0.010
Utd Utilities	0	0.006	0.006	0.008	0.010	0.014	0.007
Wessex	0	0	0	0.027	0.044	0.043	0.019
Yorkshire	0.011	0.018	0.019	0.024	0.018	0.017	0.018
Mean	0.025	0.029	0.016	0.015	0.015	0.016	0.019

Table 5.14 Water Company Charitable Donations

The figures for the food retailing companies in the sample for the years under consideration are as follows:

Company	per cent of sales revenue						
	1991	1992	1993	1994	1995	1996	ave
Argyll	0.008	0.010	0.011	0.006	0.005	0.004	0.007
Asda	0.004	0.004	0.004	0.004	0.002	0.002	0.003
Iceland	0.029	0.027	0.028	0.028	0.030	0.028	0.028
Kwiksave	0.003	0.003	0.003	0.002	0.001	0.003	0.003
WMorrison	0.004	0.012	0.006	0.004	0.012	0	0.006
Nurdin&P	0.003	0.003	0.003	0.002	0.000	0.001	0.002
Sainsbury	0.017	0.016	0.019	0.018	0.018	0.016	0.017
Tesco	0.007	0.004	0.004	0.003	0.004	0.006	0.005
Mean	0.009	0.010	0.010	0.009	0.009	0.008	0.009

Table 5.15 Food Retailing Company Charitable Donations

The figures for the food manufacturing companies in the sample for the years under consideration are as follows:

| Company | per cent of sales revenue | | | | | | |
	1991	1992	1993	1994	1995	1996	ave
ALFisher	0.006	0.004	0.006	0.008	0.010	0.007	0.007
AssBrFood	0.002	0.010	0.007	0.007	0.008	0.007	0.007
Cadbury	0.017	0.018	0.017	0.017	0.016	0.016	0.017
Dalgety	0.004	0.005	0.005	0.005	0.005	0.006	0.005
Hazlewood	0.006	0.006	0.006	0.005	0.005	0.005	0.006
NorthFood	0.029	0.031	0.027	0.035	0.035	0.036	0.032
Tate&Lyle	0.008	0.008	0.035	0.015	0.015	0.011	0.015
Unigate	0.005	0.008	0.009	0.009	0.010	0.009	0.008
Unilever	0	0	0	0	0	0	0
UtdBiscuit	0.030	0.032	0.024	0.023	0.019	0.021	0.025
Mean	0.010	0.012	0.014	0.012	0.012	0.012	0.012

Table 5.16 Food Manufacturing Company Charitable Donations

There is some difference between the sectors and so the mean figures of each sector are shown as follows:

| Sector | per cent of sales revenue | | | | | | |
	1991	1992	1993	1994	1995	1996	ave
Water	0.025	0.029	0.016	0.015	0.015	0.016	0.019
Food Retailing	0.009	0.010	0.010	0.009	0.009	0.008	0.009
Food Manf	0.010	0.012	0.014	0.012	0.012	0.012	0.012

Table 5.17 Sectoral Analysis Charitable Donations

It can be seen from this data also that there is a considerable difference between sectors and even between companies within one sector. These differences also are possibly significant and so it was decided to incorporate this measure into the composite measure constructed as a measure of environmental performance.

Environmental Report / Statement

An increasing number of companies are producing environmental reports separately to the production of the annual report. Environmental reports differ from annual reports in that they are not statutorily obligated upon the companies. The production of an environmental report is therefore undertaken voluntarily by companies and such production, it is argued, is a reflection of the perceived importance of environmental issues to that company. Moreover the size and frequency of production of such reports provides further evidence of their perceived importance. Such reports are normally described as environmental reports although they also demonstrate significant concern with social activity. Indeed the term environmental generally seems to subsume the term social within its general meaning. As such all future references in this appendix merely refer to environmental and can be taken to include also the social.

There are three important issues to consider in the way in which companies decide to produce such reports:

- whether a report is produced at all;
- the frequency of production of such reports;
- the size of such reports.

It is argued that a company which produces an annual environmental report places greater emphasis upon environmental issues than one which only produces a periodic report. Such a company in turn places greater importance upon environmental issues than one which does not produce such a report at all. Again it is argued that the number of pages contained in the report also provides a proxy measure of the importance attached to such issues.

Based upon these arguments therefore the measures for the water companies in the sample are as follows:

Company	Produced y / n	annual / periodic	no of pages (average)
Anglian	y	a	25
Hyder	y	a	20
Northumbrian	y	a	48
Severn Trent	y	a	37
Southern	y	a	29
South West	y	p	36
Thames	y	a	25
Utd Utilities	y	a	29
Wessex	y	a	56
Yorkshire	y	bi-annual	40
Mean	y		34.5

Table 5.18 Water Company Environmental Reporting

The measures for the food retailer companies in the sample are as follows:

Company	Produced y / n	annual / periodic	no of pages (average)
Argyll	y	p	21
Asda	n		
Iceland	y	p	4
Kwiksave	n		
WMorrison	n		
Nurdin&P	n		
Sainsbury	n		
Tesco	n		
Mean	n		3.1

Table 5.19 Food Retailing Company Environmental Reporting

The measures for the food manufacturing companies in the sample are as follows:

Company	Produced y / n	annual / periodic	no of pages (average)
ALFisher	n		
AssBrFood	n		
Cadbury	n		
Dalgety	n		
Hazlewood	n		
NorthFood	y	p	3
Tate&Lyle	y	p	1
Unigate	y	p	6
Unilever	y	p	48
UtdBiscuit	n		
Mean	n		5.8

Table 5.20 Food Manufacturing Company Environmental Reporting

Again there is some difference between the sectors and so the sectoral details are shown, as follows:

Sector	Produced y / n	annual / periodic	no of pages (average)
Water	y		34.5
Food Retailing	n		3.1
Food Manf	n		5.8

Table 5.21 Sectoral Analysis Environmental Reporting

It can be seen from these figures that there is again a considerable difference between sectors, with the water companies all producing environmental reports and mostly producing them annually. Equally such reports are longer and more detailed than for the other two sectors. Such reporting seems to be much rarer in the other two sectors. These differences again are possibly significant and so it was decided to incorporate this measure into the composite measure constructed as a measure of environmental performance.

Number of Measures Used

Although producing an environmental report is important in its own right, of similar importance is the content of such a report. Some such reports are merely statements of perceived importance of the environment to the company while others report upon action being taken with regard to environmental issues. Indeed some, but by no means all, contain actual data measuring environmental impact and changes in such impact made by the companies as a result of their activities. This is an important feature of environmental reporting as, much as is the case for financial reporting, measurement enables comparisons to be made. One problem with such comparisons however is that the measures incorporated into the reports differ considerably from one company to another and so it is not a reasonable proposition to undertake a comparison of environmental impact between companies. Indeed it is often not possible to compare temporally the impact of a single company over time.

It can be argued however that the inclusion of measured environmental importance in such reports is important in its own right and that the greater the number of reported measures the more importance is attached to the measurement of environmental impact. For this reason it has been decided to count the number of measures used by each company and use this as a basis for comparison.

Taking the average number of reported measures for each water company this analysis shows the following:

Company	no of measures
Anglian	10
Hyder	1
Northumbrian	4
Severn Trent	7
Southern	0
South West	2
Thames	7
Utd Utilities	0
Wessex	3
Yorkshire	4
Mean	3.8

Table 5.22 Water Company Environmental Reporting Measures

The average number of reported measures for each food retailing company shows the following:

Company	no of measures
Argyll	0
Asda	-
Iceland	0
Kwiksave	-
WMorrison	-
Nurdin&P	-
Sainsbury	-
Tesco	-
Mean	0

Table 5.23 Food Retailing Company Environmental Reporting Measures

The average number of reported measures for each food manufacturing company shows the following:

Company	no of measures
ALFisher	-
AssBrFood	-
Cadbury	-
Dalgety	-
Hazlewood	-
NorthFood	0
Tate&Lyle	0
Unigate	0
Unilever	2
UtdBiscuit	-
Mean	0.2

Table 5.24 Food Manufacturing Company Environmental Reporting Measures

Again the differences between the sectors is noticeable and the sectoral averages reveal the following:

Sector	no of measures
Water	3.8
Food Retailing	-
Food Manf	0.2

Table 5.25 Sectoral Analysis Environmental Reporting Measures

Again it can be seen from these figures that there is again a considerable difference between sectors, with the water companies almost all reporting actual measures of environmental impact but with such reporting being much rarer in the other two sectors. These differences again are possibly significant and so it was decided to incorporate this measure into the composite measure constructed as a measure of environmental performance.

Measuring Environmental Impact

Each of these measures is of some importance for demonstrating the perceived concern for the environment for a company but each by itself only provides a proxy measure for environmental performance. Accordingly each in its own right is of limited value in measuring such performance. It is argued however that taken together these four measures provide an indication of environmental performance for companies which will enable a comparative analysis to be undertaken. In order to undertake such a comparative analysis however it is necessary to translate these four measures into a mechanism for undertaking such comparison. This has been achieved by translating these four measures into a single composite measure which it is argued provides such a mechanism for comparative evaluation.

Although each of these four measures has some significance in the measurement of environmental performance it is not reasonable to argue that each measure is of equal importance. It therefore seems appropriate to construct a composite measure which gives different weights to each of these four factors as deemed appropriate. No means of objectively weighting these four factors exists and no previous work has arrived at such a weighting. It is therefore inevitable that the weighting attached to each of the four factors is subjectively determined. Justification can only be arrived at through the arguments supporting those weightings.

The four measures to be weighted are as follows:

- lines of text;
- charitable donations;
- size and frequency of environmental reports;
- number of measures reported.

A consideration of the meaning and relevance of each measure is as follows:

Lines of Text

This measure is one which is extracted from the annual report, rather than any separate environmental report, and must therefore be of some importance as far as weighting is concerned. This is because the text contained within the annual report is addressed to the same audience as the figures concerning financial performance – this is inevitable as they are both within the same document.

Charitable Donations

This factor is not directly related to environmental issues but merely indicative of the existence of some environmental awareness. It must therefore be considered to be of relatively little significance in determining environmental performance.

Size and Frequency of Environmental Reports

This factor must be of some importance as the frequency and size of reports produced indicate the extent to which the company itself thinks that environmental performance is of importance.

Number of Measures Reported

This factor must be linked with the previous in that the number of measures reported indicates that the company is involved with measuring environmental impact in addition to merely expressing concern, as could be the case when only text is produced.[2] As far as the measures selected by the various companies in this survey are concerned they are extremely diverse and in the main used by just that one company. Thus any comparative analysis using these measures is almost impossible and probably meaningless. All that can be stated for the purposes of this analysis is that the use of measures indicates a concern with environmental performance and is arguably that concern is positively relational to the number of measures used.

Based upon these considerations therefore it was decided to rank the four factors under consideration as follows:

1.   lines of text.
2.   size and frequency of environmental reports.
3.   number of measures reported.
4.   charitable donations.

Rankings were attached to the four measures in that ratio of 4:3:2:1 to give a ratio as follows:

1. lines of text (in annual report)   40 per cent
2. size and frequency of environmental reports   30 per cent
3. number of measures reported   20 per cent
4. charitable donations   10 per cent

It is recognised that this is a somewhat arbitrary process of ranking and weighting but it is argued that this is sufficient for the purposes of this analysis. The analysis is only undertaken to gain some understanding of the respective performance in environmental terms of the different sectors under analysis.[3]

In order to construct a composite measure from the four independent measures and to weight them accordingly it is then necessary to convert the raw measures reported previously into measures which can be summed to provide a composite measure. This has been undertaken only for the smaller sample of companies used in the analysis of financial performance in order to facilitate comparison with the TSR analysis previously undertaken.

Data was however collected, as detailed above, for all the 28 companies which have been considered from the three sectors. Although 4 of these companies have been excluded from the statistical analyses undertaken concerning both financial performance and environmental performance, the data from the excluded companies has been reported because this data provides supporting evidence of assertions made and conclusions drawn.[4]

The creation of a composite measure was achieved as follows:

Lines of Text

The maximum number of lines of text averaged by any company in the period under consideration is 32 while the minimum is 0. As the weight attached to this factor is 40 per cent then a multiplication of the actual lines used by a factor of 1.25 will make full use of the range available while still giving a value of zero to those companies who make no reference to environmental issues in their reports.

The weighted factor for the companies was therefore as follows:

Company	No of lines	
	ave	weighted
Water sector:		
Anglian	32	40
Hyder	0	0
Severn Trent	9	11.25
South West	30	37.5
Thames	16	20
Utd Utilities	25	31.25
Wessex	31	38.75
Yorkshire	19	23.75
Mean	20.25	25.31
Food retailing sector:		
Argyll	0	0
Asda	0	0
Iceland	9	11.25
Kwiksave	5	6.25
WMorrison	0	0
Nurdin&P	0	0
Sainsbury	20	25
Tesco	19	23.75
Mean	6.62	8.28
Food manufacturing sector:		
ALFisher	4	5
AssBrFood	9	11.25
Cadbury	27	33.75
Hazlewood	15	18.75
NorthFood	0	0
Tate&Lyle	4	5
Unigate	0	0
UtdBiscuit	17	21.25
Mean	9.5	11.87
Sectoral comparison of means:		
Water	20.25	25.31
Food Retailing	6.62	8.28
Food Manf	9.5	11.87

Table 5.26 Weighted Factor for Lines of Text

Size and Frequency of Environmental Reports

There are two sets of data to consider for this factor:

- whether or not the company produces a report and if so at what frequency;
- the number of pages contained in the report.

The number of pages ranges up to 56 for those reports which are produced. While this is perhaps the most significant part of this factor it is nevertheless necessary to recognise the frequency with which reports are produced. Accordingly it was decided to allocate 20 per cent of this factor to frequency and 80 per cent to length. For length a simple multiplication of the actual number of pages by 1.4 makes full use of the range while still leaving those companies who do not produce a report with a zero score. For frequency it was decided that the score should be allocated as 20 per cent for an annual report and 10 per cent for a periodic report. This weighted score then was converted to a score for the composite measure and this was achieved by multiplying the weighted score by 0.3.

The weighted factor was therefore arrived at as follows:

Company	score a	score b	total score	weighted score
Water sector:				
Anglian	20	35	55	16.5
Hyder	20	28	48	14.4
Severn Trent	20	51.8	71.8	21.54
South West	10	50.4	60.4	18.12
Thames	20	35	55	16.5
Utd Utilities	10	40.6	50.6	15.18
Wessex	10	78.4	88.4	26.52
Yorkshire	10	56	66	19.8
Mean	15	46.9	61.9	18.57
Food retailing sector:				
Argyll	10	29.4	39.4	11.82
Asda	0	0	0	0
Iceland	10	5.6	15.6	4.68
Kwiksave	0	0	0	0
WMorrison	0	0	0	0
Nurdin&P	0	0	0	0
Sainsbury	0	0	0	0
Tesco	0	0	0	0
Mean	2.5	4.37	6.87	2.06
Food manufacturing sector:				
ALFisher	0	0	0	0
AssBrFood	0	0	0	0
Cadbury	0	0	0	0
Hazlewood	0	0	0	0
NorthFood	10	4.2	14.2	4.26
Tate&Lyle	10	1.4	11.4	3.42
Unigate	10	8.4	18.4	5.52
UtdBiscuit	0	0	0	0
Mean	3.75	1.75	5.5	1.65
Sectoral comparison of means:				
Water	15	46.9	61.9	18.57
Food Retailing	2.5	4.37	6.87	2.06
Food Manf	3.75	1.75	5.5	1.65

Table 5.27 Measure for Environmental Reporting

Number of Measures Reported

The maximum number of measures reported by any company in its environmental report is 10. A weighted measure was therefore derived by multiplying the number of measures by 2 and thereby making full use of the range for the composite measure.

The weighted factor therefore looks as follows:

Company	no of measures	weighted
Water sector:		
Anglian	10	20
Hyder	1	2
Severn Trent	7	14
South West	2	4
Thames	7	14
Utd Utilities	0	0
Wessex	3	6
Yorkshire	4	8
Mean	4.25	8.5
Food retailing sector:		
Argyll	0	0
Asda	-	0
Iceland	0	0
Kwiksave	-	0
WMorrison	-	0
Nurdin&P	-	0
Sainsbury	-	0
Tesco	-	0
Mean	0	0
Food manufacturing sector:		
ALFisher	-	0
AssBrFood	-	0
Cadbury	-	0
Hazlewood	-	0
NorthFood	0	0
Tate&Lyle	0	0
Unigate	0	0
UtdBiscuit	-	0
Mean	0	0
Sectoral comparison of means:		
Water	4.25	8.5
Food Retailing	-	0
Food Manf	0	0

Table 5.28 Number of Measures

Charitable Donations

The range of raw data for this measure varies up to 0.032 per cent. Again a simple multiplication of the raw data by 300 makes use of the range. The resultant weighted measure therefore is as follows:

Company	per cent of sales revenue		
		ave	weighted
Water sector:			
Anglian		0.005	1.5
Hyder		0.007	2.1
Severn Trent		0.019	5.7
South West		0.014	4.2
Thames		0.010	3
Utd Utilities		0.007	2.1
Wessex		0.019	5.7
Yorkshire	0.018		5.4
Mean		0.012	3.6
Food retailing sector:			
Argyll		0.007	2.1
Asda		0.003	0.9
Iceland		0.028	8.4
Kwiksave	0.003		0.9
WMorrison		0.006	1.8
Nurdin&P		0.002	0.6
Sainsbury		0.017	5.1
Tesco		0.005	1.5
Mean		0.009	2.7
Food manufacturing sector:			
ALFisher	0.007		2.1
AssBrFood		0.007	2.1
Cadbury		0.017	5.1
Hazlewood		0.006	1.8
NorthFood		0.032	9.6
Tate&Lyle		0.015	4.5
Unigate		0.008	2.4
UtdBiscuit		0.025	7.5
Mean		0.015	4.4
Sectoral comparison of means:			
Water		0.012	3.6
Food Retailing		0.009	2.7
Food Manf		0.015	4.4

Table 5.29 Charitable Donations

From these weighted individual measures it was therefore possible to create a composite measure to reflect environmental performance by the various companies in the sample. This was achieved simply by summation, as follows:

Company	no of lines	size & frequency	no of measures	charitable donations	total
Water sector:					
Anglian	40	16.5	20	1.5	78
Hyder	0	14.4	2	2.1	18.5
Severn Trent	11.25	21.54	14	5.7	52.49
South West	37.5	18.12	4	4.2	63.82
Thames	20	16.5	14	3	53.5
Utd Utilities	31.25	15.18	0	2.1	48.53
Wessex	38.75	26.52	6	5.7	76.97
Yorkshire	23.75	19.8	8	5.4	56.95
Mean	25.31	18.57	8.5	3.6	55.98
Food retailing sector:					
Argyll	0	11.82	0	2.1	13.92
Asda	0	0	0	0.9	0.9
Iceland	11.25	4.68	0	8.4	24.33
Kwiksave	6.25	0	0	0.9	7.34
WMorrison	0	0	0	1.8	1.8
Nurdin&P	0	0	0	0.6	0.6
Sainsbury	25	0	0	5.1	30.1
Tesco	23.75	0	0	1.5	25.25
Mean	8.28	2.06	0	2.7	13.04
Food manufacturing sector:					
ALFisher	5	0	0	2.1	7.1
AssBrFood	11.25	0	0	2.1	13.35
Cadbury	33.75	0	0	5.1	38.85
Hazlewood	18.75	0	0	1.8	20.55
NorthFood	0	4.26	0	9.6	13.86
Tate&Lyle	5	3.42	0	4.5	12.92
Unigate	0	5.52	0	2.4	7.92
UtdBiscuit	21.25	0	0	7.5	28.75
Mean	11.87	1.65	0	4.39	17.91

Table 5.30 Composite Environmental Measure

Having argued earlier that these four measures, when summed, produce a composite measure which is a reasonable measure of environmental performance for the companies under consideration, and having quantified the measures for the companies concerned, it is now necessary to consider the composite measure thereby produced and whether or not the quantification seems reasonable. In such a consideration therefore the first point to recognise is that in the main the four parts of the quantification are generally similar for an individual company – in other words if a company scores highly on one part of the measure then it tends also to do so on other parts of the measure. There are obviously exceptions to this similarity, such as Cadbury or Argyll which score highly on one component but not on others, which lends reinforcement to the argument that this composite measure represents a reasonable indication of environmental performance. If the four components had been similar for all companies in the sample then this would have suggested that the components did not measures different aspects of environmental performance but were merely reflections of the same aspect. The difference for some companies suggests therefore that different aspects are being measured. This is supported by the broad similarity for most companies as this suggests that the same aspect of performance (i.e. environmental performance) is being measured, but different aspects thereof by each component.

Having argued that the components included in the composite measure are appropriate, the other factor to consider in assessing the appropriateness of the composite measure so constructed is the weighting attached to each part of the measure. The reasoning for the weighting has been argued earlier and a visual observation of the resultant quantifications produced gives no reason to suggest that this is inappropriate. It seems reasonable therefore to conclude at this point that this composite measure which has been constructed provides a reasonable representation of environmental performance for these companies, and to proceed with an analysis of this performance.

Analysing Environmental Performance

The first part of the analysis undertaken was concerned entirely with reported financial performance, based upon total shareholder returns. This part of the analysis is concerned entirely with environmental performance, based upon the composite measure constructed. The purpose of this analysis is to consider any differences with respect to this performance between the different industrial sectors. This kind of analysis for the three sectors together can be made by means of a 1 way ANOVA for unrelated designs.

This shows a significance at the $p = 0.001$ level and so this suggests that the three samples are significantly different and that the level of reporting of environmental performance depends upon industrial sector. This is similar to the financial performance analysis which also demonstrated that financial performance (as measured by TSR) is dependent upon industrial sector.

It is less clear however, from merely looking at the data, if this difference in performance applies to all three sectors or, if there is a difference only between one sector and the other two. It is therefore necessary to investigate this by considering any differences between sectors in terms of the difference between each pair of two sectors. This gives three separate analyses, as follows:

- Water – Food retailing
- Water – Food manufacturing
- Food retailing – Food manufacturing

In order to investigate the possibility of differences between each of these pairs of sectors in turn analysis is required, using an appropriate statistical technique. For this kind of analysis this technique is a t test for unrelated design. The analysis is as follows:

Water – Food Retailing

When the sets of data (composite measure) for the two sectors are compared, this shows a value of $t = 0.691$ which is not significant at any level.

The fact that this difference between these two samples is not significant might be regarded as somewhat surprising given the data sets. This must be attributed to the fact that the sample size is very small and the standard deviation, for both data sets, is relatively large. This is one of the problems when dealing with small samples. One course of action would be to increase the sample size, which could therefore be expected to show a significant difference for a larger data set. This is not possible in this case as the sample size is determined by the number of companies in each industrial grouping which meet the criteria for selection.

One way to provide supporting evidence for the difference between the two groups is to treat the data sets as not parametric and again to perform a Mann - Whitney test again on the data. This gives a value of U = 3 which is significant at the 0.01 level and so it can be assumed, on the basis of this test, that the differences between these two groups of companies are such that they are from different populations. In this case this supports the assertion that for these two sectors the level of environmental performance is dependent upon sector and also supports the conclusion which would be drawn from a simple observation of the data. While not necessarily statistically valid this further analysis has been undertaken to overcome the problem of small data samples and add weight to the arguments from other analyses. The meaning of this finding also will be considered in the context of an evaluation incorporating the analysis from the other two comparisons.

Water – Food Manufacturing

When the sets of data (composite measure) for these two sectors are compared this gives a value of t = 0.649 which again is not significant at any level. again the fact that the difference between these two samples is not significant at any level different might be regarded as somewhat surprising given the nature of the data. This also must be attributed to the fact that the sample size is very small and the standard deviation, for both data sets, is relatively large. This is one of the problems when dealing with small samples. One course of action would be to increase the sample size, which could therefore be expected to show a significant difference for a larger data set. This is not possible in this case as the sample size is determined by the number of companies in each industrial grouping which meet the criteria for selection.

One way to provide supporting evidence for the difference between the two groups is to treat the data sets as not parametric and to perform a Mann - Whitney test again on the data, as was done for other comparisons. This gives a value of U = 3 which also is significant at the 0.01 level and so it can be assumed, on the basis of this test, that the differences between these two groups of companies is such that they are from different populations. In this case this supports the assertion that for these two sectors the level of environmental performance is dependent upon sector. This finding also supports the conclusion which would be drawn from a simple observation of the data. While not necessarily statistically valid this further analysis has been undertaken to overcome the problem of small data samples and add weight to the arguments from other analyses. The meaning of this finding also will be considered in the context of an evaluation incorporating the analysis from the other two comparisons.

Food Retailing – Food Manufacturing

When these sets of data (composite measure) for the two sectors are compared this gives a value of t = 0.147. This also is insignificant at the 0.2 level and so it can be assumed that the differences between these two groups of companies is such that they are not from different populations. In other words the differences within the groups are greater than the differences between the groups and there is therefore no clear distinction between the two groups. This supports the argument advanced earlier that these two sectors are related because of their sharing of common problems and issues related to packaging. It therefore seems reasonable from the point of view of analysis to consider these two sectors as belonging to a single population. The meaning of this finding will be considered in the context of an evaluation incorporating the analysis from the other two comparisons.

Having considered the problems of small data sets previously however and sought to overcome the problem by treating the data sets as not parametric and therefore performing a Mann - Whitney test on the data, it seems appropriate for this comparison to also perform the same test. This gives a results of U = 25 which is not significant at any level and so it can be assumed, on the basis of this test also, that the differences between these two groups of companies is such that they are not from different populations. In other words this test supports the findings of the t test for this comparison. Again the significance of this will be considered in the context of the meaning of all the analysis undertaken.

Interpretation

Although when undertaking an anova test of the three sectors together it was found that their was a significant difference between the sectors, it can be seen that in reality there is only a difference between the water sector and the other two sectors. These latter two sectors show no significant difference between them.

An examination of the data in isolation, by simple observation, means that it is possible to see the differences found through analysis. It is in fact not surprising that the results of the comparison of the water and the two food sectors, the retailing and manufacturing sectors, shows them to be significantly different; indeed it would be surprising if it were not the case. Nor is it surprising that there is no significant difference between the food retailing and the food manufacturing sectors. Indeed the similarity of the results in terms of environmental performance is such that it would be reasonable to treat these two sectors as one group. Given the argument for using these two sectors, ie that they shared a common problem in terms of packaging, it is not surprising that it seems possible to make this statement, at least within the context of total shareholder returns. The question as to whether or not these two sectors comprise one group or two will be returned to at various points during the subsequent analysis and discussion.

The data analysed however suggests that each of the hypotheses 1,[5] 2[6] and 3[7] can be rejected as this analysis suggests that there is intra sectoral difference in performance but not between firms along, the lines suggested by these hypotheses. Further analysis is however needed before any firm conclusions can be made.

Conclusions

These findings found in the analysis of financial performance, based upon an analysis of TSR, and from the analysis of environmental performance, based upon the composite measure constructed, and the similarities and differences between the sectors seems to suggest that performance is very similar along both dimensions of performance. Thus in general terms it can be stated that, while there are sectoral differences, if a company performs well along one dimension of performance then it also is likely to perform well along the other dimension of performance. While the data appears to support this argument there is a need for a more rigorous testing of this before any firm conclusion can be made. This can be undertaken in terms of further quantitative analysis and this is the subject matter of chapter 7. First however a qualitative analysis must be undertaken to give further data for this analysis.

Notes

[1] See chapter 3 for a justification of the use of this measure.

[2] A note of caution must be inserted here however in order to indicate that the measures used by any particular company are not necessarily the most important or most reliable determinant of environmental performance. In the first place there are numerous possible measures of environmental performance, some of which are in possible conflict with each other. It is thus relatively easy for any company to report upon a number of measures of environmental performance which reflect favourably upon that company simply by selecting measures which

support this assertion and rejecting measures which do not. Secondly the significance of any particular measure will vary from one company to another depending upon the location of the company and the nature of its business. This makes any comparison of environmental performance, even by means of using the same measures, very difficult and comparison based upon differing sets of measures almost meaningless.

[3] As the concluding argument of this part is carried forward to chapter 6 and evaluated in conjunction with the financial performance analysis, together with that from the qualitative analysis, then considerations of the reliability of measures will be further considered in that appendix.

[4] This is particularly important for chapter 5 where a semiotic analysis of this binary opposition is undertaken and in drawing the conclusions made in chapters 8 & 9. It is for these reasons that the data for these excluded companies has been included in this chapter.

[5] Hypothesis 1 states 'There is a significant difference between the financial performance of different organisations'.

[6] Hypothesis 2 states 'There is a significant difference between the environmental performance of different organisations'.

[7] Hypothesis 3 states 'There is a negative correlation between the financial performance and the environmental performance of the same organisations'.

Chapter 6

The Environmental Discourse: the Qualitative Evidence

Introduction

It has been suggested by Schaltegger et al (1996) that one of the driving forces in the development of environmental accounting was the need to placate, through the production of appropriate information, those members of society who could be classified as environmental activists. They further suggest that the environmental accounting information developed for this purpose has now been adopted into the repertoire of organisational accounting and forms an important part of the internal management control information of the organisation. It has been argued in Chapter 4 that these assertions are untrue and that environmental accounting is not directly influenced by environmental pressure groups and does not form a part of the internal accounting information and control systems. This chapter explores this assertion in greater details and so in this chapter there a semiotic analysis of environmental accounting and reporting is undertaken in order to test the hypotheses 4 and 5 developed in chapter 4.

Environmental reporting takes place not just through the annual report of the organisations under consideration but also through their environmental reports, if these are produced. The quantity of such reporting was considered in the last chapter. In this chapter therefore what is under consideration is the nature of such reporting in terms of the content and target audience. This is achieved through a semiotic analysis and interpretation of the annual and environmental reports for the companies selected.

According to Barthes (1973) a sign consists of three elements: the sign itself, a signifier and a signified such that:

Sign = signifier + signified

Signification is the act of relating the signified with its signifier to create a sign. This signification occurs not only when a sign is created but also when meaning is extracted from the sign. Meaning is not transmittable however and because of this the meaning extracted by the reader is not necessarily the same as that sent by the author. Thus a sign leaves its interpreter to supply at least a part of its meaning (Peirce 1958). This means that signification can be considered as two independent processes on the part of the author and the reader of the text. Naturally it is in the interest of the author to seek to ensure that the meaning (s)he wishes to impart through the text is the meaning extracted by the reader. As there is no direct communication in a written text, such as a corporate report, between the author and the reader then it is in the interests of the author to seek other forms of mediation to facilitate the alignment of meanings. This is one reason for the use of the press as a mediating mechanism, as a desire on the part of the authors of corporate reports to bring these two signification acts into alignment.

The extraction of meaning by the reader is always contextual and is based upon the frame of reference of that reader. This frame of reference is dependant upon the experiences of the reader, as the reader's experiences are inseparable from the current script and its interpretation. The frame of reference is however partly set by the context in which the reading takes place. Thus the reading of the script of a corporate report is undertaken in a very different context to the reading of the script of a novel. This context is set in part by the presentation of the script itself, as the two types of script look very different. The standardisation of corporate reports of one individual company in terms of format and content is one way of defining the context more closely in terms of that particular company. In doing so this provides a further means of closing the gap between these two significations, of the author and the reader, as this helps to create a more common frame of reference for interpretation. So too does comment in the press.[1] The use of accounting as one of the languages of signification also helps in this respect to create a common code of understanding and to include those who understand the language while excluding those who do not. It is in this way that the accounting language takes on cultural capital (Bourdieu 1984). This helps segregate the audience into those being addressed by the script and those who have access to the script but are not addressed. Thus the format of the script is determined to some extent by the demands of the audience being addressed (Metz 1974).

In this respect it is perhaps meaningful that the water companies analysed, as opposed to almost all the other companies in the sample, produce a separate environmental report year by year. It has been argued that this part of the script is addressed to a different audience than that to which the annual report is addressed. This argument is amplified by the exclusion of financial data from the environmental report, as this implies also that this audience is not expected to be financially literate but nevertheless is interested in the performance of the company from an environmental perspective. It is unclear just what part of the audience is being addressed through such environmental reporting. The fact that these companies, because of their privatisation process, have a large number of small investors[2], a regulator determining the format of the quasi market for their services, and a large number of critical consumers suggests that these may be the audiences being addressed through these reports. This aspect of corporate reporting will be addressed further later in this analysis.

Signification is therefore about inclusion within the selected audience for the corporate reports on the assumption that those included understand the signification in a common way with the authors. This is based upon an assumed understanding of the code of signification used in corporate reporting. As Sapir (1949: 554) states:

> ... we respond to gestures with an extreme alertness and, one might almost say, in accordance with an elaborate and secret code that is written nowhere, known by none and understood by all.

Thus it is comfortable for the authors of the script to assume this shared signification based upon a shared understanding of the language used. This signification is enhanced through the use of the images incorporated into the script, which add to the truth value of the information conveyed by the reports (Graves, Flesher & Jordan 1996), as will be considered later in this analysis. This shared signification may however be fictitious, as will also be considered later in this analysis.

The most appropriate method for developing a semiology of corporate reporting is through the consideration of the binary oppositions inherent in the text.[3] These are considered in the context of both traditional accounting and social and environmental accounting, considering both shareholders and other stakeholders. These two forms of accounting are presented as being radically different from each other and these differences will be explored in detail in this chapter, as will the question of how real is this difference. At this point therefore the differences will merely be summarised as follows:

- Traditional accounting is basically the conventional method of accounting which measures activities and performance from the perspective of the organisation itself without any attempt to measure and report upon externalities and the effect of the organisation's activities upon those externalities. As such this form of accounting can be considered to be principally from the perspective of the owners of the business, ie the shareholders, and the managers of the business. Consequently this form of accounting is referred to in this book as shareholder accounting or the internal accounting perspective.

- Social accounting and environmental accounting are similar in concept, although their differences will be explored later. Both of these forms of accounting recognise that the organisation exists and operates in a wider external environment and therefore affects that environment through its activities. This accounting incorporates the effects of the organisation which are external to itself and attempts to measure organisational activity from an external perspective of society at large, recognising that externalities are affected by organisational activity both in a spatial and a temporal sense. In this research such accounting is referred to as stakeholder accounting or the external accounting perspective.

It is recognised that this division, into internal and external perspective, and into shareholders and stakeholders, is not an absolute division and there is necessarily an overlap between the perspectives. These overlaps, and their consequences, will be explored throughout this book and these descriptions are used primarily for convenience in labelling and distinguishing the concepts and their accounting implications. Taking this into account the semiology of corporate reporting, in terms of binary oppositions, can commence to be developed through a consideration, in this chapter, of the following binarisms:

- Accounting – Non-accounting
- The City – Environmentalists
- Financial Performance – Environmental Performance

Each is considered in turn.

The Binarisms of the Environmental Discourse

Accounting – Non-accounting

Although the annual report is produced to satisfy statutory requirements, and this requires the production of the accounting information contained in the text, it is argued that this purpose has been relegated to that of a by-product of the text which is actually produced. This text is actually produced for the whole audience who might read the text. One of the main parts of that audience consists of shareholders of the business, either actual or potential. For this audience the actual accounting information required for statutory purposes has some importance,[4] and some, at least, of these shareholders must be assumed to be financially literate. The importance of the accounting part of the script is however downplayed by the authors of the script in a desire to increase the perceived importance of other parts of the script. Thus the accounting information required in order to satisfy statutory requirements has in all cases been relegated to the back of the corporate report. Moreover the font used for the annual accounts is often smaller, and certainly never larger, than the font used in the rest of the text. Equally the use of colour is prevalent throughout the rest of the text but the accounting information is presented in single colour or at most two colours.[5] The only financial information which is highlighted is that which is deemed important to the particular audience which the authors believe themselves to be addressing.

This information is generally presented both numerically and graphically, presumably in the belief that the graphical depiction will aid communication and reinforce the message, even to the financially illiterate. Indeed graphics can be a powerful method of presenting financial information regarding progress to both the literate and the illiterate. Thus for example the information highlighted is as follows:

Thames Water Annual Report and Accounts 1996:
• Pre tax profit
• Post tax profit
• Earnings per ordinary share
• Dividend per ordinary share

Asda Group plc Report and Accounts 1996:
• Turnover
• Operating profit
• Profit on ordinary activities before taxation

- Earnings per share
- Dividends per ordinary share

Cadbury Schweppes Annual Report 1993:
- Sales
- Trading profit
- Earnings per ordinary share
- Net dividend per ordinary share
- Capital expenditure
- Marketing expenditure

The financial figures highlighted in this way always compare the year being reported on with the preceding year in order to illustrate the way in which performance has improved. Presumably the highlighted figures are selected carefully to give this impression. The graphical illustrations of these financial highlights however always compare the results for several years, thereby reinforcing this message of continual improvement with the year being reported on being the 'best yet'. The implication of this message of continual improvement is that next year will be even better. The number of years selected for graphical illustration does however vary from one company to another. Thus while most companies select five years for comparative purposes, Asda selects three years, Hazlewood Foods selects between two and five years for different indicators and United Biscuits selects between four and eleven years for different indicators in different years. Again it is suggested that these selections are made with care in order to create a positive impression in the minds of the readers of the script, and to reinforce the signification in terms of continual improvement.

It is perhaps also significant that many annual reports are not even titled 'annual report and accounts' on the basis that the accounting part of the report is of less importance (or is presented by the authors to give that impression) than other parts of the script. Thus, for example, Tate & Lyle, Hazlewood Foods plc, United Biscuits and Cadbury Schweppes merely entitle their production as the 'annual report' while Unilever produce two documents, one titled the 'annual review' and the other titled the 'annual accounts'.[6] Needless to say the annual review is despatched automatically while the annual accounts are despatched on request. Thus this presentation in terms of title used, and the relegation of the statutory accounts to the end of the report, is designed to give the impression that what is important is the reporting part of the script – in other words those parts which are constructed by the authors, in an unconstrained way which the accounts cannot be, to create the desired image of the company and its management.

Some companies, from time to time, take this naming of the annual report even further in the desire to create the intended image of the company, and thus some reports are also given titles over and above 'the annual report'. For example Tate & Lyle after 1993 entitle their annual report 'A world leader in sweeteners and starches' and this title is given gradually greater prominence as the years progress. Thus by 1995 the title has become 'A world LEADER in sweeteners and starches'. Asda Group plc on the other hand make a point regarding progress by titling their 1996 report as 'The FIRST Year of BREAKOUT'.

The non-accounting part of the text makes use of both language and non-linguistic devices such as pictures, graphs and charts. Moreover the language part of the text makes use of different colours, different font sizes and different layouts, as well as including a few key accounting numbers. This part of the text is always at the beginning of the script with the accounting information relegated to the end. Over time this part of the script has gradually increased in size, largely through the inclusion of non-linguistic devices. Indeed arguably the linguistic part of this has reduced in terms of word count through the greater use of highlighted text and bullet points to reinforce the message. The image, sought by the authors to be portrayed, is that of an interesting script and consequently an interesting company – one to be involved with!

Thus the accounting pole of this binary pair, while not being portrayed as 'bad', has certainly been portrayed as of secondary importance and relegated to the back of the annual report document, or even to a secondary document. The non-accounting pole at the same time has been promoted in importance as part of the creation of the image deemed desirable by the authors of the script. This part of the script, incorporating the chairman's statement, is of course a reflection of the managers themselves whereas the accounting part of the report is a reflection of the whole company. Thus by promoting the non-accounting pole the managers are able at the same time to promote themselves, particularly when the image presented is one of desirability.

Although binary opposition is inherent in any text, and the tensions existing within the text inevitably lead to one binarism being portrayed as good while the other is portrayed as bad, this portrayal is within the interpretation of the reader. Thus the task of the author is to shape the binarisms so that the pole intended, by the author, is accepted, by the reader, as the desirable pole of the opposition. It is argued that part of the semiotic of corporate reporting is to present and continually reinforce the dialectic between the traditional internal perspective of performance and the social external perspective. This is achieved through the attempts to shape the readers' interpretation of the binary oppositions inherent in the text.

City – Environmentalist

One method of dealing with the dichotomies involved in the binarism of corporate reporting is to segregate the audience and address different parts of the audience differently. This is most apparent in the consideration of the binary opposition between financial and environmental performance and it is argued that dealing with this dichotomy requires the segregation of the audience into those assumed to be concerned with financial performance and those assumed to be concerned with environmental performance. In preceding analyses these have been considered to be the internal and the external perspectives. For this analysis these have been labelled, for the purposes of exploring this binary opposition as the City and environmentalists, with the City representing shareholders and investors and environmentalists representing societal issues.

Although social and environmental issues are considered in the annual report,[7] a full image creation of environmental concern and performance of the organisation requires a more elaborate report. It is argued therefore that the segregation of the audience in this manner also requires the separation of the script into discrete parts in order to be able to address these different audiences differently. This separation enables different messages to be given to different parts of the audience without the necessity of reconciling contradictory messages. Thus the script has been divided into the financial script, known as the Annual Report or the Annual Report and Accounts, and the environmental script, known as the Environmental Report. Thus the semiotic stage described previously looks rather different with this division of audience and script. Instead the stage looks as follows:

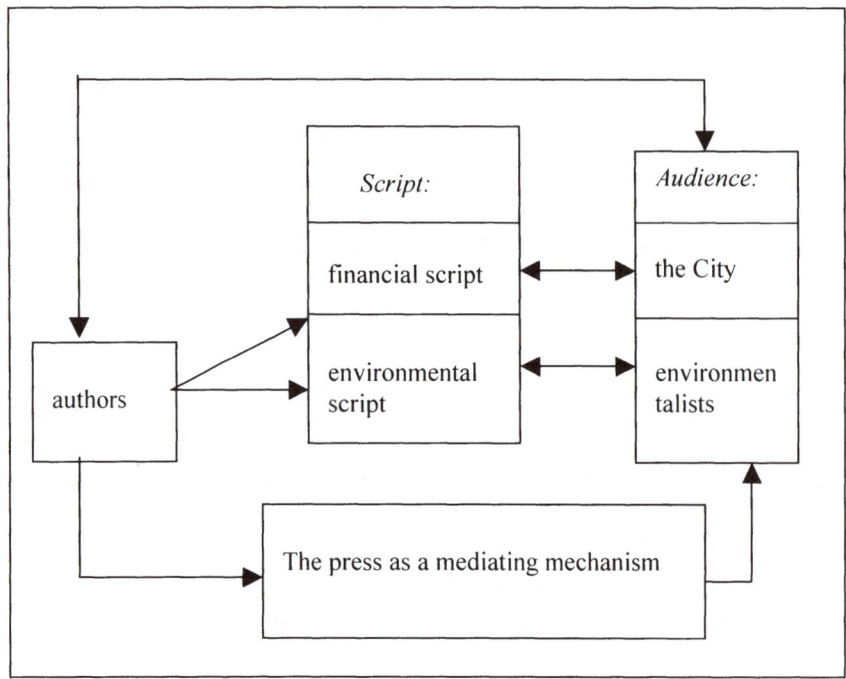

Fig 6.1 The Complete Semiotic Stage

Each different part of the script is therefore able to be written differently and needs only passing reference to the other part of the script. All reference and analysis so far has been concerned with the annual report addressing the financial reporting part of the script. The binary opposite pole is the environmental report and it is to this that attention is now turned.

The production of environmental reports is a recent phenomenon of corporate reporting. Even those companies which, in their annual report, mention their annual environmental report have only in fact produced a maximum of three such annual reports, even though the impression intended is of an extensive temporal sequence which gives added authenticity to such reporting. Such mentions of an annual report must therefore be considered to be partly a declaration of intent and partly a method of changing impressions amongst the audience. The intention of this impression creation is to create an image of an environmentally responsible organisation, which has been behaving in an environmentally responsible way for a period of time. This, of course, is part of the myth creation role of corporate reporting - to conflate the past into the present and therefore into the future.

Although it has been argued that the environmental reports are produced for that group of the audience which has been labelled, for purposes of exploring this binary opposition, as environmentalists, it is unclear among the sample being considered what part of the audience this is believed to consist of. This is in direct contrast with a company such as B & Q plc which in 1995 produced an environmental report titled 'How Green is My Front Door?' which is quite plainly addressed to customers of the company. B & Q plc have therefore identified the audience they wish to address with their environmental reporting and the script of their report unfolds appropriately for this audience.[8] This is not however the case with other companies, including all the companies in the sample considered in this research.

Indeed it appears not to be universally accepted that an environmental report is actually required. From the sample being considered only 12 companies (32%) actually produce an environmental report while another 4 companies have produced a short environmental statement. The need for the production of an environmental report is accepted however by the water companies, as all of them produce such a report. Amongst the food manufacturers and retailers however the production of such a report is the exception rather than the norm. Indeed only one manufacturer (Unilever) and one retailer (Argyll) actually produce such a report but Iceland, Northen Foods, Tate & Lyle and Unigate each produce a short environmental statement of between 1 and 6 pages in length.

These short environmental statements are not reports upon environmental performance but rather an outline of policy and a reinforcement of the message contained in the annual reports to the effect that these companies are environmentally conscious and responsible. Such a script is quite plainly concerned with image creation rather than any evaluation of, or reporting upon, performance. It is however unclear who among the audience this image creation is being addressed to as such a statement is not referred to in the annual report and is not automatically distributed to anyone but rather is available upon demand. It must be presumed therefore that the production of such a statement is a defensive measure to respond to any environmentalist who may wish to make enquiry regarding the company's environmental position. Such short statements have been excluded therefore from this consideration of environmental reports as not forming part of the script of corporate reporting.

The environmental reports which are produced range in length between 20 and 56 pages but this appears to be largely determined by the choice of layout and use of non-linguistic imagery rather than the textual content of the report. Some, such as Unilever and Wessex Water, are in the same format as the annual report and are clearly meant to be part of the same script. Others, such as Northumbrian Water, appear to be deliberately different through the use of unnecessarily poor quality recycled paper, presumably to reinforce the message about concern for the environment being translated into action. Still others such as Severn Trent and Anglian Water are different in form from the annual report without any discernible reason for this difference. This variation reinforces the argument made earlier that the audience being addressed by such reports is unclear, or possibly is different for different companies. It also leads to the suggestion that the relationship between this part of the script and the 'main' script in the form of the annual report is unclear.

As previously stated, all the water companies produce environmental reports, either annually or periodically, but very few other companies in the sample do so. It is worth, at this point, considering what the reasons for this difference between the sectors analysed might be. There seem to be three possible reasons for this difference:

- the water companies are generally progressive and are leading the way in environmental reporting; other sectors can therefore be expected to follow suit as time progresses;
- the water companies are under particular pressure from environmental pressure groups and are responding to this pressure;
- the water companies are subject to other pressures and are addressing a different audience to the other sectors.

Support can be found for two of these reasons but not for the third. Companies other than water companies, in different sectors of the economy, are producing environmental reports and this includes both companies in this sample and companies in other sectors of the economy, such as the B & Q example previously cited. It is possible to argue that such companies are the leaders in their sectors with respect to environmental reporting and that their competitors in their respective sectors can be expected to follow their lead. On this basis it is possible to argue that water and sewerage, as a sector of the economy, is in advance of other sectors of the economy in terms of environmental reporting.

The role of environmental pressure groups in influencing corporate behaviour, and in the translation of this pressure into changes in corporate reporting has been considered previously. It was argued that such pressure groups might be able to influence organisations on particular issues but that there is no evidence that such pressure groups are able to influence corporate behaviour in a way which would be reflected in their reporting systems. Thus the proposition that this might be the cause of the difference between the water companies and the rest of the companies in the sample must be rejected. The only class of environmental pressure which can be accepted to possibly cause such a change in behaviour is considered to be that from customers, particularly when those customers are individual members of society. For water companies the majority of their customers are individual members of society but so too are the customers of the food retailers and they have not, as a sector, responded through the production of such environmental reports. Conversely the customers of Unilever are not generally individuals but they have produced such an environmental report. Consequently the effect of such pressures must be dismissed as a reason for sectoral differences.

The water companies however do differ from the other sectors in this analysis in terms of the audience on the semiotic stage and this difference is very significant. This difference is in the form of an addition to the audience and that addition is the regulator, Ofwat. Moreover this part of the audience is also a mediating pressure on the performance of these companies due to its role in the regulation of both price and performance.[9] Thus addressing this part of the audience through environmental reporting may very well play a major part in the determination of the future regulatory environment, and thus financial performance, of these companies. This is of particular significance as the regulator separately assesses and reports on the performance of these companies and produces reports such as 'Leakage of water in England and Wales' (May 1996), which contains critical statements such as:

> Within the companies there seem to be serious deficiencies of knowledge as to the most cost – effective means of reducing leakage. (p5)

> The summer of 1995 demonstrated that leakage from water mains can severely exacerbate supply problems to the detriment of customers. Companies have taken action by setting themselves targets for reducing leakage. Some companies have simply reinstated previous targets... (p4)

> It is of particular concern that high levels of leakage arise in some of the largest water and sewerage companies and so account for a greater proportion of the total volume of losses. (p14)

> Companies must ensure that customers enjoy adequate supplies of water and must demonstrate through actions and processes that they are managing their distribution systems in an efficient and prudent manner. They will be

required to demonstrate that management is well-informed on the local balance between the costs of leakage reduction and resource costs. (p5)

In the July 1994 statement regarding the outcome of the periodic review, entitled 'Future Charges for Water and Sewerage Services' the following statement was made:

> We believe services can be improved by targeting expenditure on customer expectations. We would be disappointed if companies were to take the view that there is little scope for service improvements or use the Periodic Review as an excuse for justifying lapses in present standards. We know that customers will be looking for maintenance and improvement of services. (p58)

These statements in formal reports were reinforced by the issue of press releases such as 'Ofwat publishes proposals to improve company trading practices' (January 1997) and 'Water customers should expect a reduction in prices at the next review' (February 1997). The detail from such press releases were also taken up by the press, acting as a mediating mechanism in the discourse. This resulted in press reporting with such headlines as:

- 'Tough changes to water regulation'
  (*Guardian*, 10/3/92)
- 'Water company complaints double. High salaries and charges make customers see red'
  (*Guardian*, 10/6/92)
- 'The river of cash returns'
  (*Guardian*, 12/7/94)
- 'Consumer watchdog lukewarm on plans to stem flow of leaks'
  (*Guardian*, 22/5/96)
- 'Watchdog uncovers water profits misuse'
  (*Independent*, 25/9/96)
- 'Pay bonanza for privatised utility bosses'
  (*Independent*, 2/10/96)
- 'Severn Trent cuts leaks and lifts dividends'
  (*Times*, 11/6/97)
- 'Water firms spend less on leaks since privatisation'
  (*Sunday Times*, 11/5/97)
- '£46 on water bills for clean up puts pressure on Prescott'
  (*Guardian*, 3/7/98)

Thus the discourse in the press, stemming from the comments and actions of the regulator has been continual over time. It is clear therefore that the regulator is firmly on the semiotic stage not just as part of the audience but also as an actor in the play (Crowther et al 2001). Indeed the regulator must be considered to be a significant actor in the reporting play because of his power to affect the future of the individual water companies through his actions at the next, and all subsequent, regulatory reviews. These reviews are concerned not just with setting prices (which naturally affect financial performance) but also with setting performance targets, which affect costs and hence also financial performance. It is argued therefore that the universality of the production of environmental reports by the water companies is due to this place on the stage of the regulator. Moreover it is argued that this part of the script is addressed to the regulator alone, with other readers of the script being incidental to this. This argument is supported by the fact that some of the information contained in such reports, as detailed below, may be of meaning to the regulator but to very few other readers. Thus it is argued that the third proposition regarding the addressing of a different audience is the real reason for the difference between the water and sewerage sector and the other sectors.

The semiotic stage for water companies therefore looks as follows:

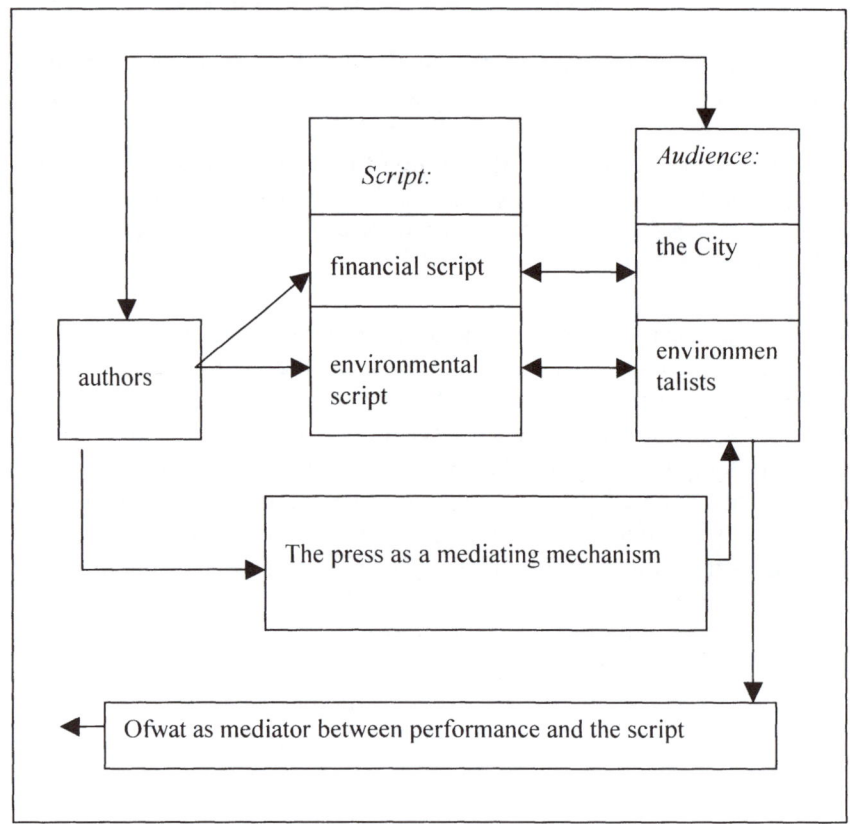

Fig 6.2 The Semiotic Stage of Water Companies

When looking at the actual content of the environmental reports themselves, these scripts contain both image building messages and actual reported measures of performance. It is argued however that these reported measures are not designed to enable an evaluation to take place but rather to create an impression of a rigorous scientific control and measurement of performance. This it is argued is the real purpose of the inclusion of such actual measures. This is because the measures actually selected for reporting have little meaning to anyone without the necessary detailed technical background in the area being reported upon for each specific measure. Thus when considering such environmental reports, it is not surprising to find:

- scene setting images showing pictures of the local countryside (Yorkshire Water Environmental Protection and Stewardship 1996) or people enjoying leisure activities (Southern Water Report 1995/96);
- images of the normal activity of the organisation such as repairs to water pipes (Severn Trent Environmental Report 1996) or the creation of a new reservoir (Wessex Water Environmental Performance Report 1994/95);
- graphical depiction of continuous improvement in areas such as distribution leakage (South West Water Environmental Report 1996) and number of sewer collapses (Northumbrian Water Group's Second Environmental Performance Report 1994/95).
- textual messages of action taken such as:

> We aim continually to reduce our impact upon the environment.
> To achieve this aim we have:
> - established a uniform methodology to identify and quantify the environmental impact
> - of our manufacturing operations;
> - developed a database to measure the contribution our packaging makes to the waste stream;
> - identified a number of potentially controversial materials and drawn up plans for their reduction or elimination;
> - worked with our operating companies to set reduction targets for these parameters and to integrate environmental measurement and targets into our management reporting structure.
>
> (Unilever Environmental Report)

> We have developed an extensive environmental information system which enables us to understand the scientific aspects of our environmental performance. We recognise that for a complete business assessment we need to translate this into financial terms. We are working with accounting and educational organisations to make progress in this respect.
> (Severn Trent Environmental Report 1996)

> Our environmental performance throughout this year is described in detail in this Environmental Review. The following are key achievements of which we are particularly proud.
> - Best ever compliance with drinking water quality standards at 98.9%
> - Avoided a hosepipe ban and maintained drinking water supplies to customers despite extreme summer drought and harsh winter
> - Certificate of Endorsement for contribution to improvements in the quality of the River Thames
> - Significant improvement in sewage effluent consent compliance, rising

to 98.5%
- Best ever compliance with sewage biosolids recycling to agricultural land
- 100% compliance with sewage biosolids dispersal at sea
- Won eight environmental awards
- Achieved and exceeded policy target to improve energy efficiency by 10% by 1996, against projected levels from 1992 baseline

(Thames Water Environmental Review 1996)

It is interesting to note that the latter company feels able to congratulate itself on the non – achievement of compliance targets and present this as a key achievement. Thus the image of environmental responsibility and achievement can be fostered whatever the actual level of performance.

As stated earlier an evaluation of performance is always comparative, either temporally with previous periods or spatially with comparable organisations. The temporal evaluation is undertaken within the company using the measures which each company decides itself are the most appropriate. It is perhaps unsurprising that all the measures used by all companies show an improvement over past periods.

Thus Thames Water (1996) reports upon measures such as:
- Abatement notices served;
- Renewable energy generated through combined heat and power;
- Fuel use;
- Waste recycling.

Severn Trent (1996) reports upon the following measures:
- Production of methane;
- Nitrogen oxide emissions;
- Biochemical oxygen discharged to rivers after treatment;
- Type of fuel used;
- Trees planted;
- Properties flooded by sewage.

Southern Water (1995/96) reports upon such measures as:
- Drinking water microbiological compliance;
- Bathing water compliance;
- Leisure use of reservoirs.

Anglian Water (1996) reports upon such measures as:
- Number of sewage samples tested;
- Classification of water quality samples;
- Sewage sludge disposal;
- Number of capital schemes assessed for environmental impact.

Thus each company is able to select measures which create the myths of social concern and environmental responsibility and of continual progress, through the selective use of measures which support these myths. As a consequence of the individual selection of measures to be reported upon, a spatial evaluation of performance, through a comparison of the performance with other water companies, is not possible and the temporal evaluation is all that remains. This temporal evaluation has of course been determined by the authors of the script, through their choice of measures for reporting upon, in order to support the myth of continual improvement. It is true however that any measure of environmental performance does not have universal acceptance as a measurement tool, and so each company must determine its own priorities for environmental performance and develop appropriate measures for reporting upon impact. It is convenient however that these companies, all undertaking very similar operations, have chosen different measures of performance which all show their performance as being not just good but, by implication, the best that can be achieved. Significantly the only companies which chose to measure and report upon leakages were those such as Anglian, which had been singled out by Ofwat for praise in this regard.

The use of titles to the reports for some of the companies is also used to help create the desired image of responsibility. Thus the following titles are used:

- Environmental Protection and Stewardship (Yorkshire Water 1996)
- Safeguarding the Environment (North West Water 1995)
- Enhancing the Environment (South West Water 1996)
- Stewardship (Severn Trent 1996)
- Conservation and the Environment (Southern Water 1994/95, 1995/96)

Thus the script for the environmental reporting part of the text closely parallels the financial reporting part of the text. Each is designed to look forwards and to create appropriate images of a dynamic active organisation with an irrelevant past, a good present and an even more promising future. This is achieved through the use of linguistic and non-linguistic devices to create an image of the organisation and a continual recreation of the myth of existence and purpose. Facts, and particularly accounting and other quantitative facts, are largely irrelevant to the text unless they are useful in supporting the image being created. The only difference between environmental reporting, as constituted through the environmental reports, and financial reporting, as constituted through the annual report, is that there is no overlap between the message and no overlap between the part of the segregated audience which is addressed. The question of the possibility of such audience segregation must however be addressed, and will be the subject of later consideration.

Financial Performance – Environmental Performance

Although environmental performance is a separate topic in accounting and has developed its own body of literature, it can also be considered to be subsumed within the broader considerations of social performance. For the purposes of this analysis this is taken to be the case and that both social accounting and environmental accounting are manifestations of an attempt to account for, and report upon, the impact of an organisation upon its wider environment.[10] Thus for this analysis the polar opposition is between traditional accounting, which purports to measure the effect of an organisation upon itself, and social accounting, which attempts to measure and report upon the effects of organisational activity upon the external environment. The discourse of corporate reporting, as manifest in corporate reports, tends to classify this external perspective as environmental reporting, as evidenced by the production of environmental reports rather than social reports, and so this binary opposition has been labelled as financial performance – environmental performance.

Financial performance and environmental performance can be considered to be different dimensions of performance, each responding to different pressures from different stakeholders of the organisation. Implicit within the discourse and practice of corporate reporting is an assumption that a focus upon one must be at the expense of the other. One outcome of such an assumption is that only one of these two dimensions of performance can be adequately met, and good performance in terms of the one selected to be met necessitates the sacrificing of performance along the other dimension. Thus, according to this assumption, for the organisation's owners and investors financial performance would be represented as good while environmental performance would be represented as bad. For the societal and environmentalist stakeholders however the opposite would be the case as good financial performance could only be achieved through the sacrifice of environmental performance. The actuality is of course that neither of these two dimensions of performance is maximised,[11] and cannot be maximised because of other pressures upon corporate operational performance originating from other stakeholders of the organisation. Thus financial performance, from the point of view of shareholders, is sacrificed for the needs of other stakeholders such as employees and society at large. The extent to which environmental performance is sacrificed is however more problematical as it is unclear what exactly constitutes good environmental performance.

Adopting the view that good environmental behaviour is concerned with sustainability and with negating the effect of the activities of the organisation upon choices available for future generations does not make the position any clearer.[12] Environmental activity normally represents a trade off between one environmental effect and another.[13] Evaluating the net effect of such activity depends upon the perspective of the person undertaking the evaluation as different weightings would be attached to each effect depending upon their respective utility to the person undertaking that evaluation. Moreover it is impractical to determine the environmental impact of any corporate activity merely by the summation of the impact upon all individuals. Thus the net environmental impact of many corporate activities is impossible to assess and evaluate. It is accepted however that the general ethical position of society at large determines that some types of performance are environmentally bad, such as poisoning the local environment through emissions from the organisation as a result of its activities, while some are good, such as landscaping the local environment of the organisation's location. Any such assessment is however temporally determined depending upon the mores of the time; an evaluation undertaken in the nineteenth century, for example, would give a very different evaluation of environmental performance to one undertaken in the present. Similarly the activities of the present will most likely be evaluated differently in the future on the basis of the knowledge and attitudes prevailing at that time.

Given the difficulties of evaluating environmental performance it might be expected that the organisations studied would make reference to this difficulty as a means of obviating the need to report upon such environmental performance. This is not however the case and all organisations in this study actually comment, to a greater or lesser extent, upon environmental issues surrounding the organisational performance. This reporting of environmental performance does not segregate environmental performance from social performance, which tends to be subsumed within the reporting of environmental performance, and both together are considered to be aspects of environmental performance. This reporting is undertaken in the same way as the comments made upon financial performance considered earlier. Thus the organisations through their annual reports seek to represent their environmental performance as good in the present but expected to be even better in the future, and this promised improved future is because of actions taken in the present by the authors of the script.

It must be recognised that no measures of environmental performance exist which have gained universal acceptability, as good environmental performance is subjectively based upon the perspective of the evaluator and the mores of the temporal horizon of reporting. Consequently any messages concerning environmental performance cannot easily be made which allow a comparative evaluation to be undertaken. This is helpful to the image creation activity of the corporate reporting as the authors of the script are able to create an image which cannot be refuted through quantificatory comparative evaluation. Instead such images can be created through the use of linguistic and non-linguistic means. The non-linguistic mechanisms employed are mostly the use of pictures. Examples of such non-linguistic means of creating the image of an environmentally concerned organisation include pictures of:

- crop growing in developing countries to imply partnership development activity(Tate & Lyle 1995);
- carnival activity to imply social concern (Unilever 1995);
- staff in shops engaged in displaying fresh produce or in butchery to imply environmentally friendly farming activity (Asda Group 1996);
- teaching children to swim or local children pond dipping to imply environmentally sound water (Southern Water 1996);
- local crops growing to imply environmentally friendly sources of supply (J Sainsbury 1994).

Such images are part of the creation of a semiotic of environmentally friendly organisations. In most cases the illustrations are only of peripheral relevance to the actual activities of the organisation. Thus the relationship of these images to the actual activities of the organisations concerned is sometimes tenuous, as far as their normal activities are concerned, but the relationship of the images to the message desired to be portrayed through the script is more direct. Comfortable and picturesque images of friendly environmental and social matters convey the image of environmental concern by the organisations and an image of an organisation taking steps to conserve, and even improve, the environment. In this respect the images are symbolic and their role is part of the myth creation function of these corporate reports. They can be considered to be a non-linguistic equivalent of the jargon of authenticity (Adorno 1973). Indeed Cassirer (1946) argues that language reflects a myth making tendency, rather than rationality, which initially results in a symbolic expression. It is in this way that the images created become an established part of the desired semiotic.

The actual language used in the reports to convey environmental activity is much more direct and is used to make statements of what the organisation has actually done, and moreover is going to do in the future, to protect the environment. Examples include:

> Our strategy is to support community activities in the immediate vicinity of our operations. Overseas we have recently made donations to two education charities in Belize to mark the transfer of the majority of shares in Belize Sugar to its employees.
> In the Philippines, we support an important conservation project on an island in the south of the island group. Like the earlier Programme for Belize (a rainforest conservation project), it enables supporters to 'own' a parcel of the land being conserved.
> (Tate & Lyle Annual Report 1995)

> Kwik Save's commitment to the environment remains firm. As retailers we are well aware of our responsibilities to protect and maintain our environment and external recycling facilities available at a number of our larger stores include units for glass and bottles, paper, cans and textiles. In conjunction with Whizz - Kidz, Kwik Save participated in the Blue Peter Paperchain Appeal which resulted in over 200 tonnes of quality waste paper being collected through our stores. There are still 160 collecting skips in situ, continuing the appeal for the benefit of Whizz – Kidz and the environment.
> (Kwik Save Annual Report & Accounts 1995/96)

> Every part of our business is concerned with protecting and improving the environment. For many companies this is only a peripheral part of their responsibility; for us, it is a core one. Each year we publish an objective assessment of our environmental performance to highlight our 'green' credentials. Anglian Water is the largest investor in environmental improvement in the region with a ten year £4bn programme aimed at improving the quality of drinking water, bathing waters, and waste water treatment systems.
> (Anglian Water Annual Report 1994)

> We have continued to reduce the environmental impact of our operations and increase energy efficiency.

Water: We have increased efforts to conserve water and improve effluent
treatment. McVitie's Halifax factory is recycling 70% of its water and has
installed fat separators to reduce effluent pollution.....
Packaging: We have made an important contribution to industry proposals
for recovering waste and continue to reduce our own use of materials.
At Ashby, McVitie's reduced cardboard use by 20% while KP cut
multipack film usage by 15%. More companies in the UK and Continental
Europe are using recycled materials, reducing the volume of packaging and
recycling waste.
(United Biscuits Annual Report 1995)

Southern Water is an environmentally responsible company and the
regulated business is committed to ensuring that domestic and industrial
wastes are treated safely and effectively; this requires extreme care and
environmental sensitivity. The Company's seven – point policy, published
in its annual Conservation and Environmental Report makes clear its
determination to minimise the impact of its activities on the environment,
conserve natural resources, comply with statutory standards and ensure the
health and safety of its employees. Environmental responsibility extends
well beyond the Company's statutory obligations and there are numerous
areas where support is offered for environmental projects. These range from
creating new wildlife habitats to preserving heritage sites and practical help
aimed at improving town and village environments. A good example is
'Pond Week', Southern Water's joint scheme with the British Trust for
Conservation Volunteers which goes from strength to strength. The 1995
event involved more that 1,000 volunteers cleaning out or creating some 90
ponds – the UK's biggest wetlands conservation project.
(Southern Water plc Annual Report 1996)

As a major public company operating over some 8,000 square miles in the
centre of England, the company is conscious of its responsibilities to the
communities it serves. Much of its community affairs programme is
completely altruistic.
(Severn Trent plc Annual report and accounts 1994/95)

The need to demonstrate environmental concern and activity is
manifest in the annual reports of all companies in the sample and seems to
be an essential part of the script. Indeed similar statements can be found in
the majority of corporate reports. For example:

Large mining operations across the globe are properly accompanied by
environmental and social obligations. Full acceptance of these
responsibilities is essential to the well being of your company. The fact that
we are a welcome partner to governments and other companies in various

development areas across the world bears witness to our responsible approach.
(RTZ Annual Report and Accounts 1992)

Thus the image created is that of responsible behaviour and continual improvement towards a better future. Some of the statements are rather nebulous however, such as Severn Trent's reference to altruism. Equally some of the companies are making a virtue out of necessity by depicting their meeting of statutory obligations as environmental concern. This is particularly obvious in the cases of Southern Water, with its focus on waste treatment, and Anglian Water, with its focus on investment. Other companies have presented activities which will benefit themselves through reduced operational costs as being a concern for the environment. This applies in particular to United Biscuits whose recycling and cardboard reduction operations can clearly be seen to lead to reduced operational costs. For shareholders the effect of this activity is embedded within the reporting of increased profitability, without being separately explicit, and the organisation is therefore able to present the same activity differently to different audiences within the same report. In this way the desired image is created and claims of altruism can be made.

In the annual reports of the companies in the sample however environmental reporting is restricted to the creation of images of the companies being active in the area of environmental concern, supported by actions which are essentially trivial in terms of the scale of the companies' activities. In none of the reports is there any attempt at quantification of environmental performance or any reporting thereon. Several of the quotations used in illustration however make reference to separate environmental reports and a large number of the companies in the sample actually produce such reports, either annually or periodically. The implication to be drawn from this tendency to report upon environmental performance separately from financial performance is that the script has been divided because each part of the script is intended to be directed to a different part of the audience. Thus one way of tackling the dichotomy between the opposite poles of any particular binarism in the script is not to relegate one pole to a secondary position, represented as bad, but rather to segregate the readership and represent a different pole as the dominant pole when presenting the script to different parts of the audience.

Stakeholder Perspectives on Performance

These binarisms indicate that organisations are attempting to polarise performance reporting into two dimensions – financial performance and environmental performance. The existence of a large body of literature demonstrates the importance which is attached to the evaluation of performance. This evaluation is of importance not just to the academic community but also to the business community. Indeed it is of direct and immediate importance to the business community as the very survival of a business depends ultimately upon its ability to evaluate performance and select strategies which will enable it to achieve good performance, by whatever criteria are considered pertinent, in the future. The evaluation of performance therefore is not just concerned with the past but is also oriented towards the future in the selection of alternatives which will shape the strategic direction of the business and ensure its future viability. The ability to be able to realistically evaluate performance of the business therefore, and the ability to select suitable dimensions along which to carry out that evaluation, is critically important not just to the managers of the business, nor just to the owners of the business, but to the whole stakeholder community of that business.

Existing research has focused upon three main areas as far as the evaluation of performance is concerned:

- critical consideration of the techniques used in evaluation;
- consideration of the appropriateness of evaluation for particular purposes;
- empirical consideration of current practice.

While this existing research is voluminous in content, and wide-ranging in the areas considered, it is argued that, although this research is a necessary precursor to the consideration of appropriateness of the evaluation of performance, it is nevertheless fundamentally flawed in the conclusions drawn from the research and in the relevance of the findings to future developments. This can be demonstrated by an examination of each of the areas of research in detail.

Techniques Used

Evaluation of the techniques used for measuring performance has largely concentrated upon accounting techniques, although it has been recognised (Eccles 1991) that there has been a shift from an emphasis upon financial figures as the basis of performance measurement to the use of a broader range of measures. Nevertheless the emphasis has been upon a consideration of the technical merits of different accounting techniques.[14] While a consideration of the appropriateness of various techniques is vital to the mechanisms of evaluation, the approach taken by this research subsumes the crucial arguments which need to be resolved before this discussion becomes pertinent. These arguments concern the purpose of performance measurement and the determination of what can be considered good performance. Without a consideration of these questions the evaluation of performance becomes somewhat irrelevant. This research therefore is useful but only once the fundamental rationale underpinning the measurement has been identified.

Appropriateness of Measures

This class of research recognises that the reasons for the evaluation of performance underpin any measurement which is needed. The tendency of the research findings[15] is to consider the effectiveness of current measures of performance in evaluating performance from a particular perspective and finding these measures inadequate. Some writers go beyond this[16] and suggest ways of measuring performance which will enable it to be evaluated from the particular perspective with which they are concerned. While this has merits there is a tendency in doing so to suggest changes in performance measurement which meets these needs, but only at the expense of potentially neglecting other evaluation needs. Any consideration of measures suitable for evaluation needs to consider the whole purpose for which evaluation takes place in order to prevent the problems of meeting one need at the expense of others.

This research however has a tendency to consider the evaluation of performance for organisations in a particular sector or from a particular perspective, ignoring other needs for the evaluation of performance which, by implication, are deemed to be irrelevant. It does not however seem either helpful or appropriate to consider these aspects in isolation from each other and to devise measures for evaluation from a single perspective when organisational needs are inevitably interdependent. Such an approach tends to lead to separate measurement systems and inevitably to conflict and tension as the separate and independent systems lead to differing conclusions being drawn. The approaches taken are based upon existing paradigms for performance evaluation, which while satisfactory when taken in isolation, are not able to be combined to meet the needs of an organisation. It would appear therefore that there is a need for a new integrated paradigm to enable organisational performance to be evaluated as a whole.

In addition to considering the various perspectives on performance evaluation it is important to recognise that there are a variety of purposes for which performance is evaluated, which are concerned with the actual functioning of the company, from a planning point of view and from an operational point of view. Additionally the organisation is concerned with both the present and with its future existence and so has both a short term and a long term focus. It is also concerned with its internal operations and with its external environment and so must have both an internal and an external focus.

Empirical Research

Empirical research[17] has obvious merits in revealing current practice and the way in which this impacts upon decision making for future performance, and therefore has a place in the discourse of performance measurement. It also demonstrates the strengths and weaknesses of current practice as well as providing an opportunity to relate some of the theoretical debates to the environment in which they are operating. Such research does not however necessarily lead to any developments as far as the consideration of appropriate measures for evaluation to meet all needs is concerned.

The Measurement of Performance

The measurement of performance is central to any consideration of performance evaluation and this resolves into two areas for consideration, namely why measure and what to measure. Measurement theory states that measurement is essentially a comparative process, and comparison provides the purpose for measurement. Measurement enables the comparison of the constituents of performance in the following areas:

- temporally by enabling the comparison of one time period with another;
- geographically by enabling the comparison of one business, sector or nation with another;
- strategically by enabling alternative courses of action and their projected consequences to be compared.

Performance itself is not absolute but rather comparative and it is essential in evaluating performance to be able to assess comparatively in the nature of 'better than expected', 'worse than the competition' etc. It is not possible to assess performance in other than these terms and so a quantitative approach to performance evaluation is essential even if some aspects of performance are qualitative in nature.

It is necessary therefore that measurement is a constituent of performance evaluation and so it becomes necessary to determine what should be measured in order to evaluate performance. It is essential therefore to select appropriate measures for the purpose of the evaluation. It is argued however that appropriate measures cannot be selected until the purpose of evaluation has been determined. It is therefore again demonstrated that the foundation of performance measurement is the identification of the reasons for the evaluation of performance, and this must now be considered.

It is clear from the evaluation of the literature, and a consideration of actual practice, that the evaluation of performance takes place for several reasons. Each of these reasons exists in isolation from the other reasons, and so can be examined separately.

Evaluation for Control

In order to exercise control in the business environment it is necessary for the manager of the business to have information concerning the activities of that business. In order to determine whether or not the business, or that part of the business which is the concern of a particular manager, is operating as expected it is necessary in the first place that there is a plan for the activities of the business. It is also necessary that there be a means of evaluating the performance of the business in achieving the objectives of the plan. Evaluation is therefore necessary for the control of the business in order to measure and assess performance against the plan and to have a means of assessing any changes in control necessary to correct any deviations from that plan. The measures used for this purpose need to be appropriate and meaningful for the context in which they are used, and management accounting in particular has been developed for the control of the internal processes and activities of a business, as well as for the evaluation of internal opportunities for gain. The quantitative nature of accounting makes the comparative measurement of performance a relatively simple process and it has been suggested by Cherns (1978) that measurement equates with control. This proposition is overly simplistic but it is certainly the case that measurement facilitates evaluation, thereby enabling control to be exercised.

Evaluation for Strategy Formulation

Evaluation for control purposes is concerned primarily with past data and its present implications. Evaluation for strategy formulation purposes however has a future orientation, based upon the present, and, while taking into account past data, is rather concerned with predictions for the future. A business, in developing its strategy, is faced with a range of alternatives from which it must select those most appropriate to its current circumstances and constraints, future objectives and environmental stance. In order to select appropriate strategies it must have a means of evaluating these strategic alternatives in whatever terms it deems appropriate and relevant.[18] The criteria for evaluating possible strategies are diverse and pertinent individually to each business. The process of evaluation however, through measurement and prediction, is common to all. Measurement can be seen to be the core of this evaluation and appropriate measures are needed. There is no reason to suppose that measures developed for control purposes will be appropriate for strategy formulation purposes, and measures used must be appropriate for the purpose to which they are put. Indeed they need to be developed for this purpose if they do not exist. To evaluate performance on any other basis is to negate the process by a failure to recognise the purpose of the evaluation.

Evaluation for Accountability

Increasingly the external environment within which a business operates has changed and continues to change. While this affects both the strategy formulation and control purposes of performance evaluation it is of particular pertinence to the accountability purpose of evaluation. The increasing power and concern of all stakeholders within the wider stakeholder community of a business, and the way in which their respective power continues to change, have led to an increasing demand for the business to be accountable to them.[19] This means that organisations have increasingly tended to adopt a stakeholder approach to performance evaluation, rather than merely the much narrower traditional ownership approach. This has caused the recognition of the need for a different approach to performance measurement along the lines suggested by Eccles (1991). There is increasing concern with accountability therefore, rather than simply with accounting, with a greater emphasis upon social and environmental accounting, and with organisational accountability to its employees (Panozzo 1996). The need for suitable measures to evaluate performance in this wider context necessitates the adoption of new measures of performance, which are not necessarily appropriate for other evaluation purposes. Such measures are not necessarily always accounting based and indeed are not necessarily even quantitative, although such measures need to facilitate comparison. At the same time however the needs of ownership accountability cannot be neglected.[20] Accountability therefore is an area of performance which is increasing in importance and changing in nature thereby reflecting a changing need for the development of measures suitable for the evaluation of performance.

The Reporting of Performance

The evaluation of performance depends not just upon the appropriate measurement of performance but also upon the reporting of that performance. It is inevitable that each person or stakeholder grouping interested in the evaluation of the performance of an organisation needs a report, in some form, of the organisation's performance in order to undertake evaluation. It can be seen that the informational needs of different groups will differ considerably, depending upon their respective interests and concerns. The internal control needs, the needs of the owners, the needs of investors and potential investors, and the needs of the community as a stakeholder will all differ from each other and this poses a problem for the reporting of performance.[21] In order to meet the reporting needs of the diverse stakeholder community it is necessary first to identify those needs, and this necessitates a consideration of the perspective of each stakeholder and a consideration of the interests in evaluation of the organisation's performance which is of importance to each stakeholder. These will be different between different groupings, which will therefore increase the reporting needs which the organisation must address.

The need for new measures to evaluate performance has to be set within the context of a changing external environment. Thus organisations are increasingly being concerned with a holistic approach (whereby the needs of the whole stakeholder community are considered), together with such issues as soft systems, culture and the establishment of competencies, as well as with accountability. This has led to the need to evaluate performance against a set of diverse and often conflicting criteria which have led to the development of measures to evaluate performance for quite different purposes. These performance evaluation needs have a tendency to lead to the creation of tensions within the organisational performance measurement system as organisations have sought to evaluate performance against conflicting criteria. This in turn has led to tensions within the operational systems of an organisation, as organisations have sought to meet often incompatible needs.

Agency theory suggests that the management of an organisation is undertaken on behalf of the owners of that organisation, in other words the shareholders. Consequently the management of value created by the organisation is only pertinent insofar as that value accrues to the shareholders of the firm. Implicit within this view of the management of the firm, as espoused by Rappaport (1986) and Stewart (1991) amongst many others, is that society at large, and consequently all other stakeholders to the organisation, will also benefit as a result of managing the performance of the organisation in this manner. From this perspective therefore the concerns are focused upon how to manage performance for the shareholders and how to report upon that performance (Myners 1998).

This view of an organisation has however been extensively challenged by many writers,[22] who argue that the way to maximise performance for society at large is to both manage on behalf of all stakeholders and to ensure that the value thereby created is not appropriated by the shareholders but is distributed to all stakeholders. Others such as Kay (1998) argue that this debate is sterile and that organisations maximise value creation not by a concern with either shareholders or stakeholders but by focusing upon the operational objectives of the firm and assuming that value creation, and equitable distribution will thereby follow.

Adherents to each of these conflicting philosophies regarding the method of managing a business in order to secure maximum value creation have a tendency to adopt different perspectives on the evaluation of performance. Thus good performance for one school of thought is assumed to be poor performance for another school of thought. Performance maximising philosophies are thus polarised in the discourse and this leads to a polarisation of performance reporting. In this respect the financial and environmental polarity can be considered to epitomise this polarisation.

The Evaluation of Performance

This suggests an interaction between the various factors involved in the evaluation of performance, and recognition of this will enable an organisation to plan its measurement and reporting system to cover these needs. It is argued that a fragmented approach to the consideration of the evaluation of performance results in the using of measures which are not necessarily appropriate to the purpose for which they are being used. It is further argued that consideration of one aspect of performance, and the development of measures in that area, can lead to improvements in that area but often only at the expense of the other needs for evaluative measures.[23]

A framework which sets out to recognise all interest groups and the perspectives which they hold, together with a consideration of the purposes for which they seek to evaluate performance, suggests a logical approach to consideration of the issues involved. It is likely to lead to the development of a better system for measuring and reporting performance which addresses the needs of all parties. Given that the respective power of different stakeholders changes over time, and can be expected to continue to change, due to changing economic, social and cultural conditions, both at a national level and at a global level, this approach provides a means, not just of responding to needs, but also of anticipating such needs. It therefore facilitates a proactive stance as far as reporting and measuring is concerned rather than merely a reactive stance, and it is argued that this can lead to better economic performance.

A variety of measures exist to measure performance evaluatively, and while these have been criticised in their efficiency by some writers, it is nevertheless true that such measures have a role in this function. The efficiency of measures of performance can only be determined however by considering their use in the measurement of performance when the purpose of that measurement has been determined. It seems reasonable to argue that different purposes need different measures and that perhaps some, but by no means all, measures are universal in addressing all needs. Measurements derive their meaning however from the use to which they are applied and mismeasurement by using measures incorrectly causes conflict and misunderstanding. Once a framework has been developed which identifies and addresses needs and purposes of evaluation it is then possible to consider the efficiency and effectiveness of existing measures and identify deficiencies in the measurement system. It is then possible to develop and implement new measures which are appropriate to the purposes identified.

It can readily be seen that the differing needs of different parties in the evaluation process cause tensions within the organisation as it seeks to meet its internal control, strategy formulation and accountability functions and produce a reporting structure to meet these needs. While the basic information required to satisfy these needs is the same information, or at least derives from the same source data, the way in which it is analysed and used is different, which can lead to conflict within the organisation.[24] Such conflict is exacerbated when a measure is adapted for one need but only at the expense of a deterioration in its appropriateness for another purpose.[25]

Part of the semiotic of corporate reporting however is that managers have the ability to manage information provision in such a way that all stakeholders can be satisfied both with the information received and with the performance of the organisation.

It is argued that an integrated measurement and reporting system in an organisation will lead to better performance by that organisation, in whatever dimensions it measures performance. It is equally argued that this will be achieved through the reduction in tension within the organisation, caused through a fragmented approach to the measurement of performance. Such an organisation will be more responsive to the challenge of the external environment and will have its strategy and control functions more closely aligned with each other and with its ultimate objectives. This integrated approach is likely also to have other implications for an organisation, and one effect is that the resolution of conflicts by means of the adoption of this approach is likely to reduce tensions and lead to a more consensual approach to control and strategic planning. It is therefore suggested that the culture of an organisation is to some extent dependent upon its measurement and evaluation mechanisms. Such mechanisms therefore are not just neutral systems but have a highly positivistic role in shaping the organisation in cultural terms. A culture of conflict needs the involvement of the senior managers to resolve, thereby being part of the mechanism by which they represent their essentiality to the organisation. It can also be argued that the quality of performance is perceived by the evaluator and assessed according to the criteria which (s)he considers appropriate to his / her needs, rather than being absolute in its perceived quality. Performance therefore can also be viewed deterministically in that it can be considered to be as good as it is evaluated to be, and Fish (1989) argues that contextually, truth and belief are synonymous for all practical purposes.

One factor of importance in performance evaluation is the concept of the sustainability of performance. It is therefore important for all stakeholders to be able to ascertain, or at least project, not just current performance but its implications for the future. Performance evaluation must therefore necessarily have a future orientation for all evaluations. The appropriate measures developed through this proposed framework are likely to facilitate a better projection of the sustainability of performance levels and the future impact of current performance. This is because the addressing of the needs of all stakeholders is likely to reveal factors which will impact upon future performance and which might not be considered if a more traditional approach was taken towards performance evaluation. An example might be the degree to which raw materials from renewable resources have become significant to many industries recently but were not considered at all until recently by any stakeholders of an organisation other than community and environmental pressure groups.

Empirical research into the measurement and reporting of performance has tended to concentrate upon one particular sector or market,[26] within a national or global environment. The implication of this is that the issues of importance as far as performance evaluation is concerned are specific to that sector or market and that it is not possible to generalise globally about such issues. The framework developed however demonstrates that the issues are not sector specific but apply generally to all organisations – public or private, profit seeking or not for profit, national or multinational. A complete analysis of any particular organisation may reveal minor differences in perspectives and purposes, and will almost certainly reveal that some of the appropriate measures are specific to that organisation, and will therefore differ from one organisation to another. Fundamentally however it can be seen that the approach taken to the measurement and evaluation of performance should be the same whatever the type of organisation and whichever market it is operating in, and whatever the unique characteristics of that organisation. The basic issues are general rather than purely local and specific in their relevance.[27]

One implication of the analysis undertaken of evaluation systems is that the conflicting needs of different parties, and the different purposes for which measurements are used, are a source of tension within an organisation. Indeed it is argued that mismeasurement, by using measures for purposes for which they were not devised and are not appropriate, is itself a source of conflict within an organisation.[28] These tensions manifest themselves as power in the organisation, and while it is accepted that power is in the hands of the dominant coalition it is also argued that the stakeholders who are not part of that coalition also have power which they seek to use to enable the satisfaction of their needs. The tensions arising from this power struggle therefore make the organisation unstable and as far as performance is concerned unless all stakeholders are involved, either actively or passively, in the evaluation system the organisation wastes resources dealing with the ensuing conflict and seeking to meet the needs of excluded parties.[29]

It has also been argued that the quality of performance is not absolute according to certain measures but is necessarily comparative, and it can be further argued that the same level of performance will be evaluated differently by different stakeholders according to the perspective from which they are undertaking that evaluation. Thus measures only have meaning in their interpretation, as epitomised in the semiotic. It is however helpful to the communication process if that interpretation is broadly similar for each person undertaking that interpretation. The way in which measures are used, or as is often the case misused, for a variety of evaluative purposes exacerbates the problem of differing interpretations, thereby leading to a variety of evaluations based upon the same measures for information. This problem is made worse by the use of accounting information, which can be described using Adorno's (1973) expression of 'the jargon of authenticity'.[30]

It is therefore argued that precision in the use of measures and in the meaning attached to those measures is a crucial determinant of the evaluation system used by an organisation. The failure to develop an adequate system for measuring performance will lead to an incomplete evaluation of that performance from some perspectives. More significantly however it can result in a misleading evaluation of performance, as some measures are misused for evaluation in one dimension because of the lack of appropriate measures to give meaning to the evaluation. This applies not just to the measurement system but equally to the reporting system as it is this which provides the measured data to the evaluator. This flawed evaluation of performance can have serious consequences for an organisation and can lead not just to stakeholder alienation but more seriously to plans for the future of the organisation being made upon incorrect evaluations which can affect the future performance, and even conceivably the viability, of that organisation.[31]

In seeking empirical evidence to support the value and applicability of this model it is clear that these implications can be resolved into a sequence of issues which can be examined separately. An examination of the following issues therefore will lead to conclusions being able to be made concerning this framework for evaluation. This analysis of the framework can be summarised in terms of the following problem:

> Does organisational performance evaluation need a multiple dimensional approach in order to more effectively measure, report and evaluate performance and to plan for the future, and if so what sort of multiple dimensional approach?

It has been argued that organisations exist as a loose coalition of different interest groups and power groupings which are held together by an interplay of common objectives and tensions arising from conflicting objectives. The role in which the evaluation needs of the different groups causes, exacerbates, or even reduces these tensions is an area needing investigation.[32] Equally the structure of the organisation affects the tensions existing as does the extent of consensus or conflict. It has been argued that the evaluation system derives from the organisational structure and culture but at the same time shapes the culture of an organisation. This is perhaps reflected in the differences between the overt organisational structure and the covert structure, which is based upon the respective power of the various interest groups (Deleuze 1988). The greater the divergence between the two the greater is the likelihood of tensions existing and also of these tensions being unarticulated. This approach seems to provide a means of understanding the existence of tensions resulting from incompatible needs and must be investigated along with more overt recognition.

One approach to the resolution of such tensions however is to separate the sources of such tensions. Thus one objective of corporate reporting is to separate the tensions existing by reporting upon financial performance separately from reporting upon environmental performance. This is achieved through the representations of these two, potentially conflicting, priorities of performance as different and unrelated. Thus the semiotic of corporate reporting represents financial performance as the dominant pole of the binary opposition when reporting to shareholders and environmental performance as the dominant pole when reporting to environmentalists. This separation of the two poles of performance can be achieved to an even greater extent by the separation, physically, of the reports. Thus environmental reports are often produced as separate documents to the annual report.

It must be recognised that any measures employed are used for comparative purposes and one method of comparison is with other organisations in the same sector.[33] It is possible therefore that some measures do become sector specific because they meet the individual needs of all the organisations in the sector. These needs have however become generalised to the sector because the managers of all the organisations share the common need for inter-organisational comparison. It is nevertheless argued however that these measures have been developed uniquely for each organisation and that sectoral generalisations result from this rather than being an objective in itself. Each organisation, through the activities of its managers, is acting for itself rather than altruistically for the benefit of other organisations within the same sector.[34]

It has been proposed, using empirical evidence (Coates et al 1993), that the financial measures used by multinational companies can lead to short term decision making and risk minimising rather than performance optimising behaviour. It can be argued therefore that the measures used by an organisation depend upon the time horizon of that organisation and that short and long term horizons are incompatible.[35] It can also be argued conversely however that the time horizon of the organisation is dependant upon the measures adopted for evaluating performance. This interaction will be dependant upon the power of the various stakeholders, both perceived and actual power, and upon the composition of the dominant coalition and their purposes. The way in which these interactions affect performance and cause tensions within the stakeholder community need investigating and one approach is to investigate the strategic planning function and the time scales used both for planning operations and for investment appraisal. This will provide a surrogate measure leading to an understanding of the time horizons adopted within the organisation.

Accounting and Other Measurements

Traditionally performance has been measured in accounting terms using the annual report as the reporting mechanism for external reporting and management accounting reports for internal reporting. To some extent this has been determined by legal requirements and to some extent by the easily quantitative nature of accounting information. It has been increasingly argued however that accounting information does not provide a full picture of the performance of an organisation, and does not necessarily provide an accurate picture for those areas in which it does not report performance. One problem with accounting is that it lends itself to comparative analysis and has tended to be used for control purposes to track performance against budget. The purpose of doing so is to highlight problem areas for corrective action rather than to highlight areas of significance. Its use therefore has been essentially defensive rather than strategic. This use has been highlighted by Drucker (1985: 36-7) who argues that strategic opportunities for organisational benefit are missed because accounting information is used defensively. He states:

> Far more often, the unexpected success is simply not seen at all. Nobody pays any attention to it. Hence nobody exploits it... One reason for this blindness to the unexpected success is that our existing reporting systems do not as a rule report it, let alone clamour for management attention. Practically every company... has a monthly or quarterly report. The first sheet lists the areas in which performance is below expectations: it lists the problems and the shortfalls. At the meetings of the management group... everybody therefore focuses on the problem areas. No one even looks at the areas where the company has done better than expected. And if the unexpected success is not quantitative but qualitative... the figures will not even show the unexpected success as a rule.

This illustrates that the evaluation of performance is dependant not just upon the perspective of those evaluating performance but also upon the measurement and reporting system. It also illustrates the danger of accepting the presentation of accounting information as truth, rather than an interpretation of the situation. The increasing dissatisfaction with accounting as the sole means of measuring performance has led to the use of other measures in addition to accounting measures. Such measures include qualitative measures as well as quantitative measures. The development of new measures of performance has largely therefore, in recent times, taken place outside the arena of accounting and has reflected the increasing concerns of both organisations and society with such issues as quality and environmental impact. There is a need however to view accounting, other quantitative measures and qualitative measures not as separate systems for measuring performance but as parts of an integrated system and attention has turned to this.

At the same time the means by which an organisation has reported upon performance have undergone considerable change (Eccles 1991) and the extent of disclosure of performance has changed from an emphasis upon minimisation to one of maximisation of disclosure. This is reflected in changes to corporate reports but also in the publication of environmental impact reports, the increasing use of press releases and general informative publicity. It is possible to track these changes over time to reveal changes in the extent of disclosure and also changes in the parties to whom disclosure is made. This arguably reflects a change from an ownership reporting stance to one of a stakeholder stance.[36]

The evidence from the semiotic analysis would support this change to a stakeholder stance, but not at the expense of owners (ie shareholders); rather the two are treated as equally important and techniques have been developed[37] which enable them to be treated as of equal importance without negating the importance of each other. This would therefore support hypothesis 4 while not supporting hypothesis 5. The meaning and implications of this will be considered further in the next chapter.

Notes

[1] See for example the articles 'Cadbury on course to hit performance targets' (*The Times* 6/8/98) which is based upon the work of analysts in this area. Arguably these opinions of analysts are in turn based upon the information provided by the managers of the business. In this way therefore the press acts as a mediating mechanism between the company and its audience. This mediation is not always however in the interests of the company – see for example 'How Sainsbury lost

its way' (*Sunday Times* 27/7/97) which provides an example of press mediation which is not based upon the interests of the company. Thus it can be seen that, although the companies will attempt to use the press as mediation in order to create the desired semiotic, this is not always effective.

[2] Small = an assumption of financially illiteracy?

[3] This is based upon the work of Fish (1972) and Munro (1996).

[4] But see Lee & Tweedie (1977) concerning the use made of this information.

[5] This applies not just to the companies in the sample but also to other companies. See for example the reports of, inter alia, The Rank Group plc or BNFL. These can be contrasted with the reports of, for example, a company limited by guarantee such as the Institute of Management where this separation does not take place.

[6] Similarly the Rank Group produce two documents entitled 'Directors Report and Accounts' and 'Review and Financial Summary' while Pilkington entitle their two documents 'Directors Report and Accounts' and 'Annual Review and Summary Financial Statement'.

[7] See chapter 5 for a more detailed quantification and analysis of the environmental context of the annual report.

[8] See also a consideration of their website in chapter 10.

[9] See Crowther, Cooper & Carter (2001) where it is argued that the regulator is central to the determination of the performance of water companies.

[10] Indeed, as stated previously, the two are conflated into a single issue as far as corporate reporting is concerned.

[11] This is recognised by the press. See for example *The Times* series of company profiles which attempts to evaluate performance along a variety of dimensions. In most of these profiles (see for example J Sainsbury 24/8/98) the companies score similarly along both the financial and environmental dimensions.It is of course recognised that the dimensions used in these profiles do not exactly correspond with the dimensions of the dialectic in this book. Thus the environmental aspect of performance is subsumed in this series within the ethical aspect of performance.

[12] Indeed Popper's (1945) concept of the poverty of historicism suggests that future impact cannot be determined by extrapolation from the past and present.

[13] For example the building of a new reservoir by a water company provides not just water but also leisure facilities both in the present and in the future. At the same time however this reservoir may damage wildlife habitat for some species (albeit maybe also improving the habitat of other species) and limiting other leisure activities.

[14] Such as whether ROI or residual income is the more appropriate measure for evaluating divisional performance (eg Dearden 1969) and whether the transfer pricing mechanism interferes with the appropriateness of the technique (eg Emmanuel & Gee, 1982 and Grabski, 1985).

[15] e.g. Birnbeg (1980), Kimberley *et al.* (1983), Gray *et al.* (1987) considered previously.

[16] e.g. Rappaport (1992) in terms of shareholder value management or Kaplan and Norton (1992, 1993) in terms of the balanced scorecard.

[17] See for example Davis, Coates, Emmanuel, Longden & Stacey (1992) concerning the practice in multinational companies.

[18] These might be future benefit, resource requirements, stakeholder impact, environmental impact etc.

[19] See Carnaghan, Gibbins & Ikaheimo (1996) for a consideration of the role of financial disclosure upon accountability.

[20] Although Herremans et al (1992) have suggested that a broader approach to corporate disclosure and to the evaluation of performance can lead to better economic performance by an organisation.

[21] This was recognised by Birnbeg (1980) who suggested that an organisation through its accounting was attempting to supply diverse groups with differing needs for information and thereby failing to communicate adequately with all the groups to meet all the reporting needs.

[22] eg Herremans (1992), Tinker (1985).

[23] Indeed Kimberley *et al.* (1983) have argued that some areas of performance which are important to the future of the business are not even recognised let alone evaluated.

[24] See Kaplan & Norton (1992) concerning the balanced scorecard.

[25] It is for this reason that accounting and information systems in organisations are in a constant state of development and enhancement as the systems are designed to meet perceived needs and adapted to meet newly identified needs. One such source of conflict in an organisation therefore is caused by the different stakeholders seeking to access and use information differently, and this conflict tends to have a dysfunctional impact upon organisational cohesiveness and ultimately performance.

[26] Eg Fitzgerald *et al.* (1991), Jackson (1986).

[27] A model resulting in a theory of performance evaluation and its interaction with organisational behaviour has no purpose without this practical application. This point is elaborated by Horkheimer and Adorno (1944: 244) who state: "The belief that the truth of a theory is the same as its productiveness is clearly unfounded. There are some, however, who appear to maintain the opposite: that theory has so little need of application in thinking that it should dispense with it entirely."

[28] Although it can be argued that organisations themselves are not entities but are coalitions of interest groups (i.e. stakeholders) which are held together by the tensions between the different groups, it is also argued that such tensions are not necessarily constructive but are also destructive, wasting resources and resulting in sub-optimisation of the performance of the organisation.

[29] It has been argued that such needs are often met only at the expense of other needs and this therefore causes tensions itself with a result that the organisation tends to exist in a perpetually changing state of dynamic disequilibrium. This would be deleterious to organisational performance, which would be enhanced

by the existence of goal congruence, unless this disequilibrium can be managed – and this is the role of the managers of the organisation. It is therefore in their interests to both demonstrate the state of dynamic disequilibrium and also their ability to manage its control or resolution.

[30] He argues that belief, or opinion, is presented as fact by the language used to express that belief and by the acceptance of this presentation as truth by its recipients, stating"...a jargon of authenticity is spoken - even more so written. Its language is a trademark of societalised closeness, noble and homey at once - sub-language as superior language." (pp 5-6)

[31] It can readily be seen therefore that performance evaluation requires the construction of adequate measures which are meaningful and appropriate for the purpose for which they will be applied. Such measures can be financial or non-financial, quantitative or qualitative, and are likely to be a combination of such measures. It has been argued that performance can be evaluated along three dimensions - those of perspective, purpose and focus - and that a multiple dimensional analysis is required to enable all the needs for evaluation to be identified. Once identified, of course, it is possible to devise a system which provides measures and reporting mechanisms which meet these needs. These dimensions cannot therefore be considered in isolation from each other. Each dimension, rather than conflicting with the other dimensions, complements them. Similarly the different components within each dimension do not compete in importance, and are not mutually exclusive, but rather overlap and complement each other. Therefore the model, when resolved for an individual organisation, is likely to be simplified from the initial framework and the measures identified as needed for any organisation will be much less complex and voluminous than might be considered from a consideration of the initial framework. Nevertheless this multidimensional approach is necessary both for the control of the organisation and, perhaps more significantly, for its strategic development.

[32] Horkheimer and Adorno (1944: 110) argue that a social hierarchy is dependent ultimately upon force, stating: "Though it may seek a legalistic covering, the social hierarchy is ultimately dependant on force. Mastery over nature is reproduced within humanity." The use of power therefore in determining which needs are met at the expense of others is one factor which affects these tensions. Horkheimer and Adorno further argue that there is a tendency for stakeholders who have needs conflicting from those of the dominant coalition will tend towards acceptance of the dominant view as any articulation of those differences will lead towards coincidence; any irreconcilable needs will fail to be articulated. They state:"Anyone who resists can only survive by fitting in. Once his particular brand of deviation from the norm has been noted by the industry, he belongs to it as does the land-reformer to capitalism. Realistic dissidence is the trademark of anyone who has a new idea in business. In the public voice of modern society accusations are seldom audible: if they are, the perceptive can already detect signs that the dissident will soon be reconciled. The more measurable the gap between chorus and leaders, the more certainly there is room

at the top for everybody who demonstrates his superiority by well planned originality." (p132). This argues for a dynamic approach to identifying and meeting stakeholder needs and suggests that the ways in which needs are articulated determines the likelihood of them being met.

[33] This method of comparative measurement is one which features particularly strongly in the public sector (Midwinter 1994).

[34] One way in which comparative measurement can affect an organisation deleteriously however is when that comparison appears unfavourable to the organisation. In such circumstances therefore it would seem desirable that the organisation report upon performance in such a way that a comparative evaluation is not possible. This implies the use of measures which are distinct and unique to the organisation and thus cannot be compared with the measures used by other similar organisations. As far as financial reporting is concerned this is problematic as the generally accepted measures are based upon the use of accounting information and have gained acceptance through general use over time. This is not the case however with environmental measures of performance and thus one technique used by organisations is to use individual measures to represent performance in the desired manner.

[35] But see the counter arguments of Rappaport (1992).

[36] It is argued that this reflects a changing perception of the purpose of the reporting of performance which at least in part has been driven by changes in the power relationships between the different stakeholders. More specifically it is argued that the extension of measures of performance tends to provide a means, through the using of such measures, for managers to shape the interpretation of performance in the way they desire, and thereby to obscure other possible interpretations of performance. This facility is enhanced when the discourse considers the measurement of performance to be a complex process.

[37] For example the separation of the environmental reporting into a separate document is one such technique.

Chapter 7

Relating Financial and Environmental Performance: Interpretation of the Evidence

Introduction

The analysis of financial performance undertaken in chapter 5 was shown to be of limited statistical validity from the point of view of drawing any conclusions about differences between industry sectors. Nevertheless the analysis does indicate that the water sector is different from the food sectors but that there does not seem to be a great difference between the food manufacturing and food retailing sectors. The analysis also shows considerable differences between companies in each sector but also that the water sector appears more homogenous than the other two sectors. This situation also appears to be the case from an analysis of environmental performance, or at least the reporting of such performance, as also undertaken in chapter 5.[1]

The question therefore arises as to what makes the water industry different from the other two industrial sectors to such an extent that both the returns to shareholders and the reporting of environmental performance can be demonstrated to be significantly different. It is of course possible that the nature of the operational efficiency of this industry is such that the firms can make a higher level of profit, and hence returns to shareholders in this industry. Such an argument does not however apply to any consideration of environmental performance. Indeed it would be reasonable to suppose that the two dimensions of performance are actually diametrically opposed to one another, and this is part of the message of the semiotic as created by the authors of the script. It would therefore be expected that good performance in one dimension could only be achieved at the expense of good performance in the other. It would appear, on the basis of the analysis in the preceding chapters, that this is not in fact the case. Indeed it appears that good performance by a company leads to good performance in both dimensions. In order to test this assertion therefore it is necessary to examine the correlation between performance in both dimensions.

Analysing the Performance Polarity

The analysis of the correlation between the two dimensions of performance is undertaken by means of a Pearson Product Moment Correlation test. This gives a result of $r = 0.508$ and this is significant at the $p = 0.01$ level which suggests that there is a significant correlation between financial performance and environmental performance. This therefore supports the assertion made previously on the basis of the analysis undertaken and on the basis of a visual inspection of the data. In order to ascertain this relationship in more details it seems appropriate however to look at each sector in isolation.

An examination of the data for individual sectors through a Pearson Product Moment Correlation test shows the following results. For the water sector $r = 0.088$ which is not significant at any level. This suggests that there is no significant correlation between financial performance and environmental performance for this industrial sector. This finding must be interpreted in the light of the problems of small data samples made earlier.

For the food retailing industry a value of $r = -0.193$ is obtained. This also is not significant at any level which suggests that there is no significant correlation between financial performance and environmental performance for this industrial sector. This finding must also be interpreted in the light of the problems of small data samples made earlier.

An analysis of the data for the food manufacturing industry gives a result of $r = 0.003$ which is also not significant at any level which suggests that there is no significant correlation between financial performance and environmental performance for this industrial sector. This finding must also be interpreted in the light of the problems of small data samples made earlier.

It can therefore be seen that the samples for each individual industry sector do not produce significant correlations but when aggregated into a larger sample a significant positive correlation is produced. This suggests therefore that there is a positive correlation between financial performance, as measured by TSR, and environmental performance, as measured by the composite measured derived. An analysis looking at the means for the three industrial sectors gives a value 0f r = 0.983. While this produces a very high positive correlation the fact that the data sample consists of only three items means that it is not statistically significant. Nevertheless it provides strong collaborative evidence of the relationship between environmental and financial performance.

Conclusions Concerning Hypotheses

The statistical evidence from the data analysed in this chapter provides evidence of statistical relationships in performance but this evidence is not sufficiently robust to be considered as statistically significant. Thus it is not possible to make any comments regarding statistical significance. The purpose of this research however is not to provide demonstrable statistical relationships which purport to be proof of any relationship. Rather the purpose is to explore the relationship between financial and environmental performance as far as companies are concerned and to examine how this is reflected in the corporate reporting of such performance. In this context therefore the evidence from the analysis undertaken in the preceding two chapters does provide evidence with respect to this relationship. It therefore seems appropriate to consider the hypotheses developed in chapter 4 in the light of the analysis undertaken.

In chapter 4 a proposition was developed which stated that:

> There is a dichotomy between financial performance and environmental performance which represent two incompatible dimensions of performance.

This hypothesis was turned into a series of five testable hypotheses with the first three being subject to quantitative testing and the last two being subject to qualitative testing. Following the analysis od data undertaken in this and the last two chapters it is now possible to draw conclusions concerning the validity of these hypotheses. Thus in terms of the findings from the analysis undertaken the following can be stated:

Hypothesis 1

There is indeed a significant difference between the financial performance of different organisations. Moreover there is a difference between the performance of firms in the different sectors analysed, which can be described as a sectoral difference, and this difference has been considered to suggest that the socio-political and economic climate may be sufficiently dissimilar as to account for this difference. This hypothesis is however accepted.

Hypothesis 2

There is indeed a significant difference between the environmental performance of different organisations and the arguments concerning financial performance also apply to environmental performance. This hypothesis is therefore also accepted.

Hypothesis 3

The analysis shows that there is a negative correlation between the financial performance and the environmental performance of the same organisations, although the statistical veracity of the analysis is not strong. Nevertheless the evidence suggests that an organisation which performs well along one dimension of performance also performs well along the other dimension of performance. This hypothesis therefore is rejected thereby suggesting that the two dimensions of performance are not incompatible.

The purpose of these three hypotheses, taken together, is to demonstrate that there is no incompatibility between these two dimensions of performance and that it is possible to perform well along both dimensions. For this to be the case then the first two hypotheses need to be accepted and the third rejected. This is indeed the case and therefore it can be claimed that the discourses of traditional performance and environmental performance which claim this dichotomy are misleading. Thus it is claimed that the perceived dialectic between the two dimensions of performance is a false dialectic.

Hypothesis 4

The annual reports of companies do indeed consider and report upon both dimensions of performance in terms of the written reports.[2] Environmental performance is however dealt with in little detail and many of the companies produce a separate environmental report. The discussion in chapter 6 suggests that there is an attempt to split the audience between the financially oriented and the environmentally oriented by this means. Nevertheless the evidence shows that all companies consider both dimensions of performance to be important and this hypothesis is therefore accepted.

Hypothesis 5

The written parts of the annual report tend to presented in such a way that performance for the company seems to be not just good but also improving, with a consequent expectation of even better future performance. Thus there is a tendency for the reports to favour the dimension of performance for which performance has been better and this hypothesis is therefore accepted. It must be noted however that if one dimension of performance is good then there is a tendency for the other to also be good and thus this hypothesis does not represent an absolute but only a relative difference is performance.

The testing of these hypotheses through the analysis undertaken does therefore provide supporting evidence to the assertion that the dialectic between financial and environmental performance is more apparent than real. Thus the discourse of such accounting, considered in chapters 2 and 3, is misleading in its representation of these two dimensions of accounting as incompatible. Equally therefore the implication of the ability to only satisfy either shareholders and investors or other stakeholders must be rejected also.

The statistical evidence however suggests that the three sectors considered are different in nature. In particular it suggests that the water industry is significantly different from the food retailing and manufacturing sectors, which can arguably be treated as one sector due to their similarities. This difference applies to both financial performance and to environmental performance. The evidence from the analysis also supports a conclusion that there is a positive correlation between performance along the two dimensions of financial and environmental performance, with good performance along one dimension reflecting also in good performance along the other dimension. The implications of this must therefore be considered.

Part of the semiology of corporate reporting has been to create a dialectic between performance as considered internally to the organisation, and represented through its financial performance, and performance as considered externally to the organisation, and represented through its environmental performance. Implicit within this dialectic is that the two dimensions of performance are different and consequently that good performance along one dimension can only be achieved through the sacrifice of performance along the other dimension. The corporate reports themselves do not however report upon how such performance has been sacrificed, nor along which dimension. Indeed the reports themselves do not actually make clear whether any performance has been sacrificed at all but merely content themselves with creating a binary opposition between the two aspects of performance and an implicit assumption within the semiotic that some sacrifice is necessary due to the incompatibility of the two dimensions of performance.

If any performance along either dimension has actually been sacrificed then it is naturally in the interests of the authors of the script to obscure where this performance has been sacrificed. This is necessary in order to be able to represent performance as good along both dimensions by attempting to speak separately to different groups of the audience in different parts of the reporting script. It is therefore essential to seek to arrive at an evaluation of just how much value is sacrificed and along which dimension. This can be achieved through an empirical investigation of actual performance as reported in the corporate reports of the companies under consideration.

If this dialectic exists then it is implicit within the dialectic that those companies which have performed well in financial terms will have performed less well in environmental terms, and vice versa. What would not be expected from this dialectic is that companies should have performed well along both dimensions and that the best performing companies have performed better along both dimensions than the less well performing companies. This result is implicitly to be expected from the semiotic created in the corporate reporting script.

Due to the small samples in the three industry sectors under analysis,[3] it must be accepted that statistical analysis which leads to clear and robust results cannot be expected. It is for this reason that the general results only are incorporated into the central arguments as providing corroborating evidence rather than determining the course of the argument.

An analysis of financial performance has been undertaken using total shareholder returns as the measure for comparison. The findings from this are that there is a significant difference between the performance of the water sector and the other two sectors but not between individual companies in each sector. Equally an analysis of social and environmental performance has been undertaken for these companies using a constructed measure of environmental performance as the measure for comparison. Again the findings from this are that there is a significant difference between the performance of the water sector and the other two sectors but not between individual companies in each sector. In this analysis however it remains unclear, due to the need to construct a measure of environmental performance, whether this difference relates to the performance itself or merely the way in which this performance is reported. Indeed, one of the problems of environmental performance measurement is that it is unclear as to what actually comprises good performance. It is possible that good performance is merely a reflection of a skilled creation of the semiotic by the authors of the script.

In this chapter the financial performance and the environmental performance of all the companies are compared. The finding from this analysis is that there is a positive correlation between financial performance and environmental performance. Thus the companies which perform well along one dimension of performance also perform well along the other dimension, and the dialectic considered is a false one, as has been argued. If this is indeed the case then this raises a question about why the managers of the companies, as authors of the script, are so concerned with the creation of a dialectical opposition between the two dimensions of performance. If performance in the two dimensions is correlated then this creation of an opposition in the corporate performance would seem to be unnecessary as there is no need to explain why performance along one dimension has been sacrificed for performance along the other dimension.

One possible explanation of these actions on the part of managers is that they are actually unaware of the correlation between the two dimensions of performance and actually believe in the incompatibility of good performance along the two dimensions.[4] A further explanation is that managers are actually aware of this positive correlation between the two dimensions of performance but choose to represent the dialectic as existing for some other reason. Either of these two possibilities provides a sufficient explanation for the existence of this dialectic but it is not easy to determine which of the two represents the true explanation, or indeed if a different reason represents the true explanation.

Implications of the Findings

The implications of the analysis undertaken in terms of these hypotheses can be considered as a multi-stakeholder perspective upon the organisations. The acceptance of a stakeholder approach to organisations[5] and the existence of multiple perspectives upon the objectives of an organisation inevitably imply a rejection of a monistic view of organisations. Thus there can be no one single view of the objectives of the organisation and consequently no one single evaluation of the performance of that organisation. It is therefore inevitable within this paradigm that if monism is rejected as a view of organisations then this implies that the economic rationality view of organisations and their behaviour must also be rejected.[6] This rejection is based upon a reconsideration of classical liberal economics.

Classical liberal philosophy places an emphasis upon rationality and reason, with society being an artificial creation resulting from an aggregation of individual self interest, and with organisations being an inevitable result of such aggregations for business purposes. Thus Locke (1690, 1975) viewed societies as existing in order to protect innate natural private rights while Bentham (1789, 1982) and J S Mill (1863, 1962) emphasised the pursuit of human need. Of paramount importance to all was the freedom of the individual to pursue his[7] own ends, with a tacit assumption that maximising individual benefits would lead to the maximisation of organisational benefits and also societal benefits. In other words societal benefits can be determined by a simple summation of all individual benefits. Classical liberal economic theory extended this view of society to the treatment of organisations as entities in their own right with the freedom to pursue their own ends. Such theory requires little restriction of organisational activity because of the assumption that the market, when completely free from regulation, will act as a mediating mechanism which will ensure that, by and large, the interests of all stakeholders of the organisation will be attended to by the need to meet these free market requirements. This view however resulted in a dilemma in reconciling collective needs with individual freedom. De Tocqueville (1840, 1998) reconciled these aims by suggesting that government institutions, as regulating agencies, were both inevitable and necessary in order to allow freedom to individuals and to protect those freedoms.[8]

Thus classical liberal arguments recognise a limitation in the freedom of an organisation to follow its own ends without any form of regulation. Similarly Fukuyama (1992) argued that liberalism is not in itself sufficient for continuity and that traditional organisations have a tendency to atomise in the pursuance of the ends of the individuals who have aggregated for the purpose for which the organisation was formed to fulfil. He argued that liberal economic principles provide no support for the traditional concept of an organisation as a community of common interest which is only sustainable if individuals within that community give up some of their rights to the community as an entity and accept a certain degree of intolerance. On the other hand Fukuyama considered the triumph of liberal democracy as the final state of history, citing evidence of the break up of the eastern block as symbolising the triumph of classical liberalism.[9]

Although this classical liberal / economic rationality view of organisations can be viewed as one paradigm representing the structure and behaviour of organisations, with consequent implications for the evaluating and reporting of performance within such an organisation, it is by no means the only such paradigm. Indeed it is one which is specifically rejected within the analysis of this chapter. An alternative paradigm, predicated in the stakeholder view of organisations and the dynamic disequilibrium existing within organisations, and brought about by the conflicting needs of the various stakeholders, is a pluralistic paradigm.[10] Such a paradigm views organisations not as entities acting for a particular purpose but rather as a coalition of various interest groups acting in concert, through the resolution or subsumption of their convergent interests, for a particular purpose at a particular point in time. This purpose changes over time as the power of the various stakeholders changes and as various stakeholders join, and influence, the dominant coalition while other stakeholders leave that coalition.

Criticisms of the classical liberalism paradigm are essentially criticisms of modernity itself, while criticisms of the economic rationality necessitate a rejection of the view of an organisation as an entity which exists to serve the ends of its owners. In many respects the rejection of the two paradigms is inevitable when a multiple dimensional view of an organisation is adopted. This is recognised by Mouffe (1993) who argued that any study of organisations needs to include the political aspects of the operating of that organisation and to recognise the tensions inherent within the political processes caused by the antagonism within the power relationships of the various stakeholders, each vying to have their own agendas met. Equally Gray (1995) argued that the liberalism paradigm is self-defeating in its legitimation through rationality and that a pluralistic paradigm provides a better understanding of the operations of organisations within society at large. Such a pluralistic view of society has been adopted within this analysis as the foundation for the interpretation of organisational behaviour within the context of the various perspectives[11] of that organisation. Thus inevitably the measurement and evaluation of the performance of an organisation needs to be pluralistic also because the different perspectives on organisational performance lead to the different purposes for which that performance is evaluated and the different time frames within which that evaluation takes place.

A further paradigm which is prevalent at present as a means of providing an interpretation of society at large and the functioning of the individual constituents of that society is founded in postmodernist theory. This theory provides a different interpretation of the functioning of organisations, of their constituent parts (i.e. the various stakeholders) and of their relationship to each other and to society at large. Indeed postmodernism not only provides a different means of interpretation but also provides a different framework, in terms of the identification of the society in which an organisation is operating, upon which that interpretation is predicated. Such an alternative interpretation can have significant consequences for an organisation in terms of its operational structures and consequently in terms of its systems for measuring and evaluating performance. Such differing interpretations will also inevitably lead to different mechanisms for reporting that performance and to different structures to the reporting systems adopted.

The Implications of Postmodernity

In order to consider the nature of the changed interpretation of organisational performance, and the consequent reporting of that performance, under a postmodern analysis it is first necessary to consider the nature of postmodernity itself.[12] A multitude of aspects exist to postmodernism[13] but in this chapter it is the collapse of the metanarrative, as applied to organisations, which is considered in detail. This collapse of the metanarrative[14] calls into question the existence of the organisation, as discrete from its environment, and questions therefore the maintenance of the organisational boundary. Furthermore it calls into question the definitions of internal and external aspects of the organisation, its operations, and its reporting. The reinstatement of this organisational discreteness through the reinstatement of its boundary, is essential to managers in order to maintain both the internal v external dialectic and thereby to maintain their primacy. It is for this reason that this aspect of postmodernism has been selected as the focus of this chapter.[15]

The collapse of the metanarrative, and consequent weakening of the macroculture of society is accompanied by the rise of an increasingly robust set of subcultures. These subcultures are operating both at a local level geographically and at a local level in terms of common interest and identity even when geographically disparate. One conclusion to be drawn from this is that, rather than universal politics, the dominance of local or regional politics becomes paramount. Thus the dominance of community as the agent of local need, as manifest by the place of people within that community and operating at a local level as an integral part of each community, assumes priority as the expression of societal organisation. This applies to organisations, as micro-societies, just as it does to society at large. Consequently organisational and societal structures are needed which recognise this change.

A postmodernist stance therefore leads to a redefinition of locality and divorces it from geographical proximity. Indeed Harvey (1990) argues that one of the significant features of the postmodern era is the compression of space and time, brought about through developments in the technological and informational architecture of society. This compression of space and time has the effect of removing territorial boundaries from an organisation, and this has the effect of providing an opportunity for the redefinition of the concept of organisation in terms of organising local societal structures for the provision of local goods and services. The implication of this is that organisational structures need no longer be dictated solely by the need for transaction cost minimising models of service provision, and the ability to define afresh organisations for the provision of individual goods and services becomes possible.

This redefinition of organisations contains within itself one of the inherent contradictions of a postmodernist view of the world, namely the contradiction between the borderlessness of any organisation within the communities within which it is seen to be operating and the extreme nationalistic inclusion / exclusion criterion adopted for any performance evaluation and reporting systems. This criterion has the effect of polarising organisations away from a national focus in their operating and reporting structures, as the nation state collapses in significance, and to expand the concept to inclusion in an expanded state for some purposes while at the same time shrinking the concept of locality of operations to a local level for other purposes (Radhakrishnan 1994). Thus postmodernity suggests that different spaces are needed for different histories and purposes and that a dominant model of society has no rational meaning. When considering the question of organisations and the identity of the constituents of such an organisation therefore, and their relationship with the macroculture and with societal structure, this suggests that the local structure has dominant importance to the individual and that his / her sense of community is defined circumstantially. Thus an individual considers him / herself to be a stakeholder to an organisation as a community for a particular purpose, and a stakeholder of different organisational communities for different purposes, with this identity being defined in terms of commonality of interest for specific purposes rather than being an overriding part of a definition of self.

This redefinition of the relationship between self, as an organisational stakeholder for a particular purpose, and community is in perfect accord with the concept of liberal democratic pluralism which requires a separation of social spheres in order to maximise individual welfare (du Gay 1994). The pluralistic view of liberal democracy is not however extant in the economic rationality paradigm of societal and organisational functioning, which is predicated entirely within a monistic view of society.[16]

A postmodernist view of organisations and their behaviour is that they are sustained by the rules governing their existence and by the resource appropriation mechanisms which apply to them rather than by any real need from the people who they purport to serve. Thus the legitimation of their very existence is not founded upon this redefinition of organisational identity and community need. Rather this redefinition of community suggests that a very different type of organisational structure is needed, and indeed exists, in order to cater for the needs of the individual constituents of that organisation who aggregate for one common purpose while atomising (or aggregating with different individuals) for others.[17] This view of organisation structure can be extended to also exclude a territorial basis for existence (Nohria & Berkeley 1994) whereby the organisation, through the use of informational and communicational technology, need be little more than a virtual organisation existing in a virtual environment as the need arises. Thus the continuing existence, either temporally or geographically, of any organisation, as a unit of service provision, has no meaning in its own right, as the organisation has no purpose other than the provision of the functions mandated to it by the stakeholder community,[18] in its widest definition, which it serves.

Such an instrumental view of organisations and their constituent parts would be radically different from existing paradigms and interpretations but this would be fully consistent with any postmodernist definition, based within the concept of the revised stakeholder community. It would also be fully consistent with a classical liberal concept of societal structure and civilisation, provided that this is based upon pluralism rather than monism.[19] Such a view of historical development is also in accordance with scientific rationality as well as with postmodernity insofar as it is matched by Popper's (1945) concept of the poverty of historicism.[20]

Postmodern analysis of society and its organs is therefore fully coincidental with these views. Indeed Baudrillard (1988) claims that there is a need to break with all forms of enlightened conceptual critiques and that truth in the postmodern era is obsolete, while Fish (1985) claims that truth and belief are synonymous for all practical purposes. In terms of any measurement and evaluation of organisational performance this would suggest therefore that the meaning of any reported performance becomes whatever it is interpreted to mean. This interpretation will of course depend upon the perspective of the person performing that interpretation, and the purpose for which that interpretation is undertaken. This naturally places a heavy emphasis upon the interpretative ability of the receiver of the reported information as well as presupposing that this receiver understands the language of the reporting system sufficiently well to be able to extract meaning from this information. Thus the semiotic of organisational reporting becomes central to the understanding of that performance from the perspective of the reader of the reporting script, when acting as an individual. It is clear therefore that, in seeking to interpret organisational performance from the multiple perspectives previously identified, there is a need to consider an organisation's performance reporting structure from a postmodernist standpoint separately from that of the prevailing dominant hegemony. In order to do so this requires a reconsideration of the purpose of an organisation within the context of this redefinition of community identity from a stakeholder perspective.

The Implications for Organisational Performance

The acceptance of such a postmodernist paradigm of organisational structure and functioning will therefore lead to a radically different interpretation of the key determinants of organisational performance as well as a different significance being attached to these determinants for the purpose of the evaluation of performance. Such interpretations do not however coexist easily with the dominant paradigms – ie monism and pluralism – previously considered. Rather than accepting postmodernism as a fresh paradigm however it is possible to use postmodernism simply as a means of questioning the dominant discourse and providing fresh insights into the interpretations from this discourse. This possibility is itself accepted from within the discourse of postmodernity and indeed Derrida (1978) claims that this is inevitable as it is only possible to criticise the existing institutions of any paradigm from within the interpretative domain of that paradigm. Thus it is necessary to accept the discourse of one of the dominant paradigms in order to provide a postmodernist interpretation of the events within that paradigm. This therefore is the approach taken within the analysis in this chapter, whereby the pluralistic paradigm of organisational and societal constituency is accepted as the framework for the analysis but the events within this paradigm, so far as organisational performance measurement, evaluation and reporting are concerned, are interpreted both from within the discourse of this pluralistic paradigm and also from within the discourse of postmodernity. This dual evaluation provides greater insights than would be possible solely from evaluation from within one single discourse.

As far as organisational performance is concerned it is argued that, at the present time, organisations are faced with the prospect of their environment becoming increasingly susceptible to temporal pressures, brought about by the compression of space and time.[21] Thus many business organisations have found themselves having to adjust many of their operational features in order to cope, and in many cases just to survive. The crisis that this new age, often labelled as the postmodern age, has brought about seems to have become an accepted part of life. This is manifest in particular in the fact that business organisations accept that they have to adapt, to become more organic and flexible. It is generally considered that the speed of change will continue to increase in the future, and that what will be required of organisations, is the ability to create flexible structures in order to operate effectively. Thus while the success of organisations, and in particular business organisations, is measured through performance indicators, usually of the accounting variety,[22] it is argued that such performance indicators largely ignore several crucial factors for the successful performance of organisations in a postmodern environment. These factors include issues such as communications, flexibility, and most crucially time. It is these types of issues that performance measures need to address if business organisations are to succeed in this type of environment. Thus the representation of an organisation through its conventional performance reporting fails to adequately depict the organisation in such an environment. It follows therefore that the role of accounting must necessarily change from one dominated by the needs of reporting performance externally to one focused upon the internal measurement of performance.[23]

The argument of Derrida (1978) provides both the motivation and the means to integrate the measures of performance necessary to the successful operating of an organisation in this postmodern environment with the requirements of the organisation as a whole, as manifest in the need for traditional accounting reporting of performance. Thus rather than seeking to develop two independent reporting structures – postmodern measures at an operational level and traditional measures at an organisational level – it is desirable to integrate these two reporting structures into one to meet all needs. This can be achieved through the extended use of local measures to become manifest in the organisational reporting mechanism, thereby recognising that the continued existence of the organisational boundary, deemed irrelevant to any postmodernist analysis, is a crucial feature of any modernist interpretation of the organisational environment.

Probably one of the few constants in the business related literature today is the issue of change, and how it is manifest and effecting business organisations generally. The effects this has on traditional approaches to performance is well documented (see for example Howell & Soucy 1988, Kidd 1994, Wisner & Fawcett 1991). Another observable phenomenon is how this subject spans the management disciplines; from personnel to finance, from operations to marketing, all cannot fail to be touched in some way by this issue of change. The clearest indication of this change phenomenon, and of the importance of time, can be found in the imperatives that many customers are placing upon business organisations. Whereas 20 years ago the emphasis might have been on cost, and 10 years ago on quality, today the emphasis has swung decidedly toward time based issues. Stalk and Hout (1990) provide a temporal analysis of strategy through these concepts arriving at a contemporary supposition that time is now paramount as the competitive factor in business.

More significantly for the purposes of this analysis the collapse of the organisational boundary and the displacement of temporality as a continuum would suggest that the measurement of performance from a traditional accounting perspective and the measurement of performance from a societal and environmental perspective are not incompatible. Moreover it would also imply that these two modes of performance measurement are not seeking to measure different aspects of performance and that the reporting of such performance is not seeking to address two different parts of the audience to the organisations reporting script. Nevertheless in the semiotic of corporate reporting these two aspects of performance are distinctly separated and the reporting script seeks to set the two in binary opposition to each other in terms of a separation of the audience in the internal (i.e. shareholders and investors) and the external (i.e. society and environmentally concerned stakeholders).

Conclusions: the Outward Looking Corollary

A further proposition was developed in chapter 4, which was a corollary of the first proposition. This second proposition stated that:

> Corporate reports are intended to be outward looking and forward looking documents designed to meet the needs of a wide range of stakeholders of the organisation.

This second proposition must be viewed as a corollary of the first, stemming from the fact that environmental accounting is designed to meet the needs of this wide range of stakeholders. This in turn led to the development of three further hypotheses.

Confirmation of these hypotheses will provide evidence in support of the propositions stated above and hence evidence in support of the position of this research regarding the changed nature of corporate reporting. These hypotheses in turn can be tested through a qualitative analysis looking at the semiology of corporate reporting and this is the subject matter of the next chapter.

Notes

[1] The problems with the reliability of the statistical analysis is fully recognised. The purpose of this analysis is to add weight to the argument throughout the book that the financial and environmental dimensions of performance are not incompatible. If this is so then the dialectic thereby becomes a false dialectic.

[2] That is to say the directors' report and chairman's report part of the annual report.

[3] Although recognising that each sample actually comprises the whole population for the sector according to the criteria identified in chapter 4.

[4] This is a possibility as many of the arguments concerning managing on behalf of shareholders, considered previously, imply that this is indeed the case.

[5] See Freeman (1984), Carnaghan et al (1996) etc as previously considered for details of this discourse.

[6] Economic rationality presupposes that organisations, and the people within those organisations, behave in a rational manner in terms of maximising utility, and the underlying assumption of such rationality is that the organisation is attempting to maximise utility for its owners, or shareholders. It is assumed also that there exists a single (or at most two) utility maximising course of action. Under economic rationality this utility is presumed to be synonymous with wealth, perhaps because such wealth can be quantified in accounting terms and thereby become subject to mathematical analysis. It is also assumed unquestioningly in the discourse of economic rationality that what benefits the shareholders of a business will also benefit the other stakeholders to the organisation as well as society at large. Thus the monistic viewpoint of economic rationality is based upon a stance within the discourse of modernity and accepts the philosophy of classical liberal economics. Indeed this view also accepts the tenets of classical liberalism in general.

[7] The use of the term his here is deliberate as these writers were only concerned with a certain section of society, who were of course all male.

[8] See Barnett & Crowther (1998) for a more detailed consideration and critique of classical liberalism.

[9] Fukuyama presents these arguments as the end of history, which he does not celebrate. In actual fact it is his critique of classical liberalism which is the most significant contribution of his work. This aspect of his work is almost universally ignored in favour of his end of history argument.

[10] Pluralism was of course one of the strands of classical liberalism which was written out of the discourse of liberalism during the late nineteenth century.

[11] These perspectives are considered in detail in chapter 3.

[12] Postmodernism has a relatively long history and draws upon a variety of strands (Anderson 1998). It has been defined in a number of different manners: for example as being epochal (Collins 1989), in replacing modernity as the current time frame; or epistemological (Newton 1996), in its relativity to other interpretations of social structures; or as a negation of modernity itself (Featherstone 1988). The concept of postmodernity was first mentioned by Olson in 1951 (Anderson 1998) who defined it as post-industrial and post-West. The term was brought more into public awareness by Lyotard (1984) who questioned the use of modernist metanarratives which legitimate society as existing for the good of its members with the consequent presumption that the whole unites the parts as an expression of the common good. Thus the metanarrative of economic rationality legitimates both the existence of organisations and the liberal approach, which assumes that the free market provides a mediating mechanism which ensures that the freedom of organisations to pursue their own ends will inevitably become synonymous with that freedom leading to optimal benefit for both the owners of that organisation and for the other stakeholders to that organisation. Jameson (1991,1998) on the other hand viewed the postmodern as epochally late capitalist, marking a break with previous social forms.

[13] Indeed not only is the meaning of postmodernism debated but the very existence of the term is itself subject to dispute. In this book it is not intended to enter this debate but merely to use some of the arguments to shed more light on the corporate performance reporting dialectic.

[14] It is the contribution of Lyotard (1984) concerning the collapse of the unifying metanarrative which if of concern here. His argument concerning the unifying force of this metanarrative within society has been extended here to a consideration of organisations on the basis that they are micro-societies with the same arguments applying.

[15] The analysis starts with a consideration of society and narrows to a consideration of organisations as micro-societies.

[16] This definition of the relationship is however in perfect accordance with the concept of communitarianism (Fox & Miller 1995) which regards the self as atomistic and aiming to maximise value (in the liberal sense of welfare) to the lonely self through acting in a community for any specific purpose.

[17] Such a structure of organisations has been defined by Heckscher (1994) as a post-bureaucratic structure, with its rationale for continuing existence not being through self-referential normalising mechanisms but rather through the maintenance of an interactive dialogue, based upon consensus, with the

individual members of the stakeholder community which the organisation exists to serve.

[18] See Barnett & Crowther 1998 for a consideration of this purpose in the public sector.

[19] In this respect it is worth recognising that this view of societal progress is not a new concept from postmodernist theory but that Kidd (1902: 8) argued that the controlling centre of evolutionary progress is in the future when stating "It is the meaning, not the relation of the present to the past, but of the relation of the present to the future, to which all other meanings are subordinate." Furthermore a similar view was expressed by Giddens (1991: 144), writing from a stance firmly grounded in modernity, when he stated "One thing control means is the subordination of nature to human purposes, organised via the colonisation of the future. This process looks at first sight like an extension of 'instrumental reason': the application of humanly organised principles of science and technology to the mastery of the natural world. Looked at more closely, however, what we see is the emergence of *an internally referential system of knowledge and power.*"

[20] By which he argues that present trends do not necessarily continue into the future and that any amount of empirical evidence and economic or sociological analysis does not change this lack of predictive power of past data.

[21] See Harvey 1990 considered previously.

[22] Though in recent times these forms of measurement have been criticised and charged with irrelevance, largely due to their limitations.

[23] This is necessitated by the collapse of the organisational boundary as a determinant of organisational activity as the organisation both expands globally, to include both the whole operational value chain and the whole stakeholder community, and shrinks locally, to a focus upon individual operations in its environment.

Chapter 8

The Future Focus of Reporting: Evidence from Semiotic Analysis

The Outward Looking Corporate Report

An empirical analysis of organisational performance in terms of financial and environmental performance has been undertaken in chapters 5 – 7, in statistical and semiotic terms. The results of this analysis demonstrate the irrelevance of the separation of the financial and environmental aspects of performance. In this chapter further analysis of corporate reporting is undertaken which helps explain the polarising of performance into traditional, organisational accounting-based performance and societal, external performance. Thus a consideration of the role of accounting information in organisational decision-making provides a basis for a further consideration of the semiotic inherent in corporate reporting undertaken in this chapter. This is achieved through a consideration of further binarisms extant with the corporate reporting script. This is explored through a consideration of further binarisms to explore further inherent contradictions in the corporate reporting script.

Synchronicity – diachronicity

Binary oppositions exist in every text in a synchronic manner (Kim 1996). A consequence of this is that the binary opposite of diachronicity also exists as the counterpart of synchronicity. Synchronicity refers to the timelessness of the text and provides a way for examination of recurring themes within the text. Thus in the context of the 6 years of this study, the corporate reports produced, rather than being considered as individual texts for each company, can be considered to be a single text for each company which transcends the linearly temporal nature of corporate reporting. Thus some companies seek to depict this timelessness in their reporting through the use of a common format for the reports. For example Unilever divide their annual report into two books, entitled Annual Review and Annual Accounts for each year and the format in terms of size, layout and headings remains the same from one year to another. Similarly the look of the corporate report can be used to depict this timelessness within a single text. Thus Cadbury Schweppes use a common brown colour for all covers to their reports and common font within the reports, while Wessex Water make use of a plain white cover for their reports and show the same logo and title on each. In such manner the companies concerned seek to signal the temporal independence of the text and the presentation of an image of the company as a contiguous atemporal whole.

Diachronicity, on the other hand, refers to the constituent elements of the text which unfold temporally as time progresses. Thus the actual accounts contained in the annual reports are essentially diachronic as the results of the business are reported year by year. Equally the report by the chairman tends to be diachronic as the activities of the company, and the effects of these activities upon reported results, are considered in succession from one year to another. Diachronicity in the context of corporate reporting tends to be based upon a reference to past activities which is compared with the present and implying the future of the organisation, almost always in the context of an implied progression of events which is depicted as an improvement. Thus the present is always presented as an improvement upon the past while the future is suggested to be an improvement upon the present.

This is indicated in the following examples, all taken from the introductory chairman's message:

> Tate & Lyle continued to expand on a global basis in 1994. It was another good year for the company. Profit before tax increased 23%....Your board has recommended a final dividend of...11%.....The current year has started well and further steady growth is expected despite difficult trading conditions in the North American sugar market. The long term outlook remains positive.
> (Tate & Lyle Annual Report 1994)

> 1995 was a difficult year as the business underwent a significant change....sales from continuing business rose by 8.3%...The board is recommending a 5% increase in the final dividend...We continue to invest in the development of our information systems technology and we expect significant benefits from this, although they will not be felt until 1997. 1996 is a year when we return to managing the success of our core business. The

combination of our strong asset base, leading label brands and the first benefits from the delivery expansion gives us confidence in the future of the company.
(Nurdin & Peacock plc Report & Accounts 1995)

The principal management challenges for the year were four-fold: to increase operating efficiency in Severn Trent Water; to increase profitability in the non-regulated businesses; to deal with the problems associated with the drought; and to undertake an extensive review of the group's strategy. These challenges were successfully met and group profit before tax increased (by)....15.7%.... In November 1994, Severn Trent was the first water and sewerage company to introduce a programme of benefit sharing for customers and shareholders....The board looks to the future with confidence as the work and investment continues to increase the robustness of the company's resources and systems and its efficiency....The board remains committed to acting in the best interests of its customers and shareholders. It will continue to make additional investment to improve services and share the benefits of efficiencies.
(Severn Trent plc Annual report and accounts 1996)

Other companies seek to show this improvement not just through such statements but also through a redesign of the presentation of their annual reports. Thus, for example, Northern Foods changed the format of their report from landscape to portrait in 1996 while Kwik Save Group made the same change in 1993. Similarly United Utilities demonstrated the change from its previous incarnation as North West Water by a total redesign of the shape, look and layout of its report in 1996.

In all cases therefore the companies demonstrate both synchronicity and diachronicity in their annual reporting. Both are important to all companies but the relative importance of each pole of this binary opposition will vary from one company to another and will vary for the same company at different times. Thus there is both a spatial and a temporal dimension to this binary pair.

All binary opposition seeks to polarise the text in terms of the two opposite poles but this normally is undertaken in the context of portraying one pole as good and the other as bad. As Laclan (1990: 33) states:

Derrida has shown how an identity's constitution is always based on excluding something and establishing a violent hierarchy between the two resultant poles...

An essential part of semiotic analysis therefore is in this depiction of the poles as desirable and undesirable. An inevitable tension therefore exists when both poles are important and mediation within the text is attempted through other means when both poles are needed to appear good. This aspect of the dichotomous nature of corporate reporting will be considered further in terms of other binary oppositions.

Internal consumption – external consumption

Accounting information is naturally used by the organisation for the internal purposes of planning, control and decision making as well as for financial reporting. Thus accounting has long been acknowledged to exist at two levels as far as an organisation is concerned, and these two levels can be broadly categorised as management accounting and financial accounting. Management accounting is essentially for internal consumption and is concerned with the internal operations of the business, with the planning and control of these operations, and with making decisions regarding the allocation of resources within the organisation. The information sources of management accounting permeate the organisation and managers throughout the organisation are concerned with the use of management accounting information.[1] Management accounting is essentially forward looking in its concerns and can be taken to provide a representation of the organisation through representations of its individual components, without any need for a meta-representation of the organisation as a whole.

Financial accounting on the other hand is essentially for external consumption. It is concerned with reporting the activities of the organisation to the external world through the production of profitability statements and of annual accounts and balance sheets which are incorporated into the corporate reports, and also with the acquisition of resources from this external world in the form of borrowings and share capital.[2] It is essentially backward looking through its emphasis upon reporting the past activities of the organisation, and is concerned with the organisation as a whole rather than the individual constituent processes within the organisation.[3] As far as this binary opposition is concerned the external consumption pole has assumed dominance with the internal consumption pole being relegated to a secondary position.[4]

Thus, although the annual reports of organisations are available to the internal stakeholders of the organisation, the structure of such reports is such that the information is of almost no value in affecting operational practices. Such reports contain only statutory accounting information, which has been compiled at aggregate level from the activities of the organisation. Those activities of the organisation which are mentioned in the annual report are mentioned individually only insofar as a reference to them can be made within the context of the general image which the organisational authors of the script wish to portray for external consumption. Examples of such reference to the needs of accounting information for internal consumption include:

> Kwik Save has made itself one of the lowest cost operators in the food retailing industry and we intend to maintain and strengthen this position. New Generation Kwik Save is designed to improve our cost ratios. For example:
> - a more effective flow of information along the supply chain will save money on everything from waste and shrinkage to warehousing
> - more effective management of our product range will improve sales and profits
> - motivated staff committed to the success of New Generation Kwik Save will mean better staff retention and improved efficiency.
>
> (Kwik Save Annual Report & Accounts 1995/96)

It is interesting to note at this point that in 1996 Kwik Save has styled itself as *New Generation Kwik Save* in its report in order to promote the desired image of a break with the past. Responding to the poor performance of the last two years the Chairman states:

> We will not allow the setback to the Group's financial performance over the past two years to continue and we recognise that Kwik Save needs to adapt more quickly to the changing demands and rising expectations of our customers.

He continues later:

> We now have a clear vision of the way forward: New Generation Kwik Save – still committed to providing unbeatable value, but even more responsive to customers' service expectations and their desire for innovative products.

This message of the new future ahead is reinforced throughout the report with such quotes as:

> New Generation Kwik Save represents the way forward to a rewarding future.

This is presumably on the basis that such repetition will enhance the credibility of the message. This message is highlighted through printing in red type and large font throughout the script.

Other examples of such reference to the needs of accounting information for internal consumption include:

> It needs to be emphasised that, of the total water and sewerage capital expenditure to date of about £760 million, 30% has came from retained profit and 70% has been secured through the original shareholders' investment, external borrowings and other sources.
> We are continuing to forge ahead with the capital programme of improvements – at a level of about £200 million for the year. During the year we completed 88 major projects with more than 350 in planned progress at the end of the year. Over two thirds of the schemes in our £900 million 'Clean Sweep' coastal sewage treatment programme are now complete or under construction, and we have executed more than one third of all the planned schemes in the ten year capital programme.
> (South West Water plc Annual Report and Accounts 1994)

> If we are to become truly customer focused we will have to reduce our costs so that we can minimise price increases while maintaining a value added services. The service our customers receive must not only be the best but also be seen to be the best. We aim to make Anglian Water a benchmark company against which others will be judged.
> The rationale of the strategic systems review is therefore to focus ourselves on out customers, streamline decision making by reducing bureaucracy, and reduce costs by removing duplication and unnecessary activities in order to encourage an approach that is flexible and responsive to changing demands...
> The process will involve a substantial change in company culture as well as in its structure...
> There have to be job losses over the next two to three years but we will endeavour to achieve this on a voluntary basis.
> (Anglian Water Annual Report 1994)

This is set within the context of a report which gives a map as pictorial image of the size of the organisation as well as pictures giving images regarding the need for quality and the need for efficiency.

These non-linguistic devices are of course for external consumption rather than internal consumption and are designed to portray the company in a way which supports the linguistic part of the text. All the facts presented are of course available internally for consumption by the internal members of the organisation as and when desired. Thus for external consumption purposes the image created is of the organisation as a whole rather than any processes which are taking place within the organisation. These individual processes within the organisation are part of the information for internal consumption and have hence been relegated to secondary importance within the semiotic of organisational reporting. The overriding need for external consumption is a concentration upon the global, aspatial polarity of organisational existence through a representation of that organisation as a unified whole.[5]

When results are good however the semiotic can be created differently, although again always for external consumption. Thus the Chairman of GKN is able to report a 60% increase in profit before tax but to state:

> Of perhaps greater importance than the financial results were the strategic achievements of 1995. These have gone a long way towards repositioning the Group with three core activities and a number of other businesses rather smaller in scale but all capable of delivering good financial performance.
> (GKN plc report & Accounts 1995)

A postmodernist view of the organisation however concentrates upon the increased importance of localisation, in the form of the individual processes taking place within the organisation, and globalisation in the form of the market as a whole. It is the relationship of the different processes to each other, and to external components of the value chain, which is significant from the point of view of value creation by the organisation. This value chain, when mentioned in the annual report,[6] is merely implied in total for the organisation as a whole. Taking this localising view of the organisation however means that these internal relationships between processes, both internal and external to the organisation, are what determine organisational existence and success or failure. The organisation as a whole ceases to matter from the point of view of organisational success and the need to aggregate these performances of individual processes into an organisational metanarrative becomes an irrelevance. The organisation becomes merely a boundary mechanism artificially constructed around and between the activities of the organisation but in reality largely irrelevant to the performance of the organisation and its processes. Thus this boundary mechanism achieves a separation of the organisation from its environment and signals the included as distinct from the excluded as far as the sphere of organisational activity is concerned.[7]

The argument of Derrida (1978) concerning the requirement for interpretation from within the domain of the dominant language (Lakoff 1975) of the organisation however provides the means to integrate the measures of performance necessary to the successful operating of an organisation in this postmodern environment. In this environment the requirements of the organisation as a whole are manifest in the need for traditional accounting reporting of performance. This requirement is determined by the management of the organisation, as authors of the script, who need the organisation to be represented as a whole, and the external environment excluded from any consideration of organisational activity and performance. Thus rather than seeking to develop two independent reporting structures – postmodern measures at an operational level and traditional measures at an organisational level – it is desirable for the authors of the script to focus entirely upon traditional measures and traditional reporting for consumption by all stakeholders, even though a different performance measurement and reporting structure will very likely exist within the organisation. This internal to the organisation structure of reporting has merits from the point of view of managing operational performance but more importantly has the additional merit of invisibility in the corporate reporting script. Thus this approach has been taken within the domain of accounting information through the superordination, and consequent concentration upon, the use of accounting information for external consumption purposes.[8] Such reintegration does not however appear manifest in corporate reporting; instead the needs of external consumption remains paramount and internal consumption of performance measures has been relegated to internal compilation and usage. As a consequence management accounting and performance measurement, either through accounting or through other means, within the organisation remains divorced from the semiotic of external reporting. Thus the managers of an organisation are in a position to shape the semiotic of corporate performance in the way they find most desirous.[9]

The Re-creation of the Organisational Boundary

The use of financial indicators as measures of managerial performance means that the deterministic nature of accounting is central to the decision making process by which decisions will be made. Accounting has the capability to either expand or contract the decisional possibilities available to managers. Clegg and Fitter (1981) have argued however that the existence of managerial choices made within the context of environmental uncertainty leads to problems in implementing those decisions. There is inevitably therefore a tendency for managers to desire choices to be limited in order to reduce uncertainty and this desire matches the way information is structured and amalgamated in its presentation. The desire of the management team is in accordance therefore with the tendency of organisational behaviour in this respect, and this adds to the institutionalisation of the rituals of organisational religious behaviour within the organisation. This argument is in accordance with the statement of Ridgway (1956) that the use of quantitative measures of performance leads to dysfunctional behaviour within the organisation, with particular respect to decision making.[10]

A postmodernist view of the organisation however concentrates upon the increased importance of localisation, in the form of the individual processes taking place within the organisation, and globalisation, in the form of the market as a whole. It is the relationship of the different processes to each other and to external components of the value chain which is significant from the point of view of value creation by the organisation. Moreover such a postmodernist view of organisations also focuses upon a removal of both spatiality and temporality from the discourse of organisational performance. This is because these dimensions become irrelevant and the distinction between the included and the excluded, the visible and the invisible, and between the past, present and future become irrelevant. The organisation as a whole ceases to matter and becomes merely a boundary mechanism artificially constructed around and between the activities of the organisation but in reality largely irrelevant to the performance of the organisation and its processes.

The realities of organisational performance imply that, in a postmodern environment, if the organisational boundary is irrelevant, or even deleterious, to organisation performance, then so too are the managing team of that organisation. Therefore financial reporting for the external environment must be made to appear the most important function of accounting information with other purposes made subservient to this need. This is necessary in order to demonstrate the need for the continuing existence of the dominant coalition of senior managers. Thus the myth of their essential contribution to the success of the organisation (as indicated by the expensive product of that success, the corporate report) is made into reality (Barthes 1973). Accounting information therefore becomes a defensive instrument, not for the organisation, but for the senior management of the centre. It is used as a means to retain power, through using that accounting to symbolise the necessity of their continued existence, with the whole control and use of accounting information and systems being directed towards this end.

An essential dichotomy therefore exists through the use of accounting information to portray organisational existence. This reflects

one of the contradictions of the postmodern world which organisations attempt to address through their use of accounting. From an internal perspective the use of accounting within the organisation is attempting to remove the locality dimension from organisational depiction and focus upon the temporal dimension; this is achieved through the institutionalisation of the organisation's religious rituals. At the same time, from an external perspective, the use of accounting by the organisation is attempting to remove the temporal dimension of organisational existence and focus upon locality through the use of accounting information as a myth creation mechanism. The resolution of the dichotomy between the two perspectives implies the necessity of two different accounting images of the organisation, one for internal consumption and one for external consumption.[11] Problems arise however when the two seemingly discrete audiences (internal and external users of such accounting information) are able to read each others scripts and interpret them in the light of their own needs. It is perhaps fortunate therefore that only one of these scripts - the externally addressed script - is available to both audiences. In order to maintain power at the centre of the organisation it is essential that knowledge is controlled from the centre by the dominant coalition. Thus accounting information is used both to police the organisational boundary and to depict the organisation as important and immutable through the dominance of external reporting.

Legitimating Institutional Decisions

It has been stated by Birnbeg, Turopolec and Young (1983) that one of the consequences of accounting is to reduce uncertainty in the management of a business.[12] Indeed it has been demonstrated (Sridhar 1994) that the information received by senior managers is distorted by their subordinates, because of their concern for their own reputations.[13] Similarly Bhaskar and McNamee (1983) have argued that proxy measures are used as a means of quantifying performance against the planned course of action, again implying the simplification of data for decision making into a necessarily incomplete data set.

Against the argument that decisions are made based upon incomplete and simplified information is the argument that decisions are made by managers based upon their feel for the situation, and that accounting data is then used to justify the decisions already made (Brunsson 1993). In this guise accounting acts as a decision legitimation mechanism rather than a technology for decision evaluation, and in this context the use of simplified, aggregated information is either unimportant or preferable. Thus Hopper, Storey and Willmott (1987) have postulated that both accounting and decision-making are social constructs,[14] thereby implying that meaning is in the interpretation placed upon the data and the decisions made therefrom. Indeed Hopwood (1974) has stated that accounting data is subject to different interpretations according to the needs of the receiver of the data. Accounting therefore can be seen to have a legitimation role for decisions being made but it is also deterministic in nature and subject to the interpretation of the users of the information. One of the causes of tensions within an organisation is due to this deterministic nature of accounting data which leads to the existence of competing interpretations for the data (Hopwood 1983); indeed Drucker (1985) states that one of the main uses of accounting information is defensive.[15] Thus the structure and systems of an organisation can determine the effectiveness of the use of accounting data (Spicer & Ballew 1983). This can have the effect of limiting the opportunities available for the organisation, and hence the level of decision-making required by the management team, through the way in which the information is analysed, presented and interpreted.

The deterministic nature of accounting can be explained by Belkaoui's (1978) argument that accounting is not just the language of business but is actually a language in its own right, satisfying the grammatical and lexical characteristics of a language. The acceptance of accounting as a language explains some of the interpretative difficulties with accounting data, which are common problems for any language, particularly as dialects develop. These difficulties can also be explained by the way in which accounting is used in practice. Briers and Hirst (1990) state that information can be used in a variety of ways, and, in assessing the use made of accounting information, two main ways are suggested for the manner in which it is used by senior managers: defining the dominant coalition and institutionalising decisions.

The first of these uses is based upon the argument that accounting is a language and therefore that knowledge of the language and acceptance of the precepts upon which it is based can be used to give or withhold power within the organisation.[16] Decisions are made in an organisation by those with the information necessary to make the decisions (or at least by those who perceive themselves to be in possession of that information) and the power necessary to enforce that decision. Thus Finkelstein (1992) argues that strategic choice in an organisation is dependent upon the power of the top management team. Accounting information provides a mechanism for giving power to that team, or enabling the team to take power, as it provides a source of expert and referent power. This power is

however not just obtained from access to the data but also partly from understanding the framework within which the data is being interpreted. Thus the acceptance of the managerial frame of reference for decision-making is a crucial sign of the acceptance of a person within the dominant coalition of managers, with the power to make decisions. Accounting data can therefore be used as a means of signalling inclusion or exclusion of parties to that decision.

The existence of the dominant coalition within an organisation is dependant upon the power of that coalition and the use of, and interpretation of, information is one source of power. Thus Horkheimer and Adorno (1944) argue that a social hierarchy is dependant ultimately upon force. Just as this power is used to institutionalise dissident voices within the organisation so too is accounting information used as a means of institutionalising the decisions made by the dominant coalition. Thus Scapens (1994) argues that accounting, as used in practice, provides the members of an organisation with an institutional basis for making decisions within an organisational setting. Institutionalism can be described as a pattern of behaviour which is regularly used and drawn upon by the members of a community (in this case the organisation) as a means of determining, or at least informing, current behaviour. Hamilton (1932: 84) states that these patterns:

> imply a way of thought or action of some prevalence and permanence, which is embedded in the habits of a group or the customs of a people.... Institutions fix the confines of and impose forms upon the activities of human beings.

Institutionalised thought and action is embodied in the routines and rituals of an organisation: the accounting reports produced within an organisation, and the way in which they are used in decision making and the evaluation of performance, provide examples of this type of ritual. Such rituals shape organisational behaviour but also provide legitimation to the decisions made based upon these rituals.[17] The rituals can be formal routine behaviour such as the budgeting procedure but also informal behavioural patterns based upon norms for behaviour developed over time.[18] A key feature of this institutional perspective of the use of accounting information and managerial decision-making is based upon this following of precedents - the past influencing current and future behaviour. This is one way in which the uncertainty surrounding decision-making can be eliminated (or at least controlled).

The rituals of organisational behaviour need, however, to be separated into two distinct behavioural components: rote behaviour and rites. Both behavioural components of ritual are based upon past referential behaviour for legitimation, but whereas rote behaviour represents routinised actions which continue to be performed because they have always been performed,[19] regardless of meaning, rites serve a purpose in the organisation through providing symbols of the continual existence of the organisation and its movement from one stage of its existence to another.[20] Thus the rites surrounding the production of the annual budget and the annual financial report can be likened to the rites surrounding the passage of the biannual equinoxes undertaken within pagan religions (Frazer 1947) - routinised behaviour fulfilling a symbolic purpose and at the same time maintaining the social cohesiveness of the organisation through the joint participation of the members of the organisation in these rituals.[21] One of the purposes of such ritual behaviour is to remove locality from the discourse of organisational activity and to focus attention upon the temporal dimension. Thus organisational existence is legitimated in this manner as a temporal sequence proceeding from one rite of organisational existence to the next in a smooth flow of routinised ritual activity. The use of accounting information in such a ritual way serves the purpose of an organisational religion and, when used in this way, is essentially inward looking for internal consumption.

Such rituals form an essential part of the culture of an organisation and become an unquestioned part of the religion of the organisation. As Sister Teresa (1963: 23) states:

> Every society nourishes itself through rituals and ceremonies, which are all the more powerful when they are not articulated. These rituals recreate our past and speak to us about our future.

It has, however, also been argued from a Jungian perspective (Mitroff 1983) that the organisational coalitions which have evolved, together with individual behaviour patterns, produce a tendency towards institutionalised behaviour. This is because these organisational routines and rituals provide a validation of the present through its connection to the past. Thus the institutional and Jungian perspectives coincide in their interpretation of an individual's drive to interpret and legitimate the present through reference to the past. In both perspectives the symbolic functions associated with the actions provide a validating purpose for those involved, and in this context accounting routines fulfil a quasi-religious purpose within the organisation for the members of that organisation.

Accounting and Decision Ownership

Decisions are made within an organisation either by individuals or by groups of individuals acting in concert, such as the management team of the organisation. Once made however, these decisions inevitably become the property of the organisation and enter the public domain within the organisation. Ownership of the decisions made therefore needs to move from the person, or group, making the decision into organisational ownership. Indeed to be effectively implemented such decisions need to be owned by the people responsible for putting them into effect. Marcus and Pfeffer (1983) have identified that the existence of goal congruence between the dominant culture and the accounting information system is a crucial component in the implementation of decisions. It can therefore be seen that accounting information has a key role to play not just in determining who is able to make decisions but also in how those decisions can be implemented within the organisation.

Decisions, once made by the dominant coalition, need to be communicated throughout the organisation in order for ownership of these decisions to transfer from the dominant coalition to the organisation as a whole. If this communication makes use of the rituals embedded within the organisational culture then the legitimacy of the decision is increased and its acceptance into organisational ownership is facilitated. This point is made by Yates and Orlikowski (1992: 301) who argue that the means of communicating decisions within an organisation themselves become part of the social ritual of that organisation. They state:

> Adopting a concept from rhetoric and using the premises of structuration, we have interpreted organisational communication, not as the result of isolated rational actions, but as part of an embedded social process that over time produces, reproduces and modifies particular genres of communication.

Similarly Swales and Rogers (1995) consider that the language used in business affairs is important as it provides a framing context for the communication of decisions in terms of the history and culture of that organisation. The language used by the dominant coalition therefore becomes part of the institutional behaviour of the organisation but also gives power to the coalition as they set the agenda of communication. Indeed Hanna and Wilson (1984: 21) argue that language is inextricably entwined in power relationships, stating:

> Communication is almost always an attempt to control change, either by
> causing it or preventing it.

It has been argued that accounting information places power in the hands of the dominant coalition. It is also argued however that although this enables the decision agenda to be set by them, they are in fact constrained by this data and by the institutional rituals which determine which decisions can be made and how they are implemented.[22] Williamson (1970) states that the divorce of ownership and management hinders decision-making and leads to inefficiencies in the decisional process. An alternative explanation is that the decisions made are grounded in the needs and desires of the dominant coalition rather than in the needs of the business as far as the owners are concerned. Monks and Minow (1991) illustrate the way in which the power in the decision-making domain is divorced from accountability for the implementation of those decisions, and how this is deleterious to corporate performance. This too can be interpreted as an illustration of the effects of the ownership of decision-making being in the hands of the dominant coalition rather than of all the stakeholders of the organisation.

It has been argued (Dermer 1988) that organisations consist of a sustained set of beliefs and behaviours and that the existence of organisational rules, beliefs and rituals limit the extent of the control which it is possible for managers to exert in the organisation.[23] Thus the control of the decision making domain, as exercised by the dominant coalition of the management team, is constrained by the institutional nature of the organisation and the need to transfer ownership of decisions from the decision makers to the organisation as a whole for the implementation of those decisions. In this context Covalenski and Dirsmith (1986) state that organisational politics play a key role in the construction of reality as far as members of the organisation are concerned. Thus although the decision agenda is set by the decision makers, this agenda is in reality constrained by the nature of organisational behaviour. Thus, rather than having a free choice as to decisions to be made, the management team actually have a limited choice of decisions. These decisions are limited by the following:

- the available information and the way in which it is presented and interpreted, and accounting information is crucial in this respect;
- the organisational rules and rituals which determine the way decisions are put into effect;
- the need to transfer decision ownership into the public domain within the organisation.

The accounting information therefore, which is a key component of organisational decision making, provides a mechanism for putting power in the hands of the management team. At the same time however this accounting information, due to the institutional nature of organisational behaviour, also limits the choices of decisions available to these managers and shapes the way in which these decisions are made and implemented. Accounting in use therefore can be seen to be deterministic in nature rather than neutral, because of its use as a filter for original data. Thus the decisions made need to be considered in the context of managerial behaviour as far as decision-making is concerned.

Rationality and Decision Competence

The concept of rationality in managerial decision-making has been modified in organisational theory to recognise a limit to that rationality (Simon 1964), as bounded rationality. This is due to the excessive amounts of data which managers need to take into account as a part of the evaluation process prior to decision-making.[24] Mumby and Putnam (1992: 471) argue that bounded rationality does not necessarily aid decision making and that emotionality also has a part to play in the decision-making process, thereby introducing the concept of bounded emotionality as an explanation of decision making behaviour. They argue that, just as the volume of data available limits the extent of rationality managers are able to utilise, so too the organisational context of individual behaviour involves emotion in the decision making process which must also necessarily be limited in extent. They state:

> ... the components of bounded rationality (satisficing, expert knowledge, fragmented decision making and hierarchical goals) do not always facilitate decision making that serves the best interests of various groups (workers, community members and publics).

The concept of bounded rationality implies satisficing behaviour in managerial decision-making and has been used as an explanation for decision-making which does not optimise business performance. Alternative explanations however exist for the making of such decisions, and one such explanation is in the use of heuristic methods. Thus Hedberg and Jonsson (1978) argue that firms have fixed repertoires of behaviour which have been built up based on past experience. One way of reducing uncertainty in the decision-making process is to base decisions upon past experience, heuristics and the rituals of organisational behaviour. These are

grounded in the culture of the organisation and, as well as reducing uncertainty, also have the effect of providing a legitimacy to the decisions made. This legitimation provides a rationale for the making of decisions which do not necessarily optimise performance, and it can be seen that the way in which the data upon which decisions are made is structured and presented also promotes a tendency towards a heuristic basis for decision-making.

The decisions made by the management team need also to be considered however in terms of the domain of decision competence which exists within the dominant coalition. Possessing the power to make decisions, and ultimate accountability for the effect of those decisions, does not necessarily imply the competence to make those decisions. Indeed when the decisions required involve radical change to the organisation, its operations or its market focus, then it may well be that the competence to make such decisions lies outside the domain of competence of anyone in the organisation. In such circumstances it may well be considered inevitable that risk reduction through reverting to institutionalised behaviour and self-confirmatory groupthink behaviour provides a means for the acceptance of accountability for decisions made outside the domain of decision competence. In such circumstances satisficing behaviour becomes understandable and may well be regarded as inevitable.

The question of rationality in decision-making however needs to be considered not just from the viewpoint of optimising organisational performance but also from the viewpoint of the managers themselves. Given the dichotomy between the optimisation of short term performance and the optimisation of long term sustainable organisational development, and the possible incompatibility of the two, it is often unclear as to which decisions will in fact optimise performance for the organisation.[25] Indeed it can be argued that it is not possible to optimise performance in all dimensions of concern to the organisation and for all timescales, and that optimising performance for one purpose will inevitably cause sub-optimality in performance in another arena. Thus optimising financial performance can be argued to be at the expense of environmental performance, and vice versa.[26] In such a scenario the question of a single rationality in decision-making cannot exist and it becomes necessary for managers to exercise choice according to other criteria. In this context therefore it is necessary to recognise that managers are not merely functionaries of the organisation, existing merely to satisfy organisational needs, but that they are also individuals who have personal needs and their personal agendas to satisfy. It is argued therefore that in a situation in which the decisions needed to maximise organisational benefit are not

possible to make, or at least are not readily apparent, the importance of personal agendas as a mechanism for resolving the dilemma become significant.

A significant feature of the personal agenda for every one of the management team is his / her career progression and reward structure for personal and organisational performance. Increasingly the rewards for managers, and even the continuation of their services, are dependant upon the performance of the business[27] as identified according to key performance indicators. Such indicators tend to be financial in nature[28] and using such indicators is synonymous with the evaluation of short term performance only. This is increasingly the case as institutional investors form an ever increasing proportion of investors, and their performance is itself judged on short term measures.[29] In the context of uncertainty in the decision making process therefore the satisfying of personal agendas will create a tendency for managers to maximise short term performance, or at least to opt for short term rather than long term decision horizons.[30] Their focus will also be upon safety in decision making, not merely by legitimating decisions within the institutional framework, but also in opting for the most certain outcome from the decisional alternatives. They will therefore exhibit a tendency towards risk minimisation in their decision-making. Furthermore it is possible to argue that such tendencies are not just understandable but actually demonstrate rationality in decision-making within the domain of decision alternatives available to managers.

The use of financial indicators as measures of managerial performance means that the deterministic nature of accounting is central to the decision-making process by which decisions will be made. Accounting has the capability to either expand or contract the decisional possibilities available to managers,[31] and there is inevitably a tendency for managers to actually desire choices to be limited in order to reduce uncertainty; this desire matches the way information is structured and amalgamated in its presentation. Thus the desire of the management team is in accordance therefore with the tendency of organisational behaviour in this respect, and this adds to the institutionalisation of the rituals of organisational behaviour within the organisation.

As far as the reporting of organisational performance is concerned however this desire becomes manifest in a different temporality. Rather than defining the temporal dimension in terms of the short term future and the long term future, these two are subsumed into one future. This future is then contrasted with the past through the construction of a past – future polarity within the semiotic of corporate reporting. This subsumption, and consequent changed polarisation, both occludes the conflict between decision optimisation in the short term versus decision optimisation in the long term and at the same time eliminates any thought of managerial self interest from the mind of the reader. This is part of the synedoche of corporate reporting and managerial behaviour (Miller 1992) – the indistinguishability of the parts from the whole. Thus the authors of the script in this manner attempt to change the interpretation of the reader to one which focuses upon the need to achieve better performance in the future than in the past, and to one in which this can be expected to be achieved through the experienced leadership of the dominant managerial coalition within the organisation. Thereby they disguise the purpose of the reporting script through a semiotic of reinstating managers as the agents of shareholders (and possibly other stakeholders) rather than as independent actors on the semiotic stage. This must be considered through an exploration of this polarity in the corporate reporting semiology.

Past – Future

Accounting information, as produced to satisfy statutory requirements, and hence as manifest in corporate reports, provides merely a snapshot view of an organisation at a particular point in time and thereby a review of its activities over a past period. The locus of such accounting is therefore firmly entrenched in the past of the organisation. The corporate report however is designed to provide not merely a picture of the past of the organisation but more importantly a view of the present and future of that organisation. In this respect the report upon the past of the organisation provides merely a basis for painting a picture of the future of that organisation. This future must of course be painted in terms which suggest that the future will be more glorious than the past and the focus of the report is upon achieving this end. Thus the past pole of this pair of binary opposites must be portrayed as relatively bad in order to make the future pole seem good.

　　　　This can be illustrated through the following comments regarding the future:

> In the past year we have improved the competitive position of Sainsbury's supermarkets, strengthened its rate of expansion and reinforced top management structure. These changes will take time to translate fully into improved performance. Further innovation and development of our offer is under way and we are moving decisively forward.
> (J Sainsbury plc Annual Review 1996)

[NB profits declined by 5% while sales increased by 11.9% during this period]

> In 1994/95, we have met the challenges placed before us and finished the year with a creditable set of results. We have also seen a reasonable start to the new year with profits for the first two months in line with our budget and ahead of last year. With our investment in people and plant, our recent acquisitions and our strong portfolio of well – focused businesses, we look forward to further progress in the years ahead.
> (Unigate plc Report and Accounts 1995)

[NB turnover declined by 4.4% and operating profits by 3.1% during this period]

> Your Board's strategy to create a high quality asset base in value added, high growth areas, has largely been achieved. Unfortunately, we have failed to deliver acceptable financial returns from our quality and growth successes....
> We are confident, however, that we can maintain our impressive sales growth through our strong innovation. We expect to restore margins during the second half of the year.
> (Hazlewood Foods plc Annual Report 1994)

[Profits declined by 9.3% while turnover increased by 4.9%]

> Since I became Chairman on 23 April 1996, I have initiated a review of our corporate strategy. This is taking place against the following five aims: earning the trust of customers through quality, reliability and fair price of our services; being innovative in identifying customer needs and devising business solutions; making full use of the talents of our people; contributing to the protection of the environment; delivering value to shareholders through the effectiveness of our operations and financial structures.
> The vital services which the group provides to its domestic and commercial customers are all subject to major change. We will respond positively to these changes and, at the same time, deliver value to our shareholders, who are the ultimate providers of the capital needed to finance and support our development.
> (Yorkshire Water plc Annual Report and Accounts 1996)

[In this case the Chairman seems to wish to imply that his appointment alone is sufficient to take the company into the better tomorrow implied. It is interesting to note that one of the innovative business solutions devised to meet customer needs was the erection of standpipes in the streets of Bradford.]

A temporal study of such statements for one company illustrates this image creation even more fully. The following are extracted from the annual reports of United Biscuits:

> As we face the challenges of the 1990s, we will continue to operate with strategic and financial discipline and a determination to maximise shareholder value. We will ensure that we have the skills, creativity, flexibility and management strength to achieve and sustain excellent performance. (1992)

[turnover up 5% but operating profit down 14%]

> The UB of today has a well focused strategy, a number of market – leading positions, exceptional brands and an outstanding management team across all parts of the business. With these strengths, despite the probable continuation of challenging trading conditions, I am confident of future success. (1993)

[turnover up 10% and operating profit up 5%]

> I would like to take this opportunity to reiterate my belief in the prospects for UB. The business is strong, with an impressive brand portfolio and with a balance of leading positions in developed markets and an expanding presence in emerging markets. In addition, we have a talented and highly committed team and a clear strategy which has been consistently applied. I am confident that this combination will deliver good returns to shareholders in the years ahead. (1994)

[turnover static but operating profit down 3%]

> The targets we have set for improvement are challenging – as they must be for us to resume profit growth and cash generation as soon as possible. Throughout the group there is a mood of realism and absolute determination. We appreciate the patience that shareholders have shown and, in answer to the questions I asked at the beginning of this statement (can United Biscuits turn the tide and deliver the value that shareholders require?), shareholders can expect to see improvement in UB's performance in 1996 and beyond. (1995)

[turnover static but operating profit down 27%]

Thus it is possible to see from this company that the promises of a better future can continue to be made year by year without regard to the fact that the same promise made in the previous year has not been met and the improvements forecasted have not materialised. A focus upon the future as the dominant pole of this pair of binary opposites is needed to enable this to happen and this focus both obviates the need to deliver promised performance, as the outlook is always forward, and seeks to negate any possible criticism for past failures. Action has always been taken by the management team (who are always committed and capable) which will deliver benefits in the future. One way to create the desired symbolic image of the better future however is by means of repetition in a temporal series (Deleuze 1994) and so the repetition of the message helps create the desired image of improvement in the future without any need to actualise that improvement through achievement. Mere repetition of the message year by year is sufficient to create the image desired amongst the readers of the diachronically unfolding script. As the locus of attention is always forward then the past failures no longer matter – only the promise of the improved future matters. As Hollier (1995) observes, the act of repetition creates a break in discourse and thereby removes temporality from the act of continuous improvement; mere repetition suffices instead to create the image.

By 1995 however, even for the authors of the United Biscuits script, these promises must have seemed a little dubious as the authors of the script felt the need to reinforce the message of a better future. In this year therefore the first page of the report was given over entirely to the delivery of this message of a better future, the salient point of which was captured in the subheadings:

> 1995 was a very poor year – especially for shareholders. But 1995 was the turning point.

The authors of the report however still felt able to promise a better future for the organisation. Presumably they felt that this would still be credible to the readers of the script, or at least the shareholder part of the readership, who they seemed to assume would share a common view with the authors of the future. As Paris (1975: 12) states:

> Education and habit stimulate our desire to match reality with our concepts.

The authors of the script can therefore be said either to have matched reality with their concepts in order to believe this promise for the future, or they merely believed that this would apply to the readership, and therefore engaged in a reinforcement of the promises made while demonstrating the fraternity between the authors and the readers of the script through the use of common language (Derrida 1997). In either event the evidence seems to suggest that making such a promise is sufficient without any need to keep that promise and be accountable for its keeping or breaking.

The aim of the creation of this binary opposition therefore is to reinforce the idea of the dialectic between financial performance and environmental performance. Moreover it is argued that the pressures for corporate reporting are moderated by the behaviour of managers in the organisation.

The Segregation of the Corporate Reporting Script

It has already been argued that a part of the creation of the dialectic between an internal focus upon performance and an external focus, which is inherent in the corporate reporting script, is brought about by the segregation of the audience. This is necessary in order that different messages can be conveyed to different parts of the audience. The empirical evidence however suggests that the dialectic in actual performance is not real. It has also been argued, from a stakeholder perspective, that the audience itself cannot readily be segregated into different discrete sections, each with different needs.[32] All that remains therefore within the dialectic is a separation in the reporting of organisational performance. Thus, through the semiotic of corporate reporting, the authors of the script seek to create and maintain the dialectic by means of their attempt to address different audiences in different parts of the reporting script. This leads to a consideration of the ritual and myth creating roles of corporate reporting.

Myth – Ritual

The myth creation role of corporate reporting has been referred to several times in the preceding analysis. This myth creation role has several aspects but one aspect is the creation of the myth of the unified whole. As Nietsche (1956: 156) states, 'Only a horizon ringed about by myth can unify a culture.'

One of the purposes of the corporate report therefore is the creation of the myth of the unified culture of the actors on the semiotic stage – in other word the common cultural bond of identity between the authors of the script and the audience.[33] This is achieved by the creation of a symbolic order which is an autonomous order of reality independent of the things symbolised (Jenkins 1979). The myth itself is a symbolic form (Brandist

1997) which assumes a life of its own. As Cassirer (1955: 5-6) states the specificity of myth lies not in its content but rather in:

> the intensity with which it is experienced, with which it is believed – as only something endowed with objective reality can be believed.

Thus myth has the power to present a single viewpoint as directly expressive of the existence of the organisation, which consequently exists in the form presented in the annual report. The corporate report as myth therefore provides an authoritative discourse about the organisation, and as Bakhtin (1981: 342) states:

> The authoritative word demands that we acknowledge it, that we make it our own; it binds us, quite independent of any power it might have to persuade us internally; we encounter it with its authority already fused into it. The authoritative word is located in the distanced zone, organically connected with a past that is felt to be hierarchically higher.

Thus the corporate report replaces the organisation itself as the real through this power assumed from its myth creation role and the organisation becomes in the minds of both the readers and the authors (through the reflective quality of the readership) that which is presented through the corporate reporting mechanism. The concept of the corporate report can therefore be considered to have attained a life of its own through the resurrection of the myth of its origin and authenticity.[34]

In addition to the myth creation role of corporate reporting for the individual organisation, Campbell (1949) argues that all myths have an underlying commonality which transcends the individual myth. Thus as far as corporate reporting is concerned the common elements can be seen in the common format of such reporting, the common style and the use of common language – natural, accounting and non-linguistic – to provide a unified myth concerning corporate reporting as the authoritative discourse of organisational existence and activity.[35] Thus the history of organisations unfolds through this corporate reporting (Campbell 1976) but unfolds in a manner which is common to all organisations and can therefore be depicted as universal and immutable. This unfolding of history can be seen from the development of corporate reports over time (McKinstry 1996) but the mythical role of such reports ensures that, although the image of the organisation changes with the development of corporate reports (Preston, Wright & Young 1997), the image of the organisation remains immutably fixed in the present.[36]

The creation of the myth of organisational existence is an essential step along the road to the creation of the religion which binds the organisation together (Malinowski 1962) and this religion becomes manifest in the rituals of organisational behaviour which will be explored as the other pole of this binarism. Malinowski (1962: 119) defines this in the following terms:

> What is then the fact of a myth? Briefly, that all the principal tenets of religious belief have a tendency to be spun out into concrete stories; in the second place, these stories are never merely accounts of what happened in the past. Every act of ritual, every artistic representation of religious subjects, in the worship of relics and sacred places in short, in all the visual signs of past sensational acts of grace every theme is revivified. The events of the mythological past play also a leading part in moral conduct and social organisation.

One further purpose of myth creation in this context is the reinforcement of organisation boundaries, and hence the restatement of organisational existence. It has already been argued that corporate reporting is essentially for external consumption and that the accounting of organisations, together with all other information systems of those organisations, is directed within the text to this end.[37] External reporting serves the function of providing a statement to the external world that the organisation exists as a discrete entity and the production of the annual report[38] actually is designed to fulfil this role. Moreover the design of the report is carefully considered to make a statement not just that the organisation exists but also to create an image of that organisation. Thus, over time, corporate reports have become more and more full of information, statements from the chairman and others, and pictures of organisational activities.[39] These corporate reports have therefore become more of a symbolic representation of the organisation designed to give to the (by implication) 'discerning' reader the impression that this is an organisation to be interested in, with a dynamic present and an even more interesting future. The legal purpose of reporting past performance thereby becomes less significant as the focus is upon the prospects for the future. These prospects are always suggested to be an improvement upon the present and this provides a means of signalling the importance of the organisation and of its existence.

Despite the assertions of Norris (1990), language creates reality which then becomes truth. Thus, as Barthes (1988) claims, meaning is not in the linguistic structure of a message but in the image created by the recipient of the message. Accounting by its nature creates an image of the organisation, the decision making within the organisation and the future of that organisation. This is achieved though the use of the language of accounting and the perceived certainty attached to that language. One of the purposes of such external reporting is to continually recreate the myth of organisational existence as certainty in the uncertain world. This certainty is of course a myth and one important function of accounting therefore is to act as a myth creation mechanism for the organisation as a statement of organisational existence as immutable.

One of the purposes of myth making is to remove temporality from the perception of the onlooker (Levi Strauss 1966), who in this case is an external consumer of the information supplied by the organisation. Removing temporality has the effect of conflating the past and present into the present and to make this present contiguous with the future. In doing so the uncertainty of images made through accounting, from one period to the next, is disguised within the omnipresent organisational myth based upon the eternal present. Rationality and predictability through using accounting information within the metanarrative myth of organisational immutability therefore seems reasonable within any discourse of organisational reporting. This removal of temporality has the concomitant effect of focusing upon spatiality. As far as spatiality is concerned the organisation seeks to create the myth of itself as omnipresent through the attention given to both the local and the global aspects of organisational existence. This is achieved through the use of appropriate text and image. For example Severn Trent produce a map showing the whole of the UK in their 1994/5 annual report which highlights their activities throughout England and Wales.

Severn Trent is by definition territorially bounded to the central part of the UK but produces a picture indicating its existence throughout the UK. Additionally it signals its global presence through text such as:

> In addition Severn Trent water international is working with the appropriate authorities to deliver water and waste services in Swaziland, Puerto Rico, Mauritius and India.

Similarly J Sainsbury, in its 1994 annual report produces a map which shows the location of its stores throughout the UK with a map of its North American stores inset. This company also focuses upon the local and states:

> The highlight of the year was the opening of our new store in Beckton in East London.

United Biscuits in its 1995 annual report highlights its global operations by citing its sales as totalling £2.4 billion with employee number as 27,800 and operating in 24 countries. This is supported by the following text:

> In 1995 we became the first UK multinational to convene a Europe – wide employee consultative council. We broke new ground in Eastern China, where we started construction of a new factory and extended distribution and sales. We invested in major factory upgrades in Poland and Australia.

Equally Unilever (annual report 1995) describes itself as ' The multi-local multinational' while Cadbury Schweppes (annual report 1993, 1994, 1995) produces pictures of its products in use by ethnically diverse individuals in obviously remote locations. Tate & Lyle (annual report 1994) devotes 4 pages of its 16 page Report on Operations to diagrams illustrating the global nature of its activities.

Thus the myth of organisational existence is created by this means and this existence is continually recreated as atemporal and omnipresent, but also extremely local. In this manner synchronicity and diachronicity are conflated and subsumed within the myth. Likewise the past is removed in favour of the eternal present and better future as the organisation signals its existence and importance through this mythical role of corporate reporting.

This myth of organisation importance is naturally of concern to the authors of the text. If the organisation is important then, by implication, those managing the organisation, ie the authors of the script, must also be important. The form of corporate reports is designed to create an image of the importance and permanence of the organisation, and hence of those managing that organisation. This therefore explains the increased dominance, not of accounting information, but of messages from members of the dominant coalition managing the organisation and particularly the chairman, managing director and increasingly other powerful members of the management team. This message is designed to indicate the need for the organisation to exist as a discrete entity, defined through the reinforcement of the organisational boundary and reinforced through the production of appropriately constructed corporate reports. At the same time such reports demonstrate just how necessary those members of the dominant coalition are to maintenance of the organisation and to its future. The language of the statements from these people tends therefore to be used as a device for corrupting thought (Orwell 1970) by being used as an instrument to prevent thought about the various alternative realities of the organisation's existence, in terms of the multiple representations of the organisation which are apparent through the use of the technology of accounting.

These realities imply that in a postmodern environment, if the organisational boundary is irrelevant, or even deleterious, to organisation performance, then so too are the managing team of that organisation. Therefore reporting to the external environment must be made to appear the most important function of accounting information, with other purposes made subservient to this need in order to demonstrate the need for the dominant coalition of senior managers. Thus the myth of the organisation is extended to the authors of the script and their essential contribution to the success of the organisation (as indicated by the expensive product of that success, the corporate report) is made into reality (Barthes 1973). Accounting information therefore becomes a defensive instrument, not for the organisation, but for the senior management of the centre, and a means to retain power through using accounting to symbolise the necessity of their continued existence, with the whole control and use of accounting information and systems being directed towards this end.

In binary opposition to myth as far as corporate reporting is concerned is ritual. For an individual, ritual is an essential part of personality integration – a process of becoming whole (Perls 1975). Rituals therefore are steps along the way to completion of the whole.[40] So too for organisations are rituals steps to be completed along the way to wholeness. In the case of the organisation however the integration needed is not that of parts of the organisation but that of the various people involved in the organisation into a unified whole, based upon the rituals of organisational religion. This religion, of necessity, becomes institutionalised into the organisation and its culture and forms part of the way in which the organisation conducts itself both internally and in relating to its external environment.[41] As Bocock (1974: 174) states:

> Ritual action can have two sorts of consequences for the society in which it takes place: either it can provide a process whereby people become more attached to the basic way of life and values of the society, or to the major sub-groups within it of which the participants in ritual are a part, or ritual can lead to people making new demands on the way of life in their society, and a desire to see change both in action and in the values the society pursues.

It is naturally not in the interests of the organisation to allow the ritual actions of the organisation to lead to demands for changes. It therefore becomes imperative that the ritual role of corporate activity becomes subsumed within the myth creation role and this can be achieved through the institutionalisation of such ritual activity within the organisational religion.

One of the purposes of such ritual behaviour is to remove spaciality from the discourse of organisational activity and to focus attention upon the temporal dimension. Thus organisational existence is legitimated in this manner as a temporal sequence proceeding from one rite of organisational existence to the next in a smooth flow of routinised ritual activity. The use of accounting information in such a ritual way serves the purpose of an organisational religion and, when used in this way, is essentially inward looking for internal consumption. The rituals, for maximal effectiveness also need to encompass external stakeholders and the corporate reporting ritual serves in this way.[42] This reporting ritual serves to both include these external stakeholders, as audience of the script, within the rituals of organisational religion.

Thus in the corporate reports the authors signal that the organisation is moving forwards to better times in the manner previously outlined. This is achieved through the language of the report which clearly sends the message that the authors of the report are the decision makers for the organisation. At the same time it signals that their knowledge enables them to make the best decisions on behalf of the other stakeholders. Thus, for example, the following statements are made:

> I am pleased to report another successful year for the Group, with our water and sewerage business making excellent progress and our other subsidiaries operating well.

and

> The benefits of the improvements we have delivered and planned for the future are now becoming apparent.
> (South West Water plc Annual Report and Accounts 1994)
>
> Our circumstances have demanded a changed approach and the first pages of this annual report outline the actions we have taken. The first signs are encouraging....
> I am grateful for the time, support and involvement they (the non-executive directors) have committed and I share their unequivocal backing for the management team and the new way forward.
> (United Biscuits Annual Report 1995)
>
> This has been a difficult year in many of our markets, but a year in which we have made considerable progress in repositioning the group. As we anticipated, the over-supply of fresh produce, which was a key influence on our performance last year, persisted throughout the financial year. Recession and increasing competition in our major markets also made trading difficult for our European food processing businesses. Whilst our

results reflect these problems, there has been a strong underlying improvement in the position of the group, based on our programme of strengthening management, reducing costs, acquiring complementary businesses and disposing of operations which do not fall within the areas covered by our long term strategic goals.
(The Albert Fisher Group plc Annual Report and Financial Statements 1993)

Conclusions

The arguments in this chapter explore the way in which the future of organisations has become more important, and this is manifest in an outward looking and forward looking focus of the annual report. The arguments from this and preceding chapters also suggest that segregation of the audience into discrete segments, with discrete interests in and perspectives on organisational performance, is not possible. Thus it is argued that the dialectic of organisational performance created through the corporate performance reporting discourse is itself unreal. Rather the dialectic must be seen to be a creation on the parts of the authors of the performance reporting script. Nevertheless it is clear that the authors of the corporate reporting script have sought to bolster the dialectic through a separation of the two parts of the script themselves. From the analysis undertaken so far this seems surprising as there appears to be no reason to undertake this activity to ensure the creation and maintenance of this dialectic. The next chapter therefore considers the implications of this analysis in terms of the hypotheses which have been explored.

Notes

[1] The primary focus of this information is at the level of processes within the organisation, and the relationship between these individual processes and departments. It is also concerned with interactions within the value chain of the organisation, and so with the relationships between the various processes within the organisation and their suppliers and customers. These suppliers and customers may be other processes or departments within the organisation but may also be entities external to the organisation.

[2] This is achieved by taking the accounting data from the organisation and structuring it to represent the activity of the organisation as a whole.

[3] The implicit view of the organisation, derived from using financial accounting, is that the organisation as a whole is greater than the sum of its parts and that the organisation, as represented through financial reporting, provides a metanarrative

of the organisation, of greater significance than the narratives obtained from the individual processes within the organisation. In a modernist interpretation of accounting therefore financial accounting is superordinate to management accounting through its ability to represent the significant features of organisational performance via its external reporting function. This actuality is supported by Johnson and Kaplan's (1987) claim that the purpose of management accounting has been lost in the need to provide external financial reporting of organisational activity.

[4] Indeed it is possible to argue that this pair of binary opposites is in fact treated as good – bad as far as the dominant coalition of managers determining the course of action of the organisation are concerned. This assumption of the dominance of external reporting, in the form of financial accounting, over internal reporting, in the form of management accounting, can be questioned from a postmodern perspective. So too can the assumption of the ability of accounting information to provide a meaningful metanarrative of the organisation, uniting the organisation through this metanarrative.

[5] The importance, for such depictions, of cultural signs in the corporate landscape cannot be underestimated (see Carter & Crowther (2000). Thus, for example, when Cadbury Schweppes announced that in future they were to be managed on the basis of shareholder value creation the mere insertion of this cultural sign into the corporate landscape was sufficient to effect a two-thirds increase in their share price. This was achieved without reference to any internal representations of the organisation and without any need to provide any backing to the cultural sign by implementing the management technique concerned.

[6] See for example Kwik Save Annual Report & Accounts 1995/96 considered above.

[7] In this respect the organisational boundary can be likened to that of a nation state and subject to equal questioning of its meaning in an era of increased local - global polarisation.

[8] Although see the earlier argument that in actual fact this accounting is of little relevance for external reporting purposes. Thus a violent hierarchy is established (Laclan 1990) with external reporting at the top, followed by financial reporting and accounting with the internal accounting needs relegated to the bottom.

[9] But see earlier comments regarding the role of the press in mediating this semiotic. Thus for example cautionary press reporting such as 'Iceland profits slide at half time' (*The Times* 3/9/97) and 'Unigate and Dairy Crest return to talks' (*The Times* 10/6/97) make use of accounting information in considering the effects of the actions of these companies upon shareholders. Thus the accounting information is translated into its effects upon share price and earnings per share.

[10] This view is reiterated by Scapens (1984) who argues, within the context of accounting information, that the arbitrary nature of cost allocations in accounting leads to short term decisions making and sub-optimality in organisational performance.

[11] This in itself can explain the existence of two different forms of accounting - management accounting for internal control of ritualised behaviour and financial accounting for external consumption and myth creation. Two such different uses of accounting as organisational depiction is perfectly in accord with the postmodern environment as the organisation is addressing two different audiences through these different image creation uses of accounting information.

[12] This is achieved through the way in which data is structured, filtered aggregated etc, and the conclusion to be drawn from this is that decision-making is based upon incomplete information.

[13] This can be explained in terms of attribution theory, whereby a person has a tendency to exaggerate favourable results and attribute them to his / her individual efforts and abilities but minimise unfavourable results and attribute them to external factors.

[14] See also Clegg, Higgins & Spybey (1990) who argue that the temporality of accounting is also a social construct.

[15] This is both for the individual manager in justifying his actions to his superiors and for the management team through a focus upon an exception reporting approach to explaining deviations from the planned activities of the organisation. He argues that this has the effect of constraining the opportunities available to the business and reducing the available decisions open to it.

[16] See Lakoff (1975) for an analysis of the way in which the language of the powerful is adopted by others as a mark of inclusion..

[17] See also Veblen (1899) for his consideration of conspicuous consumption and Carter & Crowther (2000) for their consideration of the way in which managers consume techniques as fashion. The essential point of both arguments is that it is the observation of consumption by others which gives legitimacy, thereby sanctifying the rituals undergone.

[18] Such informal rituals will tend to become part of the culture of the organisation.

[19] For example a monthly budgetary control meeting.

[20] These rites signal changes from one stage of development to the next.

[21] Similarly the regular performance reporting rituals can be likened to the regular meeting of a church congregation, providing an opportunity for the purging of sins (of omission and commission), a reinforcement of jointly held self-belief, and an opportunity for the priesthood (ie the dominant coalition of management) to reinforce the congratulatory message of continuous improvement.

[22] Thus Morgan (1988) has argued that accountants are not purveyors of universal and rationalist truth but in fact have a very one-sided view of the world, and construct and interpret data accordingly. Swanson (1978), on the other hand, states that accounting data is two faced and can not only be used to help organisational learning and planning but can also be used as a means of organisational self delusion. Thus it is relatively easy for the dominant coalition to become victims of groupthink (Janis 1972) and make decisions based upon their self-reinforcing ideas and interpretations of the information within the decision domain, which are not rational when evaluated using alternative criteria.

This possibility is particularly likely if the power of the dominant coalition is strong and the mechanisms for excluding others from the decision are particularly effective.

[23] Similarly Abernethy & Stoelwinder (1995) have found that formal administrative controls in organisations have needed to be replaced by less obtrusive forms of control due to the increasingly complex nature of the tasks which managers perform.

[24] Thus the concept of bounded rationality has been introduced into the description of managerial behaviour and Williamson (1975) considers the concept in the context of budgeting while Hogarth (1993) considers bounded rationality in accounting.

[25] The question of the identification of optimal performance has been considered in previous chapters. The conclusion to be drawn is that one single definition of optimal performance does not exist.

[26] But the analysis previously undertaken produces evidence to negate this argument.

[27] See for example the article 'Legal battle against ousted boss' (*The Observer* 8/3/99) which recounts the reasons why Brian Staples was ousted as chief executive of United Utilities and the subsequent argument (and legal battle) as to who was liable for the performance of the company.

[28] Such as return on capital employed or returns to investors.

[29] Not only are the fund managers themselves (as individuals) judged in this manner but increasingly also the funds themselves are so judged. See 'Unilever pension fund sues MAM for £100m damages' (*The Times* 8/10/99) which recounts the claim by Unilever because their pension fund performance was below benchmark during 1997.

[30] See also Coates *et al.* (1993) for a consideration of this tendency towards short term behaviour.

[31] Clegg & Fitter (1981) have argued however that the existence of managerial choices made within the context of environmental uncertainty leads to problems in implementing those decisions.

[32] This is inevitable as the same person is likely to have multiple interests in the performance of any organisation and hence multiple perspectives upon the measurement and reporting of that performance.

[33] See Crowther, Cooper & Carter (2001) for a consideration of the symbiotic relationship between the actors on the water company stage.

[34] It can therefore be considered to have attained hyperreality through becoming more real than reality (Baudrillard 1981).

[35] It is recognised of course that legislation and GAAP requires a considerable element of this commonality but it is argued that this is subsumed within the image creation requirements of corporate reporting.

[36] Levi Strauss (1955) contends that myth is different from language and so the techniques used to analyse myth must be different from those used to analyse language. This point is refuted however through the use of semiotic tools of

analysis, which it is argued are equally appropriate to this study when considering the language used in corporate reporting and the myth creation role of such reporting.

[37] Corporate reporting for external consumption can be considered as a myth creation mechanism for the redefinition and reinforcement of organisational boundaries which are in reality obsolete for performance determining purposes.

[38] It is recognised that this reporting is actually required by law for all public limited companies, but argued that this reason has been relegated in importance.

[39] That is to say the reports of large UK plcs rather that other companies (public or private) as considered earlier in this book. Equally the contrast can be made with foreign companies reporting in other environments. Thus for example the annual report and accounts of VEBA (German company aiming to satisfy the reporting requirements of the USA) contain large amounts of legally required information but nothing else – certainly no pictures and no colour.

[40] These can be considered to be the rites of passage (Beit-Hallahmi & Argyle 1997) which mark the way to that wholeness.

[41] This institutionalisation of religion becomes part of the culture of the organisation and socialises the individual who assimilates the cultural givens of the organisation (Dollimore 1984).

[42] The inclusion of the press in the reporting rituals of the organisation also serves to include the press into the religious activities of the organisation while at the same time seeking to use them as acolytes in the mediation and promotion of the corporate message.

Chapter 9

The Semiology of External Reporting: an Evaluation of the Evidence

Introduction

Throughout the preceding chapter the semiology of corporate reporting has been considered and it has been argued that, through this semiology, the authors of the corporate reporting script have created a dialectic between the internal perspective on corporate performance, as epitomised by traditional financial reporting of performance, and the external perspective on corporate reporting, as epitomised by social and environmental reporting. This has become manifest in such reports becoming more outward and forward looking as a means of maintaining this dialectic. In considering this semiology of corporate reporting it has been argued that the dialectic created through this reporting does not in reality exist but is merely a construct created by the authors of the reporting script. It therefore becomes necessary to consider the implications of this.

It has already been concluded that the financial and environmental dimensions of performance were perfectly compatible and thus that the first five hypotheses tested were incorrect. A second proposition was however developed as a corollary of this, stemming from the fact that environmental accounting is designed to meet the needs of this wide range of stakeholders. From this proposition a further three hypotheses were developed. Confirmation of these hypotheses will provide evidence in support of the propositions stated above and hence evidence in support of the position of this research regarding the changed nature of corporate reporting. Thus these hypotheses must be examined in detail.

Hypothesis 6

The analysis undertaken shows that the written reports[1] have greater prominence than the financial reports[2] in the corporate report. This is evidenced both by the scale of each part of the report and by its relative positioning, together with the colours and images used. Thus this hypothesis must be accepted.

Hypothesis 7

The analysis undertaken shows that the written reports consider future prospects to a greater extent than past performance. Past performance is mentioned only when it has been particularly good (to extract praise) or when it has been problematical (to show that corrective action has bee taken). The orientation of the report is firmly towards the future and this hypothesis must be accepted.

Hypothesis 8

The analysis undertaken shows that the reporting documents as a whole show evidence of being designed to meet the needs of a wide range of external stakeholders. This is evidenced both within the annual report and by the use of separate environmental reports. Moreover the recognition of the different needs, in terms of acceptable performance, of different stakeholders is recognised through an attempt to segregate the audience and direct attention towards different parts of the reporting script. Thus this hypothesis must also be accepted.

The acceptance of these hypotheses shows an acceptance of the second proposition, regarding the changed focus of corporate reporting. The implications of this must therefore be considered.

A Semiotic of External Reporting

Approaching this semiotic analysis through the mechanism of exploring the concept of binary opposition[3] has given insights into the semiology of such reporting. It can be seen that an attempt is made in the semiotic to show that one pole of each binarism can be relegated into insignificance even when it cannot be portrayed as bad. This is necessary in order to present the opposite pole as the important pole.[4] Depending upon the purpose of each particular part of the script it is necessary that an appropriate part of the script can be relegated into insignificance, even when this is in conflict with another part of the semiotic. Thus returning to the sets of binary opposites it can be seen that they can be represented as follows:

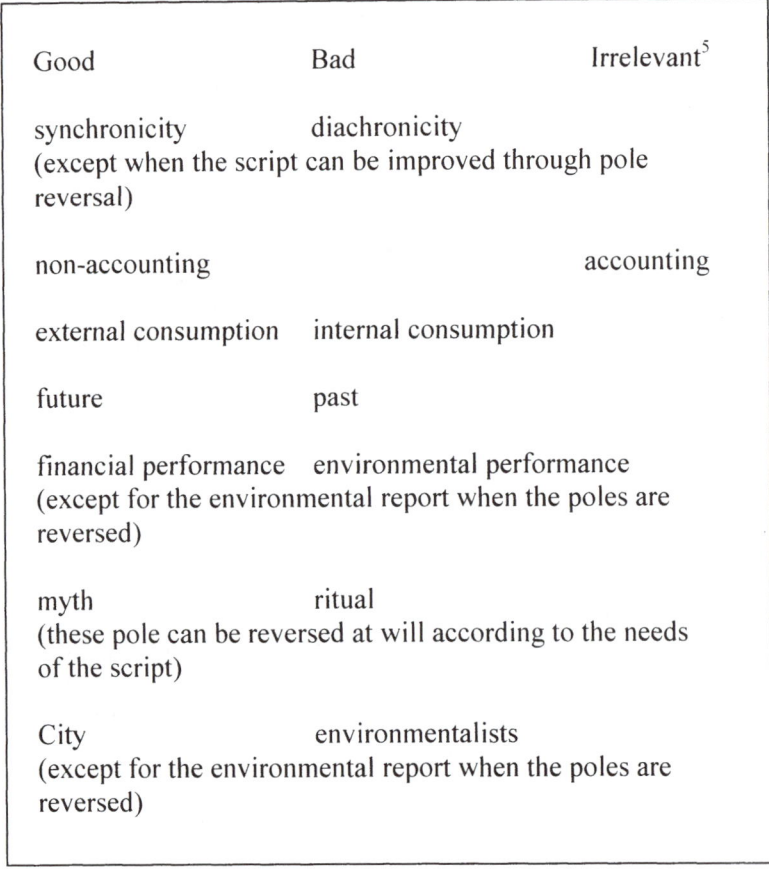

Good   Bad   Irrelevant[5]

synchronicity   diachronicity
(except when the script can be improved through pole reversal)

non-accounting   accounting

external consumption   internal consumption

future   past

financial performance   environmental performance
(except for the environmental report when the poles are reversed)

myth   ritual
(these pole can be reversed at will according to the needs of the script)

City   environmentalists
(except for the environmental report when the poles are reversed)

Fig 9.1 Polarised Binary Oppositions

Segregating the audience however means that these poles can be reversed and replaced according to the section of the audience being addressed. Moreover it enables that pole which are represented as indifferent[6] to become represented as either good or bad[7] as the needs of that part of the audience demand. Thus the accounting polarity can become important when the statutory return is required and the rest of the report becomes bad. Equally it can become good when the ritual pole of the myth – ritual binary opposition – is paramount as it can provide legitimation for shareholder rewards in the form of either increased or reduced dividends payable.

The understanding of the semiotic of corporate reporting in this manner is of importance as it allows the consideration of the relationship between the audience and the authors of the script to be explored. From the analysis undertaken it can be seen that there is in fact a dialogue going on between these parties who are all in fact actors on the semiotic stage, albeit performing different roles.[8] It is equally clear however that the authors of the script are also behaving as directors of the play taking place on the stage, and are seeking to control the way in which the other actors perform their parts. The other actors have essentially supporting roles. Occasionally however these other actors have cameo roles in a starring part such as, for example, when the shareholders are called to the centre of the stage to approve the actions of the authors and at the same time approve and accept their rewards for good performance.[9] The authors of the script are of course the dominant coalition of management who control not just the script of corporate reporting but also the activities of the company whose performance determines the corporate report.

Given the data considered in the preceding chapters, the semiotic analysis undertaken on this data, and the interpretations placed upon this analysis, it now becomes necessary to consider these separate analyses together in the context of the purpose for corporate reporting being constituted in such a manner. This is necessary in order to draw some conclusions out of the analysis and to consider the applicability of those conclusions in a general business context. This is the subject matter of this section and these considerations bring out the central question which has yet to be addressed. This question concerns the role of the dominant coalition, which has been argued to be management, in any organisation in the determination of performance and the reporting upon that performance.

Agency theory argues that managers merely act as custodians of the organisation and its operational activities[10] and places upon them the burden of managing in the best interest of the owners of that business.[11] According to agency theory all other stakeholders of the business are largely irrelevant and if they benefit from the business then this is coincidental to the activities of management in running the business to serve shareholders. This focus upon shareholders alone as the intended beneficiaries of a business has been questioned considerably from many perspectives, which argue that it is either not the way in which a business is actually run or that it is a view which does not meet the needs of society in general. Conversely stakeholder theory argues that there are a whole variety of stakeholders involved in the organisation and each deserves some return for their involvement. According to stakeholder theory therefore benefit is maximised if the business is operated by its management on behalf of all stakeholders and returns are divided appropriately amongst those stakeholders, in some way which is acceptable to all. Unfortunately a mechanism for dividing returns amongst all stakeholders which has universal acceptance does not exist, and stakeholder theory is significantly lacking in suggestions in this respect. Nevertheless this theory has some acceptance and is based upon the premise that operating a business in this manner achieves as one of its outcomes the maximisation of returns to shareholders, as part of the process of maximising returns to all other stakeholders. This maximisation of returns is achieved in the long run through the optimisation of performance for the business to achieve maximal returns to all stakeholders.[12] Consequently the role of management is to optimise the long term performance of the business in order to achieve this end and thereby reward all stakeholders, including themselves as one stakeholder community, appropriately.

These two theories can be regarded as competing explanations of the operations of a firm, which lead to different operational foci and to different implications for the measurement and reporting of performance. It is significant however that both theories have one feature in common. This is that the management of the firm is believed to be acting on behalf of others, either shareholders or stakeholders more generally.[13] This must be considered in the context of the semiotic analysis which has been undertaken.

In the preceding chapters it has been argued that one of the aims of corporate reporting is to bring about a segregation of the audience for such reports in order to systematically raise the importance of various poles in the binary oppositions identified, and as a corollary lower the importance of the opposite poles.[14] It was argued that different parts of the script were intended by the authors to semiotically interact with different sections of the audience and to create an image of the organisation which would appeal to that part of the audience. In other words this requires the creation of multiple images of the organisation within the same text such that each person can construct from the text the most appealing image of the organisation for his / her needs and perspective.[15] This approach will only work if it is possible to segregate the script so that different parts of the script are read by different parts of the audience. Moreover it is also necessary to segregate the audience appropriately so that the right part of the script is read by the right part of the audience. Both of these two requirements are problematical.

It has been demonstrated that the script can be separated into an environmental script and a financial script and this approach has been taken by a number of companies in the sample.[16] Almost half the companies in the sample produce either an environmental report or an environmental statement. The rest of the sample presumably either feel sufficiently secure to have no need to address this part of the audience separately or feel that they can meet their needs through one single report. These environmental reports or statements contain details and images of social and environmental performance and activity but no reference to financial performance.[17] Financial information is contained in the annual report (which contains the statutory reporting requirements), together with information believed to be of interest to financial stakeholders.[18] Indeed Unilever has recognised that the statutory reporting requirements are incidental to the purpose of the annual report and have therefore segregated their script further through the production of two documents – the Annual Review and the Annual Accounts.[19]

All of the companies however recognise that total segregation of the audience is not possible and include reference to environmental matters in their annual report while excluding any quantitative evaluation of environmental performance. The annual report is sent as a matter of course to all shareholders[20] as part of the ritual element of the corporate religion and to all other interested parties. The environmental report is however made available but not sent to any part of the audience as a matter of course. Thus the shareholders are an essential part of the audience, for statutory purposes, and their interaction with the script is of importance to the authors. It is mainly however the large, and hence most powerful, shareholders (primarily the investment institutions) which are of importance to the authors of the script, together with the analysts[21] who are believed to influence those shareholders. Thus companies such as Severn Trent have declared to all shareholders that they will only be given the statutory minimum of a summary financial statement, unless they explicitly declare their requirement otherwise. This seems to be an attempt to clear the semiotic stage of the insignificant supporting cast and enable the authors to interact with the most powerful parts of the audience.[22]

It has been previously argued, in the context of a consideration of the stakeholders of the organisation and their respective perspectives upon organisational performance, that an individual is likely to belong to more than one stakeholder community and hence have more than one perspective upon organisational performance.[23] As such this person will have different perspectives upon the performance of the organisation and will be interested in both environmental performance and financial performance, as well as the short term performance and the longer term performance of the organisation from both these perspectives. This makes audience segregation problematical unless it can be arranged that each person will read the script only from a single perspective at any particular time and will fail to integrate the images extracted from these different perspectives – a highly unlikely situation. It also demonstrates that, despite the best efforts of the authors to segregate the script, it remains in fact one complete script[24] accessible to all.

This problem of audience segregation is particularly problematical when the company is one which deals with individuals as consumers of its products and this is the case with the water companies and the food retailers. The consumers of their corporate script are by definition multiple stakeholders – societally, as customers, possibly also territorially through their domicile, and as shareholders. This situation is particularly severe for the water companies who, due to the nature of the privatisation process, find themselves with large numbers of customers as shareholders. For example Southern Water has 96.4% of its shareholders owning less than 1,000 shares each but comprising only 14.2% of its total share ownership while Severn Trent has 98.7% of its shareholders owning less than 5,000 shares each but comprising only 18.1% of its total share ownership. These small shareholders must be assumed to be almost entirely private individuals but also, more importantly, due to the privatisation process, almost entirely customers of the respective companies. Moreover these individuals will reside in the geographical area encompassed by the water company concerned and hence have a particular interest in the environmental effects of the activities of that company.

It is therefore argued that audience segregation is impossible for purposes of reading different parts of the script, and any attempt to do so is destined for failure. The criticism received by water companies for benefiting shareholders at the expense of customers provides evidence in support of this impossibility. The question therefore arises as to whether or not there is a need to segregate the script and what benefits might arise from so doing. The semiotic analysis suggests that there must be a strong motivation for the authors of the script to attempt this task of segregation given the impossibility of any complete form of audience segregation. Instead such segregation is based around the need to segregate the two aspects of performance – the internal traditional accounting perspective and the external societal perspective – rather than the need to separate the audience.

This separation can therefore be considered to be a dialectic,[25] which is created by the authors of the script, and the exploration of the meaning and purpose of this dialectic becomes important to the understanding of corporate reporting.[26] The semiology of corporate reporting is designed to reinforce the impression that these two dimensions of performance[27] are incompatible and that good performance in one dimension necessitates poor performance in the other. The semiotic created by the authors of the corporate reporting script is based upon this implicit assumption of incompatibility.

Techniques for Maintaining the Dialectic

It has been argued that this dialectic does not in reality exist and must therefore be created in the minds of the readers of the corporate reporting script. It has also been argued that this creation of the dialectic also creates the reality of the dialectic in the minds of the authors of the script.[28] It is by this means therefore that the dialectic is brought into existence and becomes real because it is believed to be real – belief and reality becoming thereby inseparable. In maintaining the dialectic of the difference between financial performance and social performance the authors of the script need to make use of a variety of techniques to continually reinforce the existence of the dialectic. The following techniques, which have been considered in the preceding analysis, can be seen to exist:

- audience segregation is maintained through separate financial and environmental reporting in separate documents;
- appropriate activities and measures are selected for reporting to the different audience, making direct comparison problematical for the readers;
- the same activity is reported differently to the different audiences as part of the semiotic;
- mediation through the press is attempted for image reinforcement;
- non-linguistic devices are used extensively for image building.

The way in which different images are created can be considered through the pictures used in the reporting of companies. Thus for example for Unigate images in the environmental statement show the environment without being specifically related to the company and are used to create a picture of environmental friendliness while images in the annual report create a picture of a technologically developed, and hence financially careful organisation. In the reports of Yorkshire Water the environmental report seeks to create an image of good citizenship through the use of pictures which show the local community alongside captions such as 'Building Better Environments for the Community'. In the annual report however an attempt is made to create an image of responsible management through the use of a picture of the board of the company. The use of the board as an image is in accordance with the statements made by the chairman, as detailed previously.[29]

The semiotic developed in the preceding analysis has been based upon a sample of corporate reports for a sample of companies. It is argued however that the semiotic would not change if a different set of companies had been used for analysis, and this will be elaborated upon in the concluding chapter. Furthermore it is argued that the dialectic created by the authors of such corporate reports would not be changed if a different set of corporate reports for a different set of companies had been used as the basis for analysis.

Creating a Synthesis

It has been argued that audience segregation is impossible for purposes of reading different parts of the script, and any attempt to do so is destined for failure. The question therefore arises as to whether or not there is actually a need to segregate the script and what benefits might arise from so doing.[30] The statistical analysis undertaken shows that the two dimensions of performance are not incompatible, thereby negating one purpose of this segregation. Care must be taken however in drawing this conclusion as the statistical analysis is based upon a small sample of companies. An analysis of a much larger data set would be needed to provide firmer evidence to strengthen this conclusion, and this is one way in which the work undertaken in this book could benefit by extension. Additionally it must be recognised that the relationships found are relatively weak and provide support for the arguments made elsewhere rather than firm statistical evidence in their own right.

It is also recognised that the measure constructed for environmental performance may well be of limited value until tested more rigorously for validity both through testing latitudinally upon other companies and longitudinally with the same companies over an extended period of time. Again this suggests scope for further work arising from this research. Such further work may well lead to the development of better measures of environmental performance, but at the present time, as already identified, such measures fail to exist, as does a universal definition of what constitutes good environmental performance. Nevertheless the evidence gathered from this analysis is sufficiently suggestive to continue with this argument for the integration of environmental reporting with financial reporting. The other argument for such integration however is based upon the semiotic analysis undertaken.

One synthesis which could be argued from the analysis undertaken in this work therefore is the integration of the different perspectives upon performance into one unified performance measurement and reporting system, embodied in a unified corporate annual report. Plainly this is not the case as far as the measurement and reporting of performance is concerned in actuality. It therefore becomes necessary to seek another synthesis as a means of integrating the dialectic.

The Conflation of Financial and Environmental Performance

One view of good environmental performance is that of stewardship and thus just as the management of an organisation is concerned with the stewardship of the financial resources of the organisation so too would management of the organisation be concerned with the stewardship of environmental resources. The difference however is that environmental resources are mostly located externally to the organisation. Stewardship in this context therefore is concerned with the resources of society as well as the resources of the organisation. As far as stewardship of external environmental resources is concerned then the central tenet of such stewardship is that of ensuring sustainability. Sustainability is focused on the future and is concerned with ensuring that the choices of resource utilisation in the future are not constrained by decisions taken in the present. This necessarily implies such concepts as generating and utilising renewable resources, minimising pollution and using new techniques of manufacture and distribution. It also implies the acceptance of any costs involved in the present as an investment for the future.

Not only does such sustainable activity however impact upon society in the future; it also impacts upon the organisation itself in the future. Thus good environmental performance by an organisation in the present is in reality an investment in the future of the organisation itself. This is achieved through the ensuring of supplies and production techniques which will enable the organisation to operate in the future in a similar way to its operations in the present and so to undertake value creation activity in the future much as it does in the present. Financial management also however is concerned with the management of the organisation's resources in the present so that management will be possible in a value creation way in the future. Thus the internal management of the firm, from a financial perspective, and its external environmental management coincide in this common concern for management for the future. Good performance in the financial dimension leads to good future performance in the environmental dimension and vice versa. Thus there is no dichotomy between environmental performance and financial performance and the two concepts conflate into one concern. This concern is of course the management of the future as far as the firm is concerned.[31] The role of social and environmental accounting and reporting and the role of financial accounting and reporting therefore can be seen to be coincidental. Thus the work required needs be concerned not with arguments about resource distribution but rather with the development of measures which truly reflect the activities of the organisation upon its environment. These techniques of measurement, and consequently of reporting, are a necessary precursor to the concern with the management for the future.

Similarly the creation of value within the firm is followed by the distribution of value to the stakeholders of that firm, whether these stakeholders are shareholders or others. Value however must be taken in its widest definition to include more than economic value as it is possible that economic value can be created at the expense of other constituent components of welfare such as spiritual or emotional welfare.[32] This creation of value by the firm adds to welfare for society at large, although this welfare is targeted at particular members of society rather than treating all as equals. This has led to arguments by Tinker (1988), Herremans et al (1992) and Gray (1992), amongst others, concerning the distribution of value created and to whether value is created for one set of stakeholders at the expense of others. Nevertheless if, when summed, value is created then this adds to welfare for society at large, however distributed. Similarly good environmental performance leads to increased welfare for society at large, although this will tend to be expressed in emotional and community terms rather than being capable of being expressed in quantitative terms. This will be expressed in a feeling of wellbeing, which will of course lead to increased motivation. Such increased motivation will inevitably lead to increased productivity, some of which will benefit the organisations, and also a desire to maintain the pleasant environment which will in turn lead to a further enhanced environment, a further increase in welfare and the reduction of destructive aspects of societal engagement by individuals.

Thus increased welfare leads to its own self-perpetuation. In the context of welfare also therefore financial performance and environmental performance conflate into a general concern with an increase in welfare. It

is therefore argued that environmental performance and financial performance are not different dimensions of performance which must inevitably be in opposition to each other. Rather they are both facets of the same dimension of concern for the future. The conflation of financial performance and environmental performance into the same concept does not of course mean that environmental accounting becomes irrelevant. Rather it raises the profile of such accounting and places it at the centre of organisational accounting alongside management accounting. Furthermore it means that more work is needed to develop the embryonic concepts of environmental accounting and make the quantification of environmental effect more effective and meaningful and comparative. Thus it becomes apparent that more work is needed in the area of environmental accounting but moreover it becomes apparent that this is work which is vital for the understanding of corporate performance and the future of that performance. Thus environmental accounting and performance must inevitably become the concern of corporate management.

It has already been identified that the dominant coalition of managers at the centre of an organisation, called for the sake of simplicity management, are the authors of the script which becomes the corporate report. Thus as authors they shape that script and decide its contents.[33] Furthermore they, as editors, determine the image of the organisation which is portrayed to the readers of the script. They are then able to operationalise the production of that image through the corporate reporting mechanisms which are instituted within the organisation, and through determining the format of the report actually produced. The purported nature of that corporate report is to inform shareholders, and other interested parties (who are thereby considered to be readers of the script and consequently stakeholders to the corporate reporting process), of the actions which have been taken by management in the preceding period on behalf of the shareholders, and the outcomes of those actions in terms of performance. It has already been identified that the actual purpose of the report is much more than that. Indeed it has been argued that reporting upon past performance is almost inconsequential as far as such corporate reporting is concerned. Such reporting would require a past focus in the corporate report and, although reference is made to the past, not just for statutory reporting purposes, this is set in the context of the implications of that past for the future of the organisation.

Instead it has been argued that the report is intended to be forward looking and to signal to the readers of the script that the future will be an improvement on the present. Indeed it has been demonstrated, particularly in the case of United Biscuits, that the past has continually been dismissed as almost an irrelevance and certainly no basis for judgement concerning the future. Instead the future will be an improvement upon that past; thus the following statement is made in the 1995 report:

> The group has been organised into three regions with their chief executives based at group headquarters, sharing central services. Group management can now concentrate on formulating strategy and monitoring performance more rigorously. Layers of management have been removed and the result is better communication, integration and allocation of resources.

Interestingly enough this suggests that these senior executives have not been performing optimally in the past if they are able to focus on performance monitoring more rigorously in the future. This meaning is however disguised in the more important image that strategy formulation is the most significant and most difficult role of management. Indeed this role is so demanding that it requires the separation of these executives, both spatially and in terms of obligations, from their actual areas of operation. Management also demonstrates the power to reconstitute itself without reference to the owners of the business. Thus in addition to the restructuring mentioned above the following statement is also made by the chairman:

> As announced in last year's annual report, my predecessor Sir Robert Clarke retired in June 1995. Two non-executive directors have left the board, having contributed valuably to the debate on reshaping the business: Sir Charles Fraser has retired, and Tom Wyman resigned in March following our withdrawal from the USA. Executive directors David Hearn and Brian Chadbourne have also left the company. We welcomed as an executive director Malcolm Little, who has a solid record of achievement both in United Biscuits and elsewhere, and whose steadying hand is already felt across our UK businesses. Gordon Hourston, formerly chairman of Boots The Chemist, has joined us as a non-executive director.

This kind of statement is common throughout all the annual reports of the organisations in the sample and indicates the general ability of management to reconstitute itself and determine its own succession without reference to anyone else. This example has been quoted because of the relatively extreme position of United Biscuits in the sample considered in this analysis, in terms of poor past performance. It reinforces the argument made earlier that reference to the past has no place in determining the future of the organisation. Instead the future is all that matters.

Thus, for example, in 1995 the chairman of Northern Foods makes the following statements:

> I have referred in recent reports to the intensity of competition and resultant structural changes in UK food retailing. Our performance this year reflects a marked acceleration of this change, which has led to significant sales and profit reductions in our businesses...
>
> We have clear strategies in place in both our operating areas. In dairy, we lead the growing supermarket milk sector and are completing major investments which will give us significant competitive advantage...
>
> The food retailing climate in the UK remains intensely competitive and the decline of the doorstep and small shop sectors continues. Nevertheless, our scale, low cost base, product profile, financial strength and management capability gives us confidence that we are in a strong position to meet these continuing challenges and to achieve long term growth in shareholder value.

Such statements can be found throughout the landscape of corporate reporting. This then provides a clue as to the reason for the reports giving the message that environmental performance and financial performance are incompatible and that one must trade off with the other, despite the argument above that the two conflate into a common concern. The reason for the image of incompatibility is in the myth creation role of corporate reporting and the need to continually create and recreate afresh the myth of the organisation. Thus the corporate myth is intended to portray the organisation as atemporal and omnipresent.

It must be remembered however that managers are not only the authors of the script but are also part of the audience, not only as managers but also as other stakeholders. Thus one way in which the other stakeholders interact with the script and its authors is through the managers themselves acting as representatives of those other stakeholders. Thus managers are able to interpret the response of those other stakeholders to their own actions by considering their own responses. This gives the motivation and means to legitimate their actions, as managers, being undertaken on behalf of the other stakeholders to the organisation. Legitimation of activity in this way, by means of self-referential discourse, is of course dangerous and can lead to self-delusion. The fact that such discourse is unquestioned among the rest of the audience however supports the validity of legitimation in such a manner. Thus the audience is included in the community of the organisation as a part of the organisation and the horizon is ringed by the unifying myth of organisational existence (Nietsche 1956).

The Performance Reporting System Revisited

In the performance reporting model developed previously the managers of an organisation were argued to be a moderating factor between the organisation and its performance measurement and reporting systems. This can be developed into a simplified model and depicted thus:

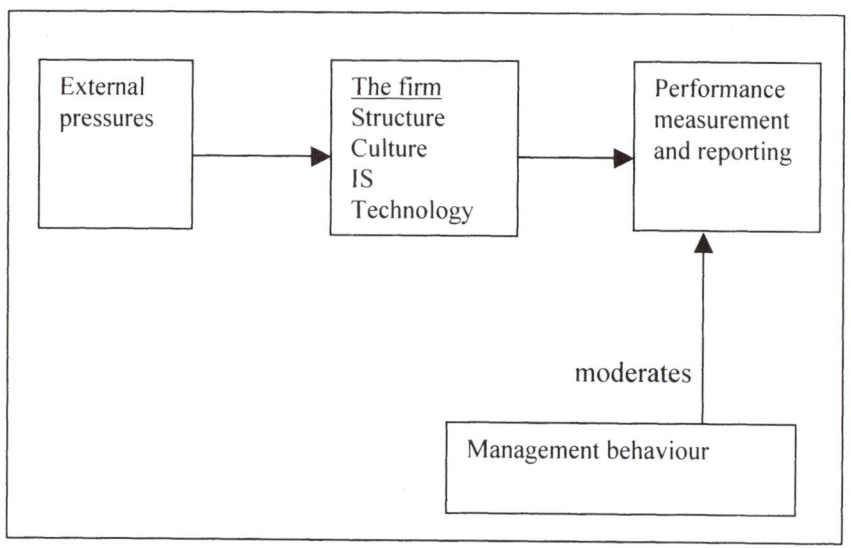

Fig 9.2 Determining the Performance Reporting System

In this model the role of management is to interpret pressures from the external environment (i.e. stakeholders or audience of the corporate reporting script) and to shape the performance reporting system in such a way that it meets the requirements of these external stakeholders and that these requirements are reflected in the corporate reporting system. The internal organisation of the firm is also determined by management, and subsequently affirmed by the external stakeholders (albeit often by default). Thus the managers, rather than acting as a moderating factor between the performance measurement and reporting system and the firm, actually determine the nature of the performance reporting system which in turn leads to particular requirements of performance measurement which determines the nature of this system. At the same time this need determines the required culture, structure, systems and technologies of the organisation.

From the viewpoint of organisational effectiveness, and resource utilisation within its accounting technologies and systems, it seems essential that the different accountings, of financial and environmental, are realigned and that only one accounting should exist for an organisation. This would involve the integration of the best features of each type of accounting in order to present a unified picture of the organisation, its processes and its external environment. It is only in this way that the planning and control of performance both in the present and in the future can be optimised.

The way in which this integration should take place depends upon a consensual understanding of the purpose of organisational existence. There are three possible views of the ownership of an organisation. These are:

- The managers;
- The shareholders;
- All stakeholders.

The implications for each view will be considered in turn.

The managers

It has been argued that the reason for organisational existence has been subverted to the needs of management and that they are the true owners of the organisation. Although shareholders are generally regarded as the owners of a business, and certainly have legal status as such, in this model their position has been relegated to that of investors. Under this model the very activities in which the organisation will engage will be determined by the needs of management and this determination will be according to the myth creation requirements and will need to support the notion of managerial essentiality. In this model the past and future disappear and only the eternal present remains. Thus the concerns of the organisation, as a reflection of the needs of management, will be focused upon the present and the immediate future and decisions will be made based upon this time frame.

Under such a model the performance measurement system will need to report upon successes as highlights and failures will be relegated to obscurity. The primary focus of accounting will be upon accounting for the organisation as a whole and any management accounting will need to exist merely to support this accounting for the whole organisation. Value creation and distribution will be minor parts of the evaluation of performance and the prime focus will be upon the present and the promise of a better future. Such a model will therefore be essentially short term in its focus.[34] There would of course be no point in the representation of environmental performance and financial performance as being in conflict with each other and so both the external reporting and the internal performance measurement could be reintegrated.

The shareholders

Under such a model the focus will naturally be upon creating value in the business and distributing that value to the shareholders either in the form of immediate dividends or in the form of growth in the value of their investment. The split between these two forms of distribution would be determined by the shareholders themselves. Their focus could therefore be either long term or short term depending upon their wishes at any particular point in time. The role of managers would therefore under this model revert to that of acting as agents of the owners and managing according to the dictates of those owners. Part of their responsibility as agents would naturally be to advise as to the consequences of various alternative courses of action and thus to ensure that the owners consider the long term as well as the short term consequences of their actions. This would involve the representation of environmental performance as an essential part of long term performance and the suggestion of a need for the integration of both types of performance measurement.

This model also implies accountability on the part of managers to the owners of the organisation and, despite the current concerns with corporate governance, the consensual view is that this is lacking.[35] The re-imposition within this model of the purpose of organisational existence therefore would require some changes in organisational behaviour and may need to be supported by legislative changes. At the very least it would require the shareholders of the organisation to reclaim some of their responsibilities and take a more active part in the management of the organisation, holding the managers accountable for the outcomes of their actions. Given that the majority of shares in large corporations are held in trust on behalf of either investors or embryonic pensioners this poses a particular problem, as the ownership of the shares and the ownership of the rights in those shares are divorced from each other. The ethical investment movement has perhaps pointed the way to the resolution of this problem but it appears at the moment to be a major problem to the re-adoption of this model of organisational existence.

Under this model the major concerns of accounting would seem to reside in management accounting, as adapted and expanded to include other measures of performance, and with concern for value creation at an individual process level. The kinds of accounting currently existing at this level would need to be refined however to incorporate environmental accounting and information. Such postmodern accounting however already transcends organisational boundaries and so the integration of such accounting need not be too problematical.

All stakeholders

The principle difference between a shareholder model of organisational existence and a stakeholder model concerns the way in which value is appropriated and distributed. One of the principal concerns is the way in which value is extracted from the organisation's external environment and appropriated within the organisation for distribution to its beneficiaries.[36] In theory if it is accepted that the organisation is run on behalf of all stakeholders then the question of value distribution should be of little concern. The problem arises because all of the stakeholders to the organisation, if even recognised in the first place, do not have an equal voice in the activities of the firm. Indeed some have no voice at all and the notion of stakeholders having a part in the management of a firm is a recent one with the definition of who comprises those stakeholders being subject to change as the values of society at large continue to change. Theoretically the managers of the firm are in the position of being able to act as mediators in this respect and to ensure that the voice of all stakeholders is heard and listened to. In practice this does not remove the difficulty of identifying stakeholders in the first place nor does it obviate the problem of unequal voices. Additionally the ability of management to represent these stakeholders must be questioned in the light of the preceding arguments.

The question of giving a voice which can be heard to all stakeholders[37] is one of the most pressing concerns of society as a whole at this point in time and there appears, at present, to be no viable suggestion for the resolution of this problem.[38] It appears of little value therefore to suggest a means of resolution for an individual organisation when the problem seems without solution for society as whole. Instead however the implications for the technologies of accounting and performance measurement and reporting can be considered. These technologies would naturally involve the inclusion of accounting for, and measuring the effects of, the actions of the firm upon its external environment in its broadest possible meaning. They would also be able to measure and report upon these effects in both the present and the long term. Accounting for the environment would therefore need to be placed alongside environmental accounting as one of the principle platforms of this technology.

Notes

[1] That is the chairman's and directors' reports.

[2] That is the balance sheet and profit & loss annual account and associated notes.

[3] This is based upon the uncovering of the Kantian inconsistencies inherent in the messages of such reports and is based upon the arguments of Fish (1972) and Munro (1996).

[4] Important normally equates to good in the semiotic, although it has been argued that in some circumstances each pole of a binarism is needed to appear good for different purposes. This is achieved through the segregation of the report and / or the audience, as considered in previous chapters.

[5] Although these poles exist within the script they are not pertinent to the semiotic and have therefore been dismissed as irrelevant.

[6] That is to say not constantly signed in one direction.

[7] The term good is used to signify desired while the term bad is used to signify undesired.

[8] See also Crowther, Cooper & Carter (2001) who liken this to an enactment of a film script.

[9] These rewards, in the form of dividends, are of course recommended by the managers and the role of the shareholders is merely to approve this recommendation. It is interesting that the rewards of the dominant coalition are not approved by the shareholders (despite their being employees of the shareholders) but recommended through other mechanisms – thereby indicating where the real power lies within an organisation. It also leads to unwanted press mediation when the press comment upon the excessive pay awarded to directors – see for example 'Pay bonanza for privatised utilities' bosses' (*The Independent* 21/10/96) and 'fat cats who find the real cream' (*Sunday Times* 25/9/99).

[10] See for example Emmanuel, Otley & Merchant (1985) for an explanation of this argument.

[11] Such owners are of course the legal owners of the business, that is the shareholders.

[12] See for example Rappaport (1986, 1992) who argues that performance can only be judged against long term criteria.

[13] They do so, not because they are the kind of people who behave altruistically, but because they are rewarded appropriately and much effort is therefore devoted to the creation of reward schemes which motivate these managers to achieve the desired ends. Similarly much literature is devoted to the consideration of the effects of reward schemes on managerial behaviour (see for example Briers & Hirst 1990, Child 1974, 1975, Coates et al 1993, Fitzgerald et al 1991) and suggestion for improvements.

[14] Thus it was argued that focusing upon environmental performance and financial performance separately in separate parts of the script, the annual report and the environmental report, was part of a mechanism of achieving this end.

[15] See Habermas (1971). The separation of the report is designed to assist this individual semiotic creation to coincide with that desired by the authors of the script.

[16] But particularly by the water companies for the reasons suggested in the preceding analysis.

[17] The only financial information contained in these reports relates to the spending on environmental improvement activities.

[18] Such as shareholders, other investors, potential investors and analysts.

[19] Other companies, such as for example Pilkington, also separate their report in this manner. Thus the statutory reporting obligation of these companies, which requires accounting information, has been separated from the annual report.

[20] Except when this annual report has itself been replaced by a summary report. Such summary reports are becoming increasingly common.

[21] And the financial press.

[22] This is part of the treating of the small shareholders resulting from privatisation as both financially illiterate and insignificant. The expectation is that these will be satisfied with a summary financial statement.

[23] Thus an individual may well be a shareholder, a customer and a member of the local spatial community surrounding an operational site of the organisation, and will certainly also be a member of society at large.

[24] At least it remains potentially one single script for those who choose to read it in this manner.

[25] It has been previously demonstrated that this dialectic does not actually exist.

[26] This dialectic was considered in terms of a Hegelian dialectic comprising of thesis and antithesis. This dialectic was explained in chapter 1 and although the existence of a Hegelian dialectic, which would be resolved through history, was rejected in favour of a Kantian approach it is important to remember this historical flow when the future is considered in chapter 10.

[27] The internal traditional accounting perspective and the external societal perspective.

[28] On the basis of truth becoming synonymous with belief (see Fish 1985).

[29] Given the critical external image of this company, however, brought about by its actions the effectiveness of this image creation must be questioned, at least when presented for external consumption. This suggests that the creation of the appropriate image to the authors of the script themselves has more importance than the creation of an external image.

[30] The statistical analysis undertaken in preceding chapters shows that companies which perform well financially also perform well environmentally. This in itself suggests that there is no need to segregate environmental performance from financial performance. Indeed it rather suggests the opposite in that the two sets

of performance should be integrated as this will enhance the script for the whole audience and improve the image of the company created by so doing.

[31] Financial reporting is of course premised upon the continuing of the company – the going concern principle.

[32] See for example Mishan (1967), Ormerod (1994) and Crowther, Davies & Cooper (1998). This can be equated to the concept of utility from the discourse of classical liberalism.

[33] It is recognised that this work involves the contributions of others both internal to the organisation (e.g. accountants) and external (e.g. publishing experts). The guiding force is however the dominant coalition who act as editors of the script.

[34] See Davis *et al.* (1992), Coates *et al.* (1993) for arguments concerning the short term focus of managerial behaviour.

[35] Indeed Monks & Minow (1991) provide cogent arguments and examples regarding the dangers of divorcing power from accountability as far as such governance is concerned.

[36] This question of value distribution has been one of the principal concerns of Tinker (1985) and many others from Karl Marx onwards.

[37] See Crowther (2000) for considerations of this in respect to the future developments of the accountability of corporations.

[38] This is despite the claims from Blair and the Labour Government regarding the merits of 'The Third Way'.

Chapter 10

The Future of Corporate Reporting

Introduction

The central argument of this research is that the corporate reports of organisations have changed because of the need to satisfy a range of stakeholders, and this is evidenced in the discourse of environmental accounting. This argument has been developed over the preceding chapters but it has also been stated that this argument is culturally bounded to the UK. It is therefore necessary to consider the implications of this limitation and this is one of the purposes of this chapter. It has also been argued however that the development of corporate reporting is continuing to unfold and it is necessary to consider the possible implications of this for the argument regarding managerial primacy. These factors, together with other changes in corporate reporting, form the subject matter of this chapter.

The primary purpose for the publication of annual reports by organisations was initially to satisfy the statutory purpose of publishing the annual accounts of the company[1] and at the same time to inform the shareholders, as the legal owners of the business, regarding the actions taken by the managers of the business on their behalf, and of the results of those action. It is clear however that over time these publications have changed in nature. Thus the annual publication of an organisation is no longer merely a version of the annual accounts, published to satisfy statutory requirements, but is now a corporate publication detailing the actions taken by the managers and their plans for future activities which will be of benefit to the shareholders of the organisation. Indeed it has been argued that the temporal focus of such reports has changed from the backward looking emphasis upon reporting actions and results to a forward looking emphasis upon the future and the desirability of that future. This change is particularly evident in publicly quoted companies whereas for private companies[2] such reports remain primarily designed merely to satisfy the statutory requirements.

It has also been argued that the annual reports produced by companies are primarily communication vehicles promulgated in the desire to enter into a discourse between the managers of the company and its owners.[3] This can be evidenced by the trend towards wider content in the annual reports including messages from the chairman and other senior executives. It can also be evidenced by the trend to publish interim publications, between the annual publications, outlining the results to date and expectations for the future.[4] Increasingly also there is a perceived need to enter into a discourse with a wider set of stakeholders, other than shareholders and potential investors. Thus the content of the annual report has been widened to include societal, environmental and employee information. Indeed this trend has been extended through the publication of separate reports to employees[5] and concerning environmental performance, and increasingly companies are publishing environmental reports in parallel with their annual financial report. These changes have not been driven by legislation but rather have been driven by other factors. In this book it has been argued that these factors are concerned primarily with external pressures from a wider variety of stakeholders, who are becoming more vociferous and influential, as well as by the operating environment. These needs, it has been argued, are based upon the incompatibilities, assumed within the discourse, of financial and social performance. It has been argued that this dialectic is not actually real but is made real by its acceptance by all parties to the discourse of corporate performance (Fish 1985).

Limitations of Sample Selection

The analysis upon which these arguments are based has been undertaken through a semiotic analysis of a sample of companies within the FTSE top 500 companies. The companies have been selected from three different industry groupings and have comprised the whole population from each of these industry groupings which satisfies the criteria for selection. The main limitation to the selection from within these industry groupings was concerned with the length of time for which the companies have existed as discrete entities as the study has been based upon a longitudinal study over a six year period. The rationale for the selection of the industry groupings was based upon the selection of industries for which social and environmental issues plainly existed but for which they did not have an overwhelming significance which might shape the conclusions to be drawn from the analysis. Thus for example the oil industry, for which environmental issues have a particularly high profile, has been excluded from the selection upon which the analysis is based.

Social and environmental issues affect all companies to some extent and this extent can be expected to change over time with probably a greater importance being attached to such issues as their importance to society changes over time.[6] Thus although the sample upon which the analysis is based has been restricted in size it is argued that they represent an approximation to the modal state of importance of such issues for companies as a whole, and this has been a prime reason for their selection. As such it is argued that the analysis undertaken, and the conclusions drawn from that analysis, can be extended to all companies within the population of UK Stock Exchange publicly quoted companies without any concern that the analysis might be biased by the sample selected. This is argued to be true for all UK domiciled companies which are subject to UK legislation as the primary constraint upon the production of annual reports.[7]

It is recognised however that companies which are based in different countries are subject to the reporting regulations of those different countries. Indeed companies very often operate in more than one country and hence are subject to the reporting regulations of more than one country. This means that the format of reports may be slightly different for different companies, even within the sample selected. These differences chiefly concern the extent of disclosure which is required within the annual report. Thus for example the environmental reporting requirements of the USA, or at least of certain states within the USA, are more extensive than in the UK and this may affect the content of the annual reports of different companies in different ways, depending upon the requirements of the countries for which the reports are produced. It is equally accepted that the cultures of different countries is also different and that the emphasis placed upon such matters as environmental or social concerns may affect different companies[8] differently because of this variation in emphasis. For example Pearce, Markandya and Barbier (1989) demonstrate within the context of the EC that countries such as Germany and France are more concerned with environmental protection than is the UK, while Italy and Ireland are less concerned. Cultural differences therefore may also affect the way in which company reports are presented and the information which is contained in such reports. Such reporting is also made in the natural language of the country for which the report is produced and this also may make a difference. All the companies in the sample produce their reports in

English, with the exception of Hyder which produces a bilingual report in English and in Welsh.

It is accepted therefore that the different reporting requirements of different countries, the different cultural constraints and mores of these different countries, and the different natural languages used by different countries, may mean that the generaliseability of the arguments in this work cannot readily be extended beyond the UK based companies. This suggests that further work involving the analysis of corporate reports from a variety of different countries and using a variety of different natural languages is needed before the universal generaliseability of the arguments in this book can be established. This therefore suggests one area in which this work can be extended. It must be recognised however that the trends towards globalisation of the competitive environment of companies (Bromley 1999), together with the moves towards the harmonisation of accounting and reporting standards which are taking place, at least as far as the EC is concerned, mean that the differences based upon domicile, and associated reporting regulations, are lessening over time. Thus it is possible that the importance of such factors in causing possible differences, which limit the generaliseability of the arguments, may be overstated for these reasons.

Other factors are however also changing for corporate reporting and these changes are driven to a large extent by the requirements of the various stakeholders to an organisation. Thus one issue which is of concern is that of accountability, and Epstein and Pava (1993) demonstrate that shareholders are interested in accountability of the managers of an organisation in a wide context. Thus they are not just interested in the actions of the managers upon their own investment but recognise obligations to society at large and expect accountability in this context.[9] They also found a lack of trust by shareholders in the information supplied by managers and an expectation of transparency. In must be recognised however that transparency is a paradoxical concept (Bankowski 1999) based upon simplification of the semiotic.

Of greater significance however in the consideration of the limits to the generaliseablity of the arguments contained in this work is the fact that much of the argument is not based upon reporting and disclosure requirements but rather is based upon a semiotic analysis. These restrictions to generaliseability tend to affect the annual accounts[10] themselves which are the backward looking part of the report, and hence have been argued to be of less importance in the creation of the semiotic myth of universality. The semiotic itself is forward-looking into the improved future of the organisation and therefore is based upon the images used in the corporate report and the information contained in the chairman's report. These are not subject to reporting requirements[11] but may be subject to cultural differences depending upon the motivations of the managers of the organisation themselves. Such motivations may be affected by, amongst other things, the managerial reward systems which are in existence in the companies and which may be nationally based. It has been argued however that the analysis undertaken in the preceding chapters has primarily a universal application although it is accepted that further work, along the lines outlined above, would be needed to establishment a sounder footing to this argument of universal generalisation of the arguments.

The Evolution of Corporate Reporting

It has been argued that the nature of corporate reporting is continuing to evolve and that the advent of the electronic technologies of the Internet and the World Wide Web (WWW) have affected this evolution. The increasing availability of access to the Internet has instigated a discourse which considers the present and likely future impact of this means of communication upon the construction of society and upon the lives of individual members of that society (Rushkoff 1997). Much of this discourse is based upon an expectation that the Internet and the World Wide Web will have a significant impact upon the way in which society operates.[12] Thus Sobchack (1996) argues that this technology will be more liberating, participatory and interactive than previous cultural forms while Axford (1995) argues that it will lead to increasing globalisation of politics, culture and social systems. Postmodernist arguments suggest that the technological capability of the Internet will lead a duality of social structures. This will be manifest in increasing globalisation of social structures and concurrently the increased localisation of these structures (Eade 1997).

Much of this discourse is concerned at a societal level with the effects of Internet technology[13] upon society, and only by implication, upon organisations and individuals within society. It is however only at the level of the individual that these changes can take place. Indeed access to the Internet, and the ability to communicate via this technology to other individuals, without regard to time and place, can be considered to be a revolutionary redistribution of power (Russell 1975). Moreover the disciplinary practices of society (Foucault 1977) break down when the Internet is used, because of the lack of spatial contiguity between communicants[14] and because of the effective anonymity of the communication which prevents the normalising surveillance mechanisms of society (Clegg 1989) to intercede in that communication. Thus the internet provides a space for resistance to foment (Robins 1995) but also provides a psychotic space in which all wishes are (or can be) fulfilled (Weibel 1990).

The Internet provides the ideal environment for a community of resistance to exist: the web structured organisation of the Internet means that no separate geographical existence is necessary for a web-based community, and the nature of the Internet is such that people are only part of an Internet community when they actually choose to participate in the activities of that community. Thus an Internet community is a truly postmodern virtual community.[15] The information architecture of the Internet means that it is relatively easy for such a community to establish its existence (Rheingold 1994) and therefore examples of such communities abound. It is relevant to observe however that such communities have existed for a considerable period of time in such areas as academic life and social life. One essential feature of postmodernity however is the changing informational architecture of society and this both makes virtual communities more prevalent and also provides one possible infrastructure for determining community identity. Thus both the territorial and temporal constituents of community disappear, or at least assume diminished significance, in a postmodern environment. At the same time this argument has been extended (Barnett & Crowther 1998) to the proposition that any community need not have either any discrete geographical existence nor any continuous temporal existence but may exist as a virtual community having sporadic temporal existence and no territorial existence.

Technology as Liberation

Of particular interest however is the way in which access to the technology to use the Internet can redefine the corporate landscape and change the power relationship between large corporations and individuals, and more particularly from the viewpoint of this book between the dominant coalition and other stakeholders. Indeed Munro (1999b: 437) has argued that one of the most effective ways of effecting change is 'to stay outside and seek to affect the stream of conduct at a distance.' The technology of the Internet makes this possible and thereby provides a means of liberation which affects the dominant power relations of the corporate world. In this respect the changes in these power relationships can be profound and even revolutionary. The technology provides a potential challenge to legitimacy and can give individuals the ability to confront large corporations and to have their voice heard with equal volume within the discourse facilitated by cyberspace. Thus, for example, without access to the Internet the trial of Helen Steel and Dave Morris would have been unnoticed by all but a few close friends, and their protest would have been effectively silenced by McDonalds (http://www.mcdonalds.com) in the way expected when all power is accrued by the large corporation rather than the individual. Because of the Internet however this balance of power has shifted in favour of the individual. Indeed this power has shifted to such an extent in this particular case that the McLibel case has become world renowned and although McDonalds eventually won the legal case it is questionable as to whether or not they won the moral and publicity cases.

It is the Internet, and the widespread access of individuals to the Internet, which brought this case to prominence and enabled the defendants to communicate with a large number of people scattered throughout the world. Moreover it enabled these people, while spatially disparate and unconnected, to join together in their expressions of support and their publicising of the actions of McDonalds. This would not have been possible without such ready access to the Internet, whereas its advent has enabled mass individualised communication, together with information dissemination mechanisms in the form of websites related to the trial. Perhaps more significantly it empowers the people involved through a transformation of their skills (Holmes 1995) who become more powerful when transferred to this electronic domain. There are many such sites relating to McDonalds and this trial but perhaps one of the more interesting in terms of exploring the power redistribution potential of the technology can be found at http://www.McSpotlight.org. This site not only gives a large amount of information of relevance to the case but also provides a debating room which anyone can enter and makes any comments he / she wishes. Thus the technology gives complete access to anyone in the world to enter a debate and make a contribution on an equal basis. Thus people who might be excluded from a debate requiring physical presence, either for spatial or temporal reasons, can be included; people who might not be able to speak in public can enter the debate; and age, gender and race provide no barrier to entry. Moreover in a virtual environment every person has an equal voice, and no-one can be silenced. This is one of the liberating aspects of the Internet which allows the redistribution of power within society, in that the new electronic form has provided a mechanism for the forging of a new global solidarity.

On this site however there are further illustrations of the ability of Internet technology to change power relationships and to give power to the individual at the expense of a large corporation. Thus there is one part of the website which allows Helen Steel and Dave Morris to give visitors to the site a guided tour around the Mcdonalds site and to deconstruct what appears on that site. This tour runs alongside an official tour to allow visitors to compare and contrast. Thus web technology can be subversive in allowing individuals to appropriate information and use it for their own purposes.

The McLibel trial was a high profile case, which provides a good example of the way in which Internet technology can be used to change power relationships, but there are numerous other examples from around the world. Indeed one of the features of the freedom of access to the Internet has been a proliferation of websites dedicated to protest about particular companies and their activities. These sites have been labelled as rogue sites (Chipchase 1999) and in many ways tend to be parodies of the official company site about which they are protesting. Examples include the anti Microsoft site, Microsucks (http://www.notagoth.com/microsucks) (which resembles the official Microsoft site, http://www.microsoft.com), the anti Walmart site (http://www.walmartsucks.com) and the anti British Airways site, British Scareways (http://www.aviation-uk.com).

The ease with which such sites can be created and accessed might suggest that they pose a threat to the hegemony of the dominant coalition of managers. When considering the corporate world however there are various other technologies which are used by corporations to expropriate power from other individuals and stakeholders and one of the most significant (Crowther 1996b, 1997) is the technology of accounting. As far as most individuals are concerned this accounting is represented through the external reporting of such corporations, in other words the annual reports produced by companies. The arguments in this work show that these reports are used by managers to assume primacy over all other stakeholders and the question therefore, with respect to the technology of the internet, becomes to what extent this technology can be liberating from this hegemony.

If the Internet is a truly liberating technology it should be effective in combating the power of such other technologies. In this chapter therefore the effect of the technological and communicative capabilities of the Internet are considered from the viewpoint of the evolving nature of corporate reporting. This is considered in terms of the way in which Internet technology produces either a globalising imperative or a localisation imperative, through a study of the effect of the medium upon

corporate reporting. In order to do so it is first necessary to consider the way in which such corporate reporting has developed and is continuing to develop in response to the changing use of the Internet.

Over the last 25 years the corporate report itself has changed from a plain statement to an increasingly glossy product containing maps, charts and pictures in a multicoloured production designed to have mass appeal. It is this modern form of corporate reporting, in the way produced and used by large publicly quoted companies which has lent itself to transfer onto the Internet and to incorporation into a wealth of other material about a company which appears of that company's website.[16] These changes have not however affected private companies in the same way, arguably because the ownership and management of such companies are much more closely intertwined, and the use of the Internet for promotional and informational purposes is different for such companies.[17]

If the preceding arguments concerning the liberating nature of the technology are correct then the ability of managers to continually recreate the image of the organisation will be limited by the inevitable transfer of power from such companies to other individual stakeholders.[18] Such individuals, it has been argued, have increasing access to this information and the ability to combine virtually in order to act as pressure groups to effect changes in corporate behaviour. The technology enables a challenge to the images produced and thereby an opening up of the dialectic. Thus it becomes necessary to explore these corporate websites, and the use made of them, in some detail in order to consider the effects of the technology upon the landscape of corporate reporting.

Traversing Corporate Cyberspace

In many respects much of the corporate reporting information that is contained on the websites of corporations is the same information, similarly presented, as appears in the paper version of the annual report. This is particularly true as far as the accounting information – the balance sheet, profit and loss account etc. – is concerned. In this respect the company satisfies its legal requirements, referred to previously, in its virtual space as well as through its paper reporting. What is different in cyberspace however is that this information is incorporated into a host of further information about itself in an environment which is designed to be visually appealing to its readers, to satisfy its other purposes of an electronic presence and to facilitate a carefully constructed and controlled dialogue with its readers.

Thus BP (http://www.bpamoco.com)[19] uses its space to announce the implications of its merger with Amoco as well as to report its past and projected future performance. One aspect of performance which is of importance to this company, given the nature of its operations, is its environmental and social performance and this is announced through its reporting. Readers of its environmental report are asked to engage in a dialogue with the company about its environmental and social performance but significantly they are asked to do so in a controlled manner by responding by means of a questionnaire which is attached, thereby ensuring that the responses received are carefully structured to give the expected (and required) feedback. No space is allowed for a more open dialogue.

J Sainsbury plc (http://www.sainsburys.co.uk) also provides details about its performance and operations and attaches to its site a statement about genetically modified food as well as details about food safety information – all designed to show a concerned face to its readers, who it expects to be both investors (with a share buying service detailed) and customers. Customers are encouraged to purchase from the company through its online ordering service which is part of its website.[20] At the same time this company presents a caring semiotic of interest in its customers while using this image to capture details about such customers. Thus its Reward card scheme features prominently on its website and customers are encouraged to register for such a card and given the facility to interrogate the state of their Reward card account. Again this site is carefully designed and orchestrated to allow interaction with its customers and investors, but only in a way determined by the company itself.

One company which promoted itself as caring for its customers, its employees and the environment is B & Q. This company produces a detailed environmental statement designed for its customers and entitled 'How Green is my Front Door?' which contains detailed environmental information concerning the company and its activities. This company has a website (http://www.diy.co.uk) designed especially for customers. On this site can be found details of its employment policy, with the possibility of applying for jobs, details about its environmental policy, and a helpline for customers. This helpline provides an interactive facility whereby customers (it assumes that all visitors to the site are actual or potential customers) can ask for advice concerning DIY projects and receive 'expert' advice[21] from members of the company. Significantly this customer site is divorced from the site which contains details of its financial performance. This site is located separately at http://www.kingfisher co.uk, the parent company and there is no direct navigation from one site to the other.

An exploration of the websites of other companies shows this pattern repeated, with a semiotic created of inclusion through the possibility if interaction with the company through cyberspace. This interaction is of course carefully orchestrated and controlled to give the appearance of concern without any need to respond to any criticisms; indeed the possibility of criticism is effectively removed through the construction of the dialogic possibilities.

Thus from these examples it is possible to see that corporations have made use of internet technology to redesign their corporate space and include within their space the virtual environment provided by the Internet. At the same time they have adopted the technology to create themselves as interested in people as customers and investors, or potentially either, to provide a semiotic of being willing and interested to engage in dialogue with such people. This dialogue is of course more apparent than real as it is carefully constructed and controlled by the organisations themselves. This raises a question therefore as to the liberating effect of technology, and it is to this that we now turn.

The Internet – Liberation or Servitude?

What is clear about the internet is that it provides a facility to give a voice to people who would otherwise find difficulty in obtaining that voice (see Grieco 1996) and as far as the technology is concerned that voice is equal to all other voices. The technology of the Internet makes no differentiation between the different voices which are present. In other words it provides a space in which all voices can be present and it is clear that it has enabled some voices, such as those of Helen Steel and Dave Morris, to have been heard by a much wider audience than would otherwise have been possible. Equally however it is clear that these voices function in much the same way as in normal speech, and in this respect some voices can be heard much more clearly than others. This is of course dependant upon the power of the language at one's command[22] and upon access to the microphone. It is in this respect that the internet, rather than providing a vehicle for liberation, in actual fact serves to reinforce the prevailing hegemony, as the more powerful have the louder and more eloquent voices.[23] Indeed one of the ways to silence the voice of protest is to incorporate that voice within one's own hegemony and to either silence it or to recognise the value of such protest and turn it to advantage. Thus Dunkin Donuts (http://www.dunkindonuts.org) has responded to the protests arising from the rogue site (http://www.dunkindonuts.com) by acquiring the site and using the complaints received on the site as a monitor of customer satisfaction. Thus it is possible to use the Internet to preserve the dominant hegemony and even protest can be incorporated into this hegemony and used to advantage.

This preservation of the dominant hegemony has been one of the concerns of the Virtual Society? research programme (http://www.brunel.ac.uk/research/virtsoc/) whose initial finding support the idea that the internet is currently no more egalitarian and equal that any other organ of society. Indeed, as has been argued, the dominant structures are actually reinforced by cyberspace rather than discarded. It must be acknowledged however that the popular use of the internet is still only in its infancy and as Wall (1998: 211) observes 'the social impact of cyberspace upon the individual is only beginning to be understood'. Thus it is possible to observe some changes which are currently taking place; for example it is reasonable to maintain that the internet does give access to quieter voices, such as small or new businesses, organisations in less developed countries, and purveyors of innovative concepts, in a way which would not otherwise be easily possible. Equally it provides a vehicle for subversion (as in the Mclibel case) which is perhaps more powerful that other vehicles and is likely to gain less public hostility than other means of protest.[24] It cannot however yet be claimed to be egalitarian; indeed it is argued that it currently provides a reinforcement rather than a dispersion of power within society. This is however a Foucauldian view of history which identifies 'the disordered flaring up and passing away of new formations of discourse' (Habermas, p61). Habermas is of course critical of this view of discourse and power and argues in favour of the arriving of an ideal speech situation from which justice can be derived. Such justice includes necessarily the giving of voice to all and it can be seen that the Internet provides an arena in which this becomes possible. At the moment however this arena is in its infancy and so currently the technology does not redefine that corporate landscape. It does however show ways in which this landscape is beginning to be transformed and thereby gives grounds for optimism for the future, rather than the pessimism of the Virtual Society (http://www.brunel.ac.uk/research/virtsoc/) analysis. This then is an area for future research.

Conclusion

An understanding of corporate reporting and the function and purposes of such reporting is an important factor in the understanding of corporate behaviour and decision-making. Equally, the understanding of the roles of the respective players in this reporting, including organisational managers, shareholders, society and other stakeholders, is an important prerequisite for that understanding. This research has added to the understanding of these issues in the context of performance measurement and reporting in three area:

- A better understanding of the determinants of corporate performance;
- An integration of the literature concerning traditional and environmental accounting;
- The development of a semiology of corporate reporting.

A model of corporate performance has been developed during this work which shows the involvement of managers as mediators in the process of managing performance. Moreover it has been demonstrated how the pressures from shareholders, investors and a wide range of other stakeholders are manifest in a concern both for financial performance and for environmental performance. The analysis has demonstrated that, despite the discourse, these are not incompatible dimensions of performance and that in the long term all interests coincide. This led to the consideration of the merits of an integrated performance measurement system. This in turn led to a discussion concerning the three possibilities of who a company should be managed on behalf of – the shareholders, all stakeholders or the managers themselves. The merits of each were considered but the selection of one must be on ideological grounds and so no preference was expressed. Nevertheless the analysis in this book opens up a discussion of the determinants and objectives of managing corporate performance.

The literature concerning traditional accounting and reporting and environmental accounting and reporting has developed as two independent, and competing, discourses with the implication that managing performance along the two dimensions of financial and environmental performance cannot be satisfactorily achieved without compromising one dimension of performance for the benefit of the other. The analysis undertaken has demonstrated that this is not the case and that a company which is performing well (by whatever criteria are selected to measure that performance) will tend to be performing well in both dimensions of performance. This also argues for the integration of performance measurement and management to accommodate both dimensions. Moreover it shows that both strand of the literature are inadequate by failing to recognise what can be learned from each other. It is therefore proposed that more integration of these two strands of literature is needed and that this will lead to a richer and more fruitful discourse of accounting and performance management.

Semiology has a significant role to play in the development of an understanding of corporate performance and its reporting. One of the most important aspects of this book is the development of a semiology of corporate reporting which enhances the understanding of the role and purpose of such reporting. This semiology shows the inconsistencies in such reporting and moreover shows that one significant purpose of such reporting is to manage the expectations of all stakeholders. Furthermore this semiotic leads to an opening up of the questions regarding the purpose of corporate reporting and performance measurement. As such therefore it is claimed that this analysis adds to this discourse through increasing the understanding of organisational behaviour, decision-making and performance through the following:

- An increase in the understanding of the importance of environmental accounting and its relationship to organisation performance measurement and reporting;
- A different perspective upon and increased understanding of the drivers of corporate performance and the role of management in this respect;
- The development of an understanding of the relationship between corporate structure and reporting and the consequent effects upon corporate accounting.

These understandings are based upon the analysis undertaken in this work, the interpretations placed upon the data used for analysis and the arguments which are developed from this analysis. It is naturally accepted that this interpretation is just one interpretation and that alternative interpretations are possible. Nevertheless the evidence in this work provides ample support for this interpretation. It is argued therefore that this research is significant in that this provides a new interpretation which adds to the understanding of corporate performance, and its reporting, and thereby adds to the understanding of managerial behaviour in shaping such performance. Moreover these arguments both add to the discourse and show where further work is would be beneficial. As such it opens up avenues for this further work and this adds to the significance of the work.

Notes

[1] See the archaeology of corporate reporting developed previously. It should be noted that this statutory purpose still remains, albeit no longer as the primary purpose.

[2] This applies also to smaller family dominated plcs and to companies limited by guarantee (e.g. the Institute of Management) and charities (e.g. Derbyshire Wildlife Trust). In all cases the reports are mush simpler and focus more upon the legal requirements. As a consequence the actual accounts tend not to be as relegated in significance within the accounts.

[3] These owners are of course not just the legal owners (shareholders) but also other stakeholders as quasi-owners (Gray *et al.* 1987, Rubenstein 1992).

[4] Indeed so dominant is the need to provide expectations that these are always announced in the press (either as fact or as the projection of an informed expert) prior to their formal announcement. When this is good news then this raising of expectations is welcomed by the managers but if it is bad news it is less welcome. In extreme circumstances the carefully constructed semiotic of an ever improving future collapses into its negative of a disastrous future (see for example the press reporting of Marks & Spencer during 1998-99 or of Sainsbury during 1999 (e.g. 'Sainsbury faces a slide in shares, *The Guardian* 11/10/99)).

[5] Although the zenith of employee reporting was during the 1970s and subsequently became less popular, they are still issued in the present.

[6] See for example the details provided by Azzone *et al.* (1996).

[7] This claim is of course subject to a limitation concerning family dominated companies.

[8] See for example Deegan & Rankin (1999) regarding Australian expectations.

[9] They also recognise that one of the driving issues of this concern is the possibility of liability for any consequences of the action of the organisation.

[10] That is to say the actual accounts and notes to the accounts which are produced according to GAAP and fulfil a statutory requirement.

[11] In terms of form and content.

[12] See for example Holmes & Grieco (1999) for a consideration of possibilities.

[13] In using the term internet this is meant to encompass all related electronic communications media such as email and the world wide web (www). Equally the word technology is used to mean hardware, software and communications mechanisms. It is not the intention to debate these technologies but rather to consider their use by individuals. Consequently terms such as the internet, the web and cyberspace are used generically in this chapter, without any intention to attach specific and separate meanings to each.

[14] See Carter & Grieco (1999) regarding the emerging electronic ontologies.

[15] See Barnett & Crowther (1998) for a consideration of the features of such a community.

[16] Internet shopping is one of these features of a company's website. See for example 'Tesco to expand its online stores' (*The Guardian* 11/10/99).

[17] Although increasingly all companies are tending to have their own website and internet shopping is becoming a standard feature of UK life.

[18] The concept of the Hegelian dialect has been previously mentioned. This form of dialect is based upon a resolution as it flows through history. It would be reasonable to argue that the evolution of corporate reporting and the changing power structures of society due to internet technology are effecting such a resolution at the present time. As this is still unfolding it is not claimed to be the case in this book but merely considered to be a possibility.

[19] The companies used to illustrate the use of websites are not all within the sample chosen for analysis in this research. Rather they have been selected to illustrate the uses to which the technology has been put by different companies.

[20] Due to the restricted service provided however, only a small minority of customers located in the greater London area are actually serviced in this manner. The semiotic of the website however suggests the universality of this very local service. This is one of the ways in which the internet can redefine the local and the global in accordance with the wishes of the authors of the site. Contrast this with the images of locality and globality in the paper reports.

[21] See Adorno (1973) concerning the nature of such expertise.

[22] See Belkaoui (1978) concerning accounting as a language.

[23] Thus the managers who edit the corporate script also act as editors for the web based corporate script and ensure the design of the semiotic in the same way. Moreover the more powerful have better access to the technologies used in design to assist them to shape that semiotic.

[24] Contrast the sympathy gained by Helen Steel and Dave Morris with the hostility generated by the actions of Reclaim the Streets.

Bibliography

Abernethy M A & Stoelwinder J U (1995); The role of professional control in the management of complex organisations; *Accounting, Organizations & Society,* 20 (1), 1-17.

Accounting Standards Board; *Reporting Financial Performance*; FRS3; London.

Accounting Standards Steering Committee (1975); *The Corporate Report*; London.

Ackerman R W (1975); *The Social Challenge to Business*; Cambridge, Ma; Harvard University Press.

Ackoff J (1974); The systems revolution; *Long Range Planning,* 7 (6), 2-5.

Adams R (1992); Green reporting and the consumer movement; in D Owens (ed); *Green Reporting*; London; Chapman & Hall.

Adorno T W (1973); *The Jargon of Authenticity*; trans K Tarnowski & F Will; London; Routledge & Kegan Paul.

Anderson P (1998); *The Origins of Postmodernity*; London; Verso.

Aoki M (1984); *The Co-operative Game Theory of the Firm*; Oxford; OUP.

Argyris C (1990); The dilemma of implementing controls: the case of managerial accounting; *Accounting, Organizations & Society,* 15 (6), 503-511.

Aryana N (1979); The influences of pressure groups on financial statements in Britain; in T A Lee & R H Parker (eds); *The Evolution of Corporate Financial Reporting*; Sunbury, Middlesex; Thomas Nelson & Sons; pp 265-274.

Axford B (1995); *The Global System*; Cambridge; Polity Press.

Azzone G, Manzini R & Noci G (1996); Evolutionary trends in environmental reporting; *Business Strategy and Environment,* 5 (4), 219-230.

Bailey P E & Soyka P A (1996); Making sense of environmental accounting; *Total Quality Environmental Management,* 5 (3), 1-15.

Bakhtin M M (1981); *The Dialogic Imagination*; trans M Holquist & C Emerson; Austin; University of Texas Press.

Bankowski Z (1999); Transparency and the particular; *Cultural Values,* 3 (4), 427-444.

Barnes B (1982); *T S Kuhn and Social Science*; New York; Colombia University Press.

Barnett N J & Crowther D (1998); Community identity in the 21st century: a postmodernist evaluation of local government structure; *International Journal of Public Sector Management,* 11 (6/7), 425-439.

319

Barthes R (1967); *Elements of Semiology*; trans A Lavers & C Smith; New York; Noonday Press.

Barthes R (1973); *Mythologies*; trans A Lavers; London; HarperCollins.

Barthes R (1977); *Image Music Text*; trans S Heath; London; Fontana.

Barthes R (1988); *The Semiotic Challenge*; Oxford; Basil Blackwell.

Batley H & Tozer L E (1990); Sustainable development: an accounting perspective; *Accounting Forum*, 17 (1), 38-61.

Baudrillard J (1981); *For a Critique of the Political Economy of Signs*; St Louis; Telos.

Baudrillard J (1988); in M Poster (ed); *Jean Baudrillard: Selected Writings*; Cambridge; Polity Press.

Baudrillard J (1994); *Simulacra and Simulation*; trans S F Glaser; Ann Arbor; University of Michigan Press.

Baumol W J (1959); *Business Behaviour, Value and Growth*; London; Macmillan.

Beaver W (1989); *Financial Reporting: an Accounting Revolution*; Englewood Cliffs, N J; Prentice-Hall.

Bebbington J (1993); The EC fifth action plan: towards sustainability; *Social and Environmental Accounting*, 13 (1), 9-11.

Beit-Hallahmi B & Argyle M (1997); *The Psychology of Religious Behaviour, Belief and Experience*; London; Routledge.

Belkaoui A (1978); Linguistic relativity in accounting; *Accounting, Organizations & Society*, 3 (2), 97-104.

Bell J (1984); The effect of presentation form on judgement confidence in performance evaluation; *Journal of Business Finance & Accounting*, 11 (3), 327-346.

Belsey C (1980); *Critical Practice*; London; Routledge.

Benston G J (1982); Accounting and corporate accountability; *Accounting Organizations & Society*, 7 (2), 87-105.

Benston G J (1984); Rejoinder to 'Accounting and corporate accountability': an extended comment; *Accounting Organizations & Society*, 9 (3/4), 417-419.

Bentham J (1982); *An Introduction to the Principles of Morals and Legislation*; London; Everyman.

Berger A A (1982); *Media Analysis Techniques*; Newbury Park, Ca.; Sage.

Berger P (1974); *Pyramids of Sacrifice*; Harmondsworth; Penguin.

Bernstein B (1961); Social Structure, Language and Learning; *Educational Research*, 3, 163-176.

Bhaskar K & McNamee P (1983); Multiple objectives in accounting and finance; *Journal of Business Finance & Accounting*, 10 (4), 595-621.

Birkin F (1996); Environmental management accounting; *Management Accounting*, 74 (2), 34-37.

Birnbeg J G (1980); The role of accounting in financial disclosure; *Accounting, Organizations & Society*, 5 (1), 71-80.

Birnbeg J G, Turopolec L & Young S M (1983); The organizational context of accounting; *Accounting, Organizations & Society*, 8 (2/3), 111-129.

Bourdieu P (1984); *Distinction: a social critique of the judgement of taste*; trans R Nice; London; Routledge & Kegan Paul.

Brandist C (1997); Bakhtin, Cassirer and symbolic forms; *Radical Philosophy*, 85, 20-27.

Brealy R & Myers S (1991); *Principles of Corporate Finance* 4th ed; New York; McGraw Hill.

Brewster E R (1994); Measure for measure?; *Public Finance*, 2 Dec 1994 p 23.

Briers M & Hirst M (1990); The role of budgetary information in performance evaluation; *Accounting, Organizations & Society*, 15 (4), 373-398.

Bromley S (1999); The space of flows and timeless time; *Radical Philosophy*, 97, 6-17.

Brunsson N (1993); Ideas and actions: justification and hypocrisy as alternatives to control; *Accounting, Organizations & Society*, 18 (6), 489-506.

Buckley A & McKenna E (1972); Budgetary control and business behaviour; *Accounting & Business Research*, Spring 1972, 137-150.

Butler D, Frost C & Macve R (1992); Environmental Reporting; in L C L Skerratt & D J Tonkins (eds); *A Guide to UK Reporting Practice for Accountancy Students*; London; Wiley.

Button K (1990); *The Urban Environment*; Key Environmental Issues No 9; British Gas.

Byatt I C R (1997); *The regulation of public utilities: the case of the water companies*; paper presented to the Liverpool Economic and Statistical Society; 3rd March 1997.

Campbell A, Devine M & Young D (1990); *A Sense of Mission*; London; Hutchinson.

Campbell J (1949); *The Hero with a Thousand Faces*; Princeton, N J; Princeton University Press.

Campbell J (1972); *Myths to Live By*; London; Souvenir Press.

Campbell J (1976); *Creative Mythology Vol 4: The Masks of God*; London; Penguin.

Campbell J (1993); *The Mythic Dimension: Selected Essays 1959-1987*; New York; HarperCollins.

Carey A & Sancto J (1998); Thinking outside the box; in A Carey & J Sancto (eds), *Performance Measurement in the Digital Age*; London; ICAEW, pp 6-9.

Carnaghan C, Gibbins M & Ikaheimo S (1996); Managing financial disclosure: the interplay between accountability pressures; in R Munro & J Mouritsen, *Accountability*; London; International Thomson .

Carroll J M (1980); *Towards a structural psychology of cinema*; The Hague; Mouton.

Carter C & Crowther D (1999); Unravelling a profession: the case of engineers in a British Regional Electricity Company; *Critical Perspectives on Accounting* 11 (1), 23-49.

Carter C & Crowther D (2000); Organisational consumerism: the appropriation of packaged managerial knowledge; Management Decision 38 (9), 626-637.

Carter C & Grieco M (1999); *New deals, no wheels: social exclusion. tele-options and electronic ontology*; paper presented to Odyssey Workshop, Cornell University, August 1999.

Cassirer E (1946); *Language and Myth*; trans S K Langer; New York; Dover Publications.

Cassirer E (1955); *The Philosophy of Symbolic Forms Vol 2: Myth*; trans R Manheim, New Haven, Connecticut; Yale University Press.

Chakravarthy B S (1986); Measuring strategic performance; *Strategic Management Journal*, 7, 437- 458.

Chaliand G (1987); *Terrorism – From Popular Struggle to Media Spectacle*; London; Saqi.

Cherns A B (1978); Alienation and accountancy; *Accounting, Organizations & Society*, 3 (2), 105-114.

Child J (1974); Managerial and organisational factors associated with company performance - part 1; *Journal of Management Studies*, 11, 73-189.

Child J (1975); Managerial and organisational factors associated with company performance - part 2; *Journal of Management Studies*, 12, 12-27.

Child J (1984); *Organisation: A Guide to Problems and Practice*; London; Harper & Row.

Chipchase J (1999); Rogue web sites; *Internet.Works*, 25, 78-83.

Churchman C W (1967); Why measure; in C W Chuchman & P Ratoosh (eds); *Measurement: Definition and Theories*; London; Wiley; pp 83-94.

Clark J M (1957); *Economic Institutions and Human Welfare*; New York; Alfred A Knopf.

Clegg C & Fitter F (1981); Organizational and behavioural consequences of uncertainty: a case study; *Journal of Occupational Behaviour*, 2, 155-175.

Clegg S R (1989); *Frameworks of Power*; London; Sage.

Clegg S R, Higgins W & Spybey T (1990); Post-Confucianism, social democracy and economic culture; in S R Clegg & S G Reddings (eds), *Capitalism in Contrasting Cultures* pp 31-78; Berlin; Walter de Gruyter.

Coates J B, Davies M L, Davis E W, Zafar A & Zwirlein T (1995); *Adopting performance measures that count: changing to a shareholder value focus*; Aston Business School Research Paper No RP9510.

Coates J B, Davis E W, Longden S G, Stacey R J & Emmanuel C (1993); *Corporate Performance Evaluation in Multinationals*; London; CIMA.

Collins M (1989); *Post-Modern Design*; London; Academy Editions.

Cooper D J & Scherer M J (1984); The value of corporate accounting reports: arguments for a political economy of accounting; *Accounting Organizations & Society*, 9 (3/4), 207-232.

Cornforth M (1971); *Dialectical Materialism*; New York; Doubleday.

Covalenski M A & Dirsmith M W (1986); The budgetary process of power and politics; *Accounting, Organizations & Society*, 11 (3), 193-214.

Crowther D (1996a); *Management Accounting for Business*; Cheltenham; Stanley Thornes.

Crowther D (1996b); Corporate performance operates in three dimensions; *Managerial Auditing Journal*, 11 (8), 4-13.

Crowther D (1997); *Representing organisations: a semiotic interpretation of accounting technologies*; paper presented at BAA Conference; Birmingham; March 1997.

Crowther D (2000); Corporate reporting, stakeholders and the Internet: mapping the new corporate landscape; *Urban Studies* 37 (10), 1837-1848.

Crowther D & Carter C (1998); *Copernican metonymy and management accounting*; Aston Working Paper Series RP9901.

Crowther D & Cooper S (2001); Innovation through postmodern networks: the case of ecoprotestors; in O Jones, S Conway & F Steward (eds), Social Interaction and Organisational Change; London; Imperial College Press; pp 321-347.

Crowther D, Cooper S & Carter C (2001); Regulation – The Movie: a semiotic study of the periodic review of UK regulated industry; *Journal of Organizational Change Management* 14 (3), 225-238.

Crowther D, Davies M & Cooper S (1998); Evaluating corporate performance: a critique of Economic Value Added; *Journal of Applied Accounting Research*, 4 (3), 2-34.

Cyert R M & March J G (1963); *A Behavioural Theory of the Firm*; Englewood Cliffs, NJ; Prentice Hall.

Cyert R M & Ijiri Y (1974); Problems of implementing the Trueblood Report; Journal of Accounting Research supplement 1974.

Dahl R A (1972); A prelude to corporate reform; *Business & Society Review*, Spring 1972, 17-23.

Davidson S, Schindler J S & Weil R L (1974); *Accounting: the Language of Business*; New York; Thomas Horton & Daughters.

Davis E W, Coates J B, Emmanuel C R, Longden S G & Stacey R J (1992); Multinational companies performance measurement systems: international perspectives; *Management Accounting Research*, 3, 102-124.

De Tocqueville A (1998); *Democracy in America*; trans H Reeve; Ware, Herts; Wordsworth

Dearden J (1969); The case against ROI control; *Harvard Business Review*, 47 (3), 124-135.

Deegan C & Rankin M (1999); The environmental reporting expectations gap: Australian evidence; *British Accounting Review*, 31 (3), 313-346.

Deleuze G (1988); *Foucault*; London; Athlone.

Deleuze G (1994); *Difference and Repetition*; trans P Patton; New York; Colombia University Press.

Deleuze G & Guattari F (1994); *What is Philosophy?*; trans H Tomlinson & G Burchell; London; Verso.

Dermer J (1988); Control and organisational order; *Accounting, Organizations & Society*, 13 (1), 25-36.

Dermer J D & Lucas R G (1986); The illusion of managerial control; *Accounting, Organizations & Society*, 11 (6), 471-482.

Derrida J (1978); *Writing and Difference*; trans A Bass; London; Routledge & Kegan Paul.

Derrida J (1997); *Politics of Friendship*; trans G Collins; London; Verso.

Dierkes M & Preston L E (1977); Corporate social accounting reporting for the physical environment: a critical review and implementation proposal; *Accounting Organizations & Society*, 2 (1), 3-22.

Dollimore J (1984); *Radical Tragedy*; Chicago; University of Chicago Press.

Donaldson T (1982); *Corporate Morality*; New Jersey; Prentice Hall.

Drucker P F (1985); *Innovation and Entrepreneurship*; Oxford; Butterworth-Heinemann.

du Gay P (1994); Colossal immodesties and hopeful monsters: pluralism and organisational conduct; *Organization*, 1 (1), 125-148.

Eade J (1997); Reconstructing places: changing images of locality in Docklands and Spitalfields; in J Eade (ed), *Living in the Global City*; London; Routledge; pp 127-145.

Eccles R G (1991); The performance evaluation manifesto; *Harvard Business Review*, 69 (1), 131-137.

Eco U (1994); *The Limits of Interpretation*; Indianapolis; Indiana University Press.

Elkington J (1990); *Community Action: No Thanks Noah*; Key Environmental Issues No 12; British Gas.

Emmanuel C R & Gee K P (1982); Transfer pricing: a fair and neutral procedure; *Accounting & Business Research*, Autumn 1982, 273-278.

Emmanuel C R & Otley D T (1976); The usefulness of residual income; *Journal of Business Finance & Accounting*, 3 (4), 43-51.

Emmanuel C R, Otley D T & Merchant K (1985); *Accounting for Management Control*; London; Chapman & Hall.

Epstein M J & Pava M L (1993); *The Shareholder's Use of Corporate Annual Reports*; London; JAI Press.

Ezzamel M & Hart M (1989); *Advanced Management Accounting: An Organisational Emphasis*; London; Cassell.

Featherstone M (1988); In pursuit of the postmodern: an introduction; *Theory Culture and Society*, 5 (2/3), 195-215.

Fetyko D F (1975); The company social audit; *Management Accounting*, 56 (10), 645-647.

Findlay J N (1958); *Hegel: a Re-examination*; London; Allen & Unwin.

Finkelstein S. (1992). 'Power in top management teams: dimensions, measurement and validation', *Academy of Management Journal*, 35 (3), 505-538.

Fish S (1972); *Self-Consuming Artefacts: the Experience of Seventeenth-Century Literature*; Berkeley; University of California Press.

Fish S (1985); Is there a text in this class?; in W T J Mitchell (ed); *Against Theory*; Chicago; University of Chicago Press.

Fish S (1989); *Is there a text in this class? The authority to interpret communities*; Cambridge, Mass; Harvard University Press.

Fisher F M & McGowan J I (1983); On the misuse of accounting rates of return to infer monopoly profits; *American Economic Review*, 73, 82-97.

Fitzgerald L, Johnston R, Brignall S, Silvestro R & Voss C (1991); *Performance Measurement in Service Businesses*; London; CIMA.

Flamholtz E G, Das T K & Tsui A S (1985); Toward an integrative framework of organisational control; *Accounting, Organizations & Society*, 10 (1), 35-50.

Folmer H (1990); *Environmental Impacts of the Single European Market*; Key Environmental Issues No 2; British Gas.

Foucault M (1970); *The Order of Things*; London; Routledge.

Foucault M (1977); *Discipline and Punish*; trans A Sheridan; London; Penguin.

Fox A (1974); *Beyond Contract: Work, Power and Trust Relations*; London; Faber & Faber.

Fox C J & Miller H T (1995); *Postmodern Public Administration: Towards Discourse*; London; Sage.

Frazer J (1947); *The Golden Bough*; London; Macmillan.

Freedman R E & Reed D L (1983); Stockholders and stakeholders: a new perspective on corporate governance; *California Management Review*, XXV (3), 88-106.

Freeman R E (1984); *Strategic Management: A Stakeholder Approach*; Boston, Ma; Pitman.

Frost G & Wilmhurst T (1996); Going green .... But not yet; *Australian Accountant*, 66 (8), 36-37.

Fukuyama F (1992); *The End of History and the Last Man*; New York; The Free Press.

Gadamer H G (1975); *Truth and Method*; trans G Bardent & J Cumming; London; Sheed & Ward.

Gamble G O, Hsu K, Jackson C & Tollerson C D (1996); Environmental disclosure in annual reports: an international perspective; *International Journal of Accounting*, 31 (3), 293-331.

Geno B J (1995); Accounting for sustainability: an exploration of accounting needs in the ecologically rational society; *Accounting Forum*, 19 (2/3), 176-194.

Giddens A (1991); *Modernity and Self-Identity*; Cambridge; Polity Press.

Gilmore C G & Willmott H (1992); Company law and financial reporting: a sociological history of the UK experience; in M Bromwich & A Hopwood (eds), *Accounting and the Law*, pp 159-191; Hemel Hempstead; Prentice Hall.

Goold M & Campbell A (1987); *Strategies and Styles: The Role of the Centre in Managing Diversified Companies*; Oxford; Basil Blackwell.

Goold M & Quinn J J (1990); *Strategic Control*; London; Hutchinson.

Gordon L A & Miller D (1976); A contingency framework for the design of accounting information systems; *Accounting, Organizations & Society*, 1 (1), 59-69.

Govindarajan V (1984); Appropriateness of accounting data in performance evaluation: an empirical examination of environmental uncertainty as an intervening variable; *Accounting, Organizations & Society*, 9 (2), 125-135.

Govindarajan V & Gupta A K (1985); Linking control systems to business unit strategy: impact on performance; *Accounting, Organizations & Society*, 10 (1), 51-66.

Grabski S V (1985); Transfer pricing in complex organisations: a review of recent empirical and analytical research; *Journal of Accounting Literature*, 4, 33-75.

Graves O F, Flesher D L & Jordan R E (1996); Pictures and the bottom line: the television epistemology of U S annual reports; *Accounting, Organizations and Society*, 21 (1), 57-88.

Gray J (1995); *Enlightenment's Wake*; London; Routledge.

Gray R (1992); Accounting and environmentalism: an exploration of the challenge of gently accounting for accountability, transparency and sustainability; *Accounting, Organizations & Society*, 17 (5), 399-425.

Gray R, Owen D & Maunders K (1987); *Corporate Social Reporting: Accounting and Accountability*; London; Prentice-Hall.

Gray R H, Bebbington J & Walters D (1993); *Accounting for the Environment*; London; ACCA.

Gray R H & Collison D (1991); The environmental audit: green-gauge or whitewash; *Managerial Auditing Journal*, 6 (5), 17-25.

Greenberg R & Nunamaker T (1987); A generalised multiple criteria model for control and evaluation of nonprofit organisations; *Financial Accountability & Management*, 3 (4), 331-342.

Greimas A J (1990); *The Social Sciences: A Semiotic View*; Minneapolis; University of Minneapolis Press.

Greimas A J & Rastier F (1968); The interaction of semiotic constraints; *Yale French Studies*, 41, 86-105.

Grieco M (1996); *Worker's Dilemma: recruitment, reliability and repeated exchange*; London; Routledge.

Guiraud P (1975); *Semiology*; London; Routledge & Kegan Paul.

Habermas J (1971); *Knowledge and Human Interests*; trans J J Shapiro; Boston, Mass; Beacon Press.

Habermas J (1994); The critique of reason as an unmasking of the human sciences: Michael Foucault; in M Kelly (ed), *Critique and Power: Recasting the Foucault / Habermas Debate*; London; MIT Press pp 47-78.

Haka S F, Gordon L A & Pinches G E (1985); Sophisticated capital budgeting selection techniques and firm performance; *The Accounting Review*, LX (4), 651-669.

Halliday M A K (1978); *Language as Social Semiotic*; London; Edward Arnold.

Hamilton W (1932); Institution; in E Seligman & A Johnson (eds), *Encyclopedia of the Social Sciences,* pp 84-89.

Hampden-Turner C (1990); *Corporate Culture*; London; Hutchinson.

Hanna M S & Wilson G L (1984); *Communication in Business and Professional Settings*; New York; Random House.

Harris M (1979); *Cultural Materialism*; New York; Random House.

Harvey D (1990); *The Condition of Postmodernity*; Oxford; Blackwell.

Hawken P (1993); *The Ecology of Commerce*; London; Weidenfeld & Nicholson.

Heckscher C (1994); Defining the post-bureaucratic type; in Heckscher C & Donnellon A (eds); *The Post- Bureaucratic Organisation*; London; Sage pp 14-62.

Hedberg B & Jonsson S (1978); Designing semi-confusing information systems for organisations in changing environments; *Accounting, Organizations & Society*, 3 (1), 47-64.

Hegel G W F (1956); *The Philosophy of History*; New York; Dover Publications.

Hein L W (1978); *The British Companies Acts and the Practice of Accountancy 1844-1962*; New York; Arno Press.

Herremans I M, Akathaparn P & McInnes M (1992); An investigation of corporate social responsibility, reputation and economic performance; *Accounting, Organizations & Society*, 18 (7/8), 587-604.

Hervey S (1982); *Semiotic Perspectives*; London; George Allen & Unwin.

Hetherington J A C (1973); *Corporate Social Responsibility Audit: A Management Tool for Survival*; London; The Foundation for Business Responsibilities.

Hewitt J (1989); White adolescent creole users and the politics of friendship; *Journal of Multicultural and Multilingual Education*, 3 (3), 340-357.

Hjelmslev L (1963); *Prolegomena to a Theory of Language*; trans F J Whitfield; Madison; University of Wisconsin Press.

Hofstedt T R (1976); Behavioural accounting research: pathologies, paradigms and prescriptions; *Accounting, Organizations & Society*, 1 (1), 43-58.

Hogarth R M (1993); Accounting for decisions and decisions for accounting; *Accounting, Organizations & Society*, 18 (5), 407-424.

Hoggett P (1996); New modes of control in the Public Services; *Public Administration*, 74, 9-32.

Hollier D (1995); From Beyond Hegel to Nietzsche's Absence; in L A Boldt-Irons, *On Bataille* pp 61-78; Albany; SUNY.

Holmes L (1995); Skills - a social perspective; in A Assiter (ed), *Transferrable Skills in Higher Education*; London; Kogan Page.

Holmes L & Grieco M (1999); *The power of transparency: the Internet, e-mail and the Malaysian political crisis*; paper presented to Asian Management in Crisis Conference, Association of South East Asian Studies, UNL, June 1999.

Hooks J (1996); Degradation – the role of accounting; *Chartered Accountants Journal of New Zealand*, 75 (3), 63-64.

Hopper T, Storey J & Willmott H (1987); Accounting for accounting: towards the development of a dialectic view; *Accounting, Organizations & Society*, 12 (5), 437-456.

Hopwood A (1974); *Accounting and Human Behaviour*; London; Accountancy Age.

Hopwood A G (1983); On trying to study accounting in the contexts in which it operates; *Accounting, Organizations & Society*, 8 (2/3), 287-305.

Horkheimer M & Adorno T W (1944); *Dialectic of Enlightenment*; trans Cumming J 1972; New York; Herder & Herder.

Horne D (1986); *The Public Culture: An Argument with the Future*; London; Pluto Press.

Howard K (1996); Should management accounting turn soft?; *Management Accounting*, 74 (4), 58-59.

Howell R A, and Soucy S R (1988); Management reporting in the new manufacturing environment, *Management Accounting*, February, 58-59.

Hutton W (1997); *Stakeholding and its Critics*; London; IEA Health and Welfare Unit.

ICAEW (1993); *Business, Accountancy and the Environment: a policy and research agenda*; London; ICAEW.

Jackson P (1986); Performance measurement and value for money in the public sector; in *Research in Action - Performance Measurement*; ICAS & CIPFA Conference proceedings.

Jameson F (1991); *Postmodernism, or, the cultural logic of Late Capitalism*; London; Verso.

Jameson F (1998); *The Cultural Turn*; London; Verso.

Janis I. L. (1972); *Victims of Groupthink*; Boston; Houghton Miffin.

Jarrett J (1983); The rate of return from interim financial reports and the allocation problem in financial accounting; *Journal of Business Finance & Accounting*, 10 (2), 289-298.

Jenkins A (1979); *The Social Theory of Claude Levi – Strauss*; London; Macmillan.

Jensen M & Meckling W (1976); Theory of the firm: managerial behaviour, agency costs and ownership structure; *Journal of Financial Economics*, October, 305-360.

Johnson H T & Kaplan R S (1987); *Relevance Lost: The Rise and Fall of Management Accounting*; Boston, Mass; Harvard Business School Press.

Jones B (1996); Going for green; *Management Review*, 85 (10), 54.

Jones C S (1985); An empirical study of management accounting systems following takeover or merger; *Accounting, Organizations & Society*, 10 (2), 177-200.

Jones M J (1996); Accounting for biodiversity: a pilot study; *British Accounting Review*, 28 (4), 281-303.

Jordan J R (1970); Financial accounting and communication; in G G Mueller & C H Smith (eds), *Accounting: a Book of Readings*; New York; Holt, Rinehart & Winston.

Kant I (1934); *Critique of Pure Reason*; London; Everyman.

Kaplan R S (1984); The evolution of management accounting; *The Accounting Review*, LIX (3), 390-418.

Kaplan R S & Norton D P (1992); The balanced scorecard - measures that drive performance; *Harvard Business Review*, Jan/Feb, 71-79.

Kaplan R S & Norton D P (1993); Putting the balanced scorecard to work; *Harvard Business Review*, Sept/Oct, 134-147.

Kay J (1993); *Foundations of Corporate Success*; Oxford; OUP.

Kay J (1998); Good Business; *Prospect*, 28 (March), 25-29.

Kidd B (1902); *Principles of Western Civilisation*; London; Macmillan.

Kidd P T (1994); *Agile Manufacturing: Forging New Frontiers*; London; Addison-Wesley.

Kim K L (1996); *Caged in our own signs: a book about semiotics*; Norwood, N J; Ablex Publishing.

Kimberley J, Norling R & Weiss J A (1983); Pondering the performance puzzle: effectiveness in interorganisational settings; in Hall R H & Quinn R E (eds); *Organisational Theory and Public Practice*; Beverly Hills; Sage; pp 249-264.

Kinnersley D (1994); *Coming Clean: the politics of water and the environment*; London; Penguin.

Klein J (1965); *Samples from English Cultures*; London; Routledge & Kegan Paul.

Klein T A (1977); *Social Costs and Benefits of Business*; Englewood Cliffs, NJ; Prentice-Hall.

Kotter J P & Heskett J L (1992); *Corporate Culture and Performance*; New York; The Free Press.

Labov W (1966); The linguistic stratification of 'r' in New York City department stores; in W Labov (ed), *Sociolinguistic Patterns*; Philadelphia; Pennsylvania University Press.

Lacan J (1977); *Ecrits: a selection*; trans A Sheridan; London; Tavistock.

Laclan E (1990); *New Reflections on the Revolution of Our Time*; London; Verso.

Laing R D (1961); *Self and Others*; London; Tavistock.

Lakoff R (1975); *Language and Woman's Place*; Cambridge; Harper & Row.

Laughlin R C (1987); Accounting systems in organisational contexts: a case for critical theory; *Accounting, Organizations & Society*, 12 (5), 479-502.

Laughlin R C & Puxty A G (1983); Accounting regulation: an alternative perspective; *Journal of Business Finance & Accounting*, 10 (3), 451-479.

Laughlin R C & Puxty A G (1986); The social conditioning and socially conditioned nature of accounting: a review and analysis through Tinker's Paper Prophets; *The British Accounting Review*, 18 (1), 17-42.

Le Page R (1968); Problems of description in multilingual communities; *Transactions of the Philological Society*, 189-212.

Leach R G (1975); presentation at the launch of The Corporate Report, July 1975.

Lee T A & Parker R H (1973); *The Evolution of Corporate Financial Reporting*; Sunbury, Middx; Thomas Nelson & Sons.

Lee T A & Tweedie D P (1975); Accounting information: an investigation of private shareholder understanding; *Accounting & Business Research*, Autumn, 280-291.

Lee T A & Tweedie D P (1977); *The Private Shareholder and the Corporate Report*; London; ICAEW.

Levi Strauss C (1955); The structural study of myth; *Journal of American Folklore*. 28, 428-444.

Levi-Strauss C (1961); *Tristes Tropiques*; trans J Russell; New York; Atheneum.

Levi Strauss C (1966); *The Savage Mind*; London; Weidenfeld & Nicolson.

Levi-Strauss C (1972); Structure and dialectics; in *Structural Anthropology 1*; trans C Jocobson & B G Schoepf; London; Penguin.

Likert R (1967); *The Human Organisation*; New York; McGraw-Hill.

Lister R J (1984); Capital budgeting: a survey; in R W Scapens , D T Otley & R J Lister; *Management Accounting , Organisational Theory and Capital Budgeting*; Oxford; OUP; pp165-255.

Locke J (1975); *Two Treatises of Government*; London; Everyman Library.

Lovelock J (1979); *Gaia*; Oxford; Oxford University Press.

Lyotard J F (1984); *The Postmodern Condition*; trans G Bennington & B Massumi; Minneapolis; University of Minneapolis Press.

McCoy C S (1985); *Management of Values: The Ethical Difference in Corporate Policy and Performance*; Marshfield, Mass; Pitman.

McDonald D & Puxty A G (1979); An inducement - contribution approach to corporate financial reporting; *Accounting, Organizations & Society*, 4 (1/2), 53-65.

McGregor D (1960); *The Human Side of Enterprise*; New York; McGraw-Hill.

McKinstry S (1996); Designing the annual reports of Burton plc from 1930 to 1994; *Accounting, Organizations and Society*, 21 (1), 89-111.

Machin J L J (1983); Management control systems: whence and whither?; in E A Lowe & J L J Machin (eds), *New Perspectives in Management Control*; London; Macmillan; pp 22-42.

Macintosh N (1985); *The Social Software of Accounting and Information Systems*; London; Wiley.

Mak Y T (1989); Fit, internal consistency and financial performance; *Journal of Business Finance and Accounting*, 16 (2), 273-300.

Malinowski B (1962); Myth as a dramatic development of dogma; in I Strenski (ed) (1992); *Malinowski and the Work of Myth*; Princeton, N J; Princeton University Press.

Marcus M L & Pfeffer J (1983); Power and the design and implementation of accounting and control systems; *Accounting, Organizations & Society*, 8 (2/3), 205-218.

Markandya A (1990); *Green Economics*; Key Environmental Issues No 8; British Gas.

Marsh P (1990); *Short-termism on trial*; London; International Fund Managers Association.

Marshal A (1947); *Principles of Economics*; London; Macmillan & Co.

Maslow A H (1954); *Motivation and Personality*; New York; Harper & Row.

Mason R O & Swanson E B (1979); Measurement for management decision: a perspective; *California Management Review*, 21 (3), 70-81.

Mathews M R (1984); A suggested classification for social accounting research; *Journal of Accounting and Public Policy*, 3, 199-221.

Mathews M R (1993); *Socially Responsible Accounting*; London; Chapman & Hall.

Mathews M R (1997); Twenty – five years of social and environmental accounting: is there a silver jubilee to celebrate?; paper presented at the British Accounting Association National Conference, Birmingham, March 1997.

Maunders K T & Burritt R L (1991); Accounting and the ecological crisis; *Accounting Auditing & Accountability Journal*, 4 (3), 9-26.

Mauntz R H & Sharif H A (1961); *The Philosophy of Auditing*; American Accounting Association.

Metz C (1974); *Language and Cinema*; The Hague; Mouton.

Metz C (1974); *Film Language: a Semiotics of the Cinema*; Oxford; Oxford University Press.

Midwinter A (1994); Developing performance indicators for local government: the Scottish experience; *Public Money & Management*, 14 (2), 37-43.

Miles R E & Snow C C (1978); *Organisational Strategy, Structure and Process*; New York; McGraw-Hill.

Mill J S (1848); *Principles of Political Economy*; London.

Mill J S (1962); *Utilitarianism, Liberty and Representative Government*; London; Everyman Library.

Miller D F (1992); *The Reason of Metaphor*; London; Sage.

Milne M J (1996); On sustainability: the environment and management accounting; *Management Accounting Research*, 7 (1), 135-161.

Mintzberg H (1973); *The Nature of Managerial Work*; New York; Harper & Row.

Mintzberg H (1994); *The Rise and Fall of Strategic Planning*; London; Prentice Hall.

Mishan E J (1967); *The Costs of Economic Growth*; Harmondsworth; Pelican.

Mitchell T W (1906); Review of corporate reports: the report of the American Locomotive Company; *Journal of Accountancy*, 106-125.

Mitroff I I (1983); *Stakeholders of the Organisational Mind*; San Francisco; Jossey-Bass.

Monks R A G & Minow N (1991); *Power and Accountability*; Glasgow; HarperCollins.

Morgan G (1988); Accounting as reality construction: towards a new epistemology for accounting practice; *Accounting, Organizations & Society*, 13 (5), 477-483.

Mouffe C (1993); *The Return of the Political*; London; Verso.

Mumby D K & Putnam L L (1992); The politics of emotion: a feminist reading of bounded rationality; *Academy of Management Review*, 17 (3), 465-486.

Munro R (1996); Alignment and identity work: the study of accounts and accountability; in R Munro & J Mouritsen (eds) *Accountability: power ethos and the technologies of managing*; London; International Thomson Business Press; pp 1-19.

Munro R (1999a); The cultural performance of control; *Organization Studies*, 20 (4), 619-640.

Munro R (1999b); Power and discretion: membership work in the time of technology; *Organization*, 6 (3), 429-450.

Murphy G J (1979); The evolution of corporate reporting practices in Canada; in E N Goffman (ed), *Academy of Accounting Historians Working Paper Series Vol 1*, pp 329-368.

Myners P (1998); Improving performance reporting to the market; in A Carey & J Sancto (eds), *Performance Measurement in the Digital Age* pp 27-33; London; ICAEW.

Neimark M & Tinker T (1986); The social construction of management control systems; *Accounting, Organizations & Society*, 11 (4/5), 369-395.

Neu D (1992); The social construction of positive choices; *Accounting, Organizations & Society*, 17 (3/4), 223-237.

Newman M S (1979); Historical development of early accounting concepts and their relation to certain economic concepts; in E N Goffman (ed), *Academy of Accounting Historians Working Paper Series Volume 1* pp 157-186.

Newton T (1996); *Postmodernism and action*; Organization, 3 (1), 7-29.

Nietsche F (1956); *The Birth of Tragedy*; New York; Doubleday.

Nohria N & Berkley J D (1994); The Virtual Organisation; in C Heckscher & A Donnellon (eds), *The Post- Bureaucratic Organisation*; London; Sage, pp108-128.

Norris C (1990); Lost in the funhouse: Baudrillard and the politics of postmodernism; in R Boyne & A Rattansi (eds), *Postmodernism and Society*; Basingstoke; Macmillan, pp 119-153.

Oakland J S (1989); *Total Quality Management*; Oxford; Butterworth-Heineman.

Ogden S & Bougen P (1985); A radical perspective on the disclosure of accounting information to trade unions; *Accounting, Organizations & Society*, 10 (2), 211-224.

Ormerod P (1994); *The Death of Economics*; London; Faber and Faber.

Orwell G (1970); *Collected Essays, Journalism and Letters Vol 4*; Harmondsworth; Penguin.

Otley D T (1980); The contingency theory of management accounting: achievement and prognosis; *Accounting, Organizations & Society*, 5 (4), 413-428.

Otley D T (1984); Management accounting and organisation theory: a review of their interrelationship; in R W Scapens, D T Otley & R J Lister; *Management Accounting, Organisational Theory and Capital Budgeting*; Oxford; OUP; pp96-164.

Otley D T & Berry A J (1979); Risk distribution in the budgetary process;

Accounting & Business Research, 9 (3), 325-337.

Otley D T & Berry A J (1980); Control, organization and accounting; *Accounting, Organizations & Society*, 5 (2), 231-244.

Ouchi W G (1979); A conceptual framework for the design of organizational control mechanisms; *Management Science*, 25 (9), 833-848.

Ouchi W G (1981); *Theory Z: How American Business Can Meet the Japanese Challenge*; Reading, Ma; Addison-Wesley.

Owen, R. (1991); *A New View of Society and other writings*, London, Penguin.

Panozzo F (1996); Accountability and identity: accounting and the democratic organization; in R Munro & J Mouritsen, *Accountability*; London; International Thomson .

Paris J (1975); *Painting and Linguistics*; Pittsburg; Carnegie – Mellon University Press.

Pava M L & Krausz J (1996); The association between corporate social responsibility and financial performance: the paradox of social cost; *Journal of Business Ethics*, 15 (3), 321-357.

Pearce D, Markandya A & Barbier E B (1989); *Blueprint for a Green Economy*; London; Earthscan.

Peirce C S (1958); *Collected papers Vol 5*; P Weiss, C Hartshorne & A Burks (eds); Harvard; Harvard University Press.

Perls F S (1975); Theory and technique of personality integration; in J O Stevens (ed); *Gestalt Is*; Moab, Utah; Real People Press.

Peters T J & Waterman R H (1982); *In Search of Excellence*; New York; Harper & Row.

Pollitt C (1990); *Managerialism and the public services: the Anglo- American experience*; Oxford; Basil Blackwell.

Popper K R (1945); *The Open Society and Its Enemies*; London; Routledge & Kegan Paul.

Power M (1991); Auditing and environmental expertise: between protest and professionalisation; *Accounting Auditing & Accountability Journal*, 4 (3), 30-42.

Preston A M, Wright C & Young J J (1996); Imag[in]ing annual reports; *Accounting, Organizations and Society*, 21 (1), 113-137.

Purdy D E (1983); The enterprise theory: an extension; *Journal of Business Finance & Accounting*, 10 (4), 531-541.

Puxty A G (1991); Social accounting and the universal pragmatics; *Advances in Public Sector Accounting*, 4, 35-47.

Quellette J (1996); Environmental accounting; *Chemical Reporter*, 250 (3), S16.

Radhakrishnan R (1994); Postmodernism and the rest of the work; *Organization*, 1 (2), 305-340.

Ramathan K V (1976); Toward a theory of corporate social accounting; *The Accounting Review*, 51 (3), 516-528.

Ranagnathan J & Ditz D (1996); Environmental accounting: a tool for better management; *Management Accounting*, 74 (2), 38-40.

Rappaport A (1981); Selecting strategies that create shareholder value; *Harvard*

Business Review, May/Jun, 139-149.

Rappaport A (1986); *Creating Shareholder Value*; New York; The Free Press.

Rappaport A (1992); CFO's and strategists: forging a common framework; *Harvard Business Review*, May/Jun, 84-91.

Rheingold H (1994); *The Virtual Community*; ; London; Secker & Warburg.

Ridgway W F (1956); Dysfunctional consequences of performance measurement; *Administrative Sciences Quarterly*, 1 (2), 240-247.

Robins K (1995); Cyberspace and the world we live in; in M Featherstone & R Burrows (eds); *Cyberspace / Cyberbodies / Cyberpunk*; London; Sage.

Robinson J (1964); *Economic Philosophy*; Harmondsworth; Penguin.

Robson K (1992); Accounting numbers as 'inscription': action at a distance and the development of accounting; *Accounting, Organizations & Society*, 17 (7), 685-708.

Rubenstein D B (1992); Bridging the gap between green accounting and black ink; *Accounting, Organizations & Society*, 17 (5), 501-508.

Rushkoff D (1997); *Children of Chaos*; HarperCollins; London.

Russell B (1992); *Power*; London; Routledge.

Sapir E (1949); The Unconscious Patterning of Behaviour in Society; in D G Mendelbaum (ed), *Selected Writings of Edward Sapir*; Berkley, Ca.; University of California Press.

Saussure F de (1966); *Course in General Linguistics*; (trans W Baskin); New York; McGraw-Hill.

Scapens R W (1979); Profit measurement in divisionalised companies; *Journal of Business Finance & Accounting*, 6 (3), 281-305.

Scapens R W (1984); Management accounting: a survey paper; in R W Scapens, D T Otley & R J Lister, *Management Accounting, Organisational Theory and Capital Budgeting*; Oxford; OUP; pp15-95.

Scapens R W (1994); Never mind the gap: towards an institutional perspective of management accounting practices; *Management Accounting Research*, 5 (3/4), 97-104.

Schaltegger S, Muller K & Hindrichsen H (1996); *Corporate Environmental Accounting*; Chichester; John Wiley & Sons.

Schreuder H & Ramanathan K V (1984a); Accounting and corporate accountability: an extended comment; *Accounting Organizations & Society*, 9 (3/4), 409-415.

Schreuder H & Ramanathan K V (1984b); Accounting and corporate accountability: a postscript; *Accounting Organizations & Society*, 9 (3/4), 421-423.

Sebeok T A (1994); *An Introduction to Semiotics*; London; Pinter.

Selznick N (1957); *Leadership in Administration: A Sociological Interpretation*; Evanston, Ill; Row, Peterson.

Simon H A (1964); On the concept of organizational goal; *Administrative Science Quarterly*, 9 (1), 1-22.

Smith T (1992); *Accounting for Growth*; London; Century Business.

Sobchack V (1996); Democratic franchise and the electronic frontier; in Z Sardar

& J R Ravetz (eds); *Cyberfutures*; London; Pluto Press.

Solomons D (1974); Corporate social performance: a new dimension in accounting reports?; in H Edey & B S Yamey (eds), *Debits, Credits, Finance and Profits*; London; Sweet & Maxwell; pp 131-141.

Sombart, W. (1915); *The Quintessence of Modern Capitalism*, New York, E P Dutton & Co.

Spicer B H (1988); Towards an organisational theory of the transfer pricing process; *Accounting, Organizations & Society*, 13 (3), 303-322.

Spicer B H & Ballew V (1983); Management accounting systems and the economics of internal organisation; *Accounting, Organizations & Society*, 8 (1), 73-96.

Sridhar S S (1994); Managerial reputation and internal reporting; *The Accounting Review,* 69 (2), 343-363.

Stacey R D (1991); *The Chaos Frontier*; Oxford; Butterworth-Heinemann.

Stalk G and Hout T M (1991); *Competing against time*; London; The Free Press.

Sternberg E (1997); The defects of stakeholder theory; *Corporate Governance: An International Review*, 6 (3), 151-163.

Sternberg E (1998); *Corporate Governance: Accountability in the Marketplace*; London; Institute of Economic Affairs.

Stewart G B III (1991); *The Quest for Value*; New York; Harper Collins.

Stewart G B III (1994); EVA, fact and fantasy; *Journal of Applied Corporate Finance*, 7 (2), 71-87.

Swales J M & Rogers P S (1995); Discourse and the projection of corporate culture: the Mission statement; *Discourse and Society,* 6 (2), 223-242.

Swanson E B (1978); The two faces of organisational information; *Accounting, Organizations & Society*, 3 (3/4), 237-246.

Swieringa R J & Weick K E (1987); Management accounting and action; *Accounting, Organizations & Society*, 12 (3), 293-308.

Taylor N V (1989); Local authority accounting - the development of a conceptual framework; *Financial Accountability & Management*, 5 (1), 19-38.

Teresa Sister F (1963); *The Living Mirror: Reflections on Clare of Assisi*; Maryknoll, NY; Orbis.

Till C A & Symes C F (1999); Environmental disclosure by Australian mining companies: environmental conscience or commercial reality?; *Accounting Forum*, 28 (3), 137-154.

Tinker T (1985); *Paper Prophets: A Social Critique of Accounting*; London; Holt, Rinehart & Winston.

Tinker T (1988); Panglossian accounting theories: the science of apologising in style; *Accounting, Organizations & Society*, 13 (2), 165-189.

Veblen T (1899); *The Theory of the Leisure Classes*; New York; New American Library.

Vickers G (1967); *Towards a Sociology of Management*; London; Chapman & Hall.

Vygotsky L & Luria A (1994); Tool and symbol in child development; in R Van Der Veer & J Valsimer (eds), *The Vygotsky Reader*, pp 99-173; Oxford; Blackwell.

Wall D (1998); Catching cybercriminals: policing the internet; *International Journal of Law, Computers and Technology*, 12 (2), 201-218.

Watson D J H & Baumler J V (1975); Transfer pricing: a behavioural context; *The Accounting Review*, 466-474.

Weibel P (1990); Virtual worlds: The emperor's new body; in G Hattinger (ed), *Electronica 1990* Vol 2; Linz; Veritas-Verlag.

Wildavsky A (1975); *Budgeting: A Comparative Theory of Budgetary Processes*; Boston, Ma; Little Brown & Co.

Wildavsky A (1984); *The Politics of the Budgetary Process*; Boston, Ma; Little Brown & Co.

Williamson O E (1963); A model of rational managerial behaviour; in Cyert R M & March J G (eds); *A Behavioural Theory of the Firm*; Englewood Cliffs, NJ; Prentice-Hall.

Williamson O E (1967); Hierarchical control and optimum firm size; *Journal of Political Economy*, 75 (2), 123-138.

Williamson O E (1970); *Corporate Control and Business Behaviour*; Englewood Cliffs, N J; Prentice Hall.

Williamson O E (1975); *Markets and Hierarchies: Analysis and Anti-trust Implications*; New York; The Free Press.

Wisner J D & Fawcett S E (1991); Linking firm strategy to operating decisions through performance measurement; *Production and Inventory Management Journal*, Third quarter, 1-18.

Wright W (1975); *Six guns and society: a structural study of the Western*; London; University of California Press.

Yates J & Orlikowski W J (1992); Genres of organisational communication: a structuration approach to studying communication and media; *Academy of Management Review,* 17, 299-326.

Index